A HANDBOOK OF MARXISM

being
a collection of extracts from the writings of
Marx, Engels and the greatest of their followers

selected
so as to give the reader
the most comprehensive account of Marxism
possible within the limits of a single volume :

the passages
being chosen by Emile Burns, who has added
in each case a bibliographical note, & an
explanation of the circumstances in which the
work was written & its special significance in
the development of Marxism : as well as the
necessary glossaries and index

HASKELL HOUSE PUBLISHERS Ltd.
Publishers of Scarce Scholarly Books
NEW YORK. N. Y. 10012
1970

First Published 1935

HASKELL HOUSE PUBLISHERS Ltd.
Publishers of Scarce Scholarly Books
280 LAFAYETTE STREET
NEW YORK. N. Y. 10012

Library of Congress Catalog Card Number: **79-119441**

Standard Book Number 8383-1090-7

Printed in the United States of America

OUR PROGRAMME

INTERNATIONAL social democracy is at present going through a period of theoretical vacillations. Up to the present the doctrines of Marx and Engels were regarded as a firm foundation of revolutionary theory—nowadays voices are raised everywhere declaring these doctrines to be inadequate and antiquated. Anyone calling himself a social-democrat and having the intention to publish a social-democratic organ, must take up a definite attitude as regards this question, which by no means concerns German social-democrats alone.

We base our faith entirely on Marx's theory ; it was the first to transform socialism from a Utopia into a science, to give this science a firm foundation and to indicate the path which must be trodden in order further to develop this science and to elaborate it in all its details. It discovered the nature of present-day capitalist economy and explained the way in which the employment of workers—the purchase of labour power—the enslavement of millions of those possessing no property by a handful of capitalists, by the owners of the land, the factories, the mines, etc., is concealed. It has shown how the whole development of modern capitalism is advancing towards the large producer ousting the small one, and is creating the prerequisites which make a socialist order of society possible and necessary. It has taught us to see, under the disguise of ossified habits, political intrigues, intricate laws, cunning theories, the class struggle, the struggle between, on the one hand, the various species of the possessing classes, and, on the other hand, the mass possessing no property, the proletariat, which leads all those who possess nothing. It has made clear what is the real task of a revolutionary socialist party—not to set up projects for the transformation of society, not to preach sermons to the capitalists and their admirers about improving the position of the workers, not the instigation of conspiracies, but the organisation of the class struggle of the proletariat and the carrying on of this struggle, the final aim of which is the seizure of political power by the proletariat and the organisation of a socialist society.

We now ask : What new elements have the touting " renovators " introduced into this theory, they who have attracted so much notice in our day and have grouped themselves round the German socialist Bernstein ? Nothing, nothing at all ; they have not advanced by a single step the science which Marx and Engels adjured us to develop ; they have not taught the proletariat any new methods of fighting ; they are only marching backwards in that they adopt the fragments of antiquated theories and are preaching to the proletariat not the theory of struggle but the theory of submissiveness—submissiveness to the bitterest enemies of the proletariat, to the governments and bourgeois parties who never tire of finding new methods of persecuting socialists. Plekhanov, one of the founders and leaders of Russian social-democracy, was perfectly right when he subjected to merciless criticism the latest " Criticism " of Bernstein, whose views have now been rejected even by the representatives of the German workers at the Party Congress in Hanover (October, 1899.—Ed.).

We know that on account of these words we shall be drenched with a flood of accusations ; they will cry out that we want to turn the Socialist Party into a holy order of the " orthodox," who persecute the " heretics " for their aberrations from the " true dogma," for any independent opinion, etc. We know all these nonsensical phrases which have become the fashion nowadays. Yes there is no shadow of truth in them, no iota of sense. There can be no strong socialist party without a revolutionary theory which unites all socialists, from which the socialists draw their whole conviction, which they apply in their methods of fighting and working. To defend a theory of this kind, of the truth of which one is completely convinced, against unfounded attacks and against attempts to debase it, does not mean being an enemy of criticism in general. We by no means regard the theory of Marx as perfect and inviolable ; on the contrary, we are convinced that this theory has only laid the foundation stones of that science on which the socialists must continue to build in every direction, unless they wish to be left behind by life. We believe that it is particularly necessary for Russian socialists to work out the Marxist theory independently, for this theory only gives general precepts, the details of which must be applied in England otherwise than in France, in France otherwise than in Germany, and in Germany otherwise than in Russia. For this reason we will willingly devote space in our paper to articles about theoretical questions, and we call upon all comrades openly to discuss the matters in dispute.

What are the main questions which arise in applying the common programme of all social-democrats to Russia ?

We have already said that the essence of this programme consists in the organisation of the class struggle of the proletariat and in carrying on this struggle, the final aim of which is the seizure of political power by the proletariat and the construction of a socialist society. The class struggle of the proletariat is divided into : The economic fight (the fight against individual capitalists, or against the individual groups of capitalists by the improvement of the position of the workers) and the political fight (the fight against the Government for the extension of the rights of the people, i.e., for democracy, and for the expansion of the political power of the proletariat). Some Russian social-democrats (among them apparently those who conduct the paper *Rabochaia Mysl*) regard the economic fight as incomparably more important and almost go so far as to postpone the political fight to a more or less distant future. This standpoint is quite wrong. All social-democrats are unanimous in believing that it is necessary to carry on an agitation among the workers on this basis, i.e., to help the workers in their daily fight against the employers, to direct their attention to all kinds and all cases of chicanery, and in this way to make clear to them the necessity of unity. To forget the political for the economic fight would, however, mean a digression from the most important principle of international social-democracy ; it would mean forgetting what the whole history of the Labour movement has taught us. Fanatical adherents of the bourgeoisie and of the Government which serves it, have indeed repeatedly tried to organise purely economic unions of workers and thus to deflect them from the " politics " of socialism. It is quite possible that the Russian Government will also be clever enough to do something of the kind, as it has always endeavoured to throw some largesse or other sham presents to the people in order to prevent them becoming conscious that they are oppressed and are without rights.

No economic fight can give the workers a permanent improvement of their situation, it cannot, indeed, be carried on on a large scale unless the workers have the free right to call meetings, to join in unions, to have their own newspapers and to send their representatives to the National Assembly as do the workers in Germany and all European countries (with the exception of Turkey and Russia). In order, however, to obtain these rights, a political fight must be carried on. In Russia, not only the workers but all the citizens are deprived of political rights. Russia is an absolute monarchy. The Tsar alone promulgates laws, nominates officials and controls them. For this reason it seems as though in Russia the Tsar and the Tsarist Government were dependent on no class and cared for all equally. In reality, however, all the officials are chosen exclusively from the possessing class, and all are subject to the influence of the large capitalists who obtain whatever they want—the Ministers dance to the tune the large capitalists play. The Russian worker is bowed under a double yoke ; he is robbed and plundered by the capitalists and the landowners, and, lest he should fight against them, he is bound hand and foot by the police, his mouth is gagged and any attempt to defend the rights of the people is followed by persecution. Any strike against a capitalist results in the military and police being let loose on the workers. Every economic fight of necessity turns into a political fight, and social-democracy must indissolubly combine the economic with the political fight into a united class struggle of the proletariat.

The first and chief aim of such a fight must be the conquest of political rights, the conquest of political freedom. Since the workers of St. Petersburg alone have succeeded, in spite of the inadequate support given them by the socialists in obtaining concessions from the Government within a short time—the passing of a law for shortening the hours of work—the whole working class, led by a united " Russian Social-Democratic Labour Party," will be able, through obstinate fighting, to obtain incomparably more important concessions.

The Russian working class will see its way to carrying on an economic and political fight alone, even if no other class comes to its help. The workers are not alone, however, in the political fight. The fact that the people is absolutely without rights and the unbridled arbitrary rule of the officials rouses the indignation of all who have any pretensions to honesty and education, who cannot reconcile themselves with the persecution of all free speech and all free thought ; it rouses the indignation of the persecuted Poles, Finns, Jews, Russian sects, it rouses the indignation of small traders, of the industrialists, the peasants, of all who can nowhere find protection against the chicanery of the officials and the police. All these groups of the population are incapable of carrying on an obstinate political fight alone ; if, however, the working class raises the banner of a fight of this kind it will be supported on all sides. Russian social-democracy will place itself at the head of all fights for the rights of the people, of all fights for democracy, and then it will be invincible.

These are our fundamental ideas which we shall develop systematically and from every point of view in our paper.

We are convinced that in this way we shall tread the path which has been indicated by the " Russian Social-Democratic Labour Party " in its " Manifesto."

V. I. Lenin

WHAT IS TO BE DONE ?

Published 1902. English edition, Martin Lawrence Ltd., 1931.

[This work, the sub-title of which is " Burning Questions of Our Movement," was of great historical importance in the development of the Russian Social Democratic Labour Party. In his earlier articles and pamphlets, Lenin had already sharply criticised the perversions of Marxist theory which were at that time beginning to dominate the socialist movement in Western Europe and were gathering influence in Russia. In *What is to be Done ?* he showed the need for a triple struggle—theoretical, political, economic—and secondly, for a centralised revolutionary party to lead it. The sections reprinted here cover the main theoretical issue of the character and content of revolutionary agitation.]

WHAT IS TO BE DONE?

DOGMATISM AND "FREEDOM OF CRITICISM"

What is "Freedom of Criticism"?

"FREEDOM OF CRITICISM," this undoubtedly is the most fashionable slogan at the present time, and the one most frequently employed in the controversies between the Socialists and democrats of all countries. At first sight, nothing would appear to be more strange than the solemn appeals by one of the parties to the dispute for freedom of criticism. Can it be that some of the progressive parties have raised their voices against the constitutional law of the majority of European countries which guarantees freedom to science and scientific investigation ? " Something must be wrong here," an onlooker who has not yet fully appreciated the nature of the disagreement among the controversialists will say when he hears this fashionable slogan repeated at every cross-road. " Evidently this slogan is one of the conventional phrases which, like a nickname, becomes legitimatised by custom," he will conclude.

In fact, it is no secret that two separate tendencies have been formed in international Social-Democracy.[1] The fight between these tendencies now flares up in a bright flame, and now dies down and smoulders under the ashes of imposing " resolutions for an armistice." What this " new " tendency, which adopts a " critical " attitude towards " obsolete doctrinaire" Marxism represents, has been *stated* with sufficient precision by Bernstein, and *demonstrated* by Millerand.

Social-Democracy must change from a party of the social revolution into a democratic party of social reforms. Bernstein has surrounded this political demand by a whole battery of symmetrically arranged " new " arguments and

[1] This, perhaps, is the first occasion in the history of modern Socialism that controversies between various tendencies within the Socialist movement have grown from national into international controversies ; and this is extremely encouraging. Formerly, the disputes between the Lassalleans and the Eisenachers, between the Guesdists and the Possibilists, between the Fabians and the Social-Democrats, and between the Narodniki and the Social-Democrats in Russia, remained purely national disputes, reflected purely national features and proceeded, as it were, on different planes. At the present time (this is quite evident now) the English Fabians, the French Ministerialists, the German Bernsteinists, and the Russian " Critics "—all belong to the same family, all extol each other, learn from each other, and are rallying their forces against " doctrinaire " Marxism. Perhaps, in this first real battle with Socialist opportunism, international revolutionary Social-Democracy will become sufficiently hardened to be able, at last, to put an end to the political reaction, long reigning in Europe.

TM

reasonings. The possibility of putting Socialism on a scientific basis and of proving that it is necessary and inevitable from the point of view of the materialist conception of history was denied ; the fact of increasing poverty, proletarianisation, the growing acuteness of capitalist contradictions, were also denied. The very conception of " *ultimate aim* " was declared to be unsound, and the idea of the dictatorship of the proletariat was absolutely rejected. It was denied that there is any difference in principle between liberalism and Socialism. *The theory of the class struggle* was rejected on the grounds that it could not be applied to strictly democratic society, governed according to the will of the majority, etc.

Thus, the demand for a decided change from revolutionary Social-Democracy to bourgeois reformism, was accompanied by a no less decided turn towards bourgeois criticism of all the fundamental ideas of Marxism. As this criticism of Marxism has been going on for a long time now, from the political platform, from university chairs, in numerous pamphlets, and in a number of scientific works, as the younger generation of the educational classes have been systematically trained for decades on this criticism, it is not surprising that the " new, critical " tendency in Social-Democracy should spring up, all complete, like Minerva from the head of Jupiter. This new tendency did not have to grow and develop, it was transferred bodily from bourgois literature to Socialist literature.

If Bernstein's theoretical criticism and political yearnings are still obscure to anyone, the trouble the French have taken to demonstrate the " new method " should remove all ambiguities. In this instance, also, France has justified its old reputation as the country in which " more than anywhere else the historical class struggles were always fought to a finish " [Engels, in his introduction to Marx's *Eighteenth Brumaire*]. The French Socialists have commenced, not to theorise, but to act. The more developed democratic political conditions in France have permitted them to put

Bernsteinism into practice immediately, with its inevitable consequences. Millerand has provided an excellent example of practical Bernsteinism. It is not surprising that he so zealously defends and praises Bernstein and Volmar ! Indeed, if Social-Democracy, in essentials, is merely a reformist party, and must be bold enough to admit this openly, then, not only has a Socialist the right to join a bourgeois cabinet, but he ought always to strive to obtain places in it. If democracy, in essence, means the abolition of class domination, then why should not a Socialist minister charm the whole bourgeois world by orations on class co-operation ? Why should he not remain in the cabinet even after the shooting down of workers by gendarmes has exposed, for the hundredth and thousandth time, the real nature of the democratic co-operation of classes ? Why should he not personally take part in welcoming the Tsar, for whom the French Socialists now have no other sobriquet than " Hero of the Gallows, Knout and Banishment " (*knouteur, pendeur et deportateur*) ? And the reward for this humiliation and self-degradation of Socialism in the face of the whole world, for the corruption of the Socialist consciousness of the working class—the only thing that can guarantee victory—the reward for this is, imposing *plans* for niggardly reforms, so niggardly in fact, that much more has been obtained even from bourgeois governments.

He who does not deliberately close his eyes cannot fail to see that the new " critical " tendency in Socialism is nothing more nor less than a new species of *opportunism*. And if we judge people not by the brilliant uniforms they deck themselves in, not by the imposing appellations they give themselves, but by their actions, and by what they actually advocate, it will be clear that " freedom of criticism " means freedom for an opportunistic tendency in Social-Democracy, the freedom to convert Social-Democracy into a democratic reformist party, the freedom to introduce bourgeois ideas and bourgeois elements into Socialism.

" Freedom " is a grand word, but under the banner of Free Trade the most predatory wars were conducted : under the banner of " free labour," the toilers were robbed. The term " freedom of criticism " contains the same inherent falsehood. Those who are really convinced that they have advanced science, would demand, not freedom for the new views to continue side by side with the old, but the substitution of the old views by the new views. The cry " Long live freedom of criticism," that is heard to-day, too strongly calls to mind the fable of the empty barrel.

We are marching in a compact group along a precipitous and difficult path, firmly holding each other by the hand. We are surrounded on all sides by enemies, and are under their almost constant fire. We have combined voluntarily, especially for the purpose of fighting the enemy and not to retreat into the adjacent marsh, the inhabitants of which, right from the very outset, have reproached us with having separated ourselves into an exclusive group, and with having chosen the path of struggle instead of the path of conciliation. And now several in our crowd begin to cry out : Let us go into this marsh ! And when we begin to shame them, they retort : How conservative you are ! Are you not ashamed to deny us the right to invite you to take a better road !

Oh yes, gentlemen ! You are free, not only to invite us, but to go yourselves wherever you will, even into the marsh. In fact, we think that the marsh is your proper place, and we are prepared to render *you* every assistance to get there. Only, let go of our hands, don't clutch at us, and don't besmirch the grand word " freedom " ; for we too are " free " to go where we please, free, not only to fight against the marsh, but also those who are turning towards the marsh. . . .

Criticism in Russia

The peculiar position of Russia in regard to the point we are examining is that *right from the very beginning* of the spontaneous labour movement on the one hand, and the change of progressive public opinion towards Marxism on the other, a combination was observed of obviously heterogeneous elements under a common flag for the purpose of fighting the common enemy (obsolete social and political views). We refer to the heyday of " legal Marxism." Speaking generally, this was an extremely curious phenomenon, that no one in the 'eighties, or the beginning of the 'nineties, would have believed possible. Suddenly, in a country ruled by an autocracy, in which the press is completely shackled, and in a period of intense political reaction in which even the tiniest outgrowth of political discontent and protest was suppressed, a *censored* literature springs up, advocating the theory of revolutionary Marxism, in a language extremely obscure, but understood by the " interest." The government had accustomed itself to regard only the theory of (revolutionary) Populism as dangerous without observing its internal evolution as is usually the case, and rejoicing at the criticism, levelled against it *no matter from what side it came*. Quite a considerable time elapsed (according to our Russian calculations) before the government realised what had happened and the unwieldly army of censors and gendarmes discovered the new enemy and flung itself upon him. Meanwhile, Marxian books were published one after another, Marxian journals and newspapers were published, nearly every one became a Marxist, Marxism was flattered, the Marxists were courted and the book publishers rejoiced at the extraordinary ready sale of Marxian literature. It is quite reasonable to suppose that among the Marxian novices who were carried away by this stream, there was more than one " author who got a swelled head. . . ."

We can now speak calmly of this period as of an event of the past. It is no secret that the brief appearance of Marxism on the surface of our literature was called forth by the alliance between people of extreme and of extremely moderate views. In point of fact, the latter were bourgeois democrats ; and this was the conclusion (so strikingly confirmed by their subsequent " critical " development), that intruded itself on the minds of certain persons even when the " alliance " was still intact.

That being the case, does not the responsibility for the subsequent " confusion " rest mainly upon the revolutionary Social-Democrats who entered into alliance with these future " critics " ? This question, together with a reply in the affirmative, is sometimes heard from people with excessively rigid views. But these people are absolutely wrong. Only those who have no reliance in themselves can fear to enter into temporary alliances with unreliable people. Besides, not a single political party could exist without entering into such alliances. The combination with the legal Marxists was in its way the first really political alliance contracted by Russian Social-Democrats. Thanks to this alliance an astonishingly rapid victory was obtained over Populism, and Marxian ideas (even though in a vulgarised form) became very widespread. Moreover, the alliance was not concluded altogether without " conditions." The proof: The burning by the censor, in 1895, of the Marxian symposium, *Materials on the Problem of the Economic Development of Russia*. If the literary agreement with the legal Marxists can be compared with a political alliance, then that book can be compared with a political treaty.

The rupture, of course, did not occur because the " allies " proved to be bourgeois democrats. On the contrary, the representatives of the latter tendency were the natural and desirable allies of the Social-Democrats in so far as their democratic tasks that were brought to the front by the prevailing situation in Russia were concerned. But an essential condition for such an alliance must be complete liberty for Socialists to reveal to the working class that its interests are diametrically opposed to the interests of the bourgeoisie. However, the Bernsteinist and " critical " tendency to which the majority of the legal Marxists turned, deprived the Socialists of this liberty and corrupted Socialist consciousness by vulgarising Marxism, by preaching the toning down of social antagonisms, by declaring the idea of the social revolution and the dictatorship of the proletariat to be absurd, by restricting the labour movement and the class struggle to narrow trade unionism and to a " practical " struggle for petty, gradual reforms. This was tantamount to the bourgeois democrat's denial of Socialism's right to independence, and, consequently, of its right to existence ; in practice it meant a striving to convert the nascent labour movement into a tail of the liberals.

Naturally, under such circumstances a rupture was necessary. But the " peculiar " feature of Russia manifested itself in that this rupture simply meant the closing to the Social-Democrats of access to the most popular and widespread " legal " literature. The " ex-Marxists " who took up the flag of " criticism," and who obtained almost a monopoly in the " sale " of Marxism, entrenched themselves in this literature. Catchwords like : " Against orthodoxy " and " Long live freedom of criticism " (now repeated by *Rabocheye Dyelo*) immediately became the fashion, and the fact that neither the censor nor the gendarmes could resist this fashion is apparent from the publication of *three* Russian editions of Bernstein's celebrated book (celebrated in the Herostratus sense) and from the fact that the books by Bernstein, Prokopovich and others were recommended by Zubatov [*Iskra*, No. 10]. And this tendency did not confine itself to the sphere of literature. The turn towards criticism was accompanied by the turn towards Economism that was taken by Social-Democratic practical workers.

The manner in which the contacts and mutual dependence between legal criticism and illegal Economism arose and grew is an interesting subject in itself, and may very well be treated in a special article. It is sufficient to note here that these contacts undoubtedly existed. The notoriety deservedly acquired by the *Credo* was due precisely to the frankness with which it formulated these contacts and laid down the fundamental political tendencies of Economism, viz. : Let the workers carry on the economic struggle (it would be more correct to say the trade union struggle, because the latter embraces also specifically labour politics), and let the Marxist intelligentsia merge with the liberals for the political "struggle." Thus, it turned out that trade union work " among the people " meant fulfilling the first part of this task, and legal criticism meant fulfilling the second part. . . .

The question now arises : Seeing what the peculiar features of Russian " criticism " and Russian Bernsteinism were, what should those who desired, in deeds and not merely in words, to oppose opportunism have done ? First of all, they should have made efforts to resume the theoretical work that was only just commenced in the period of legal Marxism, and that has now again fallen on the shoulders of the illegal workers. Unless such work is undertaken the successful growth of the movement is impossible. Secondly, they should have actively combated legal " criticism " that was corrupting people's minds. Thirdly, they should have actively counteracted the confusion and vacillation prevailing in practical work, and should have exposed and repudiated every conscious or unconscious attempt to degrade our programme and tactics. . . .

The Importance of the Theoretical Struggle

. . . The case of the Russian Social-Democrats strikingly illustrates the fact observed in the whole of Europe (and long ago observed in German Marxism) that the notorious freedom of criticism implies, not the substitution of one theory by another, but freedom from every complete and thought-out theory ; it implies eclecticism and absence of principle. Those who are in the least acquainted with the actual state of our movement cannot but see that the spread of Marxism was accompanied by a certain deterioration of theoretical standards. Quite a number of people, with very little, and even totally lacking in, theoretical training, joined the movement for the sake of its practical significance and its practical successes. We can judge, therefore, how tactless *Robocheye Dyelo* is when, with an air of invincibility, it quotes the statement of Marx that : " A single step of the real movement is worth a dozen programmes." To repeat these words in the epoch of theoretical chaos is sheer mockery. Moreover, these words of Marx are taken from his letter on the Gotha Programme, in which he *sharply condemns* eclectism in the formulation of principles : " If you must combine," Marx wrote to the party leaders, " then enter into agreements to satisfy the practical aims of the movement, but do not haggle over principles, do not make ' concessions ' in theory." This was Marx's idea, and yet there are people among us who strive—in his name !— to belittle the significance of theory.

Without a revolutionary theory there can be no revolutionary movement. This cannot be insisted upon too strongly at a time when the fashionable preaching of opportunism is combined with absorption in the narrowest forms of practical activity. The importance of theory for Russian Social-Democrats is still greater for three reasons, which are often forgotten :

The first is that our party is only in the process of formation, its features are only just becoming outlined, and it has not yet completely settled its reckoning with other tendencies in revolutionary thought which threaten to divert the movement from the proper path. Indeed, in very recent times we have observed (as Axelrod long ago warned the Economists would happen) a revival of non-Social-Democratic revolutionary tendencies. Under such circumstances, what at first sight appears to be an " unimportant " mistake, may give rise to most deplorable consequences, and only the short-sighted would consider factional disputes and strict distinction of shades to be inopportune and superfluous. The fate of Russian Social-Democracy for many,

many years to come may be determined by the strengthening of one or the other " shade."

The second reason is that the Social-Democratic movement is essentially an international movement. This does not mean merely that we must combat national chauvinism. It means also that a movement that is starting in a young country can be successful only on the condition that it assimilates the experience of other countries. In order to assimilate this experience, it is not sufficient merely to be acquainted with it, or simply to transcribe the latest revolutions. A critical attitude is required towards this experience, and ability to subject it to independent tests. Only those who realise how much the modern labour movement has grown in strength will understand what a reserve of theoretical forces and political (as well as revolutionary) experience is required to fulfil this task.

The third reason is that the national tasks of Russian Social-Democracy are such as have never confronted any other Socialist party in the world. Farther on we shall deal with the political and organisational duties which the task of emancipating the whole people from the yoke of autocracy imposes upon us. At the moment, we wish merely to state that the *rôle of vanguard can be fulfilled only by a party that is guided by an advanced theory*. . . .

TRADE UNION POLITICS AND SOCIAL DEMOCRATIC POLITICS

Political Agitation and its Restriction by the Economists

Everyone knows that the spread and consolidation of the economic[1] struggle of the Russian workers proceeded

[1] In order to avoid misunderstanding we would state, that here, and throughout this pamphlet, by economic struggle, we mean (in accordance with the meaning of the term as it has become accepted amongst us) the " practical economic struggle " which Engels described as " resistance to capitalism," and which in free countries is known as the trade union struggle.

simultaneously with the creation of a " literature " exposing economic conditions, i.e., factory and industrial conditions. These " leaflets " were devoted mainly to the
exposure of factory conditions, and very soon a passion for
exposures was roused among the workers. As soon as the
workers realised that the Social-Democratic circles desired
to and could supply them with a new kind of leaflet that
told the whole truth about their poverty-stricken lives,
about their excessive toil and their lack of rights, correspondence began to pour in from the factories and workshops. This " exposure literature " created a sensation not
only in the particular factory dealt with and the conditions
of which were exposed in a given leaflet, but in all the factories to which news had spread about the facts exposed.
And as the poverty and want among the workers in the
various enterprises and in the various trades are pretty
much the same, the " Truth about the life of the workers "
roused the admiration *of all*. Even among the most backward workers, a veritable passion was roused to " go into
print "—a noble passion to adopt this rudimentary form
of war against the whole of the modern social system which
is based upon robbery and oppression. And in the overwhelming majority of cases these " leaflets " were in truth a
declaration of war, because the exposures had a terrifically
rousing effect upon the workers ; it stimulated them to put
forward demands for the removal of the most glaring evils,
and roused in them a readiness to support these demands
with strikes. Finally, the employers themselves were compelled to recognise the significance of these leaflets as a
declaration of war, so much so that in a large number of
cases they did not even wait for the outbreak of hostilities.
As is always the case, the mere publication of these exposures made them effective, and they acquired the significance of a strong moral force. On more than one occasion
the mere appearance of a leaflet proved sufficient to compel an employer to concede all or part of the demands put
forward. In a word, economic (factory) exposures have

been an important lever in the economic struggle and they will continue to be so as long as capitalism, which creates the need for the workers to defend themselves, exists. Even in the more progressive countries of Europe to-day, the exposure of the evils in some backward trade, or in some forgotten branch of domestic industry, serves as a starting point for the awakening of class-consciousness, for the beginning of a trade-union struggle, and for the spread of Socialism.

Recently, the overwhelming majority of Russian Social-Democrats were almost wholly engaged in this work of exposing factory conditions. It is sufficient to refer to the columns of *Rabochaya Mysl* to judge to what an extent they were engaged in it. So much so, indeed, that they lost sight of the fact that this, *taken by itself*, was not substantially Social-Democratic work, but merely trade-union work. As a matter of fact, these exposures merely dealt with the relations between the workers *in a given trade*, with their immediate employers, and all that it achieved was that the vendors of labour power learned to sell their " commodity " on better terms, and to fight the purchasers of labour power over a purely commercial deal. These exposures might have served (if properly utilised by revolutionaries) as a beginning and a constituent part of Social-Democratic activity, but they might also (and with subservience to spontaneity inevitably had to) have led to a "pure and simple " trade-union struggle and to a non-Social-Democratic labour movement. Social-Democrats lead the struggle of the working class not only for better terms for the sale of labour power, but also for the abolition of the social system which compels the propertyless class to sell itself to the rich. Social-Democracy represents the working class, not in its relation to a given group of employers, but in its relation to all classes in modern society, to the state as an organised political force. Hence, it not only follows that Social-Democrats must not confine themselves entirely to the economic struggle ; they must not even allow the organisation of economic exposures to become the predominant part of their activities. We must actively take up the political education of the working class, and the development of its political consciousness. *Now*, after *Zarya* and *Iskra* have made the first attack upon Economism " all are agreed " with this (although some agreed only nominally, as we shall soon prove).

The question now arises : What does political education mean ? Is it sufficient to confine oneself to the propaganda of working-class hostility to autocracy ? Of course not. It is not enough to *explain* to the workers that they are politically oppressed (any more than it was to *explain* to them that their interests were antagonistic to the interests of the employers). Advantage must be taken of every concrete example of this oppression for the purpose of agitation (in the same way as we began to use concrete examples of economic oppression for the purpose of agitation). And inasmuch as *political* oppression affects all sorts of classes in society, inasmuch as it manifests itself in various spheres of life and activity, in industrial life, civic life, in personal and family life, in religious life, scientific life, etc., etc., is it not evident that *we shall not be fulfilling our task* of developing the political consciousness of the workers if *we do not undertake* the organisation of the *political exposure of autocracy in all its aspects* ? In order to agitate over concrete examples of oppression, these examples must be exposed (in the same way as it was necessary to expose factory evils in order to carry on economic agitation).

One would think that this was clear enough. It turns out, however, that " all " are agreed that it is necessary to develop political consciousness *in all its aspects*, only in words. It turns out that *Rabocheye Dyelo*, for example, has not only failed to take up the task of organising (or to make a start in organising) in all-sided political exposure, but is even trying to *drag Iskra*, which has undertaken this task, *away from it*. Listen to this : " The political struggle of the working class is merely (it is precisely not " merely ") a more developed, a wider and more effective form of economic struggle." [Programme of *Rabocheye Dyelo* published in No. 1, p. 3.] " The Social Democrats are now confronted with the task of, as far as possible, giving the economic struggle itself a political character." [Martynov, *Rabocheye Dyelo*, No. 10, p. 42.] " The economic struggle is the most widely applicable method of drawing the masses into active political struggle " (resolution passed by the congress of the League and "amendments" thereto). [*Two Congresses*, pp. 11 and 17.] As the reader will observe, all these postulates permeate *Rabocheye Dyelo*, from its very first number to the recently issued Instructions by the Editorial Committee, and all of them evidently express a single view regarding political agitation and the political struggle. Examine this view from the standpoint of the opinion prevailing among all Economists, that political agitation must *follow* economic agitation. Is it true that in general the economic struggle " is the most widely applicable method " of drawing the masses into the political struggle? It is absolutely untrue. All and sundry manifestations of police tyranny and autocratic outrage, in addition to the evils connected with the economic struggle, are equally " widely applicable " as a means of " drawing in " the masses. The tyranny of the Zemstvo chiefs, the flogging of the peasantry, the corruption of the officials, the conduct of the police towards the " common people " in the cities, the fight against the famine-stricken and the suppression of the popular striving towards enlightenment and knowledge, the extortion of taxes, the persecution of the religious sects, the severe discipline in the army, the militarist conduct towards the students and the liberal intelligentsia—all these and a thousand other similar manifestations of tyranny, though not directly connected with the " economic " struggle, do they, in general, represent a *less* " widely applicable " method and subject for political agitation and for drawing the masses into the political struggle? The very opposite is the case. Of all the innumerable cases in which

the workers suffer (either personally or those closely associated with them) from tyranny, violence, and lack of
rights, undoubtedly only a relatively few represent cases
of police tyranny in the economic struggle as such. Why
then should we beforehand *restrict* the scope of political
agitation by declaring *only one* of the methods to be " the
most widely applicable," when Social-Democrats have
other, generally speaking, not less " widely applicable "
means ?

Long, long ago (a year ago ! . . .) *Rabocheye Dyelo* wrote :

> The masses begin to understand immediate political demands
> after one, or at all events, after several strikes ; immediately
> the government sets the police and gendarmerie against them
> [No. 7, p. 15, August 1900].

This opportunist theory of stages has now been rejected
by the League, which makes a concession to us by declaring : " There is no need whatever to conduct political
agitation right from the beginning, exclusively on an
economic basis." [*Two Congresses*, p. 11.] This very repudiation of part of its former errors by the League will enable
the future historian of Russian Social-Democracy to discern
the depths to which our Economists have degraded Socialism better than any number of lengthy arguments ! But
the League must be very naïve indeed to imagine that the
abandonment of one form of restricting politics will induce
us to agree to another form of restriction ! Would it not be
more logical to say that the economic struggle should be
conducted on the widest possible basis, that it should be
utilised for political agitation, but that " there is no need
whatever " to regard the economic struggle as the *most*
widely applicable means of drawing the masses into active
political struggle ? The League attaches significance to the
fact that it substituted the phrase " most widely applicable
method " by the phrase " a better method," contained in
one of the resolutions of the Fouth Congress of the Jewish
Labour League (Bund). We confess that we find it difficult

to say which of these resolutions is the better one. In our opinion *both are bad*. Both the League and the Bund fall into error (partly perhaps unconsciously, owing to the influence of tradition) concerning the economic, trade-unionist interpretation of politics. The fact that this error is expressed either by the word " better " or by the words " most widely applicable " makes no material difference whatever. If the League had said that " political agitation on an economic basis " is the most widely applied (and not " applicable ") method it would have been right in regard to a certain period in the development of our Social-Democratic movement. It would have been right in regard to the *Economists and to many* (if not the majority) of the practical Economists of 1898–1901 who have *applied* the method of political agitation (to the extent that they applied it at all) *almost exclusively on an economic basis*. Political agitation on *such* lines was recognised, and as we have seen, even recommended by *Rabochaya Mysl*, and by the Self-Emancipation group ! *Rabocheye Dyelo* should have *strongly condemned* the fact that useful economic agitation was accompanied by the harmful restriction of the political struggle, but, instead of that, it declares the method most widely *applied* (*by the Economists*) to be the most widely *applicable* ! It is not surprising, therefore, that when we describe these people as Economists, they can do nothing else but pour abuse upon us, and call us " mystifiers," " disrupters," " Papal Nuncios," and " slanderers," go complaining to the world that we have mortally offended them and declare almost on oath that " not a single Social-Democratic organisation is now tinged with Economism. Oh, these evil, slanderous politicians ! They must have deliberately invented this Economism, out of sheer hatred of mankind, in order mortally to offend other people !

What do the words " to give the economic struggle itself a political character," which Martynov uses in presenting the tasks of Social-Democracy, mean concretely ? The economic struggle is the collective struggle of the workers against their employers for better terms *in the sale of their labour power*, for better conditions of life and labour. This struggle is necessarily a struggle according to trade, because conditions of labour differ very much in different trades, and, consequently, the fight to *improve* these conditions can only be conducted in respect of each trade (trade unions in the Western countries, temporary trade associations and leaflets in Russia, etc.). To give " the economic struggle itself a political character " means, therefore, to strive to secure satisfaction for these trade demands, the improvement of conditions of labour in each separate trade by means of "legislative and adminstrative measures" (as Martynov expresses it on the next page of his article, p. 43). This is exactly what the trade unions do and always have done. Read the works of the thoroughly scientific (and " thoroughly " opportunist) Mr. and Mrs. Webb and you will find that the British trade unions long ago recognised, and have long carried out the task of " giving the economic struggle itself a political character " ; they have long been fighting for the right to strike, for the removal of all juridical hindrances to the co-operative and trade-union movement, for laws protecting women and children, for the improvement of conditions of labour by means of sanitary and factory legislation, etc.

Thus, the pompous phrase : " To give the economic struggle *itself* a political character," which sounds so " terrifically " profound and revolutionary, serves as a screen to conceal what is in fact the traditional striving to *degrade* Social-Democratic politics to the level of trade-union politics ! On the pretext of rectifying *Iskra's* onesidedness, which, it is alleged, places " the revolutionising of dogma higher than the revolutionising of life," we are presented with the *struggle for economic reform* as if it were something entirely new. As a matter of fact, the phrase " to give the economic struggle itself a political character " means nothing more than the struggle for economic reforms. And Martynov himself might have come to this simple conclusion had he only pondered over the significance of his own words. " Our party," he says, turning his heaviest guns against *Iskra*, " could and should have presented concrete demands to the government for legislative and administrative measures against economic exploitation, for the relief of unemployment, for the relief of the famine-stricken, etc." [*Rabocheye Dyelo*, No. 10, pp. 42, 43.] Concrete demands for measures—does not this mean demands for social reforms ? And again we ask the impartial reader, do we slander the *Rabocheye Dyeloists* (may I be forgiven for this clumsy expression !) when we declare them to be concealed Bernsteinists, for advancing their thesis about the necessity for fighting for economic reforms as a reason for their *disagreement* with *Iskra* ?

Revolutionary Social-Democracy always included, and now includes, the fight for reforms in its activities. But it utilises " economic " agitation for the purpose of presenting to the government, not only demands for all sorts of measures, but also (and primarily) the demand that it cease to be an autocratic government. Moreover, it considers it to be its duty to present this demand to the government, not on the basis of the economic struggle *alone*, but on the basis of all manifestations of public and political life. In a word, it subordinates the struggle for reforms to the revolutionary struggle for liberty and for Socialism, in the same way as the part is subordinate to the whole. Martynov, however, resuscitates the theory of stages in a new form, and strives to prescribe an exclusively economic so to speak, path of development for the political struggle. By coming out at this moment, when the revolutionary movement is on the up-grade, with an alleged special " task " of fighting for reforms, he is dragging the party backwards, and is playing into the hands of both " economic " and liberal opportunism.

Shamefacedly hiding the struggle for reforms behind the pompous thesis " to give the economic struggle itself a political character," Martynov advanced, as if it were a special point, *exclusively economic* (in fact, exclusively factory) *reforms*. Why he did that, we do not know. Perhaps it was due to carelessness? But if he indeed had only " factory " reforms in mind, then the whole of his thesis, which we have just quoted, loses all sense. Perhaps he did it because he thought it possible and probable that the government would agree to make " concessions " only in the economic sphere? If that is what he thought, then it is a strange error. Concessions are also possible, and are made in the sphere of legislation concerning flogging, passports, land-compensation payments, religious sects, the censorship, etc., etc. " Economic " concessions (or pseudo-concessions) are, of course, the cheapest and most advantageous concessions) to make from the government's point of view, because by these means it hopes to win the confidence of the masses of the workers. Precisely for this very reason, Social-Democrats *must under no circumstances* create grounds for the belief (or the misunderstanding) that we attach greater value to economic reforms than to political reforms, or that we regard them as being particularly important, etc. . . .

Political Exposures and "Training in Revolutionary Activity"

In advancing against *Iskra* his " theory " of " raising the activity of the masses of the workers," Martynov, as a matter of fact, displayed a striving to *diminish* this activity, because he declared the very economic struggle before which all Economists grovel to be the preferable, the most important and " the most widely applicable means of rousing this activity, and the widest field for it." This error is such a characteristic one, precisely because it is not peculiar to Martynov alone. As a matter of fact, it is possible to "raise the activity of the masses of the workers" *only* provided this activity *is not restricted entirely* to "political agitation on an economic basis." And one of the fundamental

conditions for the necessary expansion of political agitation is the organisation of *all-sided* political exposure. In
no other way can the masses be trained in political consciousness and revolutionary activity except by means of
such exposure. Hence, to conduct such activity is one of the
most important functions of international Social-Democracy
as a whole, for even in countries where political liberty
exists, there is still a field for work of exposure, although in
such countries the work is conducted in a different sphere.
For example, the German party is strengthening its position
and spreading its influence, thanks particularly to the
untiring energy with which it is conducting a campaign
of political exposure. Working-class consciousness cannot
be genuinely political consciousness unless the workers are
trained to respond to all cases of tyranny, oppression,
violence and abuse, no matter *what class* is affected. Moreover, that response must be a Social-Democratic response,
and not one from any other point of view. The consciousness of the masses of the workers cannot be genuine class
consciousness, unless the workers learn to observe from concrete, and above all from topical, political facts and events,
every other social class and *all* the manifestations of the
intellectual, ethical and political life of these classes ; unless
they learn to apply practically the materialist analysis and
the materialist estimate of *all* aspects of the life and activity
of *all* classes, strata and groups of the population. Those
who concentrate the attention, observation and the consciousness of the working class exclusively, or even mainly,
upon itself alone, are not Social-Democrats ; because, for
its self-realisation the working class must not only have a
theoretical . . . rather it would be more true to say : Not
so much theoretical as a practical understanding acquired
through experience of political life of the relationships
between *all* classes of modern society. That is why the idea
preached by our Economists, that the economic struggle is
the most widely applicable means of drawing the masses
into the political movement is so extremely harmful and

extremely reactionary in practice. In order to become a Social-Democrat, a working man must have a clear picture in his mind of the economic nature and the social and political features of the landlord, of the priest, of the high state official and of the peasant, of the student and of the tramp ; he must know their strong and weak sides ; he must understand all the catchwords and sophisms by which each class and each stratum camouflages its egotistical strivings and its real " nature " ; he must understand what interests certain institutions and certain laws reflect and how they are reflected. The working man cannot obtain this " clear picture " from books. He can obtain it only from living examples and from exposures, following hot after their occurrence, of what goes on around us at a given moment, of what is being discussed, in whispers perhaps, by each one in his own way, of the meaning of such and such events, of such and such statistics, in such and such court sentences, etc., etc., etc. These universal political exposures are an essential and *fundamental* condition for training the masses in revolutionary activity.

Why is it that the Russian workers as yet display so little revolutionary activity in connection with the brutal way in which the police maltreat the people, in connection with the persecution of the religious sects, with the flogging of the peasantry, with the outrageous censorship, with the torture of soldiers, with the persecution of the most innocent cultural enterprises, etc. ? Is it because the " economic struggle " does not " stimulate " them to this, because such political activity does not " promise palpable results," because it produces little that is " positive " ? To advance this argument, we repeat, is merely to shift the blame to the shoulders of others, to blame the masses of the workers for our own philistinism (also Bernsteinism). We must blame ourselves, our remoteness from the mass movement ; we must blame ourselves for being unable as yet to organise a sufficiently wide, striking and rapid exposure of these despicable outrages. When we do that (and we must and can do it), the most backward worker will understand, *or will feel*, that the students and religious sects, the muzhiks and the authors are being abused and outraged by the very same dark forces that are oppressing and crushing him at every step of his life, and, feeling that, he himself will be filled with an irresistible desire to respond to these things and then he will organise cat-calls against the censors one day, another day he will demonstrate outside the house of the provincial governor who has brutally suppressed peasant uprising, another day he will teach a lesson to the gen-darmes in surplices who are doing the work of the Holy Inquisition, etc. As yet we have done very little, almost nothing, to *hurl* universal and fresh exposures among the masses of the workers. Many of us as yet do not appreciate the *bounden duty* that rests upon us, but spontaneously follow in the wake of the " drab every-day struggle," in the narrow confines of factory life. Under such circumstances to say that *Iskra* displays a tendency to belittle the signifi-cance of the forward march of the drab every-day struggle in comparison with the propaganda of brilliant and com-plete ideas [Martynov, p. 61]—means to drag the party backwards, to defend and glorify our unpreparedness and backwardness.

As for calling the masses to action, that will come of itself immediately that energetic political agitation, live and strik-ing exposures are set going. To catch some criminal red-handed and immediately to brand him publicly will have far more effect than any number of "appeals to action" ; the effect very often will be such that it will be impossible to tell who exactly it was that " appealed " to the crowd, and who exactly suggested this or that plan of demonstration, etc. Calls for action, not in the general, but in the concrete, sense of the term, can be made only at the place of action ; only those who themselves go into action now can make appeals for action. And our business as Social-Democratic publicists is to deepen, expand and intensify political

exposures and political agitation. A word in passing about
" calls to action." *The only paper* that *prior to* the spring
events, *called upon* the workers actively to intervene in a
matter that certainly did *not promise* any *palpable results* for
the workers, i.e., the drafting of the students into the army
was Iskra. Immediately after the publication of the order
of January 11 " Drafting the 183 Students into the Army,"
Iskra published an article about it (in its February issue,
No. 2), and *before* any demonstration was started openly
called upon " the workers to go to the aid of the students,"
called upon the " people " boldly to take up the government's open challenge. We ask : How is the remarkable
fact to be explained that although he talks so much about
" calling for action," and even suggests " calling for action "
as a special form of activity, Martynov said not a word
about *this* call ? After this, is not Martynov's allegation, that
Iskra was *one-sided* because it did not sufficiently " call for "
the struggle for demands " promising palpable results,"
sheer philistinism ?

Our Economists, including *Rabocheye Dyelo*, were successful because they disguised themselves as uneducated
workers. But the working-class Social-Democrat, the
working-class revolutionist (and their number is growing)
will indignantly reject all this talk about fighting for demands " promising palpable results," etc., because he will
understand that this is only a variation of the old song
about adding a kopeck to the rouble. These working-class
revolutionaries will say to their counsellors of the *Rabochaya
Mysl* and *Rabocheye Dyelo* : You are wasting your time,
gentlemen ; you are interfering with excessive zeal in a job
that we can manage ourselves, and you are neglecting your
own duties. It is silly of you to say that the Social-
Democrats' task is to give the economic struggle itself a
political character, for that is only the beginning, it is
not the main task that Social-Democrats must fulfil. All
over the world, including Russia, *the police themselves often
give* the economic struggle a political character, and the

workers are beginning to understand whom the government supports.[1]

The " economic struggle between the workers and the employers and the government," about which you make as much fuss as if you had made a new discovery, is being carried on in all parts of Russia, even the most remote, by the workers themselves who have heard about strikes, but who have heard almost nothing about Socialism. The " activity " you want to stimulate among us workers by advancing concrete demands promising palpable results, we are already displaying and in our every-day, petty trade-union work, we put forward concrete demands, very often without any assistance from the intellectuals whatever. But *such* activity is not enough for us ; we are not children to be fed on the sops of " economic " politics alone ; we want to know everything that everybody else knows, we want to learn the details of *all* aspects of political life and to take part *actively* in every political event. In order that we may do this, the intellectuals must talk to us less on what we already know, and tell us more about what we do not know and what we can never learn from our factory

---

[1] The demand " to give the economic struggle itself a political character " most strikingly expresses *subservience to spontaneity* in the sphere of political activity. Very often the economic struggle *spontaneously* assumed a political character, that is to say without the injection of the " revolutionary bacilli of the intelligentsia," without the intervention of the class-conscious Social-Democrats. For example, the economic struggle of the British workers assumed a political character without the intervention of the Socialists. The tasks of the Social-Democrats, however, are not exhausted by political agitation on the economic field; their task is to *convert* trade-union politics into the Social-Democratic political struggle, to *utilise* the flashes of political consciousness which gleam in the minds of the workers during their economic struggles for the purpose of *raising* them to the level of *Social-Democratic* political consciousness. The Martynovs, however, instead of raising and stimulating the spontaneously awakening political consciousness of the workers, *bow down before spontaneity* and repeat over and over again, until one is sick and tired of hearing it, that the economic struggle " stimulates " in the workers' minds thoughts about their own lack of political rights. It is unfortunate, gentlemen, that the spontaneously awakening trade-union political consciousness does not " *stimulate* " in your minds thoughts about your Social-Democratic tasks !

and " economic " experience, that is, you must give us
political knowledge. You intellectuals can acquire this
knowledge, and it is your *duty* to bring us that knowledge
in a hundred and a thousand times greater measure than
you have done up till now ; and you must bring us this
knowledge, not only in the form of arguments, pamphlets
and articles which sometimes—excuse my frankness !—
are very dull, but in the form of live *exposures* of what our
government and our governing classes are doing at this
very moment in all spheres of life. Fulfil this duty with
greater zeal, and *talk less about " increasing the activity of the
masses of the workers ! "* We are far more active than you
think, and we are quite able to support by open street
fighting demands that do not even promise any "palpable
results " whatever ! You cannot " increase " our activity,
because *you yourselves are not sufficiently active.* Be less subser-
vient to spontaneity, and think more about increasing *your
own* activity, gentlemen ! . . .

The Working Class as Champion of Democracy

We have seen that the organisation of wide political
agitation, and, consequently, of all-sided political exposures,
is an absolutely necessary *and paramount* task of activity,
that is, if that activity is to be truly Social-Democratic.
We arrived at this conclusion *solely* on the grounds of the
pressing needs of the working class for political knowledge
and political training. But this ground by itself is too
narrow for the presentation of the question, for it ignores
the general democratic tasks of Social-Democracy as a
whole, and of modern Russian Social-Democracy in particular. In order to explain the situation more concretely
we shall approach the subject from an aspect that is
" nearer " to the Economist, namely, from the practical
aspect. " Every one agrees " that it is necessary to develop
the political consciousness of the working class. But the
question arises, How is that to be done ? What must be

done to bring this about ? The economic struggle merely brings the workers " up against " questions concerning the attitude of the government towards the working class. Consequently, *however much we may try* to " give to the economic struggle itself a political character " *we shall never be able* to develop the political consciousness of the workers (to the degree of Social-Democratic consciousness) by confining ourselves to the economic struggle, for *the limits of this task are too narrow*. The Martynov formula has some value for us, not because it illustrates Martynov's abilities to confuse things, but because it strikingly expresses the fundamental error that all the Economists commit, namely, their conviction that it is possible to develop the class political consciousness of the workers *from within*, that is to say, exclusively, or at least mainly, by means of the economic struggle. Such a view is radically wrong. Piqued by our opposition to them, the Economists refuse to ponder deeply over the origins of these disagreements, with the result that we absolutely fail to understand each other. It is as if we spoke in different tongues.

The workers can acquire class political consciousness *only from without*, that is, only outside of the economic struggle, outside of the sphere of relations between workers and employers. The sphere from which alone it is possible to obtain this knowledge is the sphere of relationships between *all* classes and the state and the government—the sphere of the inter-relations between *all* classes. For that reason, the reply to the question : What must be done in order that the workers may acquire political knowledge ? cannot be merely the one which, in the majority of cases, the practical workers, especially those who are inclined towards Economism, usually content themselves with, i.e., " go among the workers." To bring political knowledge to the workers the Social-Democrats must *go among all classes of the population*, must despatch units of their army *in all directions*.

We deliberately select this awkward formula, we deliberately express ourselves in a simple, forcible way, not

because we desire to indulge in paradoxes, but in order to
" stimulate " the Economists to take up their tasks which
they unpardonably ignore, to make them understand the
difference between trade-union and Social-Democratic
politics, which they refuse to understand. Therefore, we
beg the reader not to get excited, but to hear us patiently
to the end.

Take the type of Social-Democratic circle that has been
most widespread during the past few years, and examine its
work. It has " contact with the workers," it issues leaflets
—in which abuses in the factories, the government's partiality towards the capitalists, and the tyranny of the police
are strongly condemned—and rests content with this. At
meetings of workers, there are either no discussions or
they do not extend beyond such subjects. Lectures and
discussions on the history of the revolutionary movement,
on questions of the home and foreign policy of our government, on questions of the economic evolution of Russia and
of Europe, and the position of the various classes in modern
society, etc., are extremely rare. Of systematically acquiring
and extending contact with other classes of society, no one
even dreams. The ideal leader, as the majority of the members of such circles picture him, is something more in the
nature of a trade-union secretary than a Socialist political
leader. Any trade-union secretary, an English one, for instance, helps the workers to conduct the economic struggle,
helps to expose factory abuses, explains the injustice of the
laws and of measures which hamper the freedom of strikes
and the freedom to picket, to warn all and sundry that a
strike is proceeding at a certain factory, explains the
partiality of arbitration courts which are in the hands of
the bourgeois classes, etc., etc. In a word, every trade-union
secretary conducts and helps to conduct " the economic
struggle against the employers and the government." It
cannot be too strongly insisted that *this is not* enough to
constitute Social-Democracy. The Social-Democrat's ideal
should not be a trade-union secretary, but *a tribune of the*

people, able to react to every manifestation of tyranny and oppression, no matter where it takes place, no matter what stratum or class of the people it affects ; he must be able to group all these manifestations into a single picture of police violence and capitalist exploitation ; he must be able to take advantage of every petty event in order to explain his Socialistic convictions and his Social-Democratic demands *to all*, in order to explain to *all* and everyone the world historical significance of the struggle for the emancipation of the proletariat. . . .

We said that a Social-Democrat, if he really believes it is necessary to develop the political consciousness of the proletariat, must " go among all classes of the people." This gives rise to the questions : How is this to be done ? Have we enough forces to do this ? Is there a base for such work among all the other classes ? Will this not mean a retreat, or lead to a retreat from the class point of view ? We shall deal with these questions.

We must " go among all classes of the people " as theoreticians, as propagandists, as agitators, and as organisers. No one doubts that the theoretical work of Social-Democrats should be directed towards studying all the features of the social and political position of the various classes. But extremely little is done in this direction compared with the work that is done in studying the features of factory life. In the committees and circles, you will meet men who are immersed say in the study of some special branch of the metal industry, but you will hardly ever find members of organisations (obliged, as often happens, for some reason or other to give up practical work) especially engaged in the collection of material concerning some pressing question of social and political life which could serve as a means for conducting Social-Democratic work among other strata of the population. In speaking of the lack of training of the majority of present-day leaders of the labour movement, we cannot refrain from mentioning the point about training in this connection also, for it is also bound up with the " economic " conception of " close organic contact with the proletarian struggle." The principal thing, of course, is *propaganda and agitation* among all strata of the people. The Western-European Social-Democrats find their work in this field facilitated by the calling of public meetings, to which *all* are free to go, and by the parliament, in which they speak to the representatives of *all* classes. We have neither a parliament, nor the freedom to call meetings, nevertheless we are able to arrange meetings of workers who desire to listen to *a Social-Democrat*. We must also find ways and means of calling meetings of representatives of all and every other class of the population that desire to listen to a *Democrat* ; for he who forgets that " the Communists support every revolutionary movement," that we are obliged for that reason to emphasise *general democratic tasks before the whole people*, without for a moment concealing our Socialistic convictions, is not a Social-Democrat. He who forgets his obligation to *be in advance of everybody* in bringing up, sharpening and solving *every* general democratic question is not a Social-Democrat. . . .

To proceed. Have we sufficient forces to be able to direct our propaganda and agitation among *all* classes of the population ? Of course we have. Our Economists are frequently inclined to deny this. They lose sight of the gigantic progress our movement has made from (approximately) 1894 to 1901. Like real Khvostists, they frequently live in the distant past, in the period of the beginning of the movement. At that time, indeed, we had astonishingly few forces, and it was perfectly natural and legitimate then to resolve to go exclusively among the workers, and severely condemn any deviation from this. The whole task then was to consolidate our position in the working class. At the present time, however, gigantic forces have been attracted to the movement ; the best representatives of the young generation of the educated classes are coming over to us ; everywhere, and in all provinces, there are people who have taken part in the movement in the past, who desire to do so now, who are striving towards Social-Democracy, but who are obliged to sit idle because we cannot employ them (in 1894 you could count the Social-Democrats on your fingers). One of the principal political and organisational shortcomings of our movement is that we are *unable* to utilise all these forces, and give them appropriate work (we shall deal with this in detail in the next chapter). The overwhelming majority of these forces entirely lack the opportunity for " going to the workers," so there are no grounds for fearing that we shall deflect forces from our main cause. And in order to be able to provide the workers with real, universal, and live political knowledge, we must have " our own men," Social-Democrats, everywhere, among all social strata, and in all positions from which we can learn the inner springs of our state mechanism. Such men are required for propaganda and agitation, but in a still larger measure for organisation.

Is there scope for activity among all classes of the population ? Those who fail to see this also lag intellectually behind the spontaneous awakening of the masses. The labour movement has aroused and is continuing to arouse discontent in some, hopes for support for the opposition in others, and the consciousness of the intolerableness and inevitable downfall of autocracy in still others. We would be " politicians " and Social-Democrats only in name (as very often happens), if we failed to realise that our task is to utilise every manifestation of discontent, and to collect and utilise every grain of even rudimentary protest. This is quite apart from the fact that many millions of the peasantry, handicraftsmen, petty artisans, etc., always listen eagerly to the preachings of any Social-Democrat who is at all intelligent. Is there a single class of the population in which no individuals, groups or circles are to be found who are discontented with the state of tyranny, and therefore accessible to the propaganda of Social-Democrats as the spokesmen of the most pressing general democratic needs ? To those who desire to have a clear idea of what the

political agitation of a Social-Democrat *among all* classes
and strata of the population should be like, we would
point to *political exposures* in the broad sense of the word
as the principal (but of course not the sole) form of this
agitation.

> We must " arouse in every section of the population that is at
> all enlightened a passion for *political* exposure," I wrote in my
> article " Where to Begin " (*Iskra*, No. 4, May 1901), with which
> I shall deal in greater detail later.
> " We must not allow ourselves to be discouraged by the fact
> that the voice of political exposure is still feeble, rare and timid.
> This is not because of a general submission to political despot-
> ism, but because those who are able and ready to expose have
> no tribune from which to speak, because there is no audience
> to listen eagerly to and approve of what the orators say, and
> because the latter can nowhere perceive among the people
> forces to whom it would be worth while directing their com-
> plaint against the ' omnipotent ' Russian government. . . .
> We are now in a position to set up a tribune for the national
> exposure of the tsarist government, and it is our duty to do so.
> That tribune must be a Social-Democratic paper. . . ."

The ideal audience for these political exposures is the
working class, which is first and foremost in need of universal and live political knowledge, which is most capable of
converting this knowledge into active struggle, even if it
did not promise " palpable results." The only platform from
which *public* exposures can be made is an All-Russian newspaper. " Unless we have a political organ, a movement
deserving the name of political is inconceivable in modern
Europe." In this connection Russia must undoubtedly be
included in modern Europe. The press has long ago become
a power in our country, otherwise the government would
not spend tens of thousands of roubles to bribe it, and to
subsidise the Katkovs, and Meshcherskys. And it is no
novelty in autocratic Russia for the underground press to
break through the wall of censorship and *compel* the legal
and conservative press to speak openly of it. This was the
case in the 'seventies and even in the 'fifties. How much

broader and deeper are now the strata of the people willing to read the illegal underground press, and to learn from it " how to live and how to die," to use the expression of the worker who sent a letter to *Iskra* [No. 7]. Political exposures are as much a declaration of war against the *government* as economic exposures are a declaration of war against the employers. And the wider and more powerful this campaign of exposure will be, the more numerous and determined the social *class* which has *declared war in order to commence the war* will be, the greater will be the moral significance of this declaration of war. Hence, political exposures in themselves serve as a powerful instrument for *disintegrating* the system we oppose, the means for diverting from the enemy his casual or temporary allies, the means for spreading enmity and distrust among those who premanently share power with the autocracy.

Only a party that will *organise* real all-national exposures can become the vanguard of the revolutionary forces in our time. The word all-national has a very profound meaning. The overwhelming majority of the non-working class exposers (and in order to become the vanguard, we must attract other classes) are sober politicians and cool business men. They know perfectly well how dangerous it is to " complain " even against a minor official, let alone against the " omnipotent " Russian government. And they will come *to us* with their complaints only when they see that these complaints really have effect, and when they see that we represent a *political* force. In order to become this political force in the eyes of outsiders, much persistent and stubborn work is required to *increase* our own consciousness, initiative and energy. For this, it is not sufficient to stick the label " vanguard " on " rearguard " theory and practice.

But if we have to undertake the organisation of the real all-national exposure of the government, then in what way will the class character of our movement be expressed ? —the over-zealous advocates of " close organic contact

with the proletarian struggle " will ask us. The reply is :
In that we *Social-Democrats* will *organise* these public exposures ; in that all the questions that are brought up by the
agitation will be explained in the spirit of Social-Democracy, without any deliberate or unconscious distortions of
Marxism ; in the fact that *the party* will carry on this universal political agitation, uniting into one inseparable whole
the pressure upon the government in the name of the whole
people, the revolutionary training of the proletariat—
while preserving its political independence—the guidance
of the economic struggle of the working class, the utilisation
of all its spontaneous conflicts with its exploiters, which
rouse and bring into our camp increasing numbers of the
proletariat ! . . .

V. I. Lenin

THE REVOLUTION OF 1905

*Articles published in Bolshevik journals during 1905 and 1906,
also a lecture delivered in Zurich in January 1917. English edition,
Martin Lawrence, Ltd., 1931.*

[During the Russian revolution of 1905 Lenin was in
Geneva, where he was editing the Bolshevik journals
Vperiod and later *Proletary*, the *Iskra* (which Lenin directed
from 1901–3) having come under Menshevik control since
1903. The first article, reprinted here, was written on Jan.
25, 1905, immediately after the massacre of the workers
in St. Petersburg on " Bloody Sunday," and was published
in *Vperiod*, Jan. 31, 1905. This was followed by other articles
on the various stages of the revolution. The lecture on the
1905 revolution delivered by Lenin in Zurich on January
Um

22, 1917, covers the ground of these articles, and is therefore the second document reprinted below. It is a complete analysis of the 1905 revolution, which Lenin later described as the " dress rehearsal " of the 1917 revolution.]

THE REVOLUTION OF 1905

THE BEGINNING OF THE REVOLUTION
IN RUSSIA

Geneva.
Wednesday, January 25.

M OST important historic events are taking place in Russia. The proletariat has risen against Tsarism. The proletariat has been driven to the uprising by the Government. Now there is hardly room for doubt that the Government deliberately allowed the strike movement to develop and a wide demonstration to be started in order to bring matters to a head, and to have a pretext for calling out the military forces. Its manœuvre was successful ! Thousands of killed and wounded—this is the toll of Bloody Sunday, January 22, in Petersburg. The army vanquished unarmed workers, women and children. The army overpowered the enemy by shooting prostrate workers. " We have taught them a good lesson ! " cynically say the Tsar's henchmen and their European flunkeys, the conservative bourgeoisie.

Yes, it was a great lesson ! The Russian proletariat will not forget this lesson. The most uneducated, the most backward strata of the working class, who had naïvely trusted the Tsar and had sincerely wished to put peacefully before " the Tsar himself " the requests of a tormented nation, were all taught a lesson by the military force led by the Tsar and the Tsar's uncle, the Grand Duke Vladimir.

The working class had received a great lesson in civil

war ; the revolutionary education of the proletariat advanced in one day further than it could have advanced in months and years of drab, everyday, stupefied existence. The slogan of the heroic Petersburg proletariat, " liberty or death ! " rings like an echo throughout the whole of Russia. Events are developing with marvellous speed. The general strike in Petersburg is spreading. All industrial social and political life is paralysed. On Monday, January 23, the encounters between the workers and the military become more stubborn. Contrary to the false Government *communiqués*, blood is spilt in many parts of the capital. The Kolpino workers are rising. The proletariat is arming itself and the people. There are rumours that the workers have seized the Sestroretsk Arsenal. The workers are supplying themselves with revolvers, they are forging their tools into weapons, they are procuring bombs for a desperate fight for freedom. The general strike is spreading to the provinces. In Moscow 10,000 people have already ceased work. A general strike is to be called in Moscow to-morrow (Thursday, January 26). A revolt has broken out in Riga. The workers in Lodz are demonstrating, an uprising is being prepared in Warsaw, demonstrations of the proletariat are taking place in Helsingfors. In Baku, Odessa, Kiev, Kharkov, Kovno and Vilno, there is growing ferment among the workers and the strike is spreading. In Sebastopol the stores and arsenals of the navy department are ablaze, and the troops refuse to shoot on the rebellious sailors. There are strikes in Reval and in Saratov. In Radom, an armed encounter occurred between the workers and a detachment of reserves which had been called out.

The revolution is spreading. The government is already beginning to waver. From a policy of bloody repression it is trying to pass to economic concessions and to save itself by throwing a sop, by promising the nine-hour day. But the lesson of Bloody Sunday must not be forgotten. The demand of the rebellious Petersburg workers—the immediate convocation of a Constituent Assembly on the basis of universal, direct, equal and secret suffrage—must become the demand of all the striking workers. The immediate overthrow of the Government—such was the slogan raised in answer to the massacre of January 9, even by those Petersburg workers who believed in the Tsar ; they raised this slogan through their leader, George Gapon, who said after that bloody day : " We no longer have a Tsar. A river of blood separates the Tsar from the nation. Long live the fight for freedom ! "

Long live the revolutionary proletariat ! say we. The general strike is rousing and mobilising larger and larger masses of the working class and of the city poor. The arming of the people is becoming one of the immediate problems of the revolutionary moment.

Only an armed people can be a real stronghold of national freedom. And the sooner the proletariat succeeds in arming itself, and the longer it maintains its martial position of striker and revolutionary, the sooner will the army begin to waver, the soldiers will at last begin to understand what they are doing, they will go over to the side of the people against the monsters, against the tyrants, against the murderers of defenceless workers and of their wives and children. No matter what the outcome of the present uprising in Petersburg will be, it will, in any case, be the first step to a wider, more conscious, better prepared uprising. The government may perhaps succeed in putting off the day of reckoning, but the postponement will only make the next step of the revolutionary attack more powerful. Social-Democracy will take advantage of this postponement in order to close the ranks of the organised fighters, and to spread the news about the start made by the Petersburg workers. The proletariat will join in the fight, will desert mill and factory, and prepare arms for itself. Into the midst of the city poor, to the millions of peasants, the slogans of the struggle for freedom will be carried more and more effectively. Revolutionary committees will be formed in every factory, in every section of the city, in every village. The people in revolt will overthrow all the government institutions of the Tsarist autocracy and proclaim the immediate convocation of the Constituent Assembly.

The immediate arming of the workers and of all citizens in general, the preparation and organisation of the revolutionary forces for annihilating the Government authorities and institutions—this is the practical basis on which all revolutionaries can, and must unite, to strike a common blow. The proletariat must always go its independent way in close contact with the Social-Democrat party, always bearing in mind its great final goal, the goal of ridding mankind of all exploitation. But this independence of the Social-Democratic proletarian party will never cause us to forget the importance of a common revolutionary attack at the moment of actual revolution. We Social-Democrats can and must proceed independently of the revolutionaries of the bourgeois democracy, and guard the class independence of the proletariat. But we must go hand in hand with them in an uprising when direct blows are being struck at Tsarism, when resisting the troops, when attacking the Bastille of the accursed enemy of the entire Russian people.

The eyes of the proletariat of the whole world are anxiously turned towards the proletariat of all Russia. The overthrow of Tsarism in Russia, started so valiantly by our working class, will be the turning-point in the history of all countries, will make easier the task of the workers of all nations, in all states, in all parts of the globe. Therefore, let every Social-Democrat, let every class-conscious worker remember the great tasks of the all-national struggle that now rest on his shoulders. Let him not forget that he represents the needs and the interests of the entire peasantry too, of the entire mass of the toiling and exploited, of the entire people against the all-national enemy. The whole world is watching the example of the heroic proletarians of St. Petersburg.

Long live the Revolution !
Long live the proletariat in revolt !

LECTURE ON THE 1905 REVOLUTION

MY YOUNG FRIENDS AND COMRADES,

To-day is the twelfth anniversary of " Bloody Sunday," which is rightly regarded as the beginning of the Russian Revolution.

Thousands of workers—not Social-Democrats, but faithful, loyal people—led by the priest Gapon, stream from all parts of the city to the centre of the capital, to the square in front of the Winter Palace, in order to submit a petition to the Tsar. The workers carry ikons, and their leader, in a letter to the Tsar, has guaranteed his personal safety and asked him to appear before the people.

Troops are called out. Uhlans and Cossacks hurl themselves against the crowd with drawn swords. They fire on the unarmed workers, who on their bended knees implore the Cossacks to let them go to the Tsar. On that day, according to police reports, more than 1,000 were killed and more than 2,000 were wounded. The indignation of the workers was indescribable.

Such is the bare outline of what took place on January 22, 1905, " Bloody Sunday."

In order that you may understand more clearly the significance of this event, I will quote to you a few passages from the workers' petition. The petition begins with the following words :

> We workers, inhabitants of St. Petersburg, have come to Thee. We are unfortunate, reviled slaves. We are crushed by despotism and tyranny. At last, when our patience was exhausted, we ceased work and begged our masters to give us only that without which life is a torture. But this was refused. Everything seemed unlawful to the employers. We here, many thousands of us, like the whole of the Russian people, have no human rights whatever. Owing to the deeds of Thine officials we have become slaves."

The petition enumerates the following demands : amnesty, civic liberty, normal wages, the land to be gradually transferred to the people, convocation of a Constituent Assembly on the basis of universal and equal suffrage ; and it ends with the following words : " Sire, do not refuse aid to Thy people ! Throw down the wall that separates Thee from Thy people. Order and swear that our requests will be granted, and Thou wilt make Russia happy ; if not, we are ready to die on this very spot. We have only two roads : freedom and happiness, or the grave."

Reading it *now*, this petition of uneducated, illiterate workers, led by a patriarchal priest, creates a strange impression. Involuntarily one compares this naïve petition with the peaceful resolutions passed to-day by the social-pacifists, i.e., who claim to be Socialists, but who, in reality, are bourgeois phrase-mongers. The unenlightened workers of pre-revolutionary Russia did not know that the Tsar was the head of the *ruling class*, namely, the class of large landowners, who by a thousand ties, were already bound up with a big bourgeoisie who were ready to defend their monopoly, privileges and profits by every violent means. The social-pacifists of to-day, who—without jesting —pretend to be " highly educated " people, do not realise that it is just as foolish to expect a " democratic " peace from the bourgeois governments, which are waging an imperialist predatory war, as it was foolish to think that the bloody Tsar could be induced to grant reforms by peaceful petitions.

Nevertheless, the great difference between the two is that the present-day social-pacifists are to a large extent hypocrites, who, by mild suggestions, strive to divert the people from the revolutionary struggle, whereas the unenlightened workers in pre-revolutionary Russia proved by their deeds that they were straightforward people who, for the first time, had awakened to political con-sciousness.

It is this awakening of tremendous masses of the people to political consciousness and revolutionary struggle that marks the historic significance of January 22, 1905.

" There is not yet a revolutionary people in Russia," said Mr. Peter Struve, then leader of the Russian liberals and publisher abroad of an illegal, free organ—*two days before* " *Bloody Sunday.*" To this " highly educated," supercilious and extremely stupid leader of the bourgeois reformists the idea that an illiterate peasant country could give birth to a revolutionary people seemed utterly absurd. The reformists of those days—like the reformists of to-day—were profoundly convinced that a real revolution was impossible !

Prior to January 22 (January 9, old style), 1905, the revolutionary party of Russia consisted of a small handful of people, and the reformists of those days (like the reformists of to-day) derisively called them a " sect." Several hundred revolutionary organisers, several thousand members of local organisations, half a dozen revolutionary papers appearing not more frequently than once a month, published mainly abroad, and smuggled into Russia under extraordinary difficulties and at the price of many sacrifices—such were the revolutionary parties in Russia, and revolutionary Social-Democracy in particular, prior to January 22, 1905. This circumstance gave the narrow-minded and overbearing reformists a formal justification for asserting that there was not yet a revolutionary people in Russia.

Within a few months, however, the picture completely changed. The hundreds of revolutionary Social-Democrats " suddenly " grew into thousands ; the thousands became leaders of between two and three millions of proletarians. The proletarian struggle gave rise to a strong ferment, often to revolutionary movements, among the peasant masses, fifty to a hundred million strong ; the peasant movement had its repercussion in the army and led to soldiers' uprisings, to armed clashes between one section of the army and another. In this manner, a colossal country, with a population of 130,000,000, entered into the revolution ; in this way slumbering Russia became transformed into a Russia of a Revolutionary proletariat and a revolutionary people.

It is necessary to study this transformation to understand its possibilities, its ways and methods, so to speak.

The principal means by which this transformation was brought about was the mass strike. The peculiar feature of the Russian Revolution is that in its social content it was a *bourgeois-democratic* revolution, but in its methods of struggle it was a *proletarian* revolution. It was a bourgeois-democratic revolution, since the aim toward which it strove directly and which it could reach directly, with the aid of its own forces, was a democratic republic, an eight-hour day and the confiscation of the immense estates of the nobility—all measures achieved almost completely in the French bourgeois revolution in 1792 and 1793.

At the same time the Russian Revolution was also a proletarian revolution, not only in the sense that the proletariat was the leading force, the vanguard of the movement, but also in the sense that the specifically proletarian means of struggle—namely, the strike—was the principal instrument employed for rousing the masses and the most characteristic phenomenon in the wave-like rise of decisive events.

The Russian Revolution is the *first*, though certainly not the last, great revolution in history, in which the mass political strike played an extraordinarily great rôle. It can even be asserted that it is impossible to understand the events in the Russian Revolution and the changes that took place in its political forms, unless a study is made of the *statistics of strikes*, which alone provide the clue to these events and change in form.

I know perfectly well that statistics are very dry in a lecture and are calculated to drive an audience away.

Nevertheless, I cannot refrain from quoting a few figures, in order that you may be able to appreciate the objective foundation of the whole movement. The average number of persons involved in strikes in Russia during the last ten years preceding the revolution was 43,000 per annum. Consequently, the total number of persons involved in strikes during the whole decade preceding the revolution was 430,000. In January, 1905, which was the first month of the revolution, the number of persons involved in strikes was 440,000. There were more persons involved in strikes in one month than in the whole of the preceding decade !

In no capitalist country in the world—not even in advanced countries like England, the United States of America, or Germany, has such a tremendous strike movement been witnessed as that which occurred in Russia in 1905. The total number of persons involved in strikes rose to 2,800,000, twice the total number of factory workers in the country ! This, of course, does not prove that the urban factory workers of Russia were more educated, or stronger, or more adapted to the struggle than their brothers in Western Europe. The very opposite is true.

But it does prove how great the dormant energy of the proletariat can be. It shows that in a revolutionary epoch— I say this without exaggeration on the basis of the most accurate data of Russian history—the proletariat *can* develop fighting energy *a hundred times greater* than in normal, peaceful, times. It shows that up to 1905, humanity did not yet know what a great, what a tremendous exertion of effort the proletariat is capable of in a fight for really great aims, and when it fights in a really revolutionary manner !

The history of the Russian Revolution shows that it is the vanguard, the chosen elements of the wage-workers who fought with the greatest tenacity and the greatest self-sacrifice. The larger the enterprises involved, the more stubborn the strikes were and the more often they repeated themselves during that year. The bigger the city the more significant was the rôle the proletariat played in the struggle. In the three large cities, St. Petersburg, Riga and Warsaw, where the workers were numerous and more class-conscious, the proportion of workers involved in strikes to the total number of workers was immeasurably larger than in other cities, and, of course, much larger than in the rural districts.

The metal workers in Russia—probably the same is true also in regard to the other capitalist countries—represent the vanguard of the proletariat. In this connection we note the following instructive fact : Taking all industries combined, the number of persons involved in strikes in 1905 was 160 per hundred workers employed, but in the *metal industry* the number was 320 per hundred ! It is calculated that in 1905 every Russian factory worker lost in wages in consequence of strikes, on the average ten roubles—approximately 26 francs at the pre-war rate of exchange—sacrificing this money, as it were, for the sake of the struggle. If we take the metal workers alone, we find that the loss in wages is *three times as great* ! The best elements of the working class marched in the forefront of the battle, leading after them the hesitating ones, rousing the dormant and encouraging the weak.

An outstanding feature was the manner in which economic strikes were interlaced with political strikes during the revolution.

It is quite evident that only when these two forms of strikes are closely linked up with each other can the movement acquire its greatest power. The broad masses of the exploited could not have been drawn into the revolutionary movement had they not seen examples of how the wage workers in the various branches of industry compelled the capitalists to improve their conditions. This struggle imbued the masses of the Russian people with a new spirit. Only then did the old serf-ridden, backward, patriarchal pious and obedient Russia cast off the old Adam ; only then did the Russian people obtain a really democratic and really revolutionary education.

When the bourgeois gentry and their uncritical chorus of satellites, the social-reformists, talk priggishly about the "education" of the masses, they usually mean something schoolmasterly, pedantic, something which demoralises the masses and imbues them with bourgeois prejudices.

The real education of the masses can never be separated from the independent, political, and particularly from the revolutionary struggle of the masses themselves. Only the struggle educates the exploited class. Only the struggle discloses to it the magnitude of its own power, widens its horizon, enhances its abilities, clarifies its mind, forges its will; and therefore, even reactionaries have to admit that the year 1905, the year of struggle, " the mad year," definitely buried patriarchal Russia.

We will examine more closely the relation between the metal workers and the textile workers in Russia during the strike struggle of 1905. The metal workers were the best paid, the most class-conscious and the best educated proletarians. The textile workers, who in 1905 were two and a half times more numerous than the metal workers, were the most backward and the worst-paid mass of workers in Russia, who in very many cases had not yet definitely severed their connections with their present kinsmen in the village. In this connection a very important fact comes to light.

The metal workers' strikes in 1905 show a preponderance of political over economic strikes, although at the beginning of the year this preponderance was not so great as it was toward the end of the year. On the other hand, among the textile workers were observed a great preponderance of economic strikes at the beginning of 1905, and only at the end of the year do we get a preponderance of political strikes. From this it follows quite obviously that the economic struggle, the struggle for immediate and direct improvement of conditions, is alone capable of rousing the backward strata of the exploited masses, gives them a real education and transforms them—during a revolutionary epoch—into an army of political fighters within the space of a few months.

Of course, for this to happen, the vanguard of the workers had to understand that the class struggle was not a struggle in the interests of a small upper stratum, as the reformists too often tried to persuade the workers to believe ; the proletariat had to come forward as the real vanguard of the majority of the exploited, drawing that majority into the struggle, as was the case in Russia in 1905 and as must certainly be the case in the coming proletarian revolution in Europe.

The beginning of 1905 brought with it the first great wave of strikes throughout the entire country. Already in the spring of that year we observe the awakening of the first big, not only economic, but also political *peasant movement* in Russia. The importance of this turning-point of history will be appreciated if it is borne in mind that it was only in 1861 that the peasantry in Russia was liberated from the severest bondage of serfdom, that the majority of the peasants are illiterate, that they live in indescribable poverty, oppressed by the landlords, deluded by the priests and isolated from each other by great distances and an almost complete absence of roads.

A revolutionary movement against Tsarism arose for the first time in Russia in 1825 and that revolution was represented almost entirely by noblemen. From that moment up to 1881, when Alexander the Second was assassinated by the terrorists, the movement was led by middle class intellectuals. They displayed the greatest spirit of self-sacrifice, and they aroused the astonishment of the whole world by their heroic, terroristic methods of struggle. Those sacrifices were certainly not made in vain. They certainly contributed—directly and indirectly— to the subsequent revolutionary education of the Russian people. But they did not and could not achieve their immediate aim—to call forth a popular revolution.

This was achieved only by the revolutionary struggle of the proletariat. Only the waves of mass strikes that swept over the whole country, coupled with the severe lessons of the imperialist Russo-Japanese war, roused the broad masses of peasants from their lethargic slumber. The word " striker " acquired an entirely new meaning among the peasants : it signified a rebel, a revolutionary, a term previously expressed by the word " student." As, however, the " student " belonged to the middle class, to the " learned," to the " gentry," he was alien to the people. On the other hand a " striker " was of the people ; he belonged to the exploited class ; when deported from St. Petersburg, he often returned to the village, where he told his fellow-villagers of the conflagration that had broken out in the cities that was to destroy the capitalists and nobility. A new type appeared in the Russian village—the class-conscious young peasant. He associated with " strikers," he read newspapers, he told the peasants about events in the cities, explained to his fellow villagers the meaning of political demands and called upon them to fight against the big landowners, the priests and the government officials.

The peasants would gather in groups to discuss their conditions and gradually they were drawn into the struggle. Gathering in large crowds they attacked the big landowners, set fire to their mansions and estates and looted their stores, seized grain and other foodstuffs, killed policemen and demanded that the huge estates belonging to the nobility be transferred to the people.

In the spring of 1905, the peasant movement was only in its inception ; it spread to only a minority of the counties, approximately one-seventh of the total were affected.

But the combination of the proletarian mass strikes in the cities with the peasant movement in the villages was sufficient to shake the " firmest " and last prop of Tsarism. I refer to the *Army*.

A series of *mutinies* in the navy and in the army broke out. Every fresh wave of strikes and of peasant movements during the revolution was accompanied by mutinies among the armed forces in all parts of Russia. The most well-known of these is the mutiny on the Black Sea cruiser, *Prince Potemkin,* which, after it was seized by the revolutionaries, took part in the revolution in Odessa. After the revolution was defeated, and the attempts to seize other ports (for instance, Feodosia in the Crimea) had failed, it surrendered to the Rumanian authorities in Constanza.

Permit me to relate to you in detail one little episode in the mutiny of the Black Sea Fleet, in order to give you a concrete picture of events at the apex of their development.

Gatherings of revolutionary workers and sailors were being organised more and more frequently. Since men in the armed forces were not permitted to attend workers' meetings, the workers began in masses to visit the military meetings. They gathered in thousands. The idea of joint action found a lively response. The most class-conscious companies elected deputies.

Then the military authorities decided to take action. The attempts of some of the officers to deliver " patriotic " speeches at the meetings had failed miserably : the seamen, who were accustomed to debating, put their officers to shameful flight. After these efforts had failed, it was decided to prohibit meetings altogether. In the morning of November 24, 1905, a company of soldiers, in full war kit, was posted at the gate of the naval barracks. Rear-Admiral Pisarevsky, in a loud voice, gave the order : " Permit no one to leave the barracks ! In case of disobedience, shoot ! " A sailor, named Petrov, stepped forth from the ranks of the company that received that order, loaded his rifle in everybody's view, and with one shot killed Lieutenant-Colonel Stein of the Brest-Litovsk Regiment, and with another wounded Rear-Admiral Pisarevsky. The command was given : " Arrest him ! " Nobody budged. Petrov threw his rifle to the ground and exclaimed : " Why don't you move ? Take me ! " He was arrested. The seamen, who rushed from every side, angrily demanded his release, and declared that they vouched for him. Excitement ran high.

" Petrov, the shot was an accident, wasn't it ? " asked one of the officers, trying to find a way out of the situation.

" What do you mean, an accident ? I stepped forward, loaded and took aim. Is that an accident ? "

" They demand your release. . . ."

And Petrov was released. The seamen, however, were not content with that ; all officers on duty were arrested, disarmed, and taken to company headquarters. . . . Seamen delegates, forty in number, conferred throughout the whole night. The decision was to release the officers, but never to permit them to enter the barracks again.

This little incident shows you clearly how events developed in the majority of the mutinies. The revolutionary ferment among the people could not but spread to the armed forces. It is characteristic that the leaders of the movement came from those elements in the navy and the army which had been recruited mainly from among the industrial workers and possessed most technical training, for instance, the sappers. The broad masses, however, were still too naïve, their mood was too passive, too good-natured, too Christian. They flared up very quickly ; any case of injustice, excessively harsh conduct on the part of the officers, bad food, etc., was enough to call forth revolt. But there was no persistence in their protest ; they lacked a clear perception of aim ; they lacked a clear understanding of the fact that only the most vigorous continuation of the armed struggle, only a victory over all the military and civil authorities, only the overthrow of the government and the seizure of power throughout the whole state could guarantee the success of the revolution.

The broad masses of the seamen and soldiers lightheartedly rose in revolt. But with equal light-heartedness they foolishly released the arrested officers. They allowed themselves to be pacified by promises and persuasion on the part of their officers ; in this way the officers gained precious time, obtained reinforcements, broke the power of the rebels, and then the most brutal suppression of the movement and the execution of the leaders followed.

It is instructive to compare the mutinies in Russia in 1905 with the mutinies of the Decembrists in 1825. At that time, the leaders of the political movement belonged almost exclusively to the officer class, particularly to the officers of the nobility ; they had become infected through contact with the democratic ideas of Europe during the Napoleonic Wars. The mass of the soldiers, who at that time were still serfs, remained passive.

The history of 1905 presents a totally different picture. The mood of the officers, with few exceptions, was either bourgeois-liberal reformist, or openly counter-revolutionary. The workers and peasants in military uniform were the soul of the mutinies ; the mutinies became a movement of the people. For the first time in the history of Russia the movement spread to the majority of the exploited. But on the one hand, the masses lacked persistence and determination, they were too much afflicted with the malady of trustfulness ; on the other hand, the movement lacked an organisation of revolutionary Social-Democratic workers in military uniform. The soldiers lacked the ability to take the leadership into their own hands, to place themselves at the head of the revolutionary army, and to assume the offensive against the government authorities.

These two shortcomings—we will say in passing—will slowly, perhaps, but surely, be removed, not only by the general development of capitalism, but also by the present war.

At all events, the history of the Russian Revolution, like the history of the Paris Commune of 1871, unfailingly teaches that militarism can never, under any circumstances, be vanquished and destroyed, except by a victorious struggle of one section of the national army against the other section. It is not sufficient simply to denounce, revile and to " repudiate " militarism, to criticise and to argue that it is harmful ; it is foolish peacefully to refuse to perform military service : the task is to keep the revolutionary consciousness of the proletariat in a state of high tension and to train its best elements, not only in a general way but concretely, so that when popular ferment reaches the higher pitch, they will put themselves at the head of the revolutionary army.

This lesson is taught us by daily experience in any capitalist state. Every " minor " crisis that such a state experiences shows us in miniature the elements and embryos of the battles which must inevitably take place on a large scale during a big crisis. What else, for instance, is a strike, if not a small crisis in capitalist society ? Was not the Prussian Minister for Internal Affairs, Herr von Puttkamer, right when he uttered his famous declaration : " Every strike discloses the hydra head of revolution " ? Does not the calling out of troops during strikes in all, even the most peaceful, the most " democratic "—save the mark—capitalist countries show *how* things will work in a *really great* crisis ?

But to return to the history of the Russian Revolution.

I have endeavoured to picture to you how the workers stirred the whole country and the broadest, most backward strata of the exploited, how the peasant movement began, and how it was accompanied by military uprisings.

In the autumn of 1905, the movement reached its zenith. On August 19 the Tsar issued a manifesto on the introduction of popular representation. The so-called Bulygin Duma was to be created on the basis of a suffrage embracing a remarkably small number of electors, and this peculiar " parliament " was supposed to have, not legislative, but only *advisory* powers !

The bourgeoisie, the liberals, the opportunists, were ready to embrace wholeheartedly this " grant " of a frightened Tsar. Like all reformists, our reformists of 1905 could not understand that historic situations arise when reforms and particularly mere promises of reforms pursue *only* one aim : to allay the unrest of the people, to force the revolutionary class to cease, or at least to slacken, its struggle.

Russian revolutionary Social-Democracy perfectly understood the true nature of the grant of an illusory constitution in August, 1905. This is why, without a moment's hesitation, it issued the slogans : " Down with the advisory Duma ! Boycott the Duma ! Down with the Tsarist government ! Continue the revolutionary struggle for the overthrow of this government ! Not the Tsar, but a provisional revolutionary government must convoke the first real popular representative assembly in Russia ! "

History proved that the revolutionary Social-Democrats were right by the fact that the Bulygin Duma was never convoked. It was swept away by the revolutionary storm before it assembled ; this storm forced the Tsar to promulgate a new electoral law, which provided for an increase in the number of electors, and to recognise the legislative character of the Duma.

In October and December, 1905, the rising tide of the Russian Revolution reached its highest level. The floodgates of the revolutionary power of the people opened wider than ever before. The number of persons involved in strikes—which in January, 1905, as I have already told you, was 440,000—reached over half a million in November, 1905 (in one single month, notice !). To this number, which applies *only* to factory workers, must be added several hundreds of thousands of railway workers, postal and telegraph employees, etc.

The Russian general railroad strike stopped railway traffic and most effectively paralysed the power of the government. The doors of the universities and lecture halls which in peace-time were used only to befuddle youthful heads with pedantic professorial wisdom and to turn them into docile servants of the bourgeoisie and Tsarism, were flung wide open and served as meeting-places for thousands of workers, artisans and office workers, who openly and freely discussed political questions.

Freedom of the press was won. The censorship was simply ignored. No publisher dared send the copy to the authorities, and the authorities did not dare take any measures against this. For the first time in Russian history revolutionary papers appeared freely in St. Petersburg and other cities ; in St. Petersburg alone, three daily Social-Democratic papers, with circulations ranging from 50,000 to 100,000, were published.

The proletariat marched at the head of the movement. It set out to win the eight-hour day in a revolutionary manner. The fighting slogan of the St. Petersburg prole-tariat was then : " *An eight-hour day and arms !* " It became obvious to the growing mass of the workers that the fate of the revolution could, and would, be decided only by an armed struggle.

In the fire of battle a peculiar mass organisation was formed, the famous *Soviets of Workers' Deputies*, meetings of delegates from all factories. In several cities in Russia these *Soviets of Workers' Deputies* began to play more and more the rôle of a provisional revolutionary government, the rôle of organs and leaders of rebellion. Attempts were made to organise Soviets of Soldiers' and Sailors' Deputies, and to combine them with the Soviets of Workers' Deputies.

For a period, several cities of Russia at that time re-presented something in the nature of small, local " re-publics," the state authorities were deposed, and the Soviet of Workers' Deputies actually functioned as the new state authority. Unfortunately, these periods were all too brief, the " victories " were too weak, too isolated.

The peasant movement in the autumn of 1905 reached still greater dimensions. *Over one-third* of the counties throughout the country were affected by " peasant riots " and real peasant uprisings. The peasants burned no less than 2,000 estates and distributed among themselves the provisions that the predatory nobility had robbed from the people.

Unfortunately, this work was not done with sufficient thoroughness : unfortunately, the peasants destroyed only one-fifteenth of the total number of noblemen's estates, only one-fifteenth part of what *they should have* destroyed, in order to wipe from the face of the land of Russia the shame of large feudal land ownership. Unfortunately, the peasants were too scattered, too isolated from each other in their actions ; they were too unorganised, not aggressive enough, and therein lies one of the fundamental reasons for the defeat of the revolution.

Among the oppressed peoples of Russia there flared up a national movement for liberation. *Over one-half, almost three-fifths (to be exact, 57 per cent.)* of the population of Russia is subject to national oppression : they have not the right to employ their native language, and are forcibly Russified. For instance, the Mohammedans, who number tens of millions among the population of Russia, with astonishing rapidity, organised a Mohammedan League. Generally speaking, all kinds of organisations sprang up and grew at a colossal rate at that time.

To give the audience, particularly the youth, an example of how at that time the national movement for liberation rose in connection with the labour movement, I quote the following case :

In December, 1905, the children in hundreds of Polish schools burned all Russian books, pictures and portraits of the Tsar, and attacked and drove out of the Russian schools the Russian teachers and Russian schoolmasters, shouting : " Get out of here ! Go back to Russia ! " The Polish pupils in the secondary schools put forward the following demands : (1) all secondary schools to be under the control of a Soviet of Workers' Deputies ; (2) joint pupils' and workers' meetings to be called within the school buildings ; (3) the wearing of red blouses in the secondary schools to be permitted as a token of membership in the future proletarian republic ; etc.

The higher the tide of the movement rose, the more vigorously and decisively did the reaction arm to fight against the revolution. The Russian Revolution of 1905 confirmed the truth of what Karl Kautsky had written in 1902 in his book *Social Revolution* (at that time he was still a revolutionary Marxist and not a defender of social-patriots and opportunists as at present). He wrote the following :

> The coming revolution . . . will be less like a spontaneous uprising against the government and more like a protracted *civil war*.

This is exactly what happened ! This will, undoubtedly, also happen in the coming European revolution !

The hatred of Tsarism was directed particularly against the Jews. On the one hand, the Jews provided a particularly high percentage (compared with the total of the Jewish population) of leaders of the revolutionary movement. In passing, it should be said to their merit that to-day the Jews provide a relatively high percentage of representatives of internationalism compared with other nations. On the other hand, Tsarism knew perfectly well how to play up the most despicable prejudices of the most ignorant strata of the population against the Jews, in order to organise—if not to lead directly—pogroms, those atrocious massacres of peaceful Jews, their wives and children, which have roused such disgust throughout the whole civilised world. Of course, I have in mind the disgust of the truly democratic elements of the civilised world, and those are *exclusively* the Socialist workers, the proletarians.

It is calculated that in 100 cities at that time 4,000 were killed and 10,000 were mutilated. The bourgeoisie, even in the freest republican countries of Western Europe, know only too well how to combine their hypocritical phrases about " Russian atrocities " with the most shameless financial transactions, particularly with financial support of Tsarism and with imperialist exploitation of Russia through the export of capital, etc.

The climax of the Revolution of 1905 was reached in the December uprising in Moscow. A small handful of rebels, namely, of organised and armed workers—they numbered not more than *eight thousand*—for nine days resisted the Tsarist government. The government dared not trust the Moscow garrison ; on the contrary, it had to keep it behind locked doors, and only on the arrival of the Semenovsky Regiment from St. Petersburg was it able to quell the rebellion.

The bourgeoisie are pleased to describe the Moscow uprising as something artificial and throw scorn upon it. In the German so-called " scientific " literature, for instance, Herr Professor Max Weber, in his great work on the political development of Russia, described the Moscow uprising as a " putsch." " The Lenin group," says this " highly learned " Herr Professor, " and a section of the Social-Revolutionaries had long prepared for this *senseless* uprising."

In order properly to appraise this professorial wisdom of the cowardly bourgeoisie, it is sufficient to recall the dry strike statistics. In January, 1905, there were only 13,000 persons involved in purely political strikes in Russia, whereas in October there were 330,000 and *in December the maximum was reached of 370,000 involved in purely political strikes*—in one month alone ! Let us recall the progress of the counter-revolution, the uprisings of the peasants and the soldiers, and we will soon come to the conclusion that the dictum of bourgeois science concerning the December uprising is not only absurd, but is a subterfuge on the part of the representatives of the cowardly bourgeoisie, which sees in the proletariat its most dangerous class enemy.

In reality, the whole development of the Russian Revolution inevitably led to an armed, decisive battle between the Tsarist government and the vanguard of the class-conscious proletariat.

In my previous remarks I have already pointed out wherein lay the weakness of the Russian Revolution which led to its temporary defeat.

With the quelling of the December uprising the revolution began to subside. Even in this period, extremely interesting moments are to be observed ; suffice it to recall the twofold attempt of the most militant elements of the working class to stop the retreat of the revolution and to prepare for a new offensive.

But my time has nearly expired, and I do not want to abuse the patience of my audience. I think, however, that I have outlined the most important aspects of the revolution—its class character, its driving forces and its method of struggle—as fully as it is possible to deal with a large subject in a brief lecture.

A few brief remarks concerning the world significance of the Russian Revolution.

Geographically, economically, and historically, Russia belongs, not only to Europe, but also to Asia. This is why the Russian Revolution succeeded in finally rousing the biggest and the most backward country in Europe and in creating a revolutionary people led by a revolutionary proletariat. It achieved more than that.

The Russian Revolution gave rise to a movement throughout the whole of Asia. The revolutions in Turkey, Persia and China prove that the mighty uprising of 1905 left deep traces, and that its influence expressed in the forward movement of *hundreds and hundreds* of millions of people is ineradicable.

In an indirect way the Russian Revolution exercised influence also on the countries situated to the west. One must not forget that news of the Tsar's constitutional manifesto, reaching Vienna on October 30, 1905, played a decisive rôle in the final victory of universal suffrage in Austria.

A telegram bearing the news was delivered to the Congress of the Austrian Social-Democratic Party, which was then assembled, just as Comrade Ellenbogen—who at that time was not yet a social-patriot but a comrade—was making his report on the political strike. This telegram was placed before him on the table. The discussion was immediately stopped. Our place is in the streets !—this was the cry that resounded in the meeting hall of the delegates of Austrian Social-Democracy. The following days witnessed monster street demonstrations in Vienna and barricades in Prague. The victory of universal suffrage in Austria was decided.

Very often we meet Western Europeans who argue about the Russian Revolution as if events, relationships, and methods of struggle in that backward country have very little resemblance to Western European relationships and, therefore, can hardly have any practical significance.

There is nothing more erroneous than such an opinion.

No doubt the forms and occasions for the impending battles in the coming European revolution will, in many respects, differ from the forms of the Russian Revolution.

Nevertheless, the Russian Revolution—precisely because of its proletarian character in that particular sense to which I referred—was the *prologue* to the coming European revolution. Undoubtedly this coming revolution can only be a proletarian revolution in the profounder sense of the word : a proletarian Socialist revolution even in its content. This coming revolution will show to an even greater degree on the one hand, that only stern battles, only civil wars, can free humanity from the yoke of capital ; on the other hand, that only class-conscious proletarians can and will come forth in the rôle of leaders of the vast majority of the exploited.

The present grave-like stillness in Europe must not deceive us. Europe is charged with revolution. The monstrous horrors of the imperialist war, the suffering caused by the high cost of living, engender everywhere a revolutionary spirit ; and the ruling classes, the bourgeoisie with its servitors, the governments, are more and more moving into a blind alley from which they can never extricate themselves without tremendous upheavals.

Just as in 1905 a popular uprising against the Tsarist government commenced under the leadership of the proletariat with the aim of achieving a democratic republic, so the coming years, precisely because of this predatory war, will lead in Europe to popular uprisings under the leadership of the proletariat against the power of finance capital, against the big banks, against the capitalists ; and these upheavals cannot end otherwise than with the expropriation of the bourgeoisie, with the victory of Socialism.

We of the older generation may not live to see the decisive battles of this coming revolution. But I can certainly express the hope that the youth who are working so splendidly in the Socialist movement of Switzerland, and of the whole world, will be fortunate enough not only to fight, but also to win, in the coming proletarian revolution.

V. I. Lenin

MATERIALISM AND EMPIRIO-CRITICISM

First published 1909. English edition, Martin Lawrence Ltd., 1928

[When in exile in Siberia in 1898–9 Lenin took up the study of philosophy, intending to support Plekhanov in his defence of dialectical materialism against the neo-Kantians. In 1903–4 a new revisionist movement began among the Russian Social Democrats ; the leading figures were A. Bogdanov and A. Lunacharsky. The 1905 revolution interrupted the philosophical controversy, which was not resumed until 1907–8, when a number of anti-materialist tendencies again became prominent. Matters came to a head with the publication in St. Petersburg in 1908 of a volume called *Outlines of Marxian Philosophy*, by a number of contributors including Bogdanov and Lunacharsky. Lenin wrote to Maxim Gorki : " With the reading of each article my indignation has grown more intense. No, this is not Marxism . . ." He at once began to work on his reply, *Materialism and Empirio-Criticism*, which is a fundamental contribution to Marxist philosophy, clearly developing the principles of dialectical materialism against every form of idealism. Here it is only possible to give a few sections dealing particularly with the theory of knowledge.]

MATERIALISM AND EMPIRIO-CRITICISM

THE THEORY OF KNOWLEDGE OF EMPIRIO-CRITICISM AND OF DIALECTIC MATERIALISM

Sensations and Complexes of Sensations

THE FUNDAMENTAL tenets of the theory of knowledge of Mach and Avenarius are expounded with frankness, simplicity and clearness only in their early philosophic works. To these works we shall now turn. As to the corrections and emendations which were afterwards effected by these writers, we shall take them up later on.

" The problem of science," Mach wrote in 1872, " can be split into three parts :

" 1. The determination of the connection of presentations. This is psychology.

" 2. The discovery of the laws of the connection of sensations (perceptions). This is physics.

" 3. The clear establishment of the laws of the connection of sensations and presentations. This is psycho-physics."

This is clear enough.

The object of physics is the relation between sensations and not between things or bodies, the images of which are our sensations. And in 1883, in his *Die Mechanik in ihrer Entwickelung*, Mach repeats the very same notion : " Sensations are not ' symbols of things.' The ' thing ' is rather the mental symbol of the complex of sensations which is in a state of relative equilibrium. Not the things (bodies) but colours, sounds, pressures, spaces, times (what we usually call sensations), are the actual elements of the world."

About this word " elements," the fruit of twelve years of " reflection," we shall speak further. At present let us note that Mach is explicit in his statement that things or bodies are complexes of sensations, and that his position is the opposite of that which holds that sensations are " symbols " of things (it would be more correct to say images or reflections of things). The latter theory is philosophic materialism. For instance, Friedrich Engels—the well-known collaborator of Marx and the co-founder of Marxism—constantly and exclusively speaks in his works of things and their mental images or reflections (*Gedanken, Abbilder*). It is obvious that these mental images arise only from sensations. It would seem that the position of " philosophic Marxism " ought to be known to everyone who speaks of it, especially to one who in the name of this philosophy writes about it. But because of the great confusion which our Machians have brought with them, it is very urgent to repeat things which are generally known. We turn to the first paragraph of *Anti-Dühring* and we read : " the things and their mental reflection . . ." ; or to the first paragraph of the philosophic part which reads thus : " But how are these subjective principles derived ? [The question here is about the fundamental principles of all knowledge.] From thought itself ? No. These forms can never be created by thought nor derived from it but only from the external world. . . . Principles are not the starting points of investigation [as it is with Dühring who wishes

MATERIALISM AND EMPIRIO-CRITICISM 637

to be a materialist, but who cannot consistently carry out materialism] but the conclusion of it ; they are not to be applied to nature and history but are derived from them. Nature and Humanity are not steered by principles, but principles are, on the other hand, only correct in so far as they correspond to nature and history. That is just the materialistic conception of matter, and the opposite, that of Dühring is the idealistic conception. It turns things upside down and constructs a real world out of the world of thought " (p. 55). Engels, to repeat, applies this " sole materialistic view " everywhere and without exception, relentlessly attacking Dühring for the least deviation from materialism to idealism. Those who will pay the slightest attention in reading *Ludwig Feuerbach* and *Anti-Dühring* will find scores of examples in which Engels speaks of things and their reflection in the human brain, in our consciousness, reason, etc. Engels does not say that sensations or ideas are " symbols " of things, for a consistent materialist ought to use the term image, picture, or reflection instead of " symbol," as we shall prove when we come to consider the question. The argument here, however, is not at all about this or that formulation of materialism, but about the opposition of materialism to idealism, about the difference of two trends of thought in philosophy, that is, whether we are to proceed from things to sensations and thought, or from sensations and thought to things ? Engels sides with the first—materialism ; Mach, with the second—idealism. No tricks, no sophistry (with which we shall often meet in his later works), will obscure the clear and undisputed fact that Ernst Mach's doctrine of things as complexes of sensations is subjective idealism and a tedious repetition of Berkeleianism. If with Mach, bodies are to be reduced to " complexes of sensations," or with Berkeley, to " combinations of sensations," then from this it inevitably follows that the " world is my idea." Starting with such a supposition it is impossible to arrive at the existence of other selves except myself—and this is the purest solipsism. Much as Mach, Avenarius, Petzoldt and the others renounced solipsism, they were unable to get rid of it without falling prey to logical contradiction. To make this fundamental element of the philosophy of Machism still clearer, we shall adduce a few more citations from Mach's works. Here is a sample from the *Analysis of Sensations* :

> We see an object having a point S. If we touch S, that is bring it into connection with our body, we receive a prick. We can see S, without feeling the prick. But as soon as we feel the prick we find S on the skin. The visible point, therefore, is a permanent nucleus, to which the prick is annexed, according to circumstances, as something accidental. From the frequency of analogous occurrences we ultimately accustom ourselves to regard all properties of bodies as " effects " proceeding from permanent nuclei and conveyed to the ego through the medium of the body ; which effects we call sensations. . . .

In other words : people " accustom " themselves to materialism, to consider sensations as the result of the effect of bodies, things, or nature on our sense-organs. This harmful—for the philosophic idealist—" habit," acquired by mankind and natural science, is not at all to the liking of Mach, and he tries to break it. " By this operation, however, these nuclei are deprived of their entire sensory content and converted into a bare abstract symbol." An old song, most honourable Professor ! This is a literal repetition of Berkeley who said that matter is a bare abstract symbol. It is obviously Ernst Mach who is laid bare, for since he does not recognise the " sensory content " to be an objective reality, existing independently of us, then the sensory content remains a " bare abstract " self, an italicised and capitalised *Self* similar to " the insane pianoforte, which imagined that it was the sole existing thing in this world." If the " sensory content " of our sensation is not the outer world, then nothing exists save the bare self that indulges in empty philosophic trifling. A stupid and fruitless occupation ! " The assertion, then, is correct that the world consists only of our sensations. In which case we have knowledge *only* of sensations, and the assumption of the nuclei referred to, or of a reciprocal action between them, from which sensations proceed, turns out to be quite idle and superfluous. Such a view can only fit in with a half-hearted realism or a half-hearted philosophical criticism." (*Ibid.*)

We cited the sixth paragraph of the " anti-metaphysical utterance " of Mach in full. It is an absolute plagiarism from Berkeley. There is not a trace here of genuine thought, unless we are to regard the expression, " we perceive our perception " as original. From this it may be inferred that the " world consists of my sensations." The word " our," used by Mach, instead of " my " is illegitimately employed by him. By this word alone Mach betrays that " half-heartedness " of which he accuses others. For if the " asser-tion " of the existence of the outer world is an " idle " speculation, if the statement about the independent existence of the needle and of the interaction between my body and its point is " idle and superfluous," then the " assertion " of the existence of other selves is still more idle and superfluous. That means that only *I* exist, and our fellow men as well as the outer world come under the category of idle "nuclei." Holding such a doctrine one ought not to speak about "our" sensations; but as Mach does speak about them, it only betrays his own half-hearted method. It proves that his philosophy is a jumble of idle and shallow words in which he himself does not believe.

The following is a good example of Mach's confusion. In § 6 of Chapter II of the *Analysis of Sensations* we read : " If I can imagine that, while I am having sensations, I myself or someone else could observe my brain with all the necessary physical and chemical appliances, it would then be possible to ascertain with what process of the organism sensations of a particular kind are connected " (p. 242).

Well, then, does it mean that our sensations are connected

with a particular kind of processes which take place in the organism in general, and in our brain in particular? Mach very definitely admits this to be the case (it would be quite a task not to admit it from the standpoint of natural science !). But is this not the very same " assertion " about the very same " nuclei and their interaction " which our philosopher declared to be idle and superfluous? We are told that bodies are complexes of sensations ; to go further than that, to regard sensations as a product of the effect of bod:es upon our sense-organs is, in Mach's opinion, metaphysics, an idle and superfluous assertion, etc.—an opinion similar to Berkeley's. But the brain is a body, you will say. Yes, that means that the brain also is no more than a complex of sensations. And that means that with the help of the complexes of sensations I (and I am also nothing else than a complex of sensations) perceive the complex of sensations. What a wonderful philosophy ! At first to recognise sensations " as the real world elements " and on this to build an " original " Berkeleianism, and then secretly to import opposite views that sensations are connected in the organism with particular kinds of processes. Are not these " processes " connected with the exchange of matter between the " organism " and the external world ? Could this exchange occur, if the sensations of the organism did not present an objectively correct picture of this external world ?

Mach does not ask himself such embarrassing questions. He jumbles together fragments of Berkeleianism with views of natural science that instinctively adhere to the materialist theory of knowledge. . . . In the same paragraph Mach writes : " It is sometimes even asked whether inorganic ' matter ' has sensation . . ." Does this mean that there is no question about organic matter having sensation ? Does it mean that sensation is not something primary but that it is one of the properties of matter ? Oh ! yes, Mach leaves out all the absurdities of Berkeleianism ! " The question is natural enough, if we start from the generally current physical conception which represents matter as the immediately and undoubtedly experienced reality out of which everything, inorganic and organic, is constructed." Let us keep in mind Mach's valuable admission that the habitual and widely spread physical notions regard matter as an immediate reality, of which reality only one variety (organic matter) possesses the well defined property of sensation. " For sensation must either arise suddenly somewhere or other in this structure, or else have been present in the foundation-stones from the beginning. From our point of view the question is merely a perversion. Matter is for us not what is primarily given. What is primarily given is, rather, the elements which, when standing to one another in a certain known relation are called sensations."

What is primarily given, then, is sensation, though in organic matter it is " connected " only with a particular kind of process ! By making such an absurd statement, it seems as if Mach condemns materialism (" the generally current physical conception ") because the question as to why and how sensation " arises " has not been decided ! This is a sample of the " refutation " of materialism by the fideists and their sycophants. Can any philosophy " solve " questions if there has not been collected a sufficient amount of data for its solution ? Does not Mach himself say in the very same paragraph, " As long as this problem [i.e., what is the lower limit of sensation in the organic world ?] has not been solved in even a single special case, no decision of the question is possible " ?

The difference between materialism and Machism in this particular question is thus reduced to the following. Materialism in full agreement with natural science takes matter as the *prius*, regarding consciousness, reason and sensation as derivative, because in a well expressed form it is connected only with the higher forms of matter (organic matter). It becomes possible, therefore, to assume the existence of a property similar to sensation " in the

WM

foundation-stones of the structure of matter itself." Such, for example, is the supposition of the well-known German naturalist Ernst Haeckel, the English biologist Lloyd Morgan and others, not to speak of Diderot's conjecture, mentioned above. Machism clings to the opposite, idealistic viewpoint, which at once leads to an incongruity since, in the first place, sensation is taken as the primary entity in spite of the fact that it is connected with particular kinds of processes (in matter organised in a particular way) ; and, in the second place, the hypothesis that bodies are complexes of sensations is here destroyed by the assumption of the existence of other living beings and, in general, of other " complexes " besides the given great Self.

The word " element," which many a naïve person accepts (as we shall later see) as a new discovery, in reality only obscures the question by a meaningless and misleading term which has not the least bearing upon the solution of the problem. This term is misleading because there still remains so much to investigate, so much to find out about how matter, devoid of sensation, is related to matter which, though composed of the same atoms (or electrons), is yet endowed with a definite faculty of sensation. Materialism, by putting clearly the problem, gives impetus to continual experimentation thus making possible its solution. Machism, one variety of muddled idealism, by means of the trifling word " element," entangles this problem and sidetracks it.

In the last philosophic work of Mach there is one place that clearly betrays this idealistic trick. In his *Erkenntnis und Irrtum* we read : " While there is no difficulty in constructing any physical element out of sensation, which is a psychical element, it is impossible to imagine how we could compose a psychical experience out of elements that are current in modern physics, out of mass and motion, rigid elements that are only convenient for this special science."

Engels speaks very definitely about the rigidity of the views of many modern naturalists and about their metaphysical (in the Marxian sense, anti-dialectical) conceptions. We shall see how Mach failed in this particular point either because he was not able to grasp it, or because he was ignorant of the relationship of relativism to dialectics. But for the present we shall not concern ourselves with it. It is important for us to note here the definiteness with which Mach's idealism comes to the fore in spite of the confused, supposedly new terminology. Now we have the assurance that there will be no difficulty in building up physical elements out of sensations, that is from psychical elements ! Such constructions are, indeed, not difficult, for they are purely verbal constructions, empty scholasticisms which leave a loophole for fideism. No wonder, then, that after this discovery Mach dedicates his works to the immanentist school, no wonder that the followers of that school, the adherents of the most reactionary philosophic idealism, embrace Mach's theory. The " recent positivism " of Ernst Mach arrived only two hundred years too late. Berkeley gave numerous proofs that out of sensations, out of " psychical elements," one can " build " nothing but *solipsism* ! We have already learned something about the materialism, with which Mach contrasts his own views without naming the enemy frankly and explicitly, from the examples of Diderot. The doctrine consists not in the derivation of sensation from the movement of matter or in the identification of sensation with the movement of matter, but in the recognition that sensation is one of the properties of matter in motion. On this particular question Engels held Diderot's views. Engels opposed the " vulgar " materialists, Vogt, Büchner and Moleschott because they assumed that thought is secreted by the brain as bile is secreted by the liver, holding that in this matter, they were confused. But Mach who contrasts his views with those of the materialists, ignores, of course, all the great materialists—Diderot, Feuerbach, Marx and Engels— just as all other official professors of the official philosophy do.

To characterise the prime and fundamental conception of Avenarius let us take his first independent philosophic work. Bogdanov in his *Empirio-Monism* (Book 1, 2nd ed., 1905, p. 12, *note*) says that " in the development of Mach's views, the starting point was philosophical idealism, while the realistic tinge is characteristic of Avenarius from the very start." Bogdanov said this, for he took Mach at his word ; but in vain, for his assertion is diametrically opposed to the truth. On the contrary, the idealistic view of Avenarius is so prominent in his work of 1876, that he was himself compelled to admit it in 1891. In the Introduction to *Der Menschliche Weltbegriff* Avenarius says : " He who read my first systematic work, *Philosophie*, etc., must surely have presumed that I would attempt to treat the questions of the *Kritik der reinen Erfahrung* from the idealist standpoint," but " the sterility of idealism " compelled me to " doubt the correctness of my previous attitude " (*ibid.*, p. x.). This starting point of Avenarius is universally acknowledged in philosophic literature. Of the French writers I shall refer to Couwelaert who says that in the *Prolegomena* the philosophical standpoint of Avenarius is that of " monistic idealism." Of the German writers I shall name Rudolph Willy, Avenarius's disciple, who says that " Avenarius—in his youth, especially in his work of 1876—was totally under the influence of the so-called epistemological idealism."

It would be ridiculous to deny idealism in Avenarius' *Prolegomena*, when it openly states that " only sensation can be thought of as existing " (pp. 10 and 65 of the second German edition). That is how Avenarius himself presents the content of § 116 of his work. " We admitted," he says, " that the existing (*das Seiende*) is a substance endowed with sensation ; the substance falls off . . . [" it is more economical," as you see, " there is less effort " in thinking that there is no " substance " and that there exists no external world !] there remains sensation : we must then regard what exists as sensation through and through."

Sensation, then, exists without " substance," thought without brain ! Are there really such philosophers who are capable of defending this brainless philosophy ? Yes, there are ! And Professor Richard Avenarius is one of them. We must pause for a while on the argument advanced in defence of this philosophy, difficult as it is for a normal person to take it seriously. Here in §§ 89 and 90 of the same work is Avenarius' argument : ". . . The position that motion causes sensation is based on illusory experience alone. This experience, the separate act of which is perception, consists in the supposed fact that sensation arises in a certain kind of substance (brain) as a result of the transferred motion (excitation) and with the help of other material conditions (e.g., blood). However, regardless of the fact that this generation was never in itself observed, an empirical proof is at least necessary to show that sensation which is assumed to be caused in a certain substance by the transferred motion, did not already exist in the substance in one way or another ; so that the appearance of sensation should not be interpreted in any other way but as a creating act on the part of the transferred action. Thus only by the proof that where we have now a sensation there was none before, not even a minimal one, is it possible to ascertain the fact which, denoting as it does some act of creation, contradicts the rest of experience and radically changes our conception of nature. But it is impossible to obtain such proof through any experience ; on the contrary, the notion of a state of substance which, previously deprived of sensation, now begins to perceive, is no more than a hypothesis. And such hypothesis only complicates and obscures our knowledge instead of simplifying and clarifying it.

Should the experience, which assumes that a transmitted motion is capable of causing sensation in a substance that begins to perceive from this moment on, prove itself illusory upon more intimate acquaintance, then there would still remain sufficient material in the content of the experience to ascertain at least the relative origin of sensation from conditions of motion. It might appear that the amount of sensation, which was latent or minimal, or which did not appear to our consciousness before, now, due to the transmitted motion, frees itself, becomes more intense, or becomes known. However, even this bit of remaining content of experience is no more than illusory. Were we even in the position of ideal observers who could trace the outgoing motion from the moving substance A which, transmitted through a series of intermediate centres, reaches the substance B which is endowed with sensation, we would at best find that sensation in substance B developed simultaneously with the reception of the incoming motion, but we would not find that this occurred as a consequence of the motion.

We have purposely quoted this refutation of materialism by Avenarius in full, in order that the reader might see with what sophistry " recent " empirio-critical philosophy operates. We shall compare the argument of the idealist Berkeley with the *materialist* argument of Bogdanov, as a kind of punishment for the latter's betrayal of materialism !

In bygone days, nine years ago, when Bogdanov was still partly " a naturo-historical materialist " (that is, an adherent of the materialist theory of knowledge, which the preponderant majority of contemporary naturalists instinctively hold), when he was only partly confused by the befuddled Ostwald, he wrote : " From ancient times to the present, the classification of the facts of consciousness into three categories has still held true for descriptive psychology, namely, the domain of sensations and ideas, the domain of emotion and the domain of excitations . . . To the first category belong the images of phenomena of the outer or inner world that are taken by themselves in consciousness. . . . Such an image is called a " sensation " if it is directly caused by the intermediation of the sense-organ with its corresponding external phenomenon." And a little farther : " Sensation . . . arises in consciousness as a result of a certain external impulse transmitted by the external sense-organs " (p. 222). Or " sensation is the foundation of mental life; it is the immediate connection with the outer world "

(p. 240). " In the process of sensation the transformation of energy of external excitation into a fact of consciousness takes place at each step " (p. 133). And even in 1905 when, due to the benevolent assistance of Ostwald and Mach, Bogdanov abandoned the materialist viewpoint for the idealist, he still wrote (because of impaired memory!) in his *Empirio-Monism* : " As is well-known, the energy of external excitation is transformed at the nerve endings into a ' telegraphic ' form of the nervous current, as yet insufficiently elaborated yet devoid of mysticism. This energy reaches the neurones that are located in the so-called ' lower ' centres—ganglial, spinal, subcortical, etc." (Book 1, 2nd ed., 1905, p. 118.)

For every scientist, who is not led astray by professorial philosophy, as well as for every materialist, sensation is nothing but a direct connection of the mind with the external world ; it is the transformation of energy of external excitation into a mental state. This transformation has been observed by each of us a million times. The sophistry of idealist philosophy consists in that it takes sensation not as a connection of the mind with the outer world but as a screen, as a wall which separates the mind from the outer world ; in that it is taken not as an image corresponding to the perception of the external phenomenon but as the " only entity." Avenarius accepted the slightly changed form of this old sophistry which had already been worn thin by Bishop Berkeley. As we do not know all the conditions of the constantly observed connection of sensation with matter organised in a certain way, we recognise sensation alone as existing. The argument of Avenarius may be reduced to this. . . .

Did Nature Exist Prior to Man?

We have already seen that this question appears to be a crucial one for the philosophy of Mach and Avenarius. Natural science positively asserts that the earth once existed in a state in which no man or any other living creature existed or could have existed. Inasmuch as organic matter is a later appearance, a result of a long evolution, it follows that there could have been no perceiving matter, no " complexes of sensations," no self which is " inseparably " connected with the environment, as Avenarius would like to have it. Hence, matter is primary, and mind, consciousness, sensation are products of a very high development. Such is the materialist theory of knowledge, which natural science instinctively holds.

The question arises whether the outstanding representatives of empirio-criticism take note of this contradiction between their theory and natural science. They do take note and ask themselves by what arguments they can remove this contradiction. Three attitudes to this question are of particular interest to materialism, that of Avenarius himself and those of his disciples, Petzoldt and Willy.

Avenarius tries to eliminate the contradiction with natural science by means of the theory of the " potential " central term in the co-ordination. As we already know, co-ordination is the " inseparable " connection of the self and the environment. To remove the obvious absurdity of this theory the concept of the " potential " central term is introduced. For instance, what should be done with the hypothesis of man's development from the embryo ? Does the environment (the " counterpart of the term ") exist, if the " central term " is the embryo ? The embryonic system C—Avenarius contends—is the " potential central term in relation to the future individual environment " (*Bemerkungen*, p. 140). The potential central term is never equal to zero, not only when there are no parents but also when there are only the " integral parts of the environment" capable of becoming parents (p. 141).

The co-ordination then is continual. It is essential for the empirio-criticist to assert this in order to save the fundamentals of his philosophy—sensations and their complexes. Even when there is no human being, the central term is not equal to zero ; it only becomes the potential central term ! It is surprising that there still are people who can take a philosopher seriously who produces such arguments. Even Wundt, who asserted that he is no enemy of metaphysics (that is, fideism), was compelled to admit " the obscure mystification of the term experience " by the application of the word " potential " which destroys whatever co-ordination there is (*loc. cit.*, p. 379).

Indeed, can one take co-ordination seriously when its continuity consists in one of its members being potential ? Is this not mysticism ? Does this not lead to fideism ? If it is possible to think of the potential central term in relation to a future environment, why not think of it in relation to the past environment, that is, after man's death ? You will contend that Avenarius did not make this inference from his theory. Well, even this is not to the credit of his fallacious and reactionary theory, for it becomes thereby more cowardly. In 1894 Avenarius did not tell the whole tale, or perhaps feared to speak or even think about it consistently. Schubert-Soldern, however, referred to this theory in 1896 for theological purposes ; in 1906 he won the approval of Mach, who said that Schubert-Soldern followed a direction which was " in close proximity to Machism " (p. 4). Engels had a perfect right to attack Dühring, the open atheist, for leaving loopholes for fideism in his philosophy. He had several times justly accused the materialist Dühring for his drawing of theological inferences at least in the 'seventies. And still there now are people who wish to be considered Marxists and yet carry to the masses a philosophy which is very near fideism ! " It would seem," Avenarius wrote in *Bemerkungen*, " that from the empirio-critical standpoint natural science has no right to make queries about such periods of our present environment which precede the existence of man in time " (p. 144). Avenarius goes on to say that " he who asks questions about it cannot avoid imaginatively projecting himself there in space and time [*sich " hinzudenken "*] ;

what the natural scientist wants to know (though he is not clearly aware of it) is essentially this : How is the earth and the universe to be determined prior to the appearance of living beings or men ? Only by imagining oneself in the rôle of a spectator, just as one follows the history of another planet or solar system from the basis of our earth, with the help of perfected instruments."

An object cannot exist independently of our mind. " We shall always imaginatively project ourselves as reason endeavouring to apprehend the object."

This theory of the necessity of " projecting " the human mind into any object and into nature prior to the emergence of man, is laid down by me in the first paragraph, in the words of the " recent positivist " Avenarius, and in the second, in the words of the subjective idealist Fichte. The sophistry of this theory is so manifest that one feels uneasy in analysing it. Now then, if we " project " ourselves, our presence will be imaginary—but yet the existence of the earth prior to the emergence of man is real. To be sure, a man could not be an actual observer of the earth which was in a molten state, and to " imagine " his being present there is obscurantism. It is the same as if I were to prove the existence of hell by the argument that I could " project " myself there as an observer. The " reconciliation " of empirio-criticism with natural science may be reduced to this : Avenarius agrees to " project " something, the possibility of which is excluded by natural science. No man who has the least education, and is healthy, can doubt that the earth existed when there could be no life, no sensation or " central term." Hence, the whole theory of Mach and Avenarius, from which it follows that the earth is a complex of sensations (" bodies are complexes of sensations ") or " complexes of elements in which the mental and physical are similar," or " the counter part of the system in which the central term cannot be equal to zero," is philosophic obscurantism, a reduction of subjective idealism to absurdity.

Petzoldt, having seen the absurdity of the position into which Avenarius fell, felt ashamed. In his *Einführung in die Philosophie der reinen Erfahrung* (Vol. II) he devotes a whole paragraph (§ 65) to the problem of the reality of periods of the earth ante-dating the existence of man.

" In the teaching of Avenarius," says Petzoldt, " the self plays a rôle different from that in Schuppe [note that Petzoldt had openly and repeatedly declared : ' Our philosophy is founded on three persons—Avenarius, Mach, and Schuppe '] yet it is a rôle of determining importance for his theory." Petzoldt was evidently influenced by the fact that Schuppe had unmasked Avenarius by saying that everything was grounded on the self ; and Petzoldt wishes to correct himself. " Avenarius once said," Petzoldt continues, " that we can think of a place where no human foot as yet has trodden, but in order to *think* about it, it is necessary that that be present which we designate by the term ' self ' *whose* thought it becomes."

Petzoldt replies : " The epistemologically important question consists in, not whether we could think of such a place, but whether we have a right to think of it as existing, or having existed, independently of any individual reflection."

That is right ! People can think and " project " all kinds of hells and devils—Lunacharsky even " projected " (to use a mild expression) a religious conception—but the purpose of the theory of knowledge is to show the unreal, fantastic and reactionary character of such figments of the imagination.

" . . . That the system C [brain] is necessary for reflection, is obvious for both the philosophy of Avenarius and that which is defended by me. . . ."

It is not true ; Avenarius's theory of 1876 is a theory of mind without brain. And in the theory of 1892-4, as we shall see immediately, there is an element of idealist absurdity.

" . . . But is this system C made the *condition of existence* of, say, the Secondary period of the earth ? " And

Petzoldt, presenting the argument of Avenarius already cited, on the aim of science and on the possibility of " projecting " the spectator replies : " No, we wish to know whether we have a right to imagine the existence of the earth at that remote epoch in the same way as I would imagine it having existed yesterday or a while ago. Or must the existence of the earth be really conditioned (as Willy claimed) by our right to assume that at a certain time together with the earth there existed at least some system C, be it even on the lowest stage of its development ? " (About this idea of Willy we shall speak presently.)

" Avenarius evades Willy's queer inference by means of the argument that the person who put the question could not divorce himself from his thought (that is, imagine himself absent), otherwise he could not avoid projecting himself imaginatively into the situation. But then Avenarius makes the individual self of the person, who makes queries about such a self, the condition, not of a mere act of thought about the inhabitable earth, but of our right to think about the existence of the earth at that time.

" It would be easy to avoid these misleading paths, if we would not ascribe such importance to the self. The only thing the theory of knowledge demands, taking into consideration the various conceptions of the remote in both space and time, is that it be plausible and uniquely determined ; the rest is the affair of special sciences " (Vol. II, p. 325).

Petzoldt converted the principle of causality into that of unique determination and introduced into his theory, as we shall see below, the *a priority* of such principle. This means that Petzoldt saves himself from Avenarius's subjective idealism and solipsism (in the professorial jargon, he attributes an exaggerated importance to the self) with the help of the *Kantian* ideas. The absence of the objective element in the doctrine of Avenarius, the impossibility of reconciling it with the demands of natural science which declares the earth (object) to have existed long before the appearance of living beings (subject), compelled Petzoldt to resort to causality (unique determination). The earth existed, says Petzoldt, for its existence prior to the appearance of man is causally bound up with the present existence of the earth. But in the first place, where does the notion of causality come from? *A priori*, says Petzoldt. In the second place are not those conceptions of hell, devils and Lunacharsky's "projections" also bound by causality? In the third place, the theory " of the complexes of sensation " at any rate proves itself to be destroyed by Petzoldt. Petzoldt could not do away with the contradiction which he found in Avenarius, and entangled himself even more, for there could be only one solution—the recognition of the theory that the outer world reflected by us exists independently of our mind. Only such a materialist solution is really compatible with natural science, and only such a conception eliminates the idealist solution of the principle of causality of Petzoldt and Mach, about which we shall speak separately. . . .

Does Man Think With the Help of the Brain?

Bazarov emphatically answers this question in the affirmative. He writes : " If to Plekhanov's thesis ' that mind is an inner [Bazarov?] state of matter,' a more satisfactory qualification be added, namely, ' that each mental process is a function of the cerebral process,' then neither Mach nor Avenarius would object to it " (*Outlines*, p. 29).

For a mouse there is no stronger beast than a cat. For the Russian Machians there is no stronger materialist than Plekhanov. Was Plekhanov really the only one, or the first one, to defend the materialist thesis that mind is the inner function of matter? And if Bazarov did not like Plekhanov's formulation of materialism, why did he take cognizance of Plekhanov and not of Engels or Feuerbach? Simply because the Machians are afraid to admit the truth. They are fighting materialism, yet they pretend that they are only fighting Plekhanov. This is an unprincipled and cowardly stratagem.

Let us proceed, however, with empirio-criticism. Avenarius " would not dispute " the statement that " thought is a function of the brain," says Bazarov. These words are absolutely untrue. Avenarius not only objects to the materialist thesis, but he even invents a whole " theory " in order to refute this thesis. " Our brain," says Avenarius in *Der menschliche Weltbegriff*, " is not the locus or residue, or creator of thought ; it is not its instrument, or organ, or carrier or substratum " (p. 76—sympathetically quoted by Mach in the *Analysis of Sensations*, p. 28). " Thought is not an indweller, or master, or half, or an aspect of anything ; neither is it the product or even the physiological function cr state of the brain in general " (*ibid*). And no less emphatically does Avenarius express himself in his *Bemerkungen* : " Presentations are not functions (physiological, or mental, or psycho-physical) of the brain" (*op. cit.*, p. 419). Sensations are not " psychical functions of the brain " (§ 116).

According to Avenarius, then, the brain is not the organ of thought, and thought is not the function of the brain. Take Engels and you will immediately meet with views exactly contrary to those—views that are frankly materialistic. " Consciousness and thought," says Engels in *Anti-Dühring*, " are products of the brain of man " (p. 56, English edition). This idea is often repeated in that work. In *Ludwig Feuerbach* we have the following exposition of Feuerbach's and Engels's views: ". . . The material, perceptual universe, to which we ourselves belong, is the only reality, and . . . our consciousness and thought, however supernatural they may seem, are only evidences of a material bodily organ, the brain. Matter is not a product of mind, but mind itself is only the highest product of matter. This is, of course, pure materialism "

(p. 64). (*Cf.* p. 53) on the reflection of nature processes in the " thinking brain."

Avenarius rejects this materialist viewpoint saying that " the thinking brain " is a " fetish of natural science " (*Der menschliche Weltbegriff*, p. 70). Hence, Avenarius has no illusions concerning his absolute disagreement with natural science. He admits, as Mach and all the adherents of the immanentist school do, that natural science unconsciously upholds the materialist view. He admits and openly declares that he absolutely disagrees with the " prevailing psychology " (*Bemerkungen*, p. 150). The prevailing psychology is guilty of an inadmissible " introjection "—a new term invented by our philosopher, which means the inherence of thought in the brain, or of sensations in us. These two words (*in uns*), says Avenarius, express the fundamental proposition which empirio-criticism disputes. "This locating of the visible, etc., in man is what we call introjection " (p. 153, § 45).

This introjection rejects " on principle " the " natural conception of reality," substituting the expression " in me " instead of the expression " before me " (*vor mir*, p. 154), making " of one component part of the (real) environment an integral part of the (ideal) mind " (*ibid.*). " Out of the *amechanical* [a new word in place of ' mental '] which manifests itself freely and clearly in experience, introjection makes something which hides itself mysteriously in the central nervous system " (*ibid.*).

Here we have the same mystification which we encountered in the famous defence of " naïve realism " by the empirio-criticists and the adherents of the immanentist school. Avenarius is acting here on the advice of Turgeniev's rascal, to denounce mainly those vices which one recognises in himself. Avenarius pretends that he is combating idealism : See how ordinary philosophic idealism is inferred from introjection, how, he says, the outer world is converted into sensation, into representation and so forth, while I defend " naïve realism," and recognise everything experienced as equally real, both "self" and environment, without locating the outer world in the brain of man.

The sophistry here is the same as that which we observed in the case of his celebrated co-ordination. Distracting the reader's attention by his attacks on realism, Avenarius defends this same idealism, albeit with a somewhat changed phraseology : thought is not a function of the brain ; the brain is not the organ of thought ; sensations are not functions of the nervous system ! oh, no, sensations are "elements," psychical in one connection and physical in another—(though the elements are "identical "). Through the use of an ambiguous and pretentious terminology, ostensibly expressing a new "theory," Avenarius circled about for a while but ultimately gravitated to his fundamental idealist position.

And if our Russian Machians (Bogdanov and the others) have not noticed the "mystification" and have seen a refutation of idealism in what is really a "new" defence of it, then let us recall at least that in the analysis of empirio-criticism given by those who are experts in philosophy, we meet a sober estimation of Avenarius's trend of ideas, in which its real character is exposed once its pretentious terminology is eliminated.

Bogdanov wrote as follows in 1903 :

Richard Avenarius gave us a well drawn and most complete philosophic picture of the development of the dualistic conceptions of mind and body. The gist of his "doctrine of introjection " is that we observe directly only physical bodies, and are acquainted only by hypothetical inference with the experiences of others, that is to say, we know the mind of another person only through indirect reasoning. . . . The hypothesis is complicated by the assumption that the experiences of the other person occurring in his body, are lodged (are introjected) in his organism. Such an hypothesis is not only superfluous but gives rise in addition to numerous contradictions. Avenarius gave an account of these contradictions in a systematic fashion, thus revealing a series of successive historical stages in the development of dualism and of philosophical idealism ;

but here, we need not follow him. " Introjection serves as an explanation of the dualism of mind and body. "

Bogdanov, believing that the doctrine of " introjection " was aimed at idealism, was caught on the hook of the " professorial " philosophy. He accepted on faith the estimation of introjection given by Avenarius himself, and failed to notice the sting it contained for materialism. Introjection denies that thought is a function of the brain, that sensations are functions of the central nervous system of man ; it denies therefore the simplest truths of physiology in order to defeat materialism. " Dualism " is here refuted idealistically (in spite of Avenarius's apparent ire against idealism), for sensation and thought prove to be not secondary phenomena, not derivative from matter, but primary entities. Dualism is refuted by Avenarius much in the same manner as the existence of the object without the subject is refuted. It is the same idealist " refutation " of the possibility of the existence of matter without thought, of the existence of an external world independent of our sensations ; the absurd denial of the fact—that the visual image of the tree is a function of the retina, the nerves and the brain—was necessary for Avenarius in order to confirm his theory of the " inseparable " connection of both self and tree, subject and environment in an " all-inclusive " experience.

The doctrine of introjection is a confusion which necessarily gives rise to idealistic absurdities and contradicts the viewpoint of natural science which holds that thought is the function of the brain, that perceptions, that is, the images of the external world, are effects of external objects on our sense-organs. The materialist elimination of " the dualism of mind and body " (materialistic monism) consists in this, that the existence of the mind is shown to be dependent upon that of the body, in that mind is declared to be secondary, a function of the brain, or a reflection of the outer world. The idealist elimination of the " dualism of body and mind " (idealistic monism) consists in an attempt to show that mind is not a function of the body, that mind is primary, that the "environment" and "self" exist in an inseparable connection in the same "complex of elements." Apart from these two diametrically opposed methods of elimination of "the dualism of body and mind," there can be no third method unless it be eclecticism—an illogical confusion of materialism and idealism. And this confusion in Avenarius appears to Bogdanov and the rest "to be a truth which transcends both materialism and idealism."

Professional philosophers, however, are not as naïve and credulous as are the Russian Machians. True, each one of these expert gentlemen, generally full fledged professors, defends "his" own pet system of refutation against materialism or, at least, of "reconciliation" of materialism and idealism. But in discussing an opponent they reveal without any ceremony the incompatible elements of materialism and idealism in what is heralded as the "latest" and most "original" system. And although a few young intellectuals were enmeshed in Avenarius's net, the old bird, Wundt, however, was not enticed by such bait. Wundt, the idealist, very impolitely unmasked the buffoon Avenarius, giving him credit *en passant* for the antimaterialistic tendency of the doctrine of introjection.

"If empirio-criticism," Wundt wrote, "reproaches vulgar materialism because by means of such expressions as the brain 'has' a thought, or 'produces' reason, it expresses a relation which cannot be stated on grounds of actual observation [evidently Wundt accepts as a matter of course the assumption that a person thinks without the help of the brain !] . . . this reproach, of course, has good ground " (*loc. cit.*, pp. 47–48).

Indeed, the idealists will always proceed against materialism hand in hand with the half-hearted compromisers, Avenarius and Mach ! It is only to be regretted, Wundt goes on to say, that this theory of introjection " does not stand in any relation to the doctrine of the independent vital series, is only artificially tacked on to it " (p. 365).

" Introjection," says Ewald, " is no more than a fiction of empirio-criticism, which serves to shield its fallacies " (*loc. cit.* p. 44) " We here observe a peculiar contradiction. On the one hand the elimination of the doctrine of introjection and the restoration of the natural conception of reality would restore it to life. On the other hand, by means of the notion of essential co-ordination, empirio-criticism leads to a purely idealistic theory concerning the absolute correlation of the counter term and the central term. Thus Avenarius's thought runs in a vicious circle. He started out to do battle against idealism, but capitulated before it on the very eve of the first skirmish. He set out to liberate the realm of objects from the yoke of the subject, but ended in tying it again to the subject. What he actually destroys in his criticism, is only a caricature of idealism, and not the genuine expression of its theory of knowledge " (*loc. cit.*, pp. 64–5).

" In the frequently-quoted statement by Avenarius," Norman Smith says, " that the brain is not the seat, organ or supporter, of thought, he rejects the only terms which we possess for defining their connection " (*loc. cit.*, p. 30).

No wonder then that the theory of introjection, approved by Wundt, gained the sympathy of James Ward, the outspoken spiritualist, who waged a systematic war against " naturalism and agnosticism," and especially against Huxley (not because he was not outspoken and explicit in his materialism, which was Engels's reproach against him, but because under his agnosticism, materialism was concealed).

Let us note that Karl Pearson, the English Machian, without dodging the philosophic issues involved, and recognising neither introjection, co-ordination, nor " the discovery of the world-elements," arrives at the inevitable conclusion of Machism, namely, purely subjective idealism. Pearson knows of no " elements " ; " sense-impressions " is his first and last word. He has no doubt that man thinks with the help of the brain. And the contradiction between this thesis (which alone is in conformity with science) and the starting point of his philosophy remained open and clear to all. Pearson tries hard to combat the view that matter exists independently of our sense-perceptions.

Repeating all of Berkeley's arguments, Pearson declares that matter is a nonentity. But when he comes to speak of the relation of the mind to the brain, he is straightforward, as, for instance, in the following : " From will and consciousness associated with material machinery we can infer nothing whatever as to will and consciousness without that machinery " (*ibid.*, p. 58). He lays down the following thesis as a summary of the corresponding part of his investigation : " Consciousness has no meaning beyond nervous systems akin to our own ; it is illogical to assert that all matter is conscious [but it is logical to assert that matter contains a property of reflection which is in its essence akin to sensation], still more that consciousness or will can exist outside matter " (*ibid.*, p. 75).

Pearson commits here a terrible blunder ! Matter is nothing but groups of sense-perceptions. This is his thesis, his philosophy. This means that sensation or thought is primary ; matter, secondary. But consciousness without matter cannot exist, surely, at least not without a nervous system. So that, mind and sensation now prove to be secondary. Water on the earth, the earth on the whale, and the whale on the water. Mach's " elements," Avenarius's " co-ordination " and " introjection " do not in the least mitigate the difficulty ; they only obscure matters with erudite chatter. . . .

Absolute and Relative Truth, or on the Eclecticism of Engels Discovered by Bogdanov

Bogdanov made this discovery in 1906, announcing it in the preface of Book III of his *Empirio-Monism*. " Engels in

Anti-Dühring," writes Bogdanov, " expresses himself almost in the same sense which I characterised as ' the relativity of truth ' (p. v), that is, in the sense of the denial of eternal truth the denial of the absolute objectivity of whatever truth there is. . . . Engels mistakenly wavers in his views when he ironically recognises certain wretched eternal truths (p. viii). . . . Only inconsistency can account for Engels's eclectic reservations in this connection . . ." (p. ix). Let us cite one instance of Bogdanov's refutation of Engels's eclecticism. " Napoleon died on May 5, 1821," says Engels, in *Anti-Dühring*, in the chapter, " Eternal Truths," where he treats of the platitudes which one must encounter in pretending to find eternal truths in historical sciences. Bogdanov thus answers Engels : " What ' truth ' is it ? And what is there ' eternal ' about it ? The constancy of the one-to-one correspondence between a point-instant of time and the death of Napoleon has no longer any real significance for our generation, it cannot serve as the starting point for any activity, and it leads nowhere " (p. ix). And on p. viii : " Can you call *Plattheiten Wahrheiten* ? Are platitudes truths ? The truth is a vital organising form of experience ; it leads us somewhere in our activity and gives us a prop in the struggle of life."

It is sufficiently clear from these two quotations that, instead of refuting Engels, Bogdanov is really beating air. If you are not in a position to maintain that the proposition, " Napoleon died on May 5, 1821," is false, then you are practically acknowledging that it is true. If you do not assert that it can be refuted in the future, then you are acknowledging this truth to be eternal. But to present such phrases as that the truth is a " vital organising form of experience " as an answer is to offer a jumble of words as philosophy. Was the earth evolved in the manner taught by the science of geology, or was the earth created in seven days ? Is it really possible to dodge the question by phrases of " vital " (what does it mean ?) truth which " leads " somewhere ? Is it true that the knowledge of the earth's

history and the history of humanity " have no real significance " ? But this is only a trifle by the means of which
Bogdanov covers his retreat. Having taken it upon himself
to prove that the admission of eternal truths by Engels
is eclecticism, it is no more than a transparent dodge to
settle the question verbally and leave unrefuted the fact
that Napoleon really died on May 5, 1821. To think that
this truth can possibly be refuted in the future is absurd.

The example taken by Engels is elementary, and anybody can present scores of such truths (as e.g., the other
instance of Engels, that Paris is in France), which are
eternal and absolute, and which only insane people can
doubt. Why does Engels speak of " platitudes " ? Because
he ridicules and refutes the dogmatic, metaphysical
materialist, Dühring, who could not apply dialectics to the
question of the relation between absolute and relative
truth. To be a materialist is to acknowledge objective
truth revealed by our sense-organs. To acknowledge as
objective truth, a truth independent of man and mankind,
is to recognise in one way or another, absolute truth.
Now, this " one way or another " separates the metaphysical materialist Dühring from the dialectical materialist
Engels. Dühring juggled with the words " last, final,
eternal truth " in discussing the most complicated questions of science, and especially in discussing history. Of
course, there are eternal truths, says Engels, but it is
unwise to use " high-sounding " words (*gewaltige Worte*)
for small matters. To further materialism, we must drop
the vulgar play upon the expression " eternal truth " ; we
must know how to put, and solve dialectically, the question of the correlation between absolute and relative
truths. This was the source of the struggle between Dühring
and Engels which took place thirty years ago. And Bogdanov, who manages " not to have noticed " Engels's
explanation of the problem of absolute and relative truth
given in the same chapter, and who accuses Engels of
" eclecticism " for his admission of a proposition which is a

truism for every sort of materialism, once more reveals his complete ignorance of materialism and dialectics.

" We now come to the question," Engels writes in *Anti-Dühring*, in the chapter mentioned, " as to what product, if any, of human knowledge can especially have ' sovereign validity ' and ' unrestricted claims to truth ' " (*loc. cit.,* p. 118). Engels thus solves the problem :

" The sovereignty of thought is realised in a number of highly unsovereign men capable of thinking ; the knowledge which has unlimited pretensions to truth is realised in a number of relative blunders ; neither the one nor the other can be fully realised except through an endless eternity of human existence.

" We have here again the same contradiction as above between the necessary, as an absolute, conceived characteristic of human thought, and its reality in the very limited thinking single individual, a contradiction which can only be solved in the endless progression of the human race, that is, endless as far as we are concerned. In this sense human thought is just as sovereign as not . . . and its possibility of knowledge just as unlimited as limited. It is sovereign and unlimited as regards its nature, its significance, its possibilities, its historical end ; it is not sovereign and limited with respect to individual expression and its actuality at any particular time. It is just the same with eternal truths " (p. 119).

This discussion is very important for the question of relativism, or the principle of the relativity of our knowledge which is emphasised by all Machians. The Machians insist that they are relativists, but the Russian Machians, repeating those words after the Germans, are afraid to, or cannot, put clearly and directly the question concerning the relation of relativism to dialectics. For Bogdanov (as for all the Machians) the recognition of the relativity of our knowledge excludes the least admission of absolute truth. For Engels absolute truth is made up of relative truths. Bogdanov is a relativist ; Engels is a dialectician.

Here is another no less important discussion of Engels from the same chapter of *Anti-Dühring* :

" Truth and error, like all mutually antagonistic concepts, have only an absolute reality under very limited conditions, as we have seen, and as even Herr Dühring should know by a slight acquaintance with the first elements of dialectics, which show the insufficiency of all polar antagonisms. As soon as we bring the antagonisms of truth and error out of this limited field it becomes relative and is not serviceable for new scientific statements. If we should seek to establish its reality beyond those limits we are at once confronted by a dilemma, both poles of the antagonism come into conflict with their opposite ; truth becomes error and error becomes truth " (*ibid.*, p. 125). There follows the example of Boyle's law (that the volume of gas is inversely proportional to its pressure). . . . The " particle of truth " contained in that law is only absolute truth within certain limits. The law is proven to be a truth " only approximately."

Human reason then in its nature is capable of yielding and does yield the absolute truth which is composed of the sum-total of relative truths. Each step in the development of science adds new fragments of truth, and from this the absolute truth is constituted, but the limits of the truth of each scientific statement are relative, now expanding, now shrinking with the growth of science. " Absolute truth," says Dietzgen in his *Excursions*, " can be seen, heard, smelt, touched and, of course, also known ; but it cannot be resolved into pure knowledge, it is not pure mind . . . (p. 281). How can a picture ' conform ' with its model ? Approximately it can. What picture worth the name does not agree approximately with its object ? Every portrait is more or less of a likeness. But to be altogether alike, quite the same as the original—what a monstrous idea !

" We can only know nature and her parts relatively, since even a part, though only a relation of nature, possesses again the characteristics of the Absolute, the nature of the All-Existence which cannot be exhausted by knowledge.

" How, then, do wè know that behind the phenomena of Nature, behind the relative truths, there is a universal, unlimited, absolute nature which does not reveal itself completely to man ? . . . Whence that knowledge ? It is innate ; it is given us with consciousness " (p. 283).

This last phrase is one of Joseph Dietzgen's inexact expressions, which led Marx, in one of his letters to Kugelmann, to make note of the confusion in Dietzgen's views. Only by seizing upon these incorrect and unessential phrases can one speak of a special philosophy of Dietzgen which is supposedly different from dialectical materialism. But Dietzgen corrects himself on the same page : " When I say that the consciousness of the endless, absolute truth is innate in us, is the one and only knowledge *a priori*, I am confirmed in my statement also by the experience of this innate consciousness."

From all these statements of Engels and Dietzgen it is obvious that as far as dialectical materialism is concerned there does not exist a fixed immutable boundary between relative and absolute truth. Bogdanov did not grasp this at all, as is evident from the fact that he could bring himself to write the following : " Old-fashioned materialism sets itself up as the absolute *objective knowledge of the essence of things* [Bogdanov's italics] but this is incompatible with the historical conditioning features of any particular ideology.

From the standpoint of modern materialism, or Marxism, the relative limits of our approximation to the cognition of the objective, absolute truth are historically conditioned ; but the existence of this truth is unconditioned, as well as the fact that we are continually approaching it. The general outlines of a picture are historically conditioned, but it is unconditionally true that this picture reflects an objectively existing model. Historically conditioned are the circumstances under which we made progress in our knowledge of the essence of things. For example, the *discovery* of alizarine in coal tar was historically conditioned, or the *discovery* of the electronic structure of the atom was historically conditioned ; but it is unconditionally true that every such discovery is a step forward to " absolute objective knowledge." In a word, every ideology is historically conditioned, but it is unconditionally true that to every scientific theory (as distinct from religion), there corresponds an objective truth, something absolutely so in nature. You will say that this distinction between relative and absolute truth is indefinite. And I will reply that it is sufficiently indefinite to prevent science from becoming dogmatic, in the bad sense of the word, from becoming dead, frozen, ossified ; but it is at the same time sufficiently " definite " to preclude us from espousing any brand of fideism or agnosticism, from embracing the sophistry and philosophical idealism of the followers of Hume and Kant. Here is a boundary which you have not noticed, and not having noticed it, you have fallen into the mire of reactionary philosophy. It is the boundary between dialectical materialism and relativism.

We are relativists, declare Mach, Avenarius and Petzoldt. We are relativists, Mr. Chernov, and a few Russian Machians who wish to be Marxians, echo after them. In this, Mr. Chernov and my Machian comrades, lies your error. To make relativism the basis of the theory of knowledge is inevitably to condemn oneself to absolute scepticism, agnosticism and sophistry, or subjectivism. Relativism as the basis of the theory of knowledge is not only a recognition of the relativity of our cognition, but is tantamount to the denial of the existence of an objective limit or goal independent of humanity to which our cognition approaches. From the point of view of mere relativism one can justify any sophistry, one can even regard the statement " Napoleon died on May 5, 1821," as conditioned ; one can declare things to be true for the " convenience " of an individual or humanity, as well as recognise scientific ideology to be " convenient " in one respect and religious ideology to be very " convenient " in another, etc.

Dialectics, as Hegel explained it, includes an " element " of relativism, of negation and scepticism, but it is not thereby reduced to relativism. The materialist dialectics of Marx and Engels certainly does contain relativism, but it is not reduced to it, that is, it recognises the relativity of all our knowledge, not in the sense of the denial of objective truth, but in the sense of the historical conditions which determine the degrees of our knowledge as it approaches this truth.

Bogdanov writes in italics : " *Consistent Marxism does not admit such dogmatism and such static expressions* " as eternal truths. This is a blunder. If the world is an eternally moving and developing material mass (as the Marxians assume) which reflects a progressive human consciousness, what has all this to do with the notion of the " static " ? The question at issue here is not one concerning the intrinsic essence of things, nor of the intrinsic nature of consciousness, but of the correspondence between the consciousness which reflects nature, and the nature which is reflected by consciousness. In this question, and in this question alone, the term " dogmatism " has a special, characteristic philosophic flavour ; it is the favourite word which the idealists and the agnostics hurl against the materialists, as we have already seen from the example of the very " old " materialist, Feuerbach. The objections that are raised from the standpoint of the prominent " recent positivists " against materialism are as old as they are trashy !

The Criterion of Practice in the Theory of Knowledge

We have seen that Marx, in 1845, and Engels, in 1888 and 1891, introduced the criterion of practice into the theory of knowledge of materialism. To ask outside the realm of practice whether " the objective truth corresponds to human reason " is scholasticism, says Marx in his second thesis on Feuerbach. The best refutation of Kantian and Humean agnosticism as well as of other philosophic whims (*Schrullen*) is practice, repeats Engels. " The success of our actions proves the correspondence (*Uebereinstimmung*) of our perception with the objective nature of the objects perceived," he answers the agnostics.

Compare with this the argument of Mach regarding the criterion of practice :

> A common and popular way of thinking and speaking is to contrast "appearance" with "reality." A pencil held in front of us in the air is seen by us as straight ; dip it into the water, and we see it crooked. In the latter case we say that the pencil *appears* crooked, but is in reality straight. But what justifies us in declaring one fact rather than another to be the reality, and degrading the other to the level of appearance ? In both cases we have to do with facts which present us with different combinations of the elements, combinations which in the two cases are differently conditioned. Precisely because of its environment the pencil dipped in water is optically crooked ; but it is tactually and metrically straight. An image in a concave or flat mirror is *only* visible whereas under other and ordinary circumstances a tangible body as well corresponds to the visible image. A bright surface is brighter beside a dark surface than beside one brighter than itself. To be sure, our expectation is deceived when, not paying sufficient attention to the conditions, and substituting for one another different cases of the combination, we fall into the natural error of expecting what we are accustomed to, although the case may be an unusual one. The facts are not to blame for that. In these cases, to speak of "appearance" may have a practical meaning, but cannot have a scientific meaning. Similarly, the question which is often asked, whether the world is real or whether we merely dream it, is devoid of all scientific meaning. Even the wildest dream is a fact as much as any other.

It is true that not only is the wildest dream a fact, but the wildest philosophy as well. There can be no doubt about it after our acquaintance with the philosophy of Ernst Mach, as the last sophist, he confounds scientific-historical, psychological investigations of human errors, all kinds of " wild dreams " of humanity, such as faith in spooks, with the epistemological differentiation of truthful and " wild." It is as if an economist would say that the theory of Senior, that the whole surplus value of the capitalist is given to him at the " last hour " of the worker's labour-time, and the theory of Marx are both a fact ; and from the point of view of science there is no sense in the question as to which theory expresses objective truth and which the prejudice of the bourgeoisie and the corruption of its professors.

The tanner, Joseph Dietzgen, saw in the scientific, that is, materialist theory of knowledge a " universal weapon against religious belief," and yet for Professor Ernst Mach the difference between the materialist and the subjective-idealist theories of knowledge " is devoid of all scientific meaning." That science is impartial in the clash of materialism, idealism and religion, is a favourite idea not only of Mach, but of all modern bourgeois professors, who are, to quote Dietzgen, " graduated flunkeys using their sham idealism to keep the people in ignorance " (loc. cit., p. 130).

It is sham professorial idealism when the criterion of practice, which makes a distinction between illusion and actuality, is taken by Mach out of the realm of science, out of the theory of knowledge.

Human practice proves the correctness of the materialist theory of knowledge, said Marx and Engels, declaring as " scholastic " and " philosophic legerdemain," all attempts to solve fundamental epistemological questions which ignore practice. For Mach practice is one thing, and the theory of knowledge another. " Cognition," says Mach, in his last work, Erkenntnis und Irrtum, " is a biologically useful mental experience. Only success can separate knowledge from error (p. 116). . . . Understanding is a physical working hypothesis " (p. 183). Our Russian Machians, who wish to be Marxians, accept with a peculiar naïveté such phrases of Mach as proof that he borders very closely on Marxism. But Mach borders on Marxism as closely as Bismarck bordered on the labour movement or Bishop Yevlogy on democracy. With Mach, such assumptions stand side by side with his idealist theory of knowledge, but do not preponderantly determine the choice of a fundamental tendency or theory in epistemology. Knowledge may be biologically useful, useful in human practice, in the preservation of the species, but it is useful only when it reflects an objective truth, independent of man. For a materialist, the " success " of human practice proves the correspondence of our representations to the objective nature of the things we perceive. For a solipsist, " success " is restricted to what is needed only in practice, and can be dissevered from the theory of knowledge. To include the criterion of practice as the basis of the theory of knowledge is inevitably to come to materialism, says the Marxian. Practice has a materialistic reference, says Mach, but the theory of practice is a different article.

" Now in practice," Mach writes in the *Analysis of Sensations*, " we can as little do without the Ego-presentation when we act, as we can do without the presentation of a body when we grasp at a thing. Physiologically we remain egoists and materialists, just as we always see the sun rise again. But theoretically this way of looking at the matter cannot be maintained " (p. 357).

Egoism is beside the point here, for egoism is not an epistemological category. The question of the rising of the sun is also beside the point, for in practice, which serves us as a criterion in the theory of knowledge, we must include also the practice of astronomical observations, discoveries, etc. There remains only Mach's valuable admission that men in their practice are totally and exclusively guided by a materialist theory of knowledge; the attempt to overlook it "theoretically" is characteristic of the scholastic erudition and sham idealist endeavours of Mach.

That these attempts to eliminate practice, in order to make room for agnosticism and idealism, on the grounds that practice is irrelevant to epistemology, are by no means new, can be seen in the following example from the history of German classical philosophy. Midway between Kant and Fichte stands Schulze (in the history of philosophy, the so-called Schulze-Aenesidemus). He openly defends the sceptical alignment in philosophy, considering himself a follower of Hume (and of the ancients, Pyrrho and Sextus). He decidedly rejects the thing-in-itself and the possibility of objective knowledge, and insists that we should not go beyond " experience," beyond sensations, while he foresees the following objection from the other camp. He says : " Since a sceptic, by participating in affairs of life, recognises as indubitable the reality of objective things, behaves accordingly and admits the criterion of truth, his own behaviour is the best and most obvious refutation of his scepticism. " Such proofs," Schulze objects angrily, " are only valid for the mob ; my scepticism does not touch upon practical life, but remains within the domain of philosophy " (p. 255). But the subjective idealist Fichte, too, hopes to find room within the domain of idealism for that " realism which is inevitable for all of us and even for the most determined idealist when it comes to practice—that realism which assumes that objects exist absolutely independent of us and outside of us."

The recent positivism of Mach has not gone very far from Schulze and Fichte ! Let us note as a curiosity that for Bazarov also in this question, no one exists save Plekhanov—for him, too, there is no stronger beast than a cat. Bazarov ridicules the " salto-vitale " philosophy of Plekhanov (*Outlines*, p. 69), who really made the absurd remark, that " belief " in the existence of the outer world is an inevitable " salto-vitale " (vital leap) in philosophy. The word " belief," though put in quotation marks (after Hume), discloses a confusion of terms in Plekhanov. There can be no question about it. But what has the problem particularly to do with Plekhanov ? Why has not Bazarov taken another materialist, let us say, Feuerbach ? Is it because he does not know him ? But ignorance is no argument. Feuerbach also, like Marx and Engels, makes an inadmissible " leap " (from the viewpoint of Schulze, Fichte and Mach) to practice, in the fundamental problems of epistemology. Criticising idealism, Feuerbach presents its essence in the following significant quotation from Fichte which demolishes Machism. " You assume," writes Fichte, " that things are real, that they exist outside of you only because you see them, hear them and touch them. But vision, touch and hearing are only sensations. . . . You perceive, not the objects, but your perceptions." And Feuerbach replies : " A human being is not an abstract ego ; he is either a man or a woman. The question, whether the world is perception, can be compared to the question, whether a human being is my perception, or our relations in practical life prove the contrary ? The fundamental error of idealism is that it asks and answers the question about objectivity and subjectivity, about the reality or unreality of the world only from the theoretical view-point " (*ibid.*, p. 189). Feuerbach absorbs the sum-total of human practice into the theory of knowledge. He says : " Of course, idealists also recognise the reality of the I and Thou in practical life. For the idealists this viewpoint is good only for life and not for speculation. But a speculation which contradicts life, which sets in place of the standpoint of truth the standpoint of death, which separates the soul from the body, is a false and dead speculation (p. 192). Before perceiving we breathe ; we cannot exist without air, food and drink."

" ' Does this mean that we must deal with questions of food and drink in examining the problem of the ideality or reality of the world ? ' exclaims the indignant idealist. How base ! What an offence to good manners to scold a refined, scientific materialism from the chair of philosophy and theology, only to *practise* the crudest sort of it at the table " (p. 196). And Feuerbach exclaims, to make subjective perception equivalent to the objective world " is to identify pollution with childbirth " (p. 198).

The remark is not a polite one, but it hits the mark of those philosophers who teach that sense-perception is the reality existing outside of us.

From the standpoint of life, practice ought to be the first and fundamental criterion of the theory of knowledge. It inevitably leads to materialism, brushing aside the infinite inventions of professorial scholasticism. Of course, we must not forget that the criterion of practice, in the nature of things, neither confirms nor refutes completely any human presentation. This criterion is sufficiently indefinite not to allow human knowledge to become " absolute," and at the same time sufficiently definite to wage a bitter struggle with all varieties of idealism and agnosticism. If that which our practice confirms, is the sole, ultimate and objective truth, then it follows that the sole path to this truth is the road of science which stands by the materialist creed. For instance, Bogdanov agrees to recognise Marx's theory of the circulation of capital as an objective truth only for " our time," regarding as " dogmatism " the designation of this theory as an " historically objective " truth. This again is a blunder. No future circumstances can change the correspondence of this theory with the fact, for the simple reason that such a truth is as eternal as that Napoleon died on May 5, 1821. But inasmuch as practice, i.e., the development of capitalist countries in the last few decades, actually proves the objective truth of the whole social and economic theory of Marx in general, and not only some of its specific formulations, it is obvious that to speak here of the " dogmatism " of the Marxists, is to make an inexcusable concession to bourgeois economy. The sole inference from the proposition upheld by Marxists, that the theory of Marx is the objective truth, is this : Following in the direction of the Marxian theory, we shall draw nearer and nearer to the objective truth (without exhausting it) ; following another path, we shall arrive at confusion and falsehood.

XM

V. I. Lenin

THE HISTORICAL FATE OF THE TEACHING OF KARL MARX

Published March 14, 1913. English translation, " Communist Review," April 1933.

[This was an article written for the thirtieth anniversary of Marx's death. It traces the influence of Marxism since 1848, showing that in spite of " decaying liberalism " reviving itself in the form of socialist opportunism, the " social peace " of Europe " most nearly resembles a powder-barrel." Lenin's prophecy of " an even greater triumph to Marxism " in the coming historical epoch was fulfilled in 1917.]

THE HISTORICAL FATE OF THE TEACHING OF KARL MARX

THE CHIEF THING in the teaching of Marx is the explanation of the world-historical rôle of the proletariat as the creator of Socialist society. Has the march of events throughout the world confirmed this teaching after it had been outlined by Marx ?

Marx put it forward for the first time in 1844. *The Communist Manifesto* of Marx and Engels, which appeared in 1848, already gives a complete, systematic explanation of this teaching, an explanation which is still the best existing. Since that time world history is obviously divided into three chief periods : (1) From the revolutions of 1848 to the Paris Commune (1871) ; (2) from the Paris

Commune to the Russian revolution of 1905 ; (3) from the Russian revolution.

Let us cast a glance at the fate of Marx's teaching in each of these periods.

I

Marx's teaching at the beginning of the first period is far from prevailing. It is only one of an extraordinary number of fractions or currents in socialism. Those forms of socialism prevail which are in general akin to our own populism : lack of understanding of the materialist foundation of the historical movement, failure to remark the rôle and importance of each class in capitalist society, the concealing of the bourgeois nature of democratic changes by various pseudo-socialist phrases about " the people," " justice," " law," etc.

The revolution of 1848 deals a mortal blow at all these noisy, motley, ranting forms of *pre*-Marxist socialism. In all countries the revolution shows the different classes of society *in action*. The shooting of the workers by the republican bourgeoisie in the June days of 1848 in Paris finally defines the socialist nature of the proletariat *alone*. The liberal bourgeoisie is a hundred times more afraid of the independence of this class than of any kind of reaction : cowardly liberalism cringes before it. The peasantry is satisfied with the abolition of the remnants of feudalism and goes over to the side of order, only in a few cases hesitating between *workers' democracy and bourgeois liberalism*. All teachings of a *non*-class socialism and of *non*-class politics appear empty nonsense.

The Paris Commune (1871) completes this development of bourgeois changes ; only to the heroism of the proletariat does the republic owe its stability, that is to say, the form of state construction in which class relations act in their most concealed form.

In all other European countries a more confused and less complete development leads to the forming of the same kind of bourgeois society. At the end of the first period (1848–1871), the period of storms and revolutions, pre-Marxian socialism is *dying out*. Independent *proletarian* parties are being born : the First International (1864–1872) and German social-democracy.

II

The second period (1872–1904) differs from the first in its " peaceful " character, in the absence of revolutions. The West has finished with bourgeois revolutions. The East has not yet grown up to them.

The West enters the field of " peaceful " preparation for the period of future changes. Everywhere proletarian parties, socialist in essence, are formed which learn how to use bourgeois parliamentarism, to create their daily press, their educational institutions, their co-operatives. The teaching of Marx wins a complete victory and *spreads out*. Slowly and undeviatingly the process of selection and gathering of the proletarian forces goes forward, the preparations for coming battles.

The dialectic of history is of such a kind that the theoretical victory of Marxism compels its enemies to reclothe themselves as Marxists. Internally decaying liberalism tries to revive itself in the form of socialist *opportunism*. The period of preparation of forces for great battles is interpreted by them as turning away from these battles. The improvement of the condition of the slaves in the struggle against wage slavery they explain as the sale by the slaves for a penny of their rights to freedom. In cowardly fashion they preach " social peace " (that is, peace with the slave-owners), turning away from the class struggle, etc. They have many supporters among socialist parliamentarians, various officials of the labour movement and the " sympathetic " intelligentsia.

III

Hardly had the opportunists succeeded in boasting of " social peace " and the fact that storms were no longer inevitable under " democracy," than a new source of great world storms was discovered in Asia. The Turkish, Persian and Chinese revolutions followed on the Russian revolution. We are now living right in the midst of the epoch of these storms and their " reflex action " on Europe. Whatever may be the fate of the great Chinese revolution, against which various " civilised " hyenas are now sharpening their teeth, no forces in the world will restore the old serfdom in Asia, nor erase from the face of the earth the heroic democracy of the popular masses in the Asiatic and semi-Asiatic countries.

The long postponement of the decisive struggle against capitalism in Europe has driven a few people, inattentive to the conditions for preparing and developing the mass struggle, to despair and anarchy. We now see how short-sighted and poor-spirited was this anarchist despair.

We should not take despair, but courage from the fact of the drawing of the eight hundred millions of Asia into the fight for the same ideals as Europe.

The Asiatic revolutions have shown us the lack of character and cowardice of liberalism, as well as the exceptional importance of the independence of the democratic masses, as well as the clear differentiation of the proletariat from the bourgeoisie of all kinds. Anybody who, after the experience of Europe and Asia, talks about a *non*-class politics or *non*-class socialism, should simply be put in a cage and exhibited along with some Australian kangaroo.

After Asia, though not in an Asiatic manner, Europe also has begun to stir. The "peaceful" period 1872–1904 has for ever and beyond return gone to eternity. The high cost of living and the yoke of the trusts are causing an unheard-of sharpening of the economic struggle which is even moving the liberalism of the most corrupted sections of the

English workers. A political crisis is ripening before our eyes even in the most "die-hard" bourgeois-junker country, in Germany. Furious piling up of armaments and the policy of imperialism are creating in contemporary Europe a kind of "social peace" which most nearly resembles a powder-barrel. While the decay of *all* the bourgeois parties and the maturing of the proletariat goes unswervingly forward.

After the appearance of Marxism each of the three great epochs of world history has brought it fresh confirmation and new triumphs. But the coming historical epoch will bring an even greater triumph to Marxism as the teaching of the proletariat.

14 (1) March, 1913.

SOCIALISM AND WAR

Published August 1915. English edition, Martin Lawrence, Ltd., 1931.

[Lenin wrote this pamphlet in Switzerland in August 1915, just before the Zimmerwald Conference of those sections of the Socialist Parties which opposed the war. The passages reprinted below are typical of the series of articles and letters written by Lenin in connection with the war, showing the " betrayal of Socialism " by the leaders of the Second International who supported " their own " imperialists, and bringing out the essential Marxist attitude to imperialist war : " Turn the imperialist war into civil war."]

SOCIALISM AND WAR

PRINCIPLES OF SOCIALISM AND THE WAR OF 1914–1915

(Ch. I)

. . . The Socialists of the whole world solemnly declared in 1912, in Basle, that they considered the coming European war a " criminal " and reactionary undertaking of *all* the governments, an undertaking which must hasten the breakdown of capitalism by inevitably generating a revolution against it. The war came, the crisis was there. Instead of revolutionary tactics, the majority of the Social-Democratic parties followed reactionary tactics, siding with their government and their respective bourgeoisies. This betrayal of Socialism means the collapse of the Second (1889–1914) International. We must make clear to ourselves the causes of that collapse, the reasons for the birth and growth of social-chauvinism.

Social-Chauvinism is Opportunism brought to Completion

During the entire period of the Second International, a struggle was going on everywhere inside the Social-Democratic parties between the revolutionary and the opportunist wings. In a series of countries there was a split along this line (England, Italy, Holland, Bulgaria). There was no doubt in the mind of any Marxist that opportunism expressed a bourgeois policy inside of the labour movement, that it expressed the interests of the petty bourgeoisie and of the alliance of an insignificant section of bourgeois-like workers with " their own " bourgeoisie against the interests of the mass of proletarians, the mass of the oppressed.

The objective conditions at the end of the nineteenth century were such that they strengthened opportunism, turning the use of legal bourgeois opportunities into servile worship of legalism, creating a thin layer of bureaucracy and aristocracy in the working class, attracting to the ranks of the Social-Democratic parties many petty-bourgeois " fellow travellers."

The war hastened this development ; it turned opportunism into social-chauvinism ; it changed the alliance of the opportunists with the bourgeoisie from a secret to an open one. At the same time, the military authorities everywhere introduced martial law and muzzled the working mass, whose old leaders, almost in a body, went over to the bourgeoisie.

The economic basis of opportunism and social-chauvinism is the same : the interests of an insignificant layer of privileged workers and petty bourgeoisie who are defending their privileged positions, their " right " to the crumbs of profits which " their " national bourgeoisie receives from robbing other nations, from the advantages of its position as a great nation.

The ideological and political content of opportunism and social-chauvinism is the same : class collaboration instead of class struggle ; renunciation of revolutionary means of struggle ; aiding " one's " own government in its difficulties instead of taking advantage of its difficulties to work for a revolution. If we take all European countries as a whole, if we look not at individual persons (however authoritative), it appears that the opportunists idealogy has become the mainstay of social-chauvinism, whereas from the camp of the revolutionists we hear almost everywhere more or less consistent protests against it. If we take, for instance, the division of opinion manifested at the Stuttgart International Socialist Congress of 1907, we find that international Marxism was against imperialism while international opportunism was even then already for it.

Unity with the Opportunists is an Alliance of the Workers with "Their" National Bourgeoisie and a split in the International Revolutionary Working Class

During the period that preceded the war, opportunism was often considered a legitimate component part of a Social-Democratic party, though " deviating " and " extreme." The war has proven the inadmissibility of this combination in the future. Opportunism has ripened, it has brought to completion its rôle of an emissary of the bourgeoisie within the labour movement. Unity with the opportunists has become nothing but hypocrisy, as evidenced by the example of the German Social-Democratic Party. On all important occasions (as at the voting of August 4) the opportunists confront the party with their ultimatum, the acceptance of which is secured through their numerous connections with the bourgeoisie, through their majorities on the executive committees of the labour unions, etc. To keep *united* with opportunism at the present time means *practically* to subjugate the working class to " its " bourgeoisie, to make an alliance with it for the oppression of other nations and for the struggle for the privileges of a great nation ; at the same time it means splitting the revolutionary proletariat of all countries.

However difficult it may be in individual cases to fight the opportunists who occupy a leading position in many organisations ; whatever peculiar forms the process of purging the labour parties of the opportunists may assume in various countries, this process is inevitable and fruitful. Reformist Socialism is dying ; regenerating Socialism "will be revolutionary, non-compromising, rebellious," according to the just expression of the French Socialist, Paul Golay.

Kautskyism

Kautsky, the greatest authority of the Second International, represents the most typical and striking example

of how lip service to Marxism has in reality led to its transformation into " Struveism " or " Brentanoism." Plekhanov
represents a similar example. Those people castrate Marxism ; they purge it, by means of obvious sophisms, of its
revolutionary living soul ; they recognise in Marxism
everything except revolutionary means of struggle, except
the advocacy of, and the preparation for, such struggle,
and the education of the masses in this direction. Kautsky
quite meaninglessly " reconciles " the fundamental idea
of social-chauvinism, the defence of the fatherland in this
war, with a diplomatic sham concession to the left, such
as abstaining from voting appropriations, verbal expression
of opposition, etc. Kautsky, who in 1909 wrote a book
predicting the approach of a revolutionary period and
discussing the relation between war and revolution, Kautsky
who in 1912 signed the Basle Manifesto on revolutionary
utilisation of the coming war, now justifies and embellishes
social-chauvinism in every way. Like Plekhanov, he joins
the bourgeoisie in ridiculing the very idea of revolution,
in repudiating every step towards immediate revolutionary struggle.

The working class cannot realise its revolutionary rôle,
which is of world significance, otherwise than by waging a
merciless war against this desertion of principles, this
supineness, this servility to opportunism and this unex-
ampled theoretical vulgarisation of Marxism. Kautskyism
is not an accident but a social product of the contradictions within the Second International which combined
faithfulness to Marxism in words with submission to opportunism in deeds.

In every country this fundamental falsehood of Kautskyism assumes different forms. In Holland, Roland-Holst,
though rejecting the idea of defence of the fatherland, is
supporting unity with the party of the opportunists. In
Russia, Trotsky, apparently repudiating this idea, also
fights for unity with the opportunists and chauvinist group
Nasha Zarya. In Rumania, Rakovsky, declaring war against

opportunism which he blames for the collapse of the International, is at the same time ready to recognise the legitimacy of the idea of the defence of the fatherland. These are manifestations of the evil which the Dutch Marxists Gorter and Pannekoek have named " passive radicalism," and which reduces itself to substituting eclecticism for revolutionary Marxism in theory and to slavishness or impotence in the face of opportunism in practice.

The Slogan of Marxists is the Slogan of Revolutionary Social-Democracy

The war has undoubtedly created the acutest crisis and has incredibly intensified the sufferings of the masses. The reactionary character of this war, the shameless lie of the bourgeoisie of *all* countries which covers its predatory aims with " national " ideology, all this inevitably creates on the basis of an objective revolutionary situation, revolutionary sentiments in the masses. Our duty is to help make these sentiments conscious, to deepen them and give them form. The only correct expression of this task is the slogan, " Turn the imperialist war into civil war." *All* consistent class struggle in time of war, all " mass actions " earnestly conducted must inevitably lead to this. We cannot know whether in the first or in the second imperialist war between the great nations, whether during or after it, a strong revolutionary movement will flare up. Whatever the case may be, it is our absolute duty systematically and unflinchingly to work in that particular direction.

The Basle Manifesto directly refers to the example of the Paris Commune, i.e. to turning a war between governments into civil war. Half a century ago, the proletariat was too weak ; objective conditions for Socialism had not ripened yet ; a co-ordination and co-operation of the revolutionary movements in all the belligerent countries could not take place ; the fact that a section of the Paris workers was captivated by " national ideology " (traditions of 1792) was its petty-bourgeois weakness noted at the time by Marx, and one of the reasons for the collapse of the Commune. Now, half a century later, all the conditions that weakened the revolution are no more. At the present time it is unforgivable for a Socialist to countenance repudiation of activities in the spirit of the Paris Communards.

Example of Fraternisation in the Trenches

The bourgeois papers of all the belligerent countries have quoted examples of fraternisation between the soldiers of the belligerent nations, even in the trenches. The fact that the military authorities of Germany and England have issued severe orders against such fraternisation proves that the government and the bourgeoisie consider it of serious importance. If at a time when opportunism among the leaders of the Social-Democratic parties of Western Europe is supreme and social-chauvinism is supported by the entire Social-Democratic press as well as by all influential figures of the Second International, such cases of fraternisation are possible, how much nearer could we bring the end of this criminal, reactionary and slave-driving war and the organisation of a revolutionary international movement if systematic work were conducted in this direction, at least by the Left Socialists of all the belligerent countries !

Importance of Illegal Organisations

Like the opportunists, the most eminent Anarchists of the world have covered themselves in this war with the shame of social-chauvinism in the spirit of Plekhanov and Kautsky. One of its useful results, however, will undoubtedly be the death of both opportunism and Anarchism in this war. The Social-Democratic parties, in no case and under no conditions refusing to take advantage of the slightest legal possibility for the organisation of the masses and the preaching of Socialism, must do away with a servile attitude towards legalism. " Be the first to shoot, Messrs. Bourgeois ! " Engels wrote in reference to civil war, pointing out the necessity for us to violate legality *after* it has been violated by the bourgeoisie. The crisis has shown that the bourgeoisie is violating legality in every country, including the freest, and that it is impossible to lead the masses towards revolution without creating an illegal organisation for preaching, discussing, analysing, preparing revolutionary means of struggle. In Germany, for instance, all *honest* activities of the Socialists are being conducted against abject opportunism and hypocritical " Kautskyism," and conducted illegally. In England, men are being sentenced to hard labour for appeals to abstain from joining the army.

To think that membership in a Social-Democratic party is compatible with repudiation of illegal methods of propaganda and the ridicule of them in the legal press is to betray Socialism.

Defeat of "One's Own" Government in Imperialist War

The advocates of victory of " one's own " government in the present war, as well as the advocates of the slogan " Neither victory nor defeat," proceed equally from the standpoint of social-chauvinism. A revolutionary class in a reactionary war cannot help wishing the defeat of its government, it cannot fail to see the connection between the government's military reverses and the increased opportunity for overthrowing it. Only a bourgeois who believes that the war started by the governments will necessarily end as a war between governments, and who wishes it to be so, finds " ridiculous " or " absurd " the idea that the Socialists of *all* the belligerent countries should express their wish that *all* " their " governments be defeated. On the contrary, such expression would coincide with the hidden thoughts of every class-conscious worker, and would lie along the line of our activity which tends to turn the imperialist war into civil war.

An earnest anti-war propaganda by a section of the English, German and Russian Socialists would undoubtedly "weaken the military strength" of the respective governments, but such propaganda would be to the credit of the Socialists. The Socialists must explain to the masses that there is no salvation for them outside of a revolutionary overthrow of "their" governments and that the difficulties of those governments in the present war must be taken advantage of for just this purpose.

Pacifism and the Peace Slogan

A mass sentiment for peace often expresses the beginning of a protest, an indignation and a consciousness of the reactionary nature of the war. It is the duty of all Social-Democrats to take advantage of this sentiment. They will take the most ardent part in every movement and in every demonstration made on this basis, but they will not deceive the people by assuming that in the absence of a revolutionary movement it is possible to have peace without annexations, without the oppression of nations, without robbery, without planting the seed of new wars among the present governments and the ruling classes. Such deception would only play into the hands of the secret diplomacy of the belligerent countries and their counter-revolutionary plans. Whoever wishes a durable and democratic peace must be for civil war against the governments and the bourgeoisie.

Right of Nations to Self-Determination

The most widespread deception of the people by the bourgeoisie in the present war consists in hiding its predatory aims under an ideology of "national liberation." The English promise freedom to Belgium, the Germans to Poland, etc. As we have seen, this is in reality a war of the oppressors of the majority of the nations of the world for the deepening and widening of such oppression.

The Socialists cannot reach their great aim without fighting against every form of national oppression. They must therefore unequivocally demand that the Social-Democrats of the *oppressing* countries (of the so-called "great" nations in particular) should recognise and defend the right of the *oppressed* nations to self-determination in the political sense of the word, i.e. the right to political separation. A Socialist of a great nation or a nation possessing colonies who does not defend this right is a chauvinist.

To defend this right does in no way mean to encourage the formation of small states, but on the contrary it leads to a freer, more fearless and therefore wider and more universal formation of larger governments and unions of governments—a phenomenon more advantageous for the masses and more in accord with economic development.

On the other hand, the Socialists of the *oppressed* nations must unequivocally fight for complete unity of the *workers* of both the oppressed and the oppressor nationalities (which also means organisational unity). The idea of a lawful separation between one nationality and the other (the so-called "national cultural autonomy" of Bauer and Renner) is a reactionary idea.

Imperialism is the period of an increasing oppression of the nations of the whole world by a handful of "great" nations ; the struggle for a Socialist international revolution against imperialism is, therefore, impossible without the recognition of the right of nations to self-determination. "No people oppressing other peoples can be free" (Marx and Engels). No proletariat reconciling itself to the least violation by "its" nation of the rights of other nations can be Socialist.

V. I. Lenin

IMPERIALISM : THE HIGHEST STAGE OF CAPITALISM

Published in Petrograd, 1917. English edition, Martin Lawrence Ltd., 1933.

[This was written by Lenin in 1916, in Zurich. Its immediate aim was to show that " the war of 1914–18 was on both sides imperialist " ; that imperialism is a " direct continuation of the fundamental properties of capitalism in general." The book traces the growth of trusts and monopolies in the chief capitalist countries, and shows how this development inevitably leads to war. It is also of great importance for its examination of the sources of opportunism in the international labour movement. Parts of the later chapters are given below ; in these conclusions are drawn and the theory of imperialism stated.]

IMPERIALISM : THE HIGHEST STAGE OF CAPITALISM

IMPERIALISM AS A SPECIAL STAGE OF CAPITALISM

(Ch. VII)

WE MUST now try to draw certain conclusions, to sum up what has been said about imperialism. Imperialism emerged as a development and direct continuation of the fundamental properties of capitalism in general. But capitalism became capitalist imperialism, only at a definite, very high stage of its development, when certain of its fundamental properties had begun to change into their opposites, when the features of a period of transition from capitalism to a higher socio-economic system had begun to take shape and reveal themselves all along the line. Economically fundamental in this process is the replacement of capitalist free competition by capitalist monopolies. Free competition is the fundamental property of capitalism and of commodity production generally. Monopoly is the direct opposite of free competition ; but we have seen the latter being transformed into monopoly before our very eyes, creating large-scale production and squeezing out small-scale production, replacing large-scale by larger-scale production, finally leading to such a concentration of production and capital that monopoly has been and is the result : cartels, syndicates and trusts, and, merging with them, the capital of a dozen or so banks manipulating thousands of millions. And at the same time the monopolies, which have sprung from free competition, do not eliminate it, but exist alongside of it and over it, thereby giving rise to a number of very acute and bitter antagonisms, points of friction, and conflicts. Monopoly is the transition from capitalism to a higher order.

If it were necessary to give the briefest possible definition of imperialism, we should have to say that imperialism is the monopoly stage of capitalism. Such a definition would include the essential point, for, on the one hand, finance capital is bank capital of the few biggest monopolist banks, merged with the capital of the monopolist combines of industrialists ; on the other hand, the division of the world is the transition from a colonial policy which has extended without hindrance to territories unoccupied by any capitalist power, to a colonial policy of monopolistic possession of the territories of the world, which has been completely divided up.

But too brief definitions, although convenient, since they .sum up the main points, are nevertheless inadequate, because very fundamental features of the phenomenon to be defined must still be deduced. And so, without forgetting the conditional and relative value of all definitions, which can never include all the connections of a fully developed phenomenon, we must give a definition of imperialism that will include the following five essential features :

1. The concentration of production and capital, developed to such a high stage that it has created monopolies which play a decisive rôle in economic life.

2. The merging of bank capital with industrial capital and the creation, on the basis of this " finance capital," of a financial oligarchy.

3. The export of capital, as distinguished from the export of commodities, becomes of particularly great importance.

4. International monopoly combines of capitalists are formed which divide up the world.

5. The territorial division of the world by the greatest capitalist powers is completed.

Imperialism is capitalism in that stage of development in which the domination of monopolies and finance capital has taken shape ; in which the export of capital has acquired pronounced importance ; in which the division of the world by the international trusts has begun, and in which the partition of all the territory of the earth by the greatest capitalist countries has been completed.

We shall see later how imperialism may and must be defined differently when consideration is given not only to the fundamental, purely economic factors—to which the above definition is limited—but also to the historical place of this stage of capitalism in relation to capitalism in general, or to the relations between imperialism and the two basic tendencies in the labour movement. The point to be noted just now is that imperialism, as understood in this sense, undoubtedly represents a special stage in the development of capitalism. In order to enable the reader to obtain as well-grounded an impression of imperialism as possible we have expressly tried to quote as much as possible from *bourgeois* economists, who are obliged to admit the particularly indisputable and established facts regarding the newest capitalist economy. With the same object we have produced detailed statistics which reveal to what extent bank capital, etc., has grown, showing just how the transition from quantity to quality, from developed capitalism to imperialism, has expressed itself. Needless to say, all the boundaries in nature and in society are conditional and changing, and it would be absurd to dispute, for instance, over the year or decade in which imperialism became " definitely " established.

In defining imperialism, however, we have to enter into controversy, primarily, with Karl Kautsky, the principal Marxist theoretician of the epoch of the so-called Second International—that is, of the twenty-five years between 1889 and 1914.

Kautsky, in 1915 and even in November 1914, decisively attacked the fundamental ideas expressed in our definition of imperialism. He declared that imperialism must not be regarded as a " phase " or as an economic stage, but as a policy ; a definite policy " preferred " by finance capital ; that imperialism cannot be " identified " with " contemporary capitalism " ; that if by imperialism is meant " all the phenomena of contemporary capitalism "—cartels, protectionism, the rule of the financiers, and colonial policy— then the question whether imperialism is necessary to capitalism becomes reduced to the " rankest tautology," for in that case, imperialism is " naturally a vital necessity for capitalism," and so on. The most accurate way to present Kautsky's ideas is to quote his own definition of imperialism, which is directly opposed to the substance of the ideas which we set forth (for the objections of the German Marxists, who for many years have been propounding such ideas, have been known to Kautsky as the objections of a definite tendency in Marxism for a long time).

Kautsky's definition is as follows :

Imperialism is a product of highly developed industrial capitalism. It consists in the striving of every industrial capitalist nation to bring under its control and to annex larger and larger *agrarian* [Kautsky's italics] regions, irrespective of what nations inhabit them.

This definition is utterly worthless because it is one-sided, i.e., it arbitrarily brings out the national question alone (admittedly, it is extremely important in itself as well as in its relation to imperialism) ; arbitrarily and *incorrectly* it connects this question *only* with the industrial capital in the countries which annex other nations ; in an equally arbitrary and incorrect manner it emphasises the annexation of agrarian regions.

Imperialism is a striving for annexations—this is what the *political* part of Kautsky's definition amounts to. It is correct, but very incomplete, for politically, imperialism is generally a striving towards violence and reaction. We are interested here, however, in the *economic* aspect of the question, which Kautsky *himself* introduced into *his own* definition. The errors in the definition of Kautsky are clearly evident. The characteristic feature of imperialism is *not* industrial capital, *but* finance capital. It is not an accident that in France, it was precisely the extraordinarily rapid development of *finance* capital and the weakening of industrial capital, that, from 1880 onwards, gave rise to a sharpening of annexationist (colonial) policy. The characteristic feature of imperialism is precisely the fact that it strives to annex *not only* agrarian but even the most industrialised regions (the German appetite for Belgium ; the French appetite for Lorraine), first, because the fact that the world is already partitioned makes it necessary, in the event of a *re-partition*, to stretch out one's hand to *any* kind of territory, and second, because an essential feature of imperialism is the rivalry between a number of great powers in striving for hegemony, i.e., for the seizure of territory, not so much for their own direct advantage as to weaken the adversary and undermine *his* hegemony (for Germany, Belgium is chiefly necessary as a base against England ; for England, Bagdad as a base against Germany, etc.).

Kautsky refers especially—and repeatedly—to the Englishmen who, he alleges, have established the purely political meaning of the word " imperialism " in his, Kautsky's, sense. We take up the work by the Englishman, Hobson, *Imperialism*, which appeared in 1902, and therein we read (p. 324) :

> The new imperialism differs from the older, first, in substituting for the ambition of a single growing empire the theory and the practice of competing empires, each motived by similar lusts of political aggrandisement and commercial gain ; secondly in the dominance of financial or investing over mercantile interests.

We see that Kautsky is absolutely wrong in factually referring to Englishmen in general (unless he meant the vulgar British imperialists, or the avowed apologists for imperialism). We see that Kautsky, while pretending that he is continuing to defend Marxism, is really taking a step backward in comparison with the *social-liberal* Hobson, who rightly takes account of two " historically concrete " (Kautsky virtually ridicules historical concreteness by his definition) features of modern imperialism : (1) the competition between *several* imperialisms and (2) the predominance of the financier over the merchant. Yet if it were chiefly a question of the annexation of an agrarian country by an industrial one, the rôle played by the merchant would be predominant.

But Kautsky's definition is not only wrong and un-Marxian. It serves as a basis for a whole system of views which all along the line run counter to Marxian theory and practice ; we shall refer to this again. The argument about words which Kautsky raises as to whether the newest stage of capitalism should be called imperialism or the stage of finance capital is really not serious. Call it what you will, it makes no difference. The important thing is that Kautsky detaches the policy of imperialism from its economics, speaks of annexations as being a policy " preferred " by finance capital, and opposes to it another bourgeois policy which he alleges to be possible on the same basis of finance capital. It would follow that monopolies in economics are compatible with methods which are neither monopolistic, nor violent, nor annexationist, in politics. It would follow that the territorial division of the world, which was completed precisely during the period of finance capital and which represents the main feature of the present peculiar forms of rivalry between the greatest capitalist states, is compatible with a non-imperialist policy. The result is a slurring-over and a blunting of the most profound contradictions of the newest stage of capitalism, instead of an exposure of their depth. The result is bourgeois reformism instead of Marxism.

Kautsky enters into controversy with the German apologist of imperialism and annexations, Cunow, who clumsily and cynically argues that : imperialism is modern capitalism ; the development of capitalism is inevitable and progressive ; therefore imperialism is progressive ; therefore we should bow down before imperialism and chant its praises. This is something like the caricature of the Russian Marxists which the Narodniks drew in 1894–1895. They used to argue that if the Marxists considered capitalism inevitable and progressive in Russia, they ought to open up a public-house and start breeding capitalism ! Kautsky retorts to Cunow : No, imperialism is not modern capitalism, but only one of the forms of the policy of modern capitalism. This policy we can and must fight ; we can and must fight against imperialism, annexations, etc.

The retort sounds quite plausible. But in effect it is a more subtle and disguised (and, therefore, more dangerous) preaching of conciliation with imperialism, for unless the " struggle " against the policy of the trusts and banks strikes at the economic bases of the trusts and banks, it reduces itself to bourgeois reformism and pacifism, to an innocent and benevolent expression of pious hopes. Kautsky's theory, which has nothing in common with Marxism, avoids mentioning existing conditions, and ignores the most important of them instead of revealing them in their full depth. Naturally, such a " theory " can only serve the purpose of defending unity with the Cunows !

From a purely economic point of view, says Kautsky, it is not impossible that capitalism will pass through yet another new phase, that of the extension of the policy of the cartels to foreign policy, the phase of ultra-imperialism, i.e., of a super-imperialism, a union of world imperialisms and not struggles among them ; a phase when wars shall cease under capitalism, a phase of " the joint exploitation of the world by an internationally combined finance capital."

We shall have to deal with this " theory of ultra-imperialism " later to show in detail how decisively and utterly it departs from Marxism. Meanwhile, in keeping with the general plan of the present work, we must examine the exact economic data on this question. Is " ultra-imperialism " possible " from the purely economic point of view," or is this ultra-nonsense ?

If by the purely economic point of view is meant a " pure " abstraction, then all that can be said resolves itself into the following proposition : evolution is proceeding towards monopoly ; therefore the trend is towards a single world monopoly, single world trust. This is indisputable, but it is also as completely devoid of meaning as is the statement that " evolution is proceeding " towards the manufacture of foodstuffs in laboratories. In this sense the " theory " of ultra-imperialism is no less absurd than a " theory of ultra-agriculture " would be.

If, on the other hand, we are discussing the " purely economic " conditions of the epoch of finance capital as an historically concrete epoch of the beginning of the twentieth century, then the best reply to the lifeless abstractions of " ultra-imperialism " (which serve an exclusively reactionary aim : that of diverting attention from the depth of *existing* contradictions) is to contrast them with the concrete economic realities of present-day world economy. Kautsky's meaningless talk about ultra-imperialism encourages, amongst other things, the profoundly mistaken idea, which only brings grist to the mill of the apologists of imperialism, that the domination of finance capital *weakens* the unevenness and contradictions within world economy, whereas in reality it *strengthens* them.

Richard Calver, in his little book, *An Introduction to World Economy*, attempted to compile the chief, purely economic data necessary to understand, in a concrete way, the inter-relations within world economy at the turn of the nine-teenth century. He divides the world into five " main economic regions " : (1) Central Europe (the whole of Europe with the exception of Russia and Great Britain) ; (2) Great Britain ; (3) Russia ; (4) Eastern Asia ; (5) America. He includes the colonies in the " regions " of the states to which they belong and " puts aside " a few coun-tries not distributed according to regions, such as Persia, Afghanistan and Arabia in Asia, Morocco and Abyssinia in Africa, etc.

We observe three regions with highly developed capital-ism (with a high development of means of communication, trade and industry) : the Central European, the British, and the American. Among them are three states which dominate the world : Germany, Britain, the United States. Imperialist rivalry and the struggle between these countries have become very keen because Germany has only an insignificant area and a few colonies ; the creation of " Central Europe " is still a matter for the future, and it is being born in the midst of desperate struggles. For the moment the distinctive feature of all Europe is political disintegration. In the British and American regions, on the contrary, political concentration is very highly developed, but there is a tremendous disparity between the immense colonies of the former and the insignificant colonies of the latter. In the colonies, capitalism is only beginning to develop. The struggle for South America becomes more and more bitter.

Here is a summary of the economic data he gives on these regions :

Principal Econ. Regions of the World	Area (in mill. sq. km.)	Pop. (in mills.)	Transport		Trade Imp. and Exp. (in bill. Mks.)	Industry		
			Rlwys. (in thous. km.)	Merch. fleet (in mill. tons)		Yearly Output of Coal (in mill. tons)	Output of Pig Iron (in mill. tons)	No. of Cotton Spindles (in mills.)
1. Cent. European . .	27·6 (23·6)[1]	388 (146)	204	8	41	251	15	26
2. British .	28·9 (28·6)	398 (355)	140	11	25	249	9	51
3. Russian .	22·	131	63	1	3	16	3	7
4. East. Asian .	12·	389	8	1	2	8	0·02	2
5. American .	30·	148	379	6	14	245	14	19

There are two regions where capitalism is poorly developed : Russia and Eastern Asia. In the former the density of population is low, in the latter it is very high ; in the former, political concentration is high, in the latter it does not exist. The partition of China has only just begun, and the struggle for it between Japan, the U.S.A., etc., is continually gaining in intensity.

Compare this reality, the vast diversity of economic and political conditions, the extreme disparity in the rate of growth of the various countries, the frenzied struggles among the imperialist states, with Kautsky's stupid little fable about " peaceful " ultra-imperialism. Is this not the reactionary attempt of a frightened petty-bourgeois to hide from stern reality ? Do not the international cartels, which seem to Kautsky to be the embryos of " ultra-imperialism " (as the manufacture of tablets in a laboratory " might " seem to be ultra-agriculture in embryo) present an example of the division and the re-division of the world, the transition from peaceful division to non-peaceful and vice versa ? Is not American and other finance capital, which peacefully divided up the whole world, with Germany's participation (for instance in the international rail syndicate, or in the international mercantile shipping trust) now re-dividing the world on the basis of a new alignment of forces

[1] The figures in parentheses show the area and population of the colonies.

which are being changed by methods altogether *non-peaceful*?

Finance capital and the trusts are aggravating instead of diminishing the differences between the rates of development of the various parts of world economy. When the alignment of forces is changed, how else, *under capitalism*, can a solution of the contradictions be found, except through *force*?

Railway statistics provide remarkably exact data on the different rates of growth of capitalism and finance capital in world economy. In the last decades of imperialist development, the total length of railways has changed as follows:

RAILROADS
(in thousands of kilometres)

	1890	1913	Increase
Europe . . .	224	346	122
United States . .	268	411	143
Colonies (total) . .	82 ⎱ 125	210 ⎱ 347	128 ⎱ 222
Independent or semi-dependent states of Asia and America . .	43 ⎰	137 ⎰	94 ⎰
Total . .	617	1,104	487

The development of railways has been most rapid in the colonies and in the independent (and semi-independent) states of Asia and America. It is known that here the finance capital of the four or five biggest capitalist states reigns fully. Two hundred thousand kilometres of new railway lines in the colonies and in the other countries of Asia and America represent more than 40 billion marks in capital, newly invested on particularly advantageous terms, with special guarantees of a good return, with profitable orders for steel mills, etc., etc.

Capitalism is growing most rapidly in the colonies and in trans-oceanic countries. Amongst the latter *new* imperialist powers are emerging (Japan). The struggle of world imperialisms is becoming acute. The tribute levied by

finance capital on the most profitable colonial and trans-
oceanic enterprises is increasing. In dividing up this
"booty," an exceptionally large share goes to countries
which, as far as rate of development of productive forces
is concerned, do not always stand at the top of the list. In
the case of the greatest powers, considered with their
colonies, the total length of railways (in thousands of kilometres) was as follows :

	1890	1913	Increase
United States	268	413	145
British Empire	107	208	101
Russia	32	78	46
Germany	43	68	25
France	41	63	22
Total	491	830	339

Thus, about eighty per cent of the total railways are concentrated in the hands of the five greatest powers. But the
concentration of the *ownership* of these railways, the concentration of finance capital, is immeasurably more important ;
French and English millionaires, for example, own an
enormous amount of stocks and bonds in American,
Russian and other railways.

Thanks to its colonies, Great Britain has increased " its "
network of railways by 100,000 kilometres, four times as
much as Germany. At the same time, it is known that the
development of productive forces in Germany during this
period, and especially the development of the coal and iron
industries, has been incomparably more rapid than in
England—not to mention France or Russia. In 1892,
Germany produced 4·9 million tons of pig iron, and Great
Britain 6·8 million tons ; but in 1912, Germany produced
17·6 million tons against Great Britain's 9 million, an overwhelming superiority over England ! The question arises,
is there, *under capitalism*, any means of eliminating the disparity between the development of productive forces and

the accumulation of capital on the one side, and the partition of colonies and "spheres of influence" by finance capital on the other side—other than war?

PARASITISM AND THE DECAY OF CAPITALISM

(Ch. VIII)

We have now to examine another very important aspect of imperialism, to which, usually, too little attention is paid in the majority of discussions on this subject. One of the shortcomings of the Marxist, Hilferding, is that he took a step backward in comparison with the non-Marxist, Hobson. We refer to parasitism, inherent in imperialism.

As we have seen, the most deep-rooted economic foundation of imperialism is monopoly. This is capitalist monopoly, i.e., monopoly which has grown out of capitalism, and exists in the general capitalist environment of commodity production and competition, in permanent and insoluble contradiction to this general environment. Nevertheless, like any monopoly, it inevitably gives rise to a tendency towards stagnation and decay. In proportion as monopoly prices become fixed, even temporarily, so the stimulus to technical, and consequently to all other progress, to advance, tends to disappear ; and to that extent also the *economic* possibility arises of artificially retarding technical progress. For instance, in America a certain Owens invented a machine which revolutionised the manufacture of bottles. The German bottle-manufacturing cartel purchased Owens's patents, but pigeon-holed them and held up their practical application. Certainly, monopoly under capitalism can never completely, and for any length of time, eliminate competition on the world market (and this is one of the reasons why the theory of ultra-imperialism is absurd). Of course, the possibility of reducing cost of production and increasing profits by introducing technical improvements is an influence in the direction of change.

Nevertheless, the *tendency* towards stagnation and decay, inherent in monopoly, continues in turn to operate in individual branches of industry ; in individual countries, for certain periods of time, it gains the upper hand.

The monopoly of ownership of very extensive, rich or well-situated colonies, works in the same direction.

Moreover, imperialism is an immense accumulation of money capital in a few countries, which, as we have seen, amounts to 100 or 150 billions francs in securities. Hence the extraordinary growth of a class, or rather of a stratum, of *rentiers*, i.e., persons who live by " clipping coupons," who take absolutely no part in any enterprise, and whose profession is idleness. The exportation of capital, one of the most essential economic bases of imperialism, still further isolates this rentier stratum from production and sets the seal of parasitism on the whole country living on the exploitation of the labour of several overseas countries and colonies.

> In 1893—writes Hobson—the British capital invested abroad represented about 15 per cent of the total wealth of the United Kingdom.

Let us remember that by 1915 this capital had increased about two and a half times.

> Aggressive imperialism—says Hobson further on—which costs the tax-payer so dear, which is of so little value to the manufacturer and trader . . . is a source of great gain to the investor. . . . The annual income Great Britain derives from commissions on her whole foreign and colonial trade, import and export, is estimated by Sir R. Giffen [the statistician] at £18,000,000 for 1899, taken at 2½ per cent, upon a turnover of £800,000,000.

Considerable as this sum is, it cannot entirely explain the aggressive imperialism of Great Britain. This is explained by the 90 to 100 million pounds revenue from " invested " capital, the income of the rentier class.

The income of the rentiers is *five times* as great as the venue obtained from the foreign trade of the greatest

" trading " country in the world ! This is the essence of imperialism and imperialist parasitism.

For this reason the term " rentier state " (*Rentnerstaat*) or usurer state is coming into general use in the economic literature on imperialism. The world has become divided into a handful of usurer states and a vast majority of debtor states.

> The premier place among foreign investments—says Schulze-Gaevernitz—is taken by those invested in politically dependent, or closely allied countries. England makes loans to Egypt, Japan, China, South America. Her war fleet plays the part of sheriff in case of necessity. England's political power protects her from the anger of her debtors. . . .

Sartorius von Waltershausen in his work, *The National Economic System of Foreign Capital Investments*, cites Holland as the model rentier state, and points out that England and France are now becoming such. Schilder believes that five industrial nations are " definitely avowed creditor nations " : England, France, Germany, Belgium and Switzerland. Holland does not appear on this list simply because it is " less industrialised." The United States is the creditor only of other American countries.

> England—writes Schulze-Gaevernitz—is gradually being transformed from an industrial state into a creditor state. Notwithstanding the absolute increase in industrial production and exports, the relative importance of revenue from interest and dividends, profits from issues, commissions and speculation is on the increase, when the whole national economy is taken into account. In my opinion it is this fact which is at the economic base of imperialist expansion. The creditor is more firmly tied to the debtor than the seller is to the buyer.

In regard to Germany, A. Lansburgh, the editor of *Die Bank*, in 1911, in an article entitled, " Germany As A Rentier State," wrote the following :

> People in Germany like to sneer at the inclination observed in France for people to become rentiers. But they forget meanwhile

that, as far as the middle class is concerned, the situation in Germany is becoming more and more like that in France.

The rentier state is a state of parasitic decaying capitalism, and this circumstance cannot fail to be reflected in all the social-political conditions of the affected countries in general, and particularly in the two fundamental tendencies in the working-class movement. To demonstrate this as clearly as possible, we shall let Hobson speak—a most " reliable " witness, since he cannot be suspected of partiality for " orthodox Marxism " ; moreover, he is an Englishman who is very well acquainted with the situation in the country which is richest in colonies, in finance capital, and in imperialist experience.

With the Boer War fresh in his mind, Hobson describes the connection between imperialism and the interests of the financiers, their growing profits from armaments, supplies, etc., and writes as follows :

> While the directors of this definitely parasitic policy are capitalists, the same motives appeal to special classes of the workers. In many towns most important trades are dependent upon government employment or contracts ; the imperialism of the metal and shipbuilding centres is attributable in no small degree to this fact.

In this writer's opinion there are two circumstances which weakened the power of the ancient empires : (1) " economic parasitism " and (2) the formation of armies composed of subject peoples.

> There is first the habit of economic parasitism, by which the ruling state has used its provinces, colonies, and dependencies in order to enrich its ruling class and to bribe its lower classes into acquiescence.

And we would add that the economic possibility of such corruption, whatever its form may be, requires monopolistically high profits.

As for the second circumstance, Hobson writes :

One of the strangest symptoms of the blindness of imperialism is the reckless indifference with which Great Britain, France and other imperial nations are embarking on this perilous dependence. Great Britain has gone farthest. Most of the fighting by which we have won our Indian Empire has been done by natives ; in India, as more recently in Egypt, great standing armies are placed under British commanders ; almost all the fighting associated with our African dominions, except in the southern part, has been done for us by natives.

The prospect of a dismemberment of China evokes the following economic evaluatioٍ by Hobson :

The greater part of Western Europe might then assume the appearance and character already exhibited by tracts of country in the south of England, in the Riviera, and in the tourist-ridden or residential parts of Italy and Switzerland, little clusters of wealthy aristocrats drawing dividends and pensions from the Far East, with a somewhat larger group of professional retainers and tradesmen and a large body of personal servants and workers in the transport trade and in the final stages of production of the more perishable goods : all the main arterial industries would have disappeared, the staple foods and manufactures flowing in as tribute from Asia and Africa. . . .
We have foreshadowed the possibility of even a larger alliance of Western states, a European federation of great powers which, so far from forwarding the cause of world-civilisation, might introduce the gigantic peril of a Western parasitism, a group of advanced industrial nations, whose upper classes drew vast tribute from Asia and Africa, with which they support great tame masses of retainers, no longer engaged in the staple industries of agriculture and manufacture, but kept in the performance of personal or minor industrial services under the control of a new financial aristocracy. Let those who would scout such a theory as undeserving of consideration examine the economic and social condition of districts in Southern England to-day which are already reduced to this condition, and reflect upon the vast extension of such a system which might be rendered feasible by the subjection of China to the economic control of similar groups of financiers, investors, and political and business officials, draining the greatest potential reservoir of profit the world has ever known, in order to consume it in Europe. The situation is far too complex, the play of world-forces far too incalculable, to render this or any other single interpretation.

of the future very probable ; but the influences which govern the imperialism of Western Europe to-day are moving in this direction, and, unless counteracted or diverted, make towards some such consummation.

Hobson is quite right. If the forces of imperialism were not counteracted they would lead to just that. He correctly appraises the significance of a " United States of Europe," in the present, imperialist stage. But it must be added that *even within* the labour movement, the opportunists, who for the moment have been victorious in most countries, are " working " systematically and undeviatingly in this very direction. Imperialism, which means the partition of the world and the exploitation not of China alone ; which means monopolistically high profits for a handful of very rich countries, creates the economic possibility of corrupting the upper strata of the proletariat, and thereby fosters, gives form to and strengthens opportunism. However, we must not lose sight of the forces which counteract imperialism generally and opportunism in particular, which, naturally, the social-liberal Hobson does not see.

The German opportunist, Gerhard Hilderbrand, who at one time was expelled from the party for defending imperialism, but would to-day make a good leader of the so-called " Social-Democratic " Party of Germany, serves as a good supplement to Hobson by his advocacy of a " United States of Western Europe " (without Russia) for the purpose of " joint " action against . . . the African Negroes, the " great Islamic movement " ; for the " maintenance of a powerful army and navy " against a " Sino-Japanese coalition," etc.

The description of " British imperialism " in Schulze-Gaevernitz's book reveals the same parasitical traits. The national income of Great Britain approximately doubled between 1865 and 1898, while the income " from abroad " increased *ninefold* in the same period. While the " merit " of imperialism is that it " trains the Negro to work " (not without coercion, of course . . .), the "danger" of imperialism is that Europe

Y<small>M</small>

will shift the burden of physical toil—first agricultural and mining, then heavy industrial labour—on to the coloured peoples, and itself be content with the rôle of rentier, and in this way, perhaps, pave the way for the economics and later, the political emancipation of the coloured races.

An increasing proportion of land in Great Britain is being taken out of cultivation and used for sport, for the diversion of the rich. It is said of Scotland—the most aristocratic place for hunting and other sport—that it " lives on its past and Mr. Carnegie " (an American billionaire). Britain annually spends £14,000,000 on horse-racing and fox-hunting alone. The number of rentiers in Great Britain is about a million. The percentage of producers among the population is becoming smaller.

Year	Population of England and Wales (in millions)	No. of workers employed in basic industries (in millions)	Per cent of the population
1851	17·9	4·1	23
1901	32·5	5·0	15

And, in speaking of the British working class, the bourgeois student of " British imperialism at the beginning of the twentieth century " is obliged to distinguish systematically between the " *upper stratum* " and the " *lower proletarian stratum proper.*" The upper stratum furnishes the main body of co-operators, of trade unionists, of members of sporting clubs and of numerous religious sects. The right to vote, which in Great Britain, is still " *sufficiently restricted to exclude the lower proletarian stratum proper,*" is adapted to their level ! In order to present the condition of the British working class in the best light, only this upper stratum—which constitutes only a *minority* of the proletarian—is generally spoken of. For instance : " The problem of unemployment is mainly a London problem and that of the lower proletarian stratum, *with whom politicians are little concerned. . . .*" It would be better to say : with whom the bourgeois politicians and the " Socialist " opportunists are little concerned.

Another one of the peculiarities of imperialism connected with the facts that we are describing, is the decline in emigration from imperialist countries, and the increase in immigration (influx of workers and transmigration) to these countries from the more backward countries, where wages are lower. As Hobson observes, emigration from Great Britain has been declining since 1884. In that year the number of emigrants was 242,000, while in 1900 the number was 169,000. German emigration reached its highest point in the decade 1881–1890 with a total of 1,453,000 emigrants. In the following two decades it fell to 554,000 and 341,000. On the other hand there was an increase in the number of workers entering Germany, from Austria, Italy, Russia and other countries. According to the 1907 census, there were 1,342,294 foreigners in Germany, of whom 440,800 were industrial workers and 257,329 were agricultural workers. In France, the workers employed in the mining industry are " in great part " foreigners : Polish, Italian and Spanish. In the United States, immigrants from Eastern and Southern Europe are engaged in the most poorly paid occupations, while American workers provide the highest percentage of foremen and of the better-paid workers. Imperialism has the tendency to create privileged sections even among the workers, and to separate them from the main proletarian masses.

It must be observed that in Great Britain the tendency of imperialism to split the workers, to strengthen opportunism among them, and cause temporary decay in the working-class movement, revealed itself much earlier than the end of the nineteenth and beginning of the twentieth centuries ; for two important distinguishing features of imperialism were observed in Great Britain in the middle of the nineteenth century, viz., vast colonial possessions and a monopolist position in world markets. For several decades Marx and Engels systematically traced this connection between opportunism in the labour movement and the imperialist features of British capitalism. For example, on October 7, 1858, Engels wrote to Marx :

> . . . the British working class is actually becoming more and more bourgeois, and it seems that this most bourgeois of all nations wants to bring matters to such a pass as to have a bourgeois aristocracy and a bourgeois proletariat *side by side* with the bourgeoisie. Of course this is to some extent justifiable for a nation which is exploiting the whole world.

Almost a quarter of a century later, in a letter dated August 11, 1881, Engels speaks of the " very worst English . . . [trade unions.—*Ed.*] which allow themselves to be led by men sold to, or at least paid by the middle class." In a letter to Kautsky, dated September 12, 1882, Engels wrote :

> You ask me what the English workers think of the colonial policy ? The same as they think about politics in general. There is no labour party here, there are only conservatives and liberal radicals, and the workers enjoy with them the fruits of the British world market and colonial monopoly. [Engels sets forth the same ideas in his preface to the second edition of *The Condition of the Working Class in England*, published in 1892.]

Here causes and effects are clearly shown. Causes : (1) exploitation of the whole world by this country ; (2) its monopolistic position in the world market ; (3) its colonial monopoly. Effects : (1) bourgeoisification of a part of the British proletariat ; (2) a part of the proletariat permits itself to be led by people who are bought by the bourgeoisie, or who at least are paid by it. The imperialism of the beginning of the twentieth century completed the partition of the world by a very few states, each of which to-day exploits (in the sense of drawing super-profits from) a part of the world only a little smaller than that which England exploited in 1858. Each of them, by means of trusts, cartels, finance capital, and the relations between debtor and creditor, occupies a monopoly position on the world market.

Each of them enjoys to some degree a colonial monopoly. (We have seen that out of 75 million square kilometres of *total* colonial area in the world, 65 million, or 86 per cent, is concentrated in the hands of six powers ; 61 million, or 81 per cent, belongs to three powers.)

The distinctive feature of the present situation is the prevalence of economic and political conditions which could not but intensify the irreconcilability between opportunism and the general and basic interests of the labour movement. Imperialism has grown from an embryo into a dominant system ; capitalist monopolies occupy first place in national economics and politics ; the partition of the world has been completed. On the other hand, instead of an undivided monopoly by Britain, we see a few imperialist powers fighting among themselves for the right to share in this monopoly, and this struggle is characteristic of the whole period of the beginning of the twentieth century.

Opportunism cannot now triumph completely in the labour movement of any country for many decades as it did in England in the second half of the nineteenth century, but in several countries it has finally grown ripe, over-ripe and rotten, and has become completely emerged with bourgeois policy as " social-chauvinism."

CRITIQUE OF IMPERIALISM

(Ch. IX)

By the critique of imperialism, in the broad sense of the term, we mean the attitude of the different classes of society towards imperialist policy in connection with their general ideology.

The enormous dimensions of finance capital concentrated in a few hands and creating an extremely extensive and close network of ties and relationships, which subordinates to itself not only the bulk of the medium and small, but even very smallest capitalists and petty owners, on the one hand,

and an intense struggle waged against other national-state groups of financiers for the partition of the world and domination over other countries, on the other hand—cause the possessing classes to go over as one to the side of imperialism. The signs of the times are a " general " enthusiasm regarding its prospects, a passionate defence of imperialism, and every possible camouflage of its real nature. The imperialist ideology is also permeating the working class. There is no Chinese Wall between it and the other classes. The leaders of the present so-called " Social-Democratic " Party of Germany are justly called social-imperialists ; that is, Socialists in words and imperialists in deeds ; and as early as 1902, Hobson noted the existence of " Fabian imperialists " in England who belonged to the opportunist " Fabian Society."

The bourgeois scholars and publicists usually present their defence of imperialism in a somewhat veiled form, obscure the fact that it is in complete domination, and conceal its deep roots ; they strive to concentrate attention on special aspects and characteristics of secondary importance, and do their utmost to distract attention from the main issue by advancing absolutely ridiculous schemes for " reform," such as police supervision of the trusts or banks, etc. Less frequently, cynical and frank imperialists speak out and are bold enough to admit the absurdity of the idea of " reforming " the fundamental features of imperialism.

We will give an example. The German imperialists attempt, in the *Archives of World Economy*, to trace the movements for national emancipation in the colonies, particularly, of course, in colonies other than German. They note the ferment and protest movements in India ; the movement in Natal (South Africa), in the Dutch East Indies, etc. One of them, commenting on an English report of the speeches delivered at a conference of subject peoples and races, held on June 28–30, 1910, consisting of representatives of various peoples under foreign domination in Africa, Asia and Europe, writes as follows :

We are told that we must fight against imperialism ; that the dominant states must recognise the right of subjugated peoples to self-government ; that an international tribunal should supervise the fulfilment of treaties concluded between the great powers and the weaker peoples. Beyond the expression of these pious hopes the conference does not go. We see no trace of a realisation of the fact that imperialism is indissolubly bound up with capitalism in its present form and that therefore (! !) it is hopeless to fight directly against imperialism, except perhaps if the fight is confined to protests against certain of its most hateful excesses.

Since reforming the bases of imperialism is an illusion, a " pious hope," since the bourgeois representatives of oppressed nations do not go " further," the bourgeois representatives of the oppressing nations do go " further," but backward, to servility to imperialism, concealed by a pretence to " science." " Logic," indeed !

The question as to whether it is possible to change the bases of imperialism by reforms, whether to go forward to a further aggravation and accentuation of the contradictions it engenders, or backwards towards allaying them, is a fundamental question in the critique of imperialism. The fact that the political characteristics of imperialism are reaction all along the line and increased national oppression, in connection with oppression by the financial oligarchy and the elimination of free competition, has given rise to a petty-bourgeois-democratic opposition to imperialism in almost all imperialist countries since the beginning of the twentieth century. And the break with Marxism made by Kautsky and the broad international Kautskyist tendency consists in the very fact that Kautsky not only did not trouble to, and did not know how to, take a stand against this petty-bourgeois reformist opposition, which is reactionary in its economic basis, but, on the contrary, in practice became identified with it.

In the United States, the imperialist war waged against Spain in 1898 gave rise to an " anti-imperialist " opposition by the last of the Mohicans of bourgeois democracy. They declared this war " criminal " ; they denounced the annexation of foreign territories as a violation of the Constitution, and decried the " jingo treachery " by means of which Aguinaldo, leader of the native Filipinos, was deceived (he was promised liberty for his country, but later American troops were landed there and the Philippines were annexed). They quoted the words of Lincoln :

> When the white man governs himself, that is self-government ; but when he governs himself and also governs another man, that is more than self-government—that is despotism.

But as long as all this criticism shrank from recognising the indissoluble bond between imperialism and the trusts, and, therefore, between imperialism and the foundations of capitalism ; as long as it shrank from aligning itself with the forces being engendered by large-scale capitalism and its development, it remained a " pious hope."

This also, in the main, is the position of Hobson in his criticism of imperialism. Hobson anticipated Kautsky in protesting against the " inevitability of imperialism," and in making an appeal showing the need to " raise the consuming capacity " of the people (under capitalism !). The petty-bourgeois point of view in the critique of imperialism, the omnipotence of the banks, the financial oligarchy, etc., is that adopted by authors whom we have repeatedly quoted, such as Agahd, Lansburgh, L. Eschwege, and, among French writers, Victor Bérard, author of a superficial book entitled *England and Imperialism*, which appeared in 1900. All of these, who make no claim whatever to being Marxists, contrast imperialism with free competition and democracy ; they condemn the Bagdad railway adventure as leading to disputes and war, utter " pious hopes " for peace, etc., including the compiler of international stock issue statistics, A. Neymarck, who, after calculating the hundreds of billions of francs of " international " securities, exclaimed in 1912 :

Is it possible to believe that peace can be disturbed ? . . . that, in the face of these enormous figures . . . any one would risk starting a war ?

Such simplicity of mind on the part of bourgeois economists is not surprising. Besides, *it is in their interest* to pretend to be so naïve and to talk " seriously " about peace under imperialism. But what remains of Kautsky's Marxism when, in 1914–1915–1916, he takes the same bourgeois-reformist point of view and affirms that " we are all agreed " (imperialists, pseudo-Socialists, and social-pacifists) with regard to peace ? Instead of an analysis of imperialism and an exposure of the depths of its contradictions, we have nothing but a reformist " pious hope " of side-stepping and evading them.

Here is an example of Kautsky's economic critique of imperialism. He takes the statistics of British export and import trade with Egypt for 1872 and 1912. These statistics show that this import and export trade has grown more slowly than British exports and imports as a whole. From this, Kautsky concludes :

> We have no reason to suppose that British trade with Egypt would have developed less, as a result of the operation of economic factors alone, without the military occupation of Egypt. . . . The efforts of present-day states to expand can best be satisfied not by the violent methods of imperialism, but by peaceful democracy.

This argument of Kautsky's which is repeated in every key by his Russian armour-bearer (and Russian sponsor of social-chauvinists) Mr. Spectator, constitutes the basis of Kautsky's critique of imperialism, and that is why we must deal with it in greater detail. We shall begin with a quotation from Hilferding, whose conclusions Kautsky, on many occasions, including April 1915, declared, " have been unanimously accepted by all Socialist theoreticians."

... It is not the business of the proletariat—wrote Hilferding —to contrast the more progressive capitalist policy with the policy, now overcome, of the era of free trade and of hostility towards the state. The reply of the proletariat to the economic policy of finance capital, to imperialism, cannot be free trade, but Socialism alone. The aim of proletarian policy cannot now be the idea of restoring free competition—now become a reactionary ideal—but only the complete abolition of competition by the abolition of capitalism.

Kautsky broke with Marxism by advocating what is, in the period of finance capital, a "reactionary ideal," "peaceful democracy," "the simple weight of economic factors"; for, *objectively*, this ideal drags us back from monopoly to non-monopoly capitalism, and is a reformist swindle.

Trade with Egypt (or with any other colony or semi-colony) "would have developed better" *without* military occupation, without imperialism, without finance capital. What does this mean? That capitalism would develop more rapidly if free competition were not restricted by monopolies in general, nor by the "ties" nor the yoke (i.e., again the monopoly), of finance capital, nor by the monopolist possession of colonies by individual countries?

Kautsky's arguments can have no other sense; and *this* "sense" is nonsense. But suppose that it is so, that free competition, without any sort of monopoly, *would* develop capitalism and trade more rapidly, is it not a fact that the more rapidly capitalism and trade develop, the greater is the concentration of production and capital which *gives rise* to monopoly? And monopolies have *already* come into being—precisely *out* of free competition! Even if monopolies have now begun to retard progress, this is not an argument in favour of free competition, which became impossible after it gave birth to monopolies.

However one may twist Kautsky's argument, there is nothing in it but reaction and bourgeois reformism. Even if we correct this argument and say, as Spectator says, that the trade of the British colonies with Britain is now developing more slowly than their trade with other countries, that likewise does not save Kautsky ; for Britain *also* is being beaten by monopoly, by imperialism, only by that of other countries (America, Germany). It is well known that the cartels have given rise to a new and original form of protective tariffs—goods suitable for export are protected (Engels noted this in Volume III of *Capital*). It is well known, too, that the cartels and finance capital have a system peculiar to themselves of exporting goods at "dumping prices," or " dumping," as the English call it : within the country the cartel sells its products at a monopolistically high price ; abroad it disposes of them at a fraction of this price to undermine a competitor, to increase its own production to the maximum, etc. If German trade with the British colonies is developing more rapidly than that of Britain, it only proves that German imperialism is younger, stronger, better organised, and more highly developed than the British, but this by no means proves the " superiority " of free trade, for it is not free trade fighting against protection and colonial dependence, but one imperialism fighting another, one monopoly against another, one finance capital against another. The superiority of German imperialism over British imperialism is stronger than the wall of colonial frontiers or of protective tariffs. To derive from this any " argument " *in favour* of free trade and " peaceful democracy " is insipidity, it is to vulgarise the essential features and qualities of imperialism, to substitute petty-bourgeois reformism for Marxism. . . .

Kautsky's theoretical critique of imperialism has therefore nothing in common with Marxism and serves no purpose other than as a preamble to propaganda for peace and unity with the opportunists and the social-chauvinists, for the very reason that this critique evades and obscures precisely the most profound and basic contradictions of imperialism : the contradictions of monopolies existing side by side with free competition ; the contradictions between the immense " operations " (and immense profits) of finance capital and " fair " trade on the open market ; between combines and trusts on the one hand and non-trustified industry on the other, etc.

The notorious theory of " ultra-imperialism," invented by Kautsky, is equally reactionary. Compare his arguments on this subject in 1915 with Hobson's arguments of 1902. Kautsky writes :

> . . . whether it is possible that the present imperialist policy might be supplanted by a new ultra-imperialist policy, which would introduce the joint exploitation of the world by an internationally combined finance capital in place of the mutual rivalries of national finance capitals ? Such a new phase of capitalism is at any rate conceivable. Is it realisable ? Sufficient evidence is not yet available to enable us to answer this question.

Hobson writes :

> Christendom thus laid out in a few great federal empires, each with a retinue of uncivilised dependencies, seems to many the most legitimate development of present tendencies, and one which would offer the best hope of permanent peace on an assured basis of inter-imperialism.

Kautsky called ultra-imperialism or super-imperialism what Hobson thirteen years before had called inter-imperialism. Except for coining a new and clever word by replacing one Latin prefix by another, Kautsky's progress in " scientific " thought consists only in his temerity at labelling as Marxism what Hobson in effect described as the cant of English parsons. After the Boer War it was quite natural that this most worthy caste should exert its main effort to *console* the British petty-bourgeoisie and the workers, who had lost many of their relatives on the battle-fields of South Africa and who were paying higher taxes in order to guarantee still higher profits for the British financiers. And what better consolation could there be than the theory that imperialism is not so bad, that it stands close to inter- (or ultra-) imperialism, which can assure permanent peace ? No matter what the good intentions of the British clergy or of the sugary Kautsky may have been, the objective, that is, the real social significance of his " theory," is this and this alone : a most reactionary consolation of the masses by holding out hopes for a possible permanent peace under capitalism, by distracting their attention from the sharp antagonisms and acute problems of the present and directing their attention to illusory perspectives of some sort of new " ultra-imperialism " of the future. Other than delusion of the masses, there is nothing in Kautsky's " Marxian " theory.

Indeed, it is enough to keep clearly in mind well-known and indisputable facts to become convinced of the complete falsity of the perspectives which Kautsky is trying to hold out to the German workers (and the workers of all countries). Let us take India, Indo-China and China. It is well known that these three colonial and semi-colonial countries, inhabited by six or seven hundred million human beings, are subjected to the exploitation of the finance capital of several imperialist powers : Great Britain, France, Japan, the United States, etc. Let us assume that these imperialist countries form alliances against one another in order to protect and extend their possessions, interests, and " spheres of influence " in these Asiatic states ; these will be " inter-imperialist," or " ultra-imperialist " alliances. Let us assume that all the imperialist powers conclude an alliance for the " peaceful " partition of these Asiatic countries ; this alliance would be " internationally united finance capital." Actual examples of such an alliance may be seen in the history of the twentieth century, for instance, in the relations of the powers with China. We ask, is it " conceivable," assuming that the capitalist system remains intact (and this is precisely the assumption that Kautsky does make), that such alliances would not be short-lived, that they would preclude friction, conflicts and struggles in any and every possible form ?

It suffices to state this question clearly to make any other reply than a negative one impossible ; for there can be *no other* conceivable basis, under capitalism, for partition of spheres of influence, of interests, of colonies, etc., than a calculation of the *strength* of the participants, their general economic, financial, military and other strength. Now, the relative strength of these participants is not changing uniformly, for under capitalism there cannot be an *equal* development of different undertakings, trusts, branches of industry or countries. Half a century ago, Germany was a pitiable nonentity as compared with Britain so far as capitalist strength was concerned. The same with Japan as compared with Russia. Is it " conceivable " that in ten or twenty years' time the relative strength of the imperialist powers will have remained *un*changed ? Absolutely inconceivable.

Therefore, " inter-imperialist " or " ultra-imperialist " alliances, in the realities of capitalism and not in the petty-bourgeois phantasies of English clergymen or the German " Marxist " Kautsky, no matter in what form these alliances be concluded, whether of one imperialist coalition against another or of a general alliance of *all* the imperialist powers, *inevitably* can be only " breathing spells " between wars. Peaceful alliances prepare the ground for wars and in their turn grow out of wars. One is the condition of the other, giving rise to alternating forms of peaceful and non-peaceful struggle *on one and the same* basis, that of imperialist connections and inter-relations of world economics and world politics. But the sage Kautsky, in order to pacify the workers and to reconcile them with the social-chauvinists who have deserted to the side of the bourgeoisie, *breaks* one link of a whole chain from the others, separates to-day's peaceful (and ultra-imperialist, nay ultra-ultra-imperialist) alliance of *all* the powers for the " pacification " of China (remember the suppression of the Boxer Rebellion) from the non-peaceful conflict of to-morrow, which will prepare the ground for another " peaceful " general alliance for the partition, say, of Turkey, on the day after to-morrow, etc.,

etc. Instead of showing the vital connection between periods of imperialist peace and periods of imperialist wars, Kautsky puts before the workers a lifeless abstraction solely in order to reconcile them to their lifeless leaders.

An American writer, Hill, in his *History of Diplomacy in the International Development of Europe*, points out in his preface the following periods of modern diplomatic history : (1) the revolutionary period ; (2) the constitutional movement ; (3) the present period of " commercial imperialism."

Another writer divides the history of Great Britain's " foreign policy " since 1870 into four periods : (1) the Asiatic period : struggle against Russia's advance in Central Asia towards India ; (2) the African period (approximately 1885–1902) : struggles against France over the partition of Africa (the Fashoda affair, 1898, a hair's-breadth from a war with France) ; (3) the second Asiatic period (treaty with Japan against Russia) ; and (4) the " European " period, chiefly directed against Germany.

" The political skirmishes of outposts are fought on the financial field," wrote Riesser, the banker, in 1905, showing how French finance capital operating in Italy was preparing the way for a political alliance between the two countries, how a struggle was developing between Germany and Britain over Persia, a struggle among all the European capitalists over Chinese loans, etc. Behold, the living reality of peaceful " ultra-imperialist " alliances in their indissoluble connection with ordinary imperialist conflicts !

The glossing over of the deepest contradictions of imperialism by Kautsky, which inevitably becomes a decking-out of imperialism, leaves its traces also in this writer's critique of the political features of imperialism. Imperialism is the epoch of finance capital and of monopolies which introduce everywhere the striving for domination, not for freedom. The result of these tendencies is reaction all along the line, whatever the political system, and extreme intensification of antagonisms in this domain also. Particularly acute also becomes national oppression and the striving for annexation, i.e., the violation of national independence (for annexation is nothing else than a violation of the right of nations to self-determination). Hilferding justly draws attention to the relation between imperialism and the intensification of national oppression.

> But in the newly opened-up countries—he writes—the imported capital intensifies antagonisms and excites the constantly growing resistance of the people, who are awakened to national consciousness against the intruders. This resistance can easily become transformed into dangerous measures directed against foreign capital. Former social relations become completely revolutionised. The agrarian fetters that for a thousand years have bound the " nations beyond the pale of history " are broken, and they themselves are drawn into the capitalist whirlpool. Capitalism itself gradually provides the vanquished with the ways and means for their emancipation. And they set out to achieve that goal which once was the highest for the European nations : the construction of a national united state as a means to economic and cultural freedom. This movement for independence threatens European capital precisely in its most valuable and most promising fields of exploitation, and European capital can maintain its denomination only by constantly increasing its military forces.

To this must be added that it is not only in newly opened-up countries, but also in the old ones, that imperialism is leading to annexation, to increased national oppression, and, consequently, also to more stubborn resistance. While objecting to the growth of political reaction caused by imperialism, Kautsky leaves in the dark a question which has become very urgent, that of the impossibility of unity with the opportunists in the epoch of imperialism. While objecting to annexations, he presents his objections in such a form as will be most acceptable and least offensive to the opportunists. He addresses himself directly to a German audience, yet he obscures the most timely and important points, for instance, that Alsace-Lorraine is an annexation by Germany. In order to appraise this " mental aberration " of Kautsky's, we shall take the

following example. Let us suppose that a Japanese is condemning the annexation of the Philippine Islands by the
Americans. Are there many who will believe that he is
protesting because he abhors annexations in general, and
not because he himself has a desire to annex the Philippines ? And shall we not be constrained to admit that the
" fight " the Japanese is waging against annexations can
be regarded as sincere and politically honest only if he
fights against the annexation of Korea by Japan, and
demands for Korea freedom of separation from Japan ?

Kautsky's theoretical analysis of imperialism and his
economic and political critique of imperialism are permeated *through and through* with a spirit absolutely irreconcilable with Marxism, a spirit that obscures and glosses
over the most basic contradictions of imperialism, and
strives to preserve at all costs the crumbling unity with
opportunism in the European labour movement.

V. I. Lenin

THE STATE AND REVOLUTION

First published early 1918. English edition, Martin Lawrence Ltd.,
1934.

[In the preface which he wrote in August 1917, Lenin
observed that " the question of the State is acquiring at
present a particular importance, both as theory, and from
the point of view of practical politics." This was when
Lenin was in Finland, after the July rising in Petrograd,
and less than three months before the November revolution. *The State and Revolution* is the most comprehensive
study of revolutionary theory in relation to the State, both
capitalist and proletarian. It is one of the most essential

works of Marxism ; it explains the whole development of
the revolution in Russia, the dictatorship of the proletariat, the building up of the productive forces and the
stages towards classless society—all in advance of events,
on the basis of the analysis made by Marx and Engels of
the theory of the State and the experience of previous
revolutions. It has only been possible to reprint chapters
I and V. The titles of the other chapters are : II. The
Experiences of 1848–51 ; III. Experience of the Paris
Commune of 1871 ; IV. Supplementary Explanations by
Engels ; and VI. Vulgarisation of Marx by the Opportunists. Lenin originally intended to write a seventh
chapter : Experience of the Russian Revolutions of 1905
and 1917 (i.e., March 1917). But, as he says in a post-
script, dated December 13, 1917, to the first edition :
" Outside of the title, I did not succeed in writing a single
line of the chapter ; what ' interfered ' was the political
crisis—the eve of the October revolution of 1917. . . . It
is more pleasant and useful to go through the ' experience
of the revolution ' than to write about it." This final
chapter was never written.]

THE STATE AND REVOLUTION

CLASS SOCIETY AND THE STATE
(Ch. I)

*1. The State as the Product of the Irreconcilability
of Class Antagonisms*

WHAT IS NOW HAPPENING to Marx's doctrine has,
in the course of history, often happened to the doctrines of
other revolutionary thinkers and leaders of oppressed
classes struggling for emancipation. During the lifetime of
great revolutionaries, the oppressing classes have visited

relentless persecution on them and received their teaching with the most savage hostility, the most furious hatred, the most ruthless campaign of lies and slanders. After their death, attempts are made to turn them into harmless icons, canonise them and surround their *names* with a certain halo for the " consolation " of the oppressed classes and with the object of duping them, while at the same time emasculating and vulgarising the *real essence* of their revolutionary theories and blunting their revolutionary edge. At the present time, the bourgeoisie and the opportunists within the labour movement are co-operating in this work of adulterating Marxism. They omit, obliterate, and distort the revolutionary side of its teaching, its revolutionary soul. They push to the foreground and extol what is, or seems, acceptable to the bourgeoisie. All the social-chauvinists are now " Marxists "—joking aside ! And more and more do German bourgeois professors, erstwhile specialists in the demolition of Marx, speak now of the " national-German " Marx, who, they aver, has educated the labour unions which are so splendidly organised for conducting the present predatory war !

In such circumstances, the distortion of Marxism being so widespread, it is our first task to *resuscitate* the real teachings of Marx on the State. For this purpose it will be necessary to quote at length from the works of Marx and Engels themselves. Of course, long quotations will make the text cumbersome and in no way help to make it popular reading, but we cannot possibly avoid them. All, or at any rate, all the most essential passages in the works of Marx and Engels on the subject of the State must necessarily be given as fully as possible, in order that the reader may form an independent opinion of all the views of the founders of scientific Socialism and of the development of those views and in order that their distortions by the present predominant " Kautskyism " may be proved in black and white and rendered plain to all.

Let us begin with the most popular of Engels' works,

Der Ursprung der Familie, des Privateigentums und des Staats,
the sixth edition of which was published in Stuttgart as
far back as 1894. We must translate the quotations from
the German originals, as the Russian translations, although
very numerous, are for the most part either incomplete
or very unsatisfactory.

Summarising his historical analysis Engels says :

> The State is therefore by no means a power imposed on
> society from the outside ; just as little is it " the reality of the
> moral idea," " the image and reality of reason," as Hegel
> asserted. Rather, it is a product of society at a certain stage
> of development ; it is the admission that this society has become
> entangled in an insoluble contradiction with itself, that it is
> cleft into irreconcilable antagonisms which it is powerless to
> dispel. But in order that these antagonisms, classes with con-
> flicting economic interests, may not consume themselves and
> society in sterile struggle, a power apparently standing above
> society becomes necessary, whose purpose is to moderate the
> conflict and keep it within the bounds of " order " ; and this
> power arising out of society, but placing itself above it, and
> increasingly separating itself from it, is the State.

Here we have, expressed in all its clearness, the basic
idea of Marxism on the question of the historical rôle and
meaning of the State. The State is the product and the
manifestation of the *irreconcilability* of class antagonisms.
The State arises when, where, and to the extent that the
class antagonisms *cannot* be objectively reconciled. And,
conversely, the existence of the State proves that the class
antagonisms *are* irreconcilable.

It is precisely on this most important and fundamental
point that distortions of Marxisms arise along two main
lines.

On the one hand, the bourgeois, and particularly the
petty-bourgeois, idealogists, compelled under the pressure
of indisputable historical facts to admit that the State only
exists where there are class antagonisms and the class
struggle, " correct " Marx in such a way as to make it
appear that the State is an organ for *reconciling* the classes.

According to Marx, the State could neither arise nor maintain itself if a reconciliation of classes were possible. But with the petty-bourgeois and philistine professors and publicists, the State—and this frequently on the strength of benevolent references to Marx !—becomes a conciliator of the classes. According to Marx, the State is an organ of class *domination*, an organ of *oppression* of one class by another ; its aim is the creation of " order " which legalises and perpetuates this oppression by moderating the collisions between the classes. But in the opinion of the petty-bourgeois politicians, order means reconciliation of the classes, and not oppression of one class by another ; to moderate collisions does not mean, they say, to deprive the oppressed classes of certain definite means and methods of struggle for overthrowing the oppressors, but to practise reconciliation.

For instance, when, in the Revolution of 1917, the question of the real meaning and rôle of the State arose in all its vastness as a practical question demanding immediate action on a wide mass scale, all the Socialist-Revolutionaries and Mensheviks suddenly and completely sank to the petty-bourgeois theory of " reconciliation " of the classes by the " State." Innumerable resolutions and articles by politicians of both these parties are saturated through and through with this purely petty-bourgeois and philistine theory of " reconciliation." That the State is an organ of domination of a definite class which *cannot* be reconciled with its antipode (the class opposed to it)—this petty-bourgois democracy is never able to understand. Its attitude towards the State is one of the most telling proofs that our Socialist-Revolutionaries and Mensheviks are not Socialists at all (which we Bolsheviks have always maintained), but petty-bourgeois democrats with a near-Socialist phraseology.

On the other hand, the " Kautskyist " distortion of Marx is far more subtle. " Theoretically," there is no denying that the State is the organ of class domination, or that class antagonisms are irreconcilable. But what is forgotten or glossed over is this : if the State is the product of the irreconcilable character of class antagonisms, if it is a force standing *above* society and " increasingly separating itself from it," then it is clear that the liberation of the oppressed class is impossible not only without a violent revolution, *but also without the destruction* of the apparatus of State power, which was created by the ruling class and in which this " separation " is embodied. As we shall see later Marx drew his theoretically self-evident conclusion from a concrete historical analysis of the problems of revolution. And it is exactly this conclusion which Kautsky —as we shall show fully in our subsequent remarks—has " forgotten " and distorted.

2. *Special Bodies of Armed Men, Prisons, Etc.*

Engels continues :

In contrast with the ancient organisation of the *gens*, the first distinguishing characteristic of the State is the grouping of the subjects of the State *on a territorial basis.* . . .

Such a grouping seems " natural " to us, but it came after a prolonged and costly struggle against the old form of tribal or gentilic society.

. . . The second is the establishment of a *public force*, which is no longer absolutely identical with the population organising itself as an armed power. This special public force is necessary, because a self-acting armed organisation of the population has become impossible since the cleavage of society into classes. . . . This public force exists in every State ; it consists not merely of armed men, but of material appendages, prisons and repressive institutions of all kinds, of which gentilic society knew nothing. . . .

Engels develops the conception of that "power" which is termed the State—a power arising from Society, but placing itself above it and becoming more and more separated from it. What does this power mainly consist of? It consists of special bodies of armed men who have at their disposal prisons, etc.

We are justified in speaking of special bodies of armed men, because the public power peculiar to every State is not " absolutely identical " with the armed population, with its " self-acting armed organisation."

Like all the great revolutionary thinkers, Engels tries to draw the attention of the class-conscious workers to that very fact which to prevailing philistinism appears least of all worthy of attention, most common and sanctified by solid, indeed, one might say, petrified prejudices. A standing army and police are the chief instruments of State power. But can this be otherwise ?

From the point of view of the vast majority of Europeans at the end of the nineteenth century whom Engels was addressing, and who had neither lived through nor closely observed a single great revolution, this cannot be otherwise. They cannot understand at all what this " self-acting armed organisation of the population " means. To the question, whence arose the need for special bodies of armed men, standing above society and becoming separated from it (police and standing army), the Western European and Russian philistines are inclined to answer with a few phrases borrowed from Spencer or Mikhailovsky, by reference to the complexity of social life, the differentiation of functions, and so forth.

Such a reference seems " scientific " and effectively dulls the senses of the average man, obscuring the most important and basic fact, namely, the break-up of society into irreconcilably antagonistic classes.

Without such a break-up, the "self-acting armed organisation of the population " might have differed from the primitive organisation of a herd of monkeys grasping sticks, or of primitive men, or men united in a tribal form of society, by its complexity, its high technique, and so forth, but would still have been possible.

It is impossible now, because society, in the period of civilisation, is broken up into antagonistic, and, indeed, irreconcilably antagonistic classes, which, if armed in a " self-acting " manner, would come into armed struggle with each other. A State is formed, a special power is created in the form of special bodies of armed men, and every revolution, by shattering the State apparatus, demonstrates to us how the ruling class aims at the restoration of the special bodies of armed men at *its* service, and how the oppressed class tries to create a new organisation of this kind, capable of serving not the exploiters, but the exploited.

In the above observation, Engels raises theoretically the very same question which every great revolution raises practically, palpably, and on a mass scale of action, namely, the question of the relation between special bodies of armed men and the " self-acting armed organisation of the population." We shall see how this is concretely illustrated by the experience of the European and Russian revolutions.

But let us return to Engels' discourse.

He points out that sometimes, for instance, here and there in North America, this public power is weak (he has in mind an exception that is rare in capitalist society, and he speaks about parts of North America in its pre-imperialist days, where the free colonist predominated), but that in general it tends to become stronger :

> It [the public power] grows stronger, however, in proportion as the class antagonisms within the State grow sharper, and with the growth in size and population of the adjacent States. We have only to look at our present-day Europe, where class struggle and rivalry in conquest have screwed up the public power to such a pitch that it threatens to devour the whole of society and even the State itself.

This was written as early as the beginning of the 'nineties of last century, Engels' last preface being dated June 16, 1891. The turn towards imperialism, understood to mean complete domination of the trusts, full sway of the large banks, and a colonial policy on a grand scale, and so forth, was only just beginning in France, and was even weaker in North America and in Germany. Since then the "rivalry in conquest" has made gigantic progress—especially as, by the beginning of the second decade of the twentieth century, the whole world had been finally divided up between these "rivals in conquest," i.e., between the great predatory powers. Military and naval armaments since then have grown to monstrous proportions, and the predatory war of 1914–1917 for the domination of the world by England or Germany, for the division of the spoils, has brought the "swallowing up" of all the forces of society by the rapacious State power nearer to a complete catastrophe.

As early as 1891 Engels was able to point to "rivalry in conquest" as one of the most important features of the foreign policy of the great powers, but in 1914–1917, when this rivalry, many times intensified, has given birth to an imperialist war, the rascally social-chauvinists cover up their defence of the predatory policy of "their" capitalist classes by phrases about the "defence of the fatherland," or the "defence of the republic and the revolution," etc. !

3. The State as an Instrument for the Exploitation of the Oppressed Class

For the maintenance of a special public force standing above society, taxes and State loans are needed.

> Having at their disposal the public force and the right to exact taxes, the officials now stand as organs of society *above* society. The free, voluntary respect which was accorded to the organs of the gentilic form of government does not satisfy them, even if they could have it. . . .

Special laws are enacted regarding the sanctity and the inviolability of the officials. " The shabbiest police servant . . . has more authority " than the representative of the clan, but even the head of the military power of a civilised State " may well envy the least among the chiefs of the clan the unconstrained and uncontested respect which is paid to him."

Here the question regarding the privileged position of the officials as organs of State power is clearly stated. The main point is indicated as follows : what is it that places them *above* society ? We shall see how this theoretical problem was solved in practice by the Paris Commune in 1871 and how it was slurred over in a reactionary manner by Kautsky in 1912 :

> As the State arose out of the need to hold class antagonisms in check, but as it, at the same time, arose in the midst of the conflict of these classes, it is, as a rule, the State of the most powerful, economically dominant class, which by virtue thereof becomes also the dominant class politically, and thus acquires new means of holding down and exploiting the oppressed class. . . .

Not only the ancient and feudal States were organs of exploitation of the slaves and serfs, but

> the modern representative State is the instrument of the exploitation of wage-labour by capital. By way of exception, however, there are periods when the warring classes so nearly attain equilibrium that the State power, ostensibly appearing as a mediator, assumes for the moment a certain independence in relation to both. . . .

Such were, for instance, the absolute monarchies of the seventeenth and eighteenth centuries, the Bonapartism of the First and Second Empires in France, and the Bismarck régime in Germany.

Such, we may add, is now the Kerensky government in republican Russia after its shift to persecuting the revolutionary proletariat, at a moment when the Soviets, thanks to the leadership of the petty-bourgeois democrats, have *already* become impotent, while the bourgeoisie is *not yet* strong enough to disperse them outright.

In a democratic republic, Engels continues, " wealth wields its power indirectly, but all the more effectively," first, by means of " direct corruption of the officials " (America) ; second, by means of " the alliance of the government with the stock exchange " (France and America).

At the present time, imperialism and the domination of the banks have " developed " to an unusually fine art both these methods of defending and asserting the omnipotence of wealth in democratic republics of all descriptions. If, for instance, in the very first months of the Russian democratic republic, one might say during the honeymoon of the union of the " Socialists "—Socialist-Revolutionaries and Mensheviks—with the bourgeoisie, Mr. Palchinsky obstructed every measure in the coalition cabinet, restraining the capitalists and their war profiteering, their plundering of the public treasury by means of army contracts ; and if, after his resignation, Mr. Palchinsky (replaced, of course, by an exactly similar Palchinsky) was " rewarded " by the capitalists with a " soft " job carrying a salary of 120,000 roubles per annum, what was this ? Direct or indirect bribery ? A league of the government with the capitalist syndicates, or " only " friendly relations ? What is the rôle played by the Chernovs, Tseretelis, Avksentyevs and Skobelevs ? Are they the " direct " or only the indirect allies of the millionaire treasury looters ?

The omnipotence of " wealth " is thus more *secure* in a democratic republic, since it does not depend on the poor political shell of capitalism. A democratic republic is the best possible political shell for capitalism, and therefore, once capital has gained control (through the Palchinskys, Chernovs, Tseretelis and Co.) of this very best shell, it establishes its power so securely, so firmly, that *no* change, either of persons, or institutions, or parties in the bourgeois republic can shake it.

We must also note that Engels quite definitely regards universal suffrage as a means of bourgeois domination.

Universal suffrage, he says, obviously summing up the long experience of German Social-Democracy, is " an index of the maturity of the working class ; it cannot, and never will, be anything else but that in the modern State."

The petty-bourgeois democrats, such as our Socialist-Revolutionaries and Mensheviks, and also their twin brothers, the social-chauvinists and opportunists of Western Europe, all expect " more " from universal suffrage. They themselves share, and instil into the minds of the people, the wrong idea that universal suffrage " in the *modern* State " is really capable of expressing the will of the majority of the toilers and of assuring its realisation.

We can here only note this wrong idea, only point out that this perfectly clear, exact and concrete statement by Engels is distorted at every step in the propaganda and agitation of the " official " (i.e., opportunist) Socialist parties. A detailed analysis of all the falseness of this idea, which Engels brushes aside, is given in our further account of the views of Marx and Engels on the " modern " State.

A general summary of his views is given by Engels in the most popular of his works in the following words :

> The State, therefore, has not existed from all eternity. There have been societies which managed without it, which had no conception of the State and State power. At a certain stage of economic development, which was necessarily bound up with the cleavage of society into classes, the State became a necessity owing to this cleavage. We are now rapidly approaching a stage in the development of production at which the existence of these classes has not only ceased to be a necessity, but is becoming a positive hindrance to production. They will disappear as inevitably as they arose at an earlier stage. Along with them the State will inevitably disappear. The society that organises production anew on the basis of a free and equal association of the producers will put the whole State machine where it will then belong : in the museum of antiquities, side by side with the spinning-wheel and the bronze axe.

It is not often that we find this passage quoted in the propaganda and agitation literature of contemporary Social-Democracy. But even when we do come across it, it is generally quoted in the same manner as one bows before an icon, i.e., it is done merely to show official respect for Engels, without any attempt to gauge the breadth and depth of revolutionary action presupposed by this relegating of " the whole State machine . . . to the museum of antiquities." In most cases we do not even find an understanding of what Engels calls the State machine.

4. The " Withering Away " of the State and Violent Revolution

Engels' words regarding the " withering away " of the State enjoy such popularity, they are so often quoted, and they show so clearly the essence of the usual adulteration by means of which Marxism is made to look like opportunism, that we must dwell on them in detail. Let us quote the whole passage from which they are taken :

> The proletariat seizes State power, and then transforms the means of production into State property. But in doing this, it puts an end to itself as the proletariat, it puts an end to all class differences and class antagonisms, it puts an end also to the State as the State. Former society, moving in class antagonisms, had need of the State, that is, an organisation of the exploiting class at each period for the maintenance of its external conditions of production ; therefore, in particular, for the forcible holding down of the exploited class in the conditions of oppression (slavery, bondage or serfdom, wage-labour) determined by the existing mode of production. The State was the official representative of society as a whole, its embodiment in a visible corporate body ; but it was this only in so far as it was the State of that class which itself, in its epoch, represented society as a whole : in ancient times, the State of the slave-owning citizens ; in the Middle Ages, of the feudal nobility ; in our epoch, of the bourgeoisie. When ultimately it becomes really representative of society as a whole, it makes itself superfluous. As soon as there is no longer any class of society to be held in subjection ; as soon as, along with class domination and the struggle for individual existence based on the former anarchy of production, the collisions and excesses arising from these have also been abolished, there is nothing more to be repressed, and a special repressive force,

a State, is no longer necessary. The first act in which the State really comes forward as the representative of society as a whole —the seizure of the means of production in the name of society —is at the same time its last independent act as a State. The interference of a State power in social relations becomes super-fluous in one sphere after another, and then becomes dormant of itself. Government over persons is replaced by the adminis-tration of things and the direction of the processes of production. The State is not " abolished," *it withers away*. It is from this standpoint that we must appraise the phrase " people's free State "—both its justification at times for agitational purposes, and its ultimate scientific inadequacy—and also the demand of the so-called Anarchists that the State should be abolished overnight.

Without fear of committing an error, it may be said that of this argument by Engels so singularly rich in ideas, only one point has become an integral part of Socialist thought among modern Socialist parties, namely, that, unlike the Anarchist doctrine of the " abolition " of the State, accord-ing to Marx the State " withers away." To emasculate Marxism in such a manner is to reduce it to opportunism, for such an " interpretation " only leaves the hazy concep-tion of a slow, even, gradual change, free from leaps and storms, free from revolution. The current popular concep-tion, if one may say so, of the " withering away " of the State undoubtedly means a slurring over, if not a negation, of revolution.

Yet, such an " interpretation " is the crudest distortion of Marxism, which is advantageous only to the bourgeoisie ; in point of theory, it is based on a disregard for the most important circumstances and considerations pointed out in the very passage summarising Engels' idea, which we have just quoted in full.

In the first place, Engels at the very outset of his argu-ment says that, in assuming State power, the proletariat by that very act " puts an end to the State as the State." One is " not accustomed " to reflect on what this really means. Generally, it is either ignored altogether, or it is considered as a piece of " Hegelian weakness " on Engels' part. As a matter of fact, however, these words express succinctly the experience of one of the greatest proletarian revolutions—the Paris Commune of 1871, of which we shall speak in greater detail in its proper place. As a matter of fact, Engels speaks here of the destruction of the bourgeois State by the proletarian revolution, while the words about its withering away refer to the remains of *proletarian* statehood *after* the Socialist revolution. The bourgeois State does not " wither away," according to Engels, but is " put an end to " by the proletariat in the course of the revolution. What withers away after the revolution is the proletarian State or semi-state.

Secondly, the State is a " special repressive force." This splendid and extremely profound definition of Engels' is given by him here with complete lucidity. It follows from this that the " special repressive force " of the bourgeoisie for the suppression of the proletariat, of the millions of workers by a handful of the rich, must be replaced by a " special repressive force " of the proletariat for the suppression of the bourgeoisie (the dictatorship of the proletariat). It is just this that constitutes the destruction of " the State as the State." It is just this that constitutes the " act " of " the seizure of the means of production in the name of society." And it is obvious that such a substitution of one (proletarian) " special repressive force " for another (bourgeois) " special repressive force " can in no way take place in the form of a " withering away."

Thirdly, as to the " withering away " or, more expressively and colourfully, as to the State " becoming dormant," Engels refers quite clearly and definitely to the period *after* " the seizure of the means of production (by the State) in the name of society," that is, after the Socialist revolution. We all know that the political form of the " State " at that time is complete democracy. But it never enters the head of any of the opportunists who shamelessly distort Marx that when Engels speaks here of the State " withering away," or " becoming dormant," he speaks of *democracy*.

At first sight this seems very strange. But it is " unintelli-
gible " only to one who has not reflected on the fact that
democracy is *also* a State and that, consequently, democracy will *also* disappear when the State disappears. The
bourgeois State can only be " put an end to " by a revolution. The State in general, i.e., most complete democracy,
can only " wither away."

Fourthly, having formulated his famous proposition that
" the State withers away," Engels at once explains concretely that this proposition is directed equally against the
opportunists and the Anarchists. In doing this, however,
Engels puts in the first place that conclusion from his proposition about the " withering away " of the State which
is directed against the opportunists.

One can wager that out of every 10,000 persons who
have read or heard about the " withering away " of the
State, 9,990 do not know at all, or do not remember, that
Engels did not direct his conclusions from this proposition
against the Anarchists *alone*. And out of the remaining ten,
probably nine do not know the meaning of a " people's
free State " nor the reason why an attack on this watch-
word contains an attack on the opportunists. This is how
history is written ! This is how a great revolutionary doctrine is imperceptibly adulterated and adapted to current
philistinism ! The conclusion drawn against the Anarchists
has been repeated thousands of times, vulgarised, har-
angued about in the crudest fashion possible until it has
acquired the strength of a prejudice, whereas the conclusion drawn against the opportunists has been hushed up
and " forgotten " !

The " people's free State " was a demand in the programme of the German Social-Democrats and their current
slogan in the 'seventies. There is no political substance in
this slogan other than a pompous middle-class circumlocu-
tion of the idea of democracy. In so far as it referred in a
lawful manner to a democratic republic, Engels was prepared to " justify " its use " at times " from a propaganda

point of view. But this slogan was opportunist, for it not only expressed an exaggerated view of the attractiveness of bourgeois democracy, but also a lack of understanding of the Socialist criticism of every State in general. We are in favour of a democratic republic as the best form of the State for the proletariat under capitalism, but we have no right to forget that wage slavery is the lot of the people even in the most democratic bourgeois republic. Furthermore, every State is a " special repressive force " for the suppression of the oppressed class. Consequently, *no* State is either " free " or " people's State." Marx and Engels explained this repeatedly to their party comrades in the 'seventies.

Fifthly, in the same work of Engels, from which every one remembers his argument on the " withering away " of the State, there is also a disquisition on the significance of a violent revolution. The historical analysis of its rôle becomes, with Engels, a veritable panegyric on violent revolution. This, of course, " no one remembers " ; to talk or even to think of the importance of this idea is not considered good form by contemporary Socialist parties, and in the daily propaganda and agitation among the masses it plays no part whatever. Yet it is indissolubly bound up with the " withering away " of the State in one harmonious whole.

Here is Engels' argument :

> . . . That force, however, plays another rôle (other than that of a diabolical power) in history, a revolutionary rôle ; that, in the words of Marx, it is the midwife of every old society which is pregnant with the new ; that it is the instrument with whose aid social movement forces its way through and shatters the dead, fossilised political forms—of this there is not a word in Herr Dühring. It is only with sighs and groans that he admits the possibility that force will perhaps be necessary for the overthrow of the economic system of exploitation—unfortunately ! because all use of force, forsooth, demoralises the person who uses it. And this in spite of the immense moral and spiritual impetus which has resulted from every victorious

ZM

revolution ! And this in Germany, where a violent collision—
which indeed may be forced on the people—would at least
have the advantage of wiping out the servility which has
permeated the national consciousness as a result of the humiliation of the Thirty Years' War. And this parson's mode of
thought—lifeless, insipid and impotent—claims to impose
itself on the most revolutionary Party which history has known ?

How can this panegyric on violent revolution, which
Engels insistently brought to the attention of the German
Social-Democrats between 1878 and 1894, i.e., right to
the time of his death, be combined with the theory
of the "withering away" of the State to form one
doctrine ?

Usually the two views are combined by means of eclecticism, by an unprincipled, sophistic, arbitrary selection (to
oblige the powers that be) of either one or the other argument, and in ninety-nine cases out of a hundred (if not more
often), it is the idea of the "withering away" that is
specially emphasised. Eclecticism is substituted for dialectics—this is the most usual, the most widespread phenomenon to be met with in the official Social-Democratic
literature of our day in relation to Marxism. Such a substitution is, of course, nothing new ; it may be observed
even in the history of classic Greek philosophy. When
Marxism is adulterated to become opportunism, the substitution of eclecticism for dialectics is the best method of
deceiving the masses ; it gives an illusory satisfaction ; it
seems to take into account all sides of the process, all the
tendencies of development, all the contradictory factors
and so forth, whereas in reality it offers no consistent and
revolutionary view of the process of social development at
all.

We have already said above, and shall show more fully
later, that the teaching of Marx and Engels regarding the
inevitability of a violent revolution refers to the bourgeois
State. It *cannot* be replaced by the proletarian State (the
dictatorship of the proletariat) through "withering away,"

but, as a general rule, only through a violent revolution. The panegyric sung in its honour by Engels and fully corresponding to the repeated declarations of Marx (remember the concluding passages of the *Poverty of Philosophy* and *The Communist Manifesto*, with its proud and open declaration of the inevitability of a violent revolution ; remember Marx's *Critique of the Gotha Programme* of 1875 in which, almost thirty years later, he mercilessly castigates the opportunist character of that programme)—this praise is by no means a mere " impulse," a mere declamation, or a polemical sally. The necessity of systematically fostering among the masses *this* and just this point of view about violent revolution lies at the root of the *whole* of Marx's and Engels' teaching. The neglect of such propaganda and agitation by both the present predominant social-chauvinist and the Kautskyist current brings their betrayal of Marx's and Engels' teaching into prominent relief.

The replacement of the bourgeois by the proletarian State is impossible without a violent revolution. The abolition of the proletarian State, i.e., of all States, is only possible through " withering away."

Marx and Engels gave a full and concrete exposition of these views in studying each revolutionary situation separately, in analysing the lessons of the experience of each individual revolution.

THE ECONOMIC BASE OF THE WITHERING AWAY OF THE STATE

(Ch. V)

A most detailed elucidation of this question is given by Marx in his *Critique of the Gotha Programme* (letter to Bracke, May 15, 1875, printed only in 1891 in the *Neue Zeit*, IX-1, and in a special Russian edition). The polemical part of this remarkable work, consisting of a criticism of Lassalleanism, has, so to speak, over-shadowed its positive part, namely, the analysis of the connection between the development of Communism and the withering away of the State.

1. Formulation of the Question by Marx

From a superficial comparison of the letter of Marx to Bracke (May 15, 1875) with Engels' letter to Bebel (March 28, 1875), analysed above, it might appear that Marx was much more " pro-state " than Engels, and that the difference of opinion between the two writers on the question of the State is very considerable.

Engels suggests to Bebel that all the chatter about the State should be thrown overboard ; that the word " State " should be eliminated from the programme and replaced by " community " ; Engels even declares that the Commune was really no longer a State in the proper sense of the word. And Marx even speaks of the " future State in Communist society," i.e., he is apparently recognising the necessity of a State even under Communism.

But such a view would be fundamentally incorrect. A closer examination shows that Marx's and Engels' views on the State and its withering away were completely identical, and that Marx's expression quoted above refers merely to this withering away of the State.

It is clear that there can be no question of defining the exact moment of the *future* withering away—the more so as it must obviously be a rather lengthy process. The apparent difference between Marx and Engels is due to the different subjects they dealt with, the different aims they were pursuing. Engels set out to show to Bebel, in a plain, bold and broad outline, all the absurdity of the current superstitions concerning the State, shared to no small degree by Lassalle himself. Marx, on the other hand, only touches upon *this* question in passing, being interested mainly in another subject—the *evolution* of Communist society.

The whole theory of Marx is an application of the theory of development—in its most consistent, complete, well considered and fruitful form—to modern capitalism. It was natural for Marx to raise the question of applying this theory both of the *coming* collapse of capitalism and to the *future* development of *future* Communism.

On the basis of what *data* can the future development of future Communism be considered ?

On the basis of the fact that *it has its origin* in capitalism, that it develops historically from capitalism, that it is the result of the action of a social force to which capitalism *has given birth*. There is no shadow of an attempt on Marx's part to conjure up a Utopia, to make idle guesses about that which cannot be known. Marx treats the question of Communism in the same way as a naturalist would treat the question of the development of, say, a new biological species, if he knew that such and such was its origin, and such and such the direction in which it changed.

Marx, first of all, brushes aside the confusion the Gotha Programme brings into the question of the interrelation between State and society.

" Contemporary society " is the capitalist society—he writes —which exists in all civilised countries, more or less free of mediæval admixture, more or less modified by each country's particular historical development, more or less developed. In contrast with this, the " contemporary State " varies with every State boundary. It is different in the Prusso-German Empire from what it is in Switzerland, and different in England from what it is in the United States. The " contemporary State " is therefore a fiction.

Nevertheless, in spite of the motley variety of their forms, the different States of the various civilised countries all have this in common : they are all based on modern bourgeois society, only a little more or less capitalistically developed. Consequently, they also have certain essential characteristics in common. In this sense, it is possible to speak of the " contemporary State " in contrast to the future, when its present root, bourgeois society, will have perished.

Then the question arises : what transformation will the State undergo in a Communist society ? In other words, what social functions analogous to the present functions of the State will then still survive ? This question can only be answered scientifically, and however many thousand times the word people is combined with the word State, we get not a flea-jump closer to the problem. . . .

Having thus ridiculed all talk about a " people's State," Marx formulates the question and warns us, as it were, that to arrive at a scientific answer one must rely only on firmly established scientific data.

The first fact that has been established with complete exactness by the whole theory of development, by science as a whole—a fact which the Utopians forgot, and which is forgotten by the present-day opportunists who are afraid of the Socialist revolution—is that, historically, there must undoubtedly be a special stage or epoch of *transition* from capitalism to Communism.

2. *Transition from Capitalism to Communism*

Between capitalist and Communist society—Marx continues —lies the period of the revolutionary transformation of the former into the latter. To this also corresponds a political transition period, in which the State can be no other than *the revolutionary dictatorship of the proletariat*.

This conclusion Marx bases on an analysis of the rôle played by the proletariat in modern capitalist society, on the data concerning the development of this society, and on the irreconcilability of the opposing interests of the proletariat and the bourgeoisie.

Earlier the question was put thus : to attain its emancipation, the proletariat must overthrow the bourgeoisie, conquer political power and establish its own revolutionary dictatorship.

Now the question is put somewhat differently : the transition from capitalist society, developing towards Communism, towards a Communist society, is impossible without a " political transition period," and the State in this period can only be the revolutionary dictatorship of the proletariat.

What, then, is the relation of this dictatorship to democracy ?

We have seen that *The Communist Manifesto* simply places side by side the two ideas : the " transformation of the proletariat into the ruling class " and the " establishment of democracy." On the basis of all that has been said above, one can define more exactly how democracy changes in the transition from capitalism to Communism.

In capitalist society, under the conditions most favourable to its development, we have more or less complete democracy in the democratic republic. But this democracy is always bound by the narrow framework of capitalist exploitation, and consequently, always remains, in reality, a democracy for the minority, only for the possessing classes, only for the rich. Freedom in capitalist society always remains just about the same as it was in the ancient Greek republics : freedom for the slave-owners. The modern wage-slaves, owing to the conditions of capitalist exploitation, are so much crushed by want and poverty that " democracy is nothing to them," " politics is nothing to them " ; that, in the ordinary peaceful course of events, the majority of the population is debarred from participating in social and political life.

The correctness of this statement is perhaps most clearly proved by Germany, just because in this State constitutional legality lasted and remained stable for a remarkably long time—for nearly half a century (1871–1914)—and because Social-Democracy in Germany during that time was able to achieve far more than in other countries in " utilising legality," and was able to organise into a political party a larger proportion of the working class than anywhere else in the world.

What, then, is this largest proportion of politically conscious and active wage-slaves that has so far been observed in capitalist society ? One million members of the Social-Democratic Party—out of fifteen million wage-workers ! Three million organised in trade unions—out of fifteen million !

Democracy for an insignificant minority, democracy for the rich—that is the democracy of capitalist society. If we look more closely into the mechanism of capitalist democracy, everywhere, both in the " petty "—so-called petty— details of the suffrage (residential qualification, exclusion of women, etc.), and in the technique of the representative institutions, in the actual obstacles to the right of assembly (public buildings are not for " beggars " !), in the purely capitalist organisation of the daily Press, etc., etc.—on all sides we see restriction after restriction upon democracy. These restrictions, exceptions, exclusions, obstacles for the poor, seem slight, especially in the eyes of one who has himself never known want and has never been in close contact with the oppressed classes in their mass life (and nine-tenths, if not ninety-nine hundredths, of the bourgeois publicists and politicans are of this class), but in their sum total these restrictions exclude and squeeze out the poor from politics and from an active share in democracy.

Marx splendidly grasped this *essence* of capitalist democracy, when, in analysing the experience of the Commune, he said that the oppressed were allowed, once every few years, to decide which particular representatives of the oppressing class should be in parliament to represent and repress them !

But from this capitalist democracy—inevitably narrow, subtly rejected the poor, and therefore hypocritical and false to the core—progress does not march onward, simply smoothly, and directly, to " greater and greater democracy," as the liberal professors and petty-bourgeois opportunists would have us believe. No, progress marches onward, i.e., toward Communism, through the dictatorship of the proletariat ; it cannot do otherwise, for there is no one else and no other way to *break the resistance* of the capitalist exploiters.

But the dictatorship of the proletariat—i.e., the organisation of the vanguard of the oppressed as the ruling class for the purpose of crushing the oppressors—cannot produce

merely an expansion of democracy. *Together* with an immense expansion of democracy which *for the first time*
becomes democracy for the poor, democracy for the people,
and not democracy for the rich folk, the dictatorship of
the proletariat produces a series of restrictions of liberty in
the case of the oppressors, the exploiters, the capitalists. We
must crush them in order to free humanity from wage-
slavery ; their resistance must be broken by force ; it is
clear that where there is suppression there is also violence,
there is no liberty, no democracy.

Engels expressed this splendidly in his letter to Bebel
when he said, as the reader will remember, that " as long
as the proletariat still *needs* the State, it needs it not in the
interests of freedom, but for the purpose of crushing its
antagonists ; and as soon as it becomes possible to speak
of freedom, then the State, as such, ceases to exist."

Democracy for the vast majority of the people, and suppression by force, i.e., exclusion from democracy, of the
exploiters and oppressors of the people—this is the modifica-
tion of democracy during the *transition* from capitalism to
Communism.

Only in Communist society, when the resistance of the
capitalists has been completely broken, when the capitalists
have disappeared, when there are no classes (i.e., there is
no difference between the members of society in their relation to the social means of production), *only then* " the State
ceases to exist," and " *it becomes possible to speak of freedom.*"
Only then a really full democracy, a democracy without
any exceptions, will be possible and will be realised. And
only then will democracy itself begin to *wither away* due to
the simple fact that, freed from capitalist slavery, from the
untold horrors, savagery, absurdities and infamies of
capitalist exploitation, people will gradually *become accustomed* to the observation of the elementary rules of social
life that have been known for centuries and repeated for
thousands of years in all school books ; they will become
accustomed to observing them without force, without

compulsion, without subordination, without the *special apparatus* for compulsion which is called the State.

The expression " the State *withers away*," is very well chosen, for it indicates both the gradual and the elemental nature of the process. Only habit can, and undoubtedly will, have such an effect ; for we see around us millions of times how readily people get accustomed to observe the necessary rules of life in common, if there is no exploitation, if there is nothing that causes indignation, that calls forth protest and revolt and has to be *suppressed*.

Thus, in capitalist society, we have a democracy that is curtailed, poor, false ; a democracy only for the rich, for the minority. The dictatorship of the proletariat, the period of transition to Communism, will, for the first time, produce democracy for the people, for the majority, side by side with the necessary suppression of the minority—the exploiters. Communism alone is capable of giving a really complete democracy, and the more complete it is the more quickly will it become unnecessary and wither away of itself.

In other words : under capitalism we have a State in the proper sense of the word, that is, special machinery for the suppression of one class by another, and of the majority by the minority at that. Naturally, for the successful discharge of such a task as the systematic suppression by the exploiting minority of the exploited majority, the greatest ferocity and savagery of suppression are required, seas of blood are required, through which mankind is marching in slavery, serfdom, and wage-labour.

Again, during the *transition* from capitalism to Communism, suppression is *still* necessary ; but it is the suppression of the minority of exploiters by the majority of exploited. A special apparatus, special machinery for suppression, the " State," is *still* necessary, but this is now a transitional State, no longer a State in the usual sense, for the suppression of the minority of exploiters, by the majority of the wage slaves of *yesterday*, is a matter comparatively so easy, simple and natural that it will cost far less blood-shed than the suppression of the risings of slaves, serfs or wage labourers, and will cost mankind far less. This is compatible with the population, that the need for *special machinery* of suppression will begin to disappear. The ex-ploiters are, naturally, unable to suppress the people with-out a most complex machinery for performing this task ; but *the people* can suppress the exploiters even with very simple " machinery," almost without any " machinery," without any special apparatus, by the simple *organisation of the armed masses* (such as the Soviets of Workers' and Soldiers' Deputies, we may remark, anticipating a little).

Finally, only Communism renders the State absolutely unnecessary, for there is *no one* to be suppressed—" no one " in the sense of a *class*, in the sense of a systematic struggle with a definite section of the population. We are not Utopians, and we do not in the least deny the possibility and inevitability of excesses on the part of *individual persons*, nor the need to suppress *such* excesses. But, in the first place, no special machinery, no special apparatus of re-pression is needed for this ; this will be done by the armed people itself, as simply and as readily as any crowd of civilised people, even in modern society, parts a pair of combatants or does not allow a woman to be outraged. And, secondly, we know that the fundamental social cause of excesses which consists in violating the rules of social life is the exploitation of the masses, their want and their poverty. With the removal of this chief cause, excesses will inevitably begin to " *wither away.*" We do not know how quickly and in what succession, but we know that they will wither away. With their withering away, the State will also *wither away.*

 ⸱ Without going into Utopias, Marx defined more fully what can *now* be defined regarding this future, namely, the difference between the lower and higher phases (degrees, stages) of Communist society.

3. First Phase of Communist Society

In the *Critique of the Gotha Programme*, Marx goes into some detail to disprove the Lassallean idea of the workers' receiving under Socialism the " undiminished " or " full product of their labour." Marx shows that out of the whole of the social labour of society, it is necessary to deduct a reserve fund, a fund for the expansion of production, for the replacement of worn-out machinery and so on ; then also, out of the means of consumption must be deducted a fund for the expenses of management, for schools, hospitals, homes for the aged, and so on.

Instead of the hazy, obscure, general phrase of Lassalle's —" the full product of his labour for the worker "—Marx gives a sober estimate of exactly how a Socialist society will have to manage its affairs, Marx undertakes a *concrete* analysis of the conditions of life of a society in which there is no capitalism, and says :

> What we are dealing with here [analysing the programme of the party] is not a Communist society which has *developed* on its own foundations, but, on the contrary, one which is just *emerging* from capitalist society, and which therefore in all respects—economic, moral and intellectual—still bears the birthmarks of the old society from whose womb it sprung.

And it is this Communist society—a society which has just come into the world out of the womb of capitalism, and which, in all respects, bears the stamp of the old society— that Marx terms the " first," or lower, phase of Communist society.

The means of production are no longer the private property of individuals. The means of production belong to the whole of society. Every member of society, performing a certain part of socially-necessary work, receives a certificate from society to the effect that he has done such and such a quantity of work. According to this certificate, he receives from the public warehouses, where articles of consumption are stored, a corresponding quantity of products. Deducting that proportion of labour which goes to the public fund, every worker, therefore, receives from society as much as he has given it.

" Equality " seems to reign supreme.

But when Lassalle, having in view such a social order (generally called Socialism, but termed by Marx the first phase of Communism), speaks of this as " just distribution " and says that this is " the equal right of each to an equal product of labour," Lassalle is mistaken, and Marx exposes his error.

" Equal right," says Marx, " we indeed have here " ; but it is *still* a " bourgeois right," which, like every right, *presupposes inequality*. Every right is an application of the *same* measure to *different* people who, in fact, are not the same and are not equal to one another ; this is why " equal right " is really a violation of equality, and an injustice. In effect, every man having done as much social labour as every other, receives an equal share of the social products (with the above-mentioned deductions).

But different people are not alike : one is strong, another is weak ; one is married, the other is not ; one has more children, another has less, and so on.

. . . With equal labour—Marx concludes—and therefore an equal share in the social consumption fund, one man in fact receives more than the other, one is richer than the other, and so forth. In order to avoid all these defects, rights, instead of being equal, must be unequal.

The first phase of Communism, therefore, still cannot produce justice and equality ; differences, and unjust differences, in wealth will still exist, but the *exploitation* of man by man will have become impossible, because it will be impossible to seize as private property the *means of production*, the factories, machines, land, and so on. In tearing down Lassalle's petty-bourgeois, confused phrase about " equality " and " justice " *in general*, Marx shows the *course of development* of Communist society, which is forced at first to destroy *only* the " injustice " that consists in the means of production having been seized by private individuals, and which *is not capable* of destroying at once the further injustice consisting in the distribution of the articles of consumption " according to work performed " (and not according to need).

The vulgar economists, including the bourgeois professors and also " our " Tugan-Baranovsky, constantly reproach the Socialists with forgetting the inequality of people and with " dreaming " of destroying this inequality. Such a reproach, as we see, only proves the extreme ignorance of the gentlemen propounding bourgeois ideology.

Marx not only takes into account with the greatest accuracy the inevitable inequality of men ; he also takes into account the fact that the mere conversion of the means of production into the common property of the whole of society (" Socialism " in the generally accepted sense of the word) *does not remove* the defects of distribution and the inequality of " bourgeois right " which *continue to rule* as long as the products are divided " according to work performed."

> But these defects—Marx continues—are unavoidable in the first phase of Communist society, when, after long travail, it first emerges from capitalist society. Justice can never rise superior to the economic conditions of society and the cultural development conditioned by them.

And so, in the first phase of Communist society (generally called Socialism) " bourgeois right " is *not* abolished in its entirety, but only in part, only in proportion to the economic transformation so far attained, i.e., only in respect of the means of production. " Bourgeois right " recognises them as the private property of separate individuals. Socialism converts them into common property. *To that extent*, and to that extent alone, does " bourgeois rights " disappear.

However, it continues to exist as far as its other part is concerned ; it remains in the capacity of regulator (determining factor) distributing the products and allotting labour among the members of society. " He who does not work, shall not eat "—this Socialist principle is *already* realised ; " for an equal quantity of labour, an equal quantity of products "—this Socialist principle is also *already* realised. However, this is not yet Communism, and this does not abolish " bourgeois right," which gives to unequal individuals, in return for an equal (in reality unequal) amount of work, an equal quantity of products.

This is a " defect," says Marx, but it is unavoidable during the first phase of Communism ; for, if we are not to fall into Utopianism, we cannot imagine that, having overthrown capitalism, people will at once learn to work for society *without any standards of right* ; indeed, the abolition of capitalism *does not immediately lay* the economic foundations for *such* a change.

And there is no other standard yet than that of " bourgeois right." To this extent, therefore, a form of State is still necessary, which, while maintaining public ownership of the means of production, would preserve the equality of labour and equality in the distribution of products.

The State is withering away in so far as there are no longer any capitalists, any classes, and, consequently, no *class* can be suppressed.

But the State has not yet altogether withered away, since there still remains the protection of " bourgeois right " which sanctifies actual inequality. For the complete extinction of the State, complete Communism is necessary.

4. Higher Phase of Communist Society

Marx continues :

In a higher phase of Communist society, when the enslaving subordination of individuals in the division of labour has disappeared, and with it also the antagonism, between mental and physical labour ; when labour has become not only a means of living, but itself the first necessity of life ; when, along with the all-round development of individuals, the productive forces too have grown, and all the springs of social wealth are flowing more freely—it is only at that stage that it will be possible to pass completely beyond the narrow horizon of bourgeois rights, and for society to inscribe on its banners : from each according to his ability : to each according to his needs !

Only now can we appreciate the full correctness of Engels' remarks in which he mercilessly ridiculed all the absurdity of combining the words " freedom " and " state." While the State exists there is no freedom. When there is freedom, there will be no State.

The economic basis for the complete withering away of the State is that high stage of development of Communism when the antagonism between mental and physical labour disappears, that is to say, when one of the principal sources of modern *social* inequality disappears—a source, moreover, which it is impossible to remove immediately by the mere conversion of the means of production into public property, by the mere expropriation of the capitalists.

This expropriation will make a gigantic development of the productive forces *possible*. And seeing how incredibly, even now, capitalism *retards* this development, how much progress could be made even on the basis of modern technique at the level it has reached, we have a right to say, with the fullest confidence, that the expropriation of the capitalists will inevitably result in a gigantic development of the productive forces of human society. But how rapidly this development will go forward, how soon it will reach the point of breaking away from the division of labour, of removing the antagonism between mental and physical labour, of transforming work into the " first necessity of life "—this we do not and *cannot* know.

Consequently, we have a right to speak solely of the inevitable withering away of the State, emphasising the protracted nature of this process and its dependence upon the rapidity of development of the *higher phase* of Communism ;

leaving quite open the question of lengths of time, or the concrete forms of withering away, since material for the solution of such questions is *not available*.

The State will be able to wither away completely when society has realised the rule : " From each according to his ability ; to each according to his needs," i.e., when people have become accustomed to observe the fundamental rules of social life, and their labour is so productive, that they voluntarily work *according to their ability*. " The narrow horizon of bourgeois rights," which compels one to calculate, with the hard-heartedness of a Shylock, whether he has not worked half an hour more than another, whether he is not getting less pay than another—this narrow horizon will then be left behind. There will then be no need for any exact calculation by society of the quantity of products to be distributed to each of its members ; each will take freely " according to his needs."

From the bourgeois point of view, it is easy to declare such a social order " a pure Utopia," and to sneer at the Socialists for promising each the right to receive from society, without any control of the labour of the individual citizen, any quantity of truffles, automobiles, pianos, etc. Even now, most bourgeois " savants " deliver themselves of such sneers, thereby displaying at once their ignorance and their self-seeking defence of capitalism.

Ignorance—for it has never entered the head of any Socialist to " promise " that the highest phase of Communism will arrive ; while the great Socialists, in *foreseeing* its arrival, presupposed both a productivity of labour unlike the present and a person not like the present man in the street, capable of spoiling, without reflection, like the seminary students in Pomyalovsky's book, the stores of social wealth, and of demanding the impossible.

Until the " higher " phase of Communism arrives, the Socialists demand the *strictest* control, *by society and by the State*, of the quantity of labour and the quantity of consumption ; only this control must *start* with the expropriation of the capitalists, with the control of the workers over the capitalists, and must be carried out, not by a State of bureaucrats, but by a State of *armed workers*.

Self-seeking defence of capitalism by the bourgeois ideologists (and their hangers-on like Tsereteli, Chernov and Co.) consists in that they *substitute* disputes and discussions about the distant future for the essential imperative questions of present-day policy : the expropriation of the capitalists, the conversion of *all* citizens into workers and employees of *one* huge " syndicate "—the whole State —and the complete subordination of the whole of the work of this syndicate to the really democratic State of the *Soviets of Workers' and Soldiers' Deputies*.

In reality, when a learned professor, and following him some philistine, and following the latter Messrs. Tsereteli and Chernov, talk of the unreasonable Utopias, of the demagogic promises of the Bolsheviks, of the impossibility of " introducing " Socialism, it is the higher stage or phase of Communism which they have in mind, and which no one has ever promised, or even thought of " introducing," for the reason that, generally speaking, it cannot be " introduced."

And here we come to that question of the scientific difference between Socialism and Communism, upon which Engels touched in his above-quoted discussion on the incorrectness of the name " Social-Democrat." The political difference between the first, or lower, and the higher phase of Communism will in time, no doubt, be tremendous ; but it would be ridiculous to emphasise it now, under capitalism, and only, perhaps, some isolated Anarchist could invest it with primary importance (if there are still some people among the Anarchists who have learned nothing from the Plekhanov-like conversion of the Kropotkins, the Graveses, the Cornelissens, and other " leading lights " of Anarchism to social-chauvinism or Anarcho-*Jusquaubout*-ism, as Gé, one of the few Anarchists still preserving honour and conscience, has expressed it).

But the scientific difference between Socialism and Communism is clear. What is generally called Socialism was termed by Marx the " first " or lower phase of Communist society. In so far as the means of production become *public* property, the word " Communism " is also applicable here, providing we do not forget that it is *not* full Communism. The great significance of Marx's elucidations consists in this : that here, too, he consistently applies materialist dialectics, the doctrine of development, looking upon Communism as something which evolves *out of* capitalism. Instead of artificial, " elaborate " scholastic definitions and profitless disquisitions on the meaning of words (what Socialism is, what Communism is), Marx gives an analysis of what may be called stages in the economic ripeness of Communism.

In its first phase or first stage Communism *cannot* as yet be economically ripe and entirely free of all tradition and of all taint of capitalism. Hence the interesting phenomenon of Communism retaining, in its first phase, " the narrow horizon of bourgeois rights." Bourgeois rights, with respect to distribution of articles of *consumption*, inevitably presupposes, of course, the existence of the *bourgeois State*, for rights are nothing without an apparatus capable of *enforcing* the observance of the rights.

Consequently, for a certain time not only bourgeois rights, but even the bourgeois State remains under Communism, without the bourgeoisie !

This may look like a paradox, or simply a dialectical puzzle for which Marxism is often blamed by people who would not make the least effort to study its extraordinarily profound content.

But, as a matter of fact, the old surviving in the new confronts us in life at every step, in nature as well as in society. Marx did not smuggle a scrap of " bourgeois " rights into Communism of his own accord ; he indicated what is economically and politically inevitable in a society issuing *from the womb* of capitalism.

Democracy is of great importance for the working class in its struggle for freedom against the capitalists. But democracy is by no means a limit one may not overstep ; it is only one of the stages in the course of development from feudalism to capitalism, and from capitalism to Communism.

Democracy means equality. The great significance of the struggle of the proletariat for equality, and the significance of equality as a slogan, are apparent, if we correctly interpret it as meaning the abolition of *classes*. But democracy means only *formal* equality. Immediately after the attainment of equality for all members of society *in respect of* the ownership of the means of production, that is, of equality of labour and equality of wages, there will inevitably arise before humanity the question of going further from formal equality to real equality, i.e., to realising the rule, " From each according to his ability ; to each according to his needs." By what stages, by means of what practical measures humanity will proceed to this higher aim—this we do not and cannot know. But it is important to realise how infinitely mendacious is the usual bourgeois presentation of Socialism as something lifeless, petrified, fixed once for all, whereas in reality, it is *only* with Socialism that there will commence a rapid, genuine, real mass advance, in which first the *majority* and then the whole of the population will take part—an advance in all domains of social and individual life.

Democracy is a form of the State—one of its varieties. Consequently, like every State, it consists in organised, systematic application of force against human beings. This on the one hand. On the other hand, however, it signifies the formal recognition of the equality of all citizens, the equal right of all to determine the structure and administration of the State. This, in turn, is connected with the fact that, at a certain stage in the development of democracy, it first rallies the proletariat as a revolutionary class against capitalism, and gives it an opportunity to crush,

to smash to bits, to wipe off the face of the earth the bourgeois State machinery—even its republican variety : the
standing army, the police, and bureaucracy ; then it sub-
stitutes for all this a *more* democratic, but still a State
machinery in the shape of armed masses of workers, which
becomes transformed into universal participation of the
people in the militia.

Here " quantity turns into quality " : *such* a degree of
democracy is bound up with the abandonment of the
framework of bourgeois society, and the beginning of its
Socialist reconstruction. If *everyone* really takes part in the
administration of the State, capitalism cannot retain its
hold. In its turn, capitalism, as it develops, itself creates
pre-requisites for " everyone " *to be able* really to take part
in the administration of the State. Among such pre-requisites
are universal literacy, already realised in most of the advanced capitalist countries, then the " training and dis-
ciplining " of millions of workers by the huge, complex,
and socialised apparatus of the post office, the railways, the
big factories, large-scale commerce, banking, etc., etc.

With such *economic* pre-requisites it is perfectly possible,
immediately, within twenty-four hours after the overthrow
of the capitalists and bureaucrats, to replace them, in the
control of production and distribution, in the business of
control of labour and products, by the armed workers, by
the whole people in arms. (The question of control and
accounting must not be confused with the question of the
scientifically educated staffs of engineers, agronomists and
so on. These gentlemen work to-day, obeying the capitalists ; they will work even better to-morrow, obeying the
armed workers.)

Accounting and control—these are the *cheif* things necessary for the organising and correct functioning of the *first
phase of* Communist society. *All* citizens are here transformed
into hired employees of the State, which is made up of the
armed workers. *All* citizens become employees and workers
of *one* national State " syndicate." All that is required is

that they should work equally, should regularly do their share of work, and should receive equal pay. The accounting and control necessary for this have been *simplified* by capitalism to the utmost, till they have become the extraordinarily simple operations of watching, recording and issuing receipts, within the reach of anybody who can read and write and knows the first four rules of arithmetic.

When the *majority* of the people begin everywhere to keep such accounts and maintain such control over the capitalists (now converted into employees) and over the intellectual gentry, who still retain capitalist habits, this control will really become universal, general, national ; and there will be no way of getting away from it, there will be " nowhere to go."

The whole of society will have become one office and one factory, with equal work and equal pay.

But this " factory " discipline, which the proletariat will extend to the whole of society after the defeat of the capitalists and the overthrow of the exploiters, is by no means our ideal, or our final aim. It is but a *foothold* necessary for the radical cleansing of society of all the hideousness and foulness of capitalist exploitation, *in order to advance further*.

From the moment when all members of society, or even only the overwhelming majority, have learned how to govern the State *themselves*, have taken this business into their own hands, have " established " control over the insignificant minority of capitalists, over the gentry with capitalist leanings, and the workers thoroughly demoralised by capitalism—from this moment the need for any government begins to disappear. The more complete the democracy, the nearer the moment when it begins to be unnecessary. The more democratic the " State " consisting of armed workers, which is " no longer a State in the proper sense of the word," the more rapidly does *every* State begin to wither away.

For when *all* have learned to manage, and independently

are actually managing by themselves social production, keeping accounts, controlling the idlers, the gentlefolk, the swindlers and similar " guardians of capitalist traditions," then the escape from this national accounting and control will inevitably become so increasingly difficult, such a rare exception, and will probably be accompanied by such swift and severe punishment (for the armed workers are men of practical life, not sentimental intellectuals, and they will scarcely allow anyone to trifle with them), that very soon the *necessity* of observing the simple, fundamental rules of every-day social life in common will have become a *habit*.

The door will then be wide open for the transition from the first phase of Communist society to its higher phase, and along with it to the complete withering away of the State.

V. I. Lenin

LETTERS FROM AFAR

Written in Switzerland in March and April 1917 ; only one was published in Petrograd, in the " Pravda " of April 3, 1917. Complete English edition, Martin Lawrence, Ltd., 1931.

[Between March 20 and April 8, 1917, Lenin wrote five letters from Switzerland, analysing the situation in Russia and laying down the main lines of policy for the Bolsheviks. The first letter was written soon after Lenin knew of the overthrow of the Tsar's Government on March 14, 1917, and the establishment of the Provisional Government. Lenin at once put forward the standpoint that this was only the first stage of a revolution which would only be completed by the overthrow of the Provisional Government and the establishment of a proletarian dictatorship. The second letter reprinted here was written on March 24,

1917 ; it develops the idea of the Soviets as the organs of revolutionary power which would smash the old machinery of the State.]

LETTERS FROM AFAR

The First Stage of the First Revolution

T HE FIRST revolution arising out of the imperialist World War has broken out. This first revolution will, certainly, not be the last.

The first stage of this first revolution, namely, the *Russian* revolution of March 14, 1917, is over, according to the scanty information at the writer's disposal in Switzerland. Surely this first stage of our revolution will not be the last one.

How could such a " miracle " happen, that in eight days —the period indicated by M. Miliukov in his boastful telegram to all the representatives of Russia abroad—a monarchy that had maintained itself for centuries, and continued to maintain itself during three years of tremendous national class conflicts of 1905–1907, could utterly collapse ?

There are no miracles in nature or in history, yet every sudden turn in history, including every revolution, presents such a wealth of material, it unfolds such unexpectedly peculiar co-ordinations of forms of conflict and alignment of fighting forces, that there is much that must appear miraculous to the burgher's mind.

A combination of a whole series of conditions of worldwide historic importance was required for the tsarist monarchy to collapse in a few days. Let us point out the principal ones.

Without the three years, 1905–1907, of tremendous class conflicts and of revolutionary energy of the Russian proletariat, this second revolution could not possibly have had the rapid progress indicated in the fact that its *first* phase was accomplished in a few days. The first revolution (1905) ploughed the ground deeply and uprooted the prejudices of centuries ; it awakened to political life and struggle millions of workers and tens of millions of peasants. The first revolution revealed to the workers and peasants, as well as to the world, all the classes (and all the principal parties) of Russian society in their true character ; the actual alignment of their interests, their powers and modes of action, their immediate and ultimate objectives. This first revolution, and the succeeding counter-revolutionary period (1907–1914), fully revealed the nature of the tsarist monarchy as having reached the " utmost limit " ; it exposed all the infamy and vileness, all the cynicism and corruption of the tsarist clique dominated by that monster, Rasputin ; it exposed all the bestiality of the Romanov family—that band of assassins which bathed Russia in the blood of the Jews, the workers, the revolutionaries—those landowners, " first among peers," who owned millions of acres of land and would stoop to any brutality, to any crime—ready to ruin or crush any section of the population, however numerous, in order to preserve the " sacred property rights " for themselves and for their class.

Without the revolution of 1905–1907, without the counter-revolution of 1907–1914, it would have been impossible to secure so clear a " self-determination " of all classes of the Russian people and of all the peoples inhabiting Russia, a clarification of the relation of these classes to each other and to the tsarist monarchy, as transpired during the eight days of the March revolution. This eight-day revolution, if we may express ourselves in terms of metaphors, was " performed " after a dozen informal as well as dress rehearsals ; the " actors " knew each other and their rôles, their places, and the entire setting ; they knew every detail through and through, down to the last more or less significant shade of political tendency and mode of action.

But, in order that the first great revolution of 1905, which Messrs. Guchkov and Miliukov and their satellites condemned as a " great rebellion " should, after the lapse of a dozen years, lead to the " glorious revolution " of 1917—so termed by the Guchkovs and Miliukovs because (for the *present*) it has put them into power—there was still needed a great, mighty, all-powerful " régisseur," who was, on the one hand, in a position to accelerate the course of history on a grand scale, and, on the other, to produce world-wide crisis of unheard-of intensity : economic, political, national and international. In addition to an unusual acceleration of world history, there were also needed particularly sharp historic turns so that during one of them the blood-stained chariot of tsarism might be overturned in a trice.

This all-powerful " régisseur," this mighty accelerator of events, was the imperialist World War.

Now it can no longer be doubted that this war is world-wide, for the United States and China have been half dragged in already, and to-morrow will be completely involved in it.

Nor can it any longer be doubted that the war is imperialistic on both sides. Only the capitalists and their satellites, the social-patriots and social-chauvinists, can deny or suppress this fact. Both the German and the Anglo-French bourgeoisie are waging war for the grabbing of foreign territory, for the strangulation of small nations, for financial supremacy over the world, for the division and redistribution of colonies, for saving the tottering capitalist régime by means of deceiving and disuniting the workers in the various countries.

It was objectively inevitable that the imperialist war should immensely quicken and unusually sharpen the class struggle of the proletariat against the bourgeoisie, and transform itself into a civil war between hostile classes.

This transformation has been started by the March

revolution, whose first stage has shown us, first, a joint attack on tsarism delivered by two forces : on the one hand, the whole bourgeois and landowning class of Russia, with all their unenlightened followers and very enlightened managers, in the persons of the Anglo-French ambassadors and capitalists ; and, on the other, the Soviet of Workers' and Soldiers' Deputies.

These three political camps, three fundamental political forces : (1) The tsarist monarchy, the head of the feudal landowning class, the head of the old bureaucracy and of the higher military commanders ; (2) the Russia of the bourgeoisie and landowners represented by the Octobrists and Cadets, with the petty bourgeoisie in their wake ; (3) the Soviet of Workers' and Soldiers' Deputies, seeking for allies among the entire proletariat and the whole mass of the poorest population—these three fundamental political forces have revealed themselves with utmost clarity even in the first eight days of the " first stage." This is evident even to such an observer as the present writer who is far away from the scene of events and is compelled to confine himself to the meagre dispatches of foreign papers.

But before going into further detail in this matter, I must come back to that portion of my letter which is devoted to a factor of first importance, namely, the imperialist World War.

The belligerent powers, the belligerent groups of capitalists, the " masters " of the capitalist system, and the slave-drivers of capitalist slavery, have been shackled to each other by the war with chains of iron. *One bloody lump*, that is the socio-political life of the historic period through which we are now passing.

The Socialists who deserted to the bourgeoisie at the beginning of the war, all the Davids and Scheidemanns in Germany, the Plekhanovs, Potresovs, Gvozdevs and Co. in Russia, have long been shouting lustily against the " illusions " of the revolutionists, against the " illusions "

of the Basle Manifesto, against the " dream farce " of turning the imperialist war into civil war. They have sung
hymns of praise to the alleged strength, tenacity and
adaptability of capitalism, while they were aiding the
capitalists in " adapting," taming, deceiving and disuniting
the working classes of the various countries !

But " he who laughs last laughs best." The bourgeoisie
was not able to delay for very long the coming of the
revolutionary crisis produced by the war. This crisis is
growing with irresistible force in all countries, beginning
with Germany where, according to a recent observer who
visited that country, there is " hunger organised with the
ability of genius," and down to England and France where
hunger is also looming, though it is not so " wonderfully "
organised.

It is natural that the tsarist Russia, where disorganisation
was monstrous, where the proletariat is the most revolutionary in the world (not due to any specific characteristics,
but because of the vivid traditions of " 1905 "), the
revolutionary crisis should have burst forth earlier than
anywhere else. The crisis was hastened by a number of
most serious defeats inflicted on Russia and her allies.
These defeats disorganised the entire old mechanism of
government and the entire old system ; they aroused the
indignation of *all* classes of the population ; they incensed
the army and largely wiped out the old body of commanders hailing from the backward nobility and particularly from the rotten officialdom, replacing it with a
young and buoyant one of a predominantly bourgeois,
petty-bourgeois and declassed origin.

But, if military defeats played the rôle of a negative factor
that hastened the outbreak, the alliance of Anglo-French
finance-capital, of Anglo-French imperialism, with the
Octobrist and Constitutional-Democratic capital of Russia
appeared as a factor that speeded this crisis.

This highly important phase of the situation is, for
obvious reasons, not mentioned by the Anglo-French Press

while maliciously emphasised by the German. We Marxists must face the truth soberly, being confused neither by the official lies, the sugary diplomatic and ministerial lies of one group of imperialist belligerents, nor by the sniggering and smirking of its financial and military rivals of the other belligerent group. The whole course of events in the March revolution shows clearly that the English and French embassies with their agents and " associates," who had long made the most desperate efforts to prevent a " separate " agreement and a separate peace between Nicholas II (let us hope and strive that he be the last) and Wilhelm II, strove directly to dethrone Nicholas Romanov.

Let us not harbour any illusions.

The fact that the revolution succeeded so quickly and, apparently, at the first superficial glance, so " radically," is due to an unusual historical conjuncture where there combined, in a strikingly " favourable " manner, absolutely dissimilar movements, absolutely different class interests, absolutely opposed political and social tendencies. There was the conspiracy of the Anglo-French imperialists who encouraged Miliukov, Guchkov and Co. to seize power, with the object of prolonging the imperialist war, with the object of conducting the war more savagely and obstinately, with the object of slaughtering new millions of Russian workers and peasants, in order that the Guchkovs might obtain Constantinople ; the French, Syria ; the English capitalists, Mesopotamia, etc. This, on the one side. On the other, there was a profound proletarian and popular mass movement (of the entire poorest population of the cities and villages) of a revolutionary character, for bread, for peace, for real freedom.

The revolutionary workers and soldiers have destroyed the infamous tsarist monarchy to its very foundations, being neither elated nor constrained by the fact that, at certain brief historic moments of an exceptional combination of circumstances, they are aided by the struggle of

Buchanan, Guchkov, Miliukov and Co., who simply desire to replace one monarch by another.

Thus, and only thus, did it occur. Thus, and only thus, must be the view of the politician who is not afraid of the truth, who soberly weighs the interrelation of social forces in a revolution, who evaluates every given moment not only from the viewpoint of its present peculiarities, but also from the standpoint of the more fundamental motives, the deeper interrelation of the interests of the proletariat and the bourgeoisie, in Russia as well as throughout the world.

The workers and soldiers of Petrograd, as well as the workers and soldiers of all Russia, self-sacrificingly fought against the tsarist monarchy—for freedom, for land for the peasants, for peace as against the imperialist slaughter. Anglo-French imperialist capital, in order to continue and develop the slaughter, engaged in court intrigues, it framed conspiracies, incited and encouraged the Guchkovs and Miliukovs, and contrived a new government, which, ready-made, seized power after the proletarian struggle had delivered the first blows against tsarism.

This government is not a fortuitous assemblage of persons.

They are the representatives of the new class that has risen to political power in Russia, the class of the capitalist landowners and bourgeoisie that for a long time has been ruling our country economically, and that, in the revolution of 1905–1907, in the counter-revolutionary period of 1907–1914, and then, with extraordinary rapidity, in the period of the war of 1914–1917, organised itself politically, taking into its hands local self-government, popular education, conventions of every type, the Duma, the war industries committees, etc. This new class was almost in power in 1917 ; therefore the first blows against tsarism were sufficient to destroy the latter, and to clear the ground for the bourgeoisie. The imperialist war, requiring an incredible exertion of strength, so accelerated the course of development of backward Russia that at a single stroke (at least it seems like a single stroke) we have caught up with Italy, England, even France ; we have attained a "coalition," a "national," "parliamentary" government (i.e. a government adapted to carrying on the imperialist slaughter and deceiving the people).

Alongside of this government, which, as regards the present war, is but the clerk of the billion-dollar "firms," England and France, there has arisen a new, unofficial, as yet undeveloped and comparatively weak, workers' government, expressing the interests of the workers and of all the poorer elements of the city and country population. This is the Petrograd *Soviet of Workers' and Soldiers' Deputies*.

Such is the actual political situation which we must first of all try to establish with the greatest possible objective precision, in order that we may base Marxist tactics on the only solid foundation upon which they should be based— the foundation of facts.

The tsarist monarchy has been beaten, but not destroyed.

The Octobrist-Cadet bourgeois government, wishing to carry on the imperialist war "to a finish," is in reality the agent of the financial firm "England and France" ; it is forced to promise to the people a maximum of liberties and pittances compatible with the maintenance by this government of its power over the people and the possibility of continuing the imperialist war.

The Soviet of Workers' and Soldiers' Deputies is a workers' government in embryo, a representative of the interests of all the poorest masses of the population, i.e., of nine-tenths of the population which is striving for peace, bread, and liberty.

The conflict among these three forces determines the situation as it is at present, a transition stage from the first phase of the revolution to the second.

In order that there may be a real struggle against the tsarist monarchy, in order that freedom may really be secured, not merely in words, not in the promises of rhetorical liberalism, it is necessary not that the workers should support the new government, but that this government should support the workers ! For the only guarantee of liberty and of a complete destruction of tsarism is the arming of the proletariat, the strengthening, broadening, and developing of the rôle, and significance and power of the Soviets of Workers' and Soldiers' Deputies.

All the rest is mere phrases and lies, the self-deception of the politicians of the liberal and radical stamp.

Help the arming of the workers, or, at least, do not interfere with it, and the liberty of Russia is invincible, the monarchy incapable of restoration, the republic secured.

Otherwise the people will be deceived. Promises are cheap ; promises cost nothing. It is on promises that all the bourgeois politicians in *all* the bourgeois revolutions have been feeding the people and fooling the workers.

" Our revolution is a bourgeois revolution, therefore the workers must support the bourgeoisie," say the worthless politicians among the *Liquidators*.

" Our revolution is a bourgeois revolution," say we Marxists, " therefore the workers must open the eyes of the people to the deceptive practices of the bourgeois politicians, must teach the people not to believe in words, but to depend wholly on their own strength, on their own organisation, on their own unity, and on their own arms."

The government of the Octobrists and Cadets, of the Guchkovs and Miliukovs, could give neither peace, nor bread, nor freedom, even if it were sincere in its desire to do so.

It cannot give peace because it is a government for war, a government for the continuation of the imperialist slaughter, a government of conquest, a government that has not uttered one word to renounce the tsarist policy of seizure of Armenia, Galicia, Turkey, of capturing Constantinople, of reconquering Poland, Courland, Lithuania, etc. This government is bound hand and foot by

Anglo-French imperialist capital. Russian capital is merely one branch of the world " firm " known as " England and France " manipulating hundreds of billions of roubles.

It cannot give bread, since it is a bourgeois government. At best it may give the people, as the government of Germany has done, " hunger organised with the ability of genius." But the people will not put up with hunger. The people will learn, probably very soon, that there is bread, and it can be obtained in no other way than by means that do not show any respect for the sanctity of capital and landownership.

It cannot give freedom, since it is a government of land-owners and capitalists, which is afraid of the people.

In another article we will speak of the tactical problems confronting us in our immediate behaviour towards this government. There we shall show wherein consists the peculiarity of the present moment, which is a period of transition from the first stage of the revolution to the second, and why the slogan, the " order of the day " in the *present* moment must be : " Workers, you have displayed marvels of proletarian and popular heroism in the civil war against tsarism ; you must display marvels of pro-letarian and nation-wide organisation in order to prepare your victory in the second stage of the revolution."

Limiting ourselves in the meanwhile to an analysis of the class struggle and the interrelation of class forces in this stage of the revolution, we must also raise the question : Who are the allies of the proletariat in this revolution ?

It has two allies : first, the broad mass of the semi-pro-letarian and, partly, the petty peasant population of Russia, numbering scores of millions and forming the over-whelming majority of the population. This great mass needs peace, bread, liberty, land. This mass will in-evitably be under a certain influence of the bourgeoisie, particularly of the petty bourgeoisie, which it resembles rather closely in its conditions of life, vacillating, as it does, between the bourgeoisie and the proletariat. The cruel

AAM

lessons of the war, which will become all the more cruel as Guchkov, Lvov, Miliukov and Co. carry on the war with greater energy, will inevitably push this mass toward the proletariat, compelling it to follow the proletariat. We must now, taking advantage of the freedom under the new régime and of the Soviets of Workers' and Soldiers' Deputies, strive, first of all and above all, to enlighten and organise this mass. Soviets of Peasants' Deputies, Soviets of Agricultural Workers—these are among our most urgent tasks. We shall thereby strive not only that the agricultural workers should establish special Soviets of their own, but also that the poorest and propertyless peasants should organise separately from the well-to-do peasants. The special tasks and special forms of the organisation urgently needed at present, will be dealt with in another letter.

The second ally of the Russian proletariat is the proletariat of the warring countries and of all countries in general. At present, it is to a considerable degree weighed down by the war, and by the social-chauvinists who, like Plekhanov, Gvozdev, Potresov in Russia, have deserted to the bourgeoisie, but all too often speak in the workers' name. The liberation of the workers from their influence has progressed with every month of the imperialist war, and the Russian Revolution will necessarily accelerate this process tremendously.

Hand in hand with these two allies, the proletariat of Russia can and will proceed, while utilising the peculiarities of the present transition moment, to win, first, a democratic republic and the victory of the peasantry over the landlords, then Socialism, which alone can give peace, bread, and freedom to the peoples exhausted by the war.

On Proletarian Militia

. . . I cannot judge from here, my accursed exile, how near the second revolution is. Skobelev, who is there on the spot, can see it better. I therefore do not occupy myself

with the questions for the answer to which I have no concrete data and can have none. I simply emphasise the fact
that a " stranger," i.e., one who does not belong to our
party, Skobelev, confirms the *very* conclusion that I arrived
at in the first letter, namely : that the March revolution
was only the *first stage* of the revolution. Russia is going
through a unique historical period of *transition* from the
first to the next stage of the revolution or, as Skobelev
expresses it, to " a second revolution."

If we want to be Marxists and to learn from the experience of the revolutions the world over, we must try to
understand just wherein lies the *uniqueness* of this transition
period, and what are the tactics that follow from its objective peculiarities.

The uniqueness of the situation lies in the fact that the
Guchkov-Miliukov government has won the first victory
with unusual ease because of the three following main
circumstances : 1. The help received from Anglo-French
finance capital and its agents ; 2. The help received from
the upper layers of the army ; 3. The fact that the entire
Russian bourgeoisie had been organised in zemstvo and
city institutions, in the Imperial Duma, in the war industries committees, etc.

The Guchkov government finds itself between the upper
and nether millstones. Bound by capitalist interests, it is
compelled to strive to prolong the predatory war for
plunder, to protect the monstrous profits of the capitalists
and the landlords, to restore the monarchy. Bound by its
revolutionary origin and the necessity of an abrupt change
from tsarism to democracy, finding itself under the pressure of the hungry masses that clamour for peace, the
government is forced to lie, to shift about, to procrastinate,
to make as many " declarations " and promises as possible
(promises are the only things that are very cheap even in
an epoch of insanely high prices), and to carry out as few
of them as possible, to make concessions with one hand,
and to withdraw them with the other.

Under certain conditions, if circumstances are most favourable to it, the new government, relying on the organising abilities of the entire Russian bourgeoisie and the bourgeois intelligentsia, may temporarily avert the final crash. But even under such conditions it cannot escape the crash altogether, for it is *impossible* to escape the claws of that terrible monster, begotten by world-capitalism—the imperialist war and famine—without abandoning the whole basis of bourgeois relations, without resorting to revolutionary measures, without appealing to the greatest historical heroism of the Russian and the world proletariat.

Hence the conclusion : We shall not be able to overthrow the new government with one stroke or, should we be able to do so (in revolutionary times the limits of the possible are increased a thousandfold), we could not retain power, *unless we met* the splendid organisation of the entire Russian bourgeoisie and the entire bourgeois intelligentsia with an *organisation of the proletariat* just as splendid, leading the vast mass of the city and country poor, ᵗhe semi-proletarians and the petty proprietors.

It matters little whether the " second revolution " has already broken out in Petrograd (I have stated that it would be absurd to attempt to estimate from abroad the actual tempo of its growth), whether it has been postponed for a time, or whether it has begun in isolated localities in Russia (there are some indications that this is the case)— *in any* case the slogan of the hour right now, on the eve of the revolution, during the revolution, and on the day after the revolution, must be—*proletarian organisation.*

Comrade-workers ! Yesterday you displayed wonders of proletarian heroism when you overthrew the tsarist monarchy. Sooner or later (perhaps even now, while I am writing these lines) you will inevitably be called upon again to display wonders of similar heroism in overthrowing the power of the landowners and the capitalists who are waging the imperialist war. But you will not be able to win a *permanent victory* in this forthcoming " true " revolution, unless you display *wonders of proletarian organisation* !

The slogan of the hour is organisation. But organisation in itself does not mean much, because, on the one hand, organisation is always necessary, and, hence, the mere insistence on " the organisation of the masses " does not yet clarify anything, and because, on the other hand, he who contents himself with organisation only is merely echoing the views of the liberals ; for the liberals, to strengthen their rule, desire nothing better than to have the workers refuse to go *beyond the usual " legal "* forms of organisation (from the point of view of " normal " bourgeois society), i.e., to have them *merely* become members of their party, their trade union, their co-operative society, etc., etc.

The workers, guided by their class instinct, have realised that in revolutionary times they need an entirely different organisation, of a type above the ordinary. They have taken the right attitude suggested by the experience of our revolution of 1905 and by the Paris Commune of 1871 : they have created a *Soviet of Workers' Deputies*, they have set out to develop it, widen and strengthen it, by attracting to it representatives of the soldiers and no doubt of the hired agricultural workers, as well as (in one form or another) of the entire poor section of the peasantry.

To create similar organisations in all the localities of Russia without exception, for all the trades and layers of the proletarian and semi-proletarian population without exception, i.e., for all the toilers and the exploited (to use an expression that is less exact from the point of view of economics but more popular), is our most important and most urgent task. I will note right here that to the peasant masses our party (whose specific rôle in the proletarian organisations of the new type I shall have occasion to discuss in one of the forthcoming letters) must recommend with special emphasis the organisation of Soviets of hired workers and petty agriculturists, such as do not sell their grain, those Soviets *to have no connection* with the prosperous peasants—otherwise it will be impossible to pursue a true proletarian policy, in a general sense,[1] nor will it be possible correctly to approach the most important practical question involving the life and death of millions of people, i.e., the question of an equitable assessment of food deliveries, of increasing its production, etc.

The question, then, is : What is to be the work of the Soviets of Workers' Deputies ? We repeat what we once said in No. 47 of the Geneva *Social-Democrat* (October 13, 1915) : "They must be regarded as organs of insurrection, as organs of revolutionary power."

This theoretical formula, derived from the experience of the Commune of 1871 and of the Russian Revolution of 1905, must be elucidated and concretely developed on the basis of the practical experience gained at this very stage of this very revolution in Russia.

We need revolutionary *power*, we need (for a certain period of transition) the *State*. Therein we differ from the Anarchists. The difference between revolutionary Marxists and Anarchists lies not only in the fact that the former stand for huge, centralised, communist production, while the latter are for decentralised, small-scale production. No, the difference as to government authority and the state consists in this, that we stand *for* the revolutionary utilisation of revolutionary forms of the State in our struggle for Socialism, while the Anarchists are *against* it.

We need the State. But we need none of those types of State varying from a constitutional monarchy to the most democratic republic which the bourgeoisie has established everywhere. And herein lies the difference between us and the opportunists and Kautskians of the old, decaying

[1] There will now develop in the village a struggle for the petty, and partly the middle, peasantry. The landowners, basing themselves on the well-to-do peasants, will lead them to submission to the bourgeoisie. We, basing ourselves on the hired agricultural workers and poor peasants, must lead them to the closest possible alliance with the proletariat of the cities.

Socialist parties who have distorted or forgotten the lessons of the Paris Commune and the analysis of these lessons by Marx and Engels.[1]

We need the State, but not the kind needed by the bourgeoisie, with organs of power in the form of police, army, bureaucracy, distinct from and opposed to the people. All bourgeois revolutions have merely perfected this government apparatus, have merely transferred it from one party to another.

The proletariat, however, if it wants to preserve the gains of the present revolution and to proceed further to win peace, bread, and freedom, must " *destroy*," to use Marx's word, this " ready-made " State machinery, and must replace it by another one, *merging* the police, the army, and the bureaucracy *with the universally armed people*. Advancing along the road indicated by the experience of the Paris Commune of 1871 and the Russian Revolution of 1905, the proletariat must organise and arm *all* the poorest and most exploited sections of the population, so that they *themselves* may take into their own hands all the organs of State power, that they *themselves* may constitute these organs.

The workers of Russia have already, with the very first stage of the first revolution, March 1917, *entered* on this course. The whole problem now is to understand clearly the nature of this new course and courageously, firmly, and persistently, to continue on it.

The Anglo-French and the Russian capitalists wanted " only " to displace, or merely to " scare," Nicholas II, leaving the old machinery of the State—the police, the army, the bureaucracy—intact.

---

[1]In one of the forthcoming letters or in a special article I shall dwell in detail on this analysis as given particularly in Marx's *Civil War in France*, in Engels' preface to the third edition of that work, in Marx's letter dated April 12, 1871, and in Engel's letters of March 18–28, 1875, also on the complete distortion of Marxism by Kautsky in his 1912 polemics against Pannekoek relative to the so-called " destruction of the State."

The workers have gone further ; they have smashed it. And now not only the Anglo-French, but even the German capitalists howl with rage and horror when they see Russian soldiers shooting their officers, some of whom were even supporters of Guchkov and Miliukov, as Admiral Nepenin, for example.

I have said that the workers have smashed the old State machinery. To be more precise. They *have begun* to smash it.

Let us take a concrete example.

The police of Petrograd and many other places have been partly killed off, and partly removed. The Guchkov-Miliukov government will not be able to restore the monarchy, nor even to retain power, unless it re-establishes the police as an organisation of armed men separated from and opposed to the people and under the command of the bourgeoisie. This is as clear as the clearest day.

On the other hand, the new government must reckon with the revolutionary masses, must humour them with half-concessions and promises, trying to gain time. Hence it agrees to half-measures : it institutes a " people's militia" with elected officers (this sounds terribly imposing, terribly democratic, revolutionary, and beautiful !). But . . . but . . . first of all, it places the militia under the control of the local zemstvo and city organs of self-government, i.e., under the control of landowners and capitalists elected under the laws of Nicholas the Bloody and Stolypin the Hangman ! ! Secondly, though it calls it the " people's " militia to throw dust into the eyes of the " people," it does not, as a matter of fact, call the people for *universal* service in this militia, nor does it compel the bosses and the capitalists to *pay* their employees the usual wage for the hours and the days they devote to public service, i.e., to the militia.

There is where the main trick is. That is how the land-owner and capitalist government of the Guchkovs and Miliukovs achieves its aim of keeping the " people's militia " on paper, while in reality it is quietly and step by step organising a bourgeois militia hostile to the people, first of " 8,000 students and professors " (as the foreign Press describes the present militia in Petrograd)—which is obviously a mere toy !—then, gradually, of the old and the new police.

Do not permit the re-establishment of the police ! Do not let go the local government organs ! Create a really universal militia, led by the proletariat ! This is the task of the day, this is the slogan of the present hour, equally in accord with the correctly understood require- ments of the further development of the class struggle, and further course of the revolution, and with the demo- cratic instinct of every worker, every peasant, every toiler, everyone who is exploited, who cannot but hate the police, the constables, the command of landowners and capitalists over armed men who wield power over the people.

What kind of police do *they* need, these Guchkovs and Miliukovs, these landowners and capitalists ? The same kind that existed during the tsarist monarchy. Following very brief revolutionary periods, *all* the bourgeois and bourgeois-democratic republics of the world organised or re-established precisely that kind of police—a special organisation of armed men, separated from and opposed to the people, and in one way or another subordinated to the bourgeoisie.

What kind of militia do we need, we, the proletariat, all the toilers ? A real people's militia, i.e., first of all, one that consists of the entire population, of all the adult citizens of both sexes ; secondly, one that combines the functions of a people's army with those of the police, and with the functions of the main and fundamental organ of the State system and the State administration.

To give more concreteness to these propositions, let us try a schematic example. Needless to say, the idea of laying out any " plan " for a proletarian militia would be absurd : when the workers, and all the people as a real mass, take up this task in a practical way, they will work it out and secure it a hundred times better than any theoretician can propose. I am not offering a plan—all I want is to illustrate my thought.

Petrograd has a population of about two million, more than half of which is between the ages of 15 and 65. Let us take a half—one million. Let us deduct one-fourth to allow for the sick or other instances where people cannot be engaged in public service for a valid reason. There still remain 750,000 persons, who, working in the militia one day out of every fifteen (and continuing to receive payment from their employers for this time), would make up an army of 50,000 people.

This is the type of " state " that we need !

This is the kind of militia that would be, in deed, and not only in name, a " people's militia."

This is the road we must follow if we wish to make impossible the re-establishment of a special police, or a special army, separated from the people.

Such a militia would, in ninety-five cases out of a hundred, be composed of workers and peasants, and would express the real intelligence and the will, the strength and the authority of the overwhelming majority of the people. Such a militia would actually arm and give military training to the people at large, thus making sure, in a manner not employed by Guchkov, nor Miliukov, against all attempts to re-establish reaction, against all efforts of the tsarist agents. Such a militia would be the executive organ of the " Soviets of Workers' and Soldiers' Deputies," it would enjoy the *full* respect and confidence of the population, because it would, itself, be an organisation of the entire population. Such a militia would change democracy from a pretty signboard, hiding the enslavement and deception of the people by the capitalists, into a real means for *educating the masses* so that they might be able to take part in *all* the affairs of the State. Such a militia would draw the youngsters into political life, training them not only by word, but by deed and *work*. Such a militia would develop those functions which belong, to use learned terms, to the welfare police, sanitary supervision, etc., by drawing into such activities all the adult women without exception. Without drawing the women into social service, into the militia, into political life, without tearing the women away from the stupefying domestic and kitchen atmosphere it is impossible to secure real freedom, it is impossible to build a democracy, let alone Socialism.

Such a militia would be a proletarian militia, because the industrial and the city workers would just as naturally and inevitably assume in it the leadership of the masses of the poor, as naturally and inevitably as they took the leading position in all the revolutionary struggles of the people in the years 1905–1907, and in 1917.

Such a militia would guarantee absolute order and a comradely discipline practised with enthusiasm. At the same time, it would afford a means of struggling in a real democratic manner against the crisis through which all the warring nations are now passing ; it would make possible the regular and prompt assessment of food and other supply levies, the establishment of " universal labour duty " which the French now call " civil mobilisaticn " and the Germans—" obligatory civil service," and without which, as has been demonstrated, it is impossible to heal the wounds that were and are being inflicted by this predatory and horrible war.

Has the proletariat of Russia shed its blood only to receive luxurious promises of mere political democratic reforms ? Will it not demand and make sure that every toiler should see and feel a certain improvement in his life right now ? That every family should have sufficient bread ? That every child should have a bottle of good milk, and that no adult in a rich family should dare take extra milk until all the children are supplied ? That the palaces and luxurious homes left by the Tsar and the aristocracy should not stand idle but should provide shelter to the homeless and the destitute ? What other organisation except a universal people's militia with women participating on a par with the men can effect these measures ?

Such measures *do not yet* constitute Socialism. They deal with distribution of consumption, not with the reorganisation of industry. They do not yet constitute the " dictatorship of the proletariat," but merely a " revolutionary-democratic dictatorship of the proletariat and the poorest peasantry." Theoretical classification doesn't matter now. It would indeed be a grave error if we tried now to fit the complex, urgent, rapidly unfolding practical tasks of the revolution into the Procrustean bed of a narrowly-conceived " theory," instead of regarding theory first of all and above all as a *guide to action*.

Will the mass of Russian workers have sufficient class-consciousness, self-discipline and heroism to show " wonders of proletarian organisation " after they have displayed wonders of courage, initiative and self-sacrifice in direct revolutionary struggle ? This we do not know, and to make conjectures about it would be idle, for such questions are answered *only* by life itself.

What we do know definitely and what we must as a party explain to the masses is that we have on hand an historic motive power of tremendous force that causes an unheard-of crisis, hunger and countless miseries. This motive power is the war which the capitalists of *both* warring camps are waging for predatory purposes. This " motive power " has brought a number of the richest, freest, and most enlightened nations to the brink of an abyss. It *forces* nations to strain all their strength to the breaking point, it places them in an insufferable position, it makes imperative the putting into effect not of " theories " (that is out of the question, and Marx had repeatedly warned Socialists against this illusion), but of most extreme yet practical measures, because *without* these extreme measures there is death, immediate and indubitable death for millions of people through hunger.

That revolutionary enthusiasm on the part of the most advanced class can accomplish much when objective conditions demand extreme measures from the entire people, need not be argued. *This* aspect of the case is clearly seen and felt by every one in Russia.

It is important to understand that in revolutionary times the objective situation changes as rapidly and as suddenly as life itself. We should be able to adjust our tactics and our immediate objectives to the peculiarities of every given situation. Up to March 1917, our task was to conduct a bold revolutionary-internationalist propaganda, to awaken and call the masses to struggle. In the March days there was required the courage of heroic struggle to crush tsarism —the most immediate foe. We are now going through a transition from the first stage of the revolution to the second, from a " grapple " with tsarism to a " grapple " with the imperialism of Guchkov-Miliukov, of the capitalists and the landowners. Our immediate problem is organisation, not in the sense of effecting ordinary organisation by ordinary methods, but in the sense of drawing large masses of the oppressed classes in unheard-of numbers into the organisation, and of embodying in this organisation military, State, and national economic problems.

The proletariat has approached this unique task and will approach it in a variety of ways. In some localities of Russia the March revolution has given the proletariat almost full power—in others, the proletariat will begin to build up and strengthen the proletarian militia perhaps by " usurpation "—in still others, it will, probably, work for immediate elections, on the basis of universal suffrage, to the city councils and zemstvos, in order to turn them into revolutionary centres, etc., until the growth of proletarian organisation, the *rapprochement* of soldiers and workers, the stirring within the peasantry, the disillusionment of very many about the competence of the militarist-imperialist government of Guchkov and Miliukov shall have brought nearer the hour when that government will give place to the " government " of the Soviets of Workers' Deputies.

Nor must we forget that right near Petrograd there is one of the most advanced, actually republican, countries— Finland—a country which from 1905 up to 1917, shielded by the revolutionary struggles in Russia, has developed a democracy by comparatively peaceful means, and has won the majority of its population over to Socialism. The Russian proletariat will insure the freedom of the Finnish republic, even to the point of separation (there is hardly a Social-Democrat who would hesitate on this score now, when the Cadet Rodichev is so shamefully haggling in Helsingfors over bits of privileges for the Great Russians), and thus gain the full confidence and comradely aid of the Finnish workers for the all-Russian proletarian cause. In a difficult and great cause errors are unavoidable, nor shall we avoid them ; the Finnish workers are better organisers, they will help us in this and, *in their own way*, bring nearer the establishment of a Socialist republic.

Revolutionary victories in Russia itself—quiet organisational successes in Finland shielded by the above victories— the Russian workers taking up revolutionary-organisational tasks on a new scale—conquest of power by the proletariat and the poorest strata of the population—encouraging and developing the Socialist revolution in the West—this is the path that will lead us to peace and Socialism.

V. I. Lenin

THE TASKS OF THE PROLETARIAT IN OUR REVOLUTION

Published 1917. English Edition, Martin Lawrence Ltd., 1932.

[Immediately after Lenin's arrival in Petrograd on April 16, 1917, he presented his ideas on the development of the revolution (already outlined in his letters from Switzerland), to meetings of Social Democratic members of the national conference of Soviets. The document put forward by Lenin (subsequently known as "The April Theses"), indicated the policy to be pursued by the Bolshevik Party ; together with a more detailed statement also written by Lenin at this time, these theses were the main material for the April (1917) Conference of the Bolsheviks, and guided their tactics up to the November revolution. The April theses are reprinted below, and also the section of the expanded statement which deals with changing the name of the Party from Social Democratic to Communist.]

ON THE TASKS OF THE PROLETARIAT IN THE PRESENT REVOLUTION

As I only arrived in Petrograd on the night of April 16, I could, of course, only on my own responsibility and admittedly without sufficient preparation render a report on April 17 on the problems of the revolutionary proletariat.

The only thing I could do to facilitate matters for myself and for honest opponents was to prepare written theses. I read them, and gave the text to Comrade Tsereteli.

I read them twice, very slowly : First at the meeting of the Bolsheviks, then at the joint meeting of Bolsheviks and Mensheviks.

I am publishing these personal theses, provided with very short explanatory notes, which were developed in more detail in the report :

THESES

1. In our attitude towards the war not the smallest concession must be made to " revolutionary defencism," for under the new government of Lvov and Co., owing to the capitalist nature of this government, the war on Russia's part remains a predatory imperialist war.

The class-conscious proletariat may give its consent to a revolutionary war, actually justifying revolutionary defencism, only on condition (a) that all power be transferred to the proletariat and its ally, the poorest section of the peasantry ; (b) that all annexations be renounced in deeds, not merely in words ; (c) that there be a complete break in practice, with all interests of capital.

In view of the undoubted honesty of the mass of rank and file representatives of revolutionary defencism who accept the war only as a necessity and not as a means of conquest, in view of their being deceived by the bourgeoisie, it is necessary most thoroughly, persistently, patiently to explain to them their error, to explain the inseparable connection between capital and the imperialist war, to prove that without the overthrow of capital, it is *impossible* to conclude the war with a really democratic, non-oppressive peace.

This view is to be widely propagated among the army units in the field.

Fraternisation.

2. The peculiarity of the present situation in Russia is that it represents a *transition* from the first stage of the revolution, which, because of the inadequate organisation

and insufficient class-consciousness of the proletariat, led to the assumption of power by the bourgeoisie—to its second stage which is to place power in the hands of the proletariat and the poorest strata of the peasantry.

This transition is characterised, on the one hand, by a maximum of legality (Russia is now the freest of all the belligerent countries of the world) ; on the other, by the absence of oppression of the masses, and, finally, by the trustingly ignorant attitude of the masses toward the capitalist government, the worst enemy of peace and Socialism.

This peculiar situation demands of us an ability to adapt ourselves to specific conditions of party work amidst vast masses of the proletariat just awakened to political life.

3. No support to the Provisional Government ; exposure of the utter falsity of all its promises, particularly those relating to the renunciation of annexations. Unmasking, instead of admitting, the illusion-breeding " demand " that *this* government, a government of capitalists, cease being imperialistic.

4. Recognition of the fact that in most of the Soviets of Workers' Deputies our party constitutes a minority, and a small one at that, in the face of the *bloc* of all the petty-bourgeois opportunist elements from the People's Socialists, the Socialists-Revolutionists down to the Organisation Committee (Chkheidze, Tsereteli, etc., Steklov, etc., etc.) who have yielded to the influence of the bourgeoisie and have been extending this influence to the proletariat as well.

It must be explained to the masses that the Soviet of Workers' Deputies is the only possible form of revolutionary government and, therefore, our task is, while this government is submitting to the influence of the bourgeoisie, to present a patient, systematic, and persistent analysis of its errors and tactics, an analysis especially adapted to the practical needs of the masses.

While we are in the minority, we carry on the work

of criticism and of exposing errors, advocating all along the necessity of transferring the entire power of state to the Soviets of Workers' Deputies, so that the masses might learn from experience how to rid themselves of errors.

5. Not a parliamentary republic—a return to it from the Soviet of Workers' Deputies would be a step backward—but a republic of Soviets of Workers', Agricultural Labourers' and Peasants' Deputies, throughout the land, from top to bottom.

Abolition of the police, the army, the bureaucracy.[1]

All officers to be elected and to be subject to recall at any time, their salaries not to exceed the average wage of a competent worker.

6. In the agrarian programme, the emphasis must be shifted to the Soviets of Agricultural Labourers' Deputies.

Confiscation of all private lands.

Nationalisation of all lands in the country, and management of such lands by local Soviets of Agricultural Labourers' and Peasants' Deputies. A separate organisation of Soviets of Deputies of the poorest peasants. Creation of model agricultural establishments out of large estates (from 100 to 300 desiatinas, in accordance with local and other conditions and with the estimates of local institutions) under the control of the Soviet of Agricultural Labourers' Deputies, and at public expense.

7. Immediate merger of all the banks in the country into one general national bank, over which the Soviet of Workers' Deputies should have control.

8. Not the " introduction " of Socialism as an immediate task, but the immediate placing of the Soviet of Workers' Deputies in control of social production and distribution of goods.

9. Party tasks :

A. Immediate calling of a party convention.

B. Changing the party programme, mainly :

---

[1] Substituting for the standing army the universal arming of the people.

(1) Concerning imperialism and the imperialist war.

(2) Concerning our attitude toward the state and our demand for a " commune state."[1]

(3) Amending our antiquated minimum programme.

C. Changing the name of the party.[2]

10. Rebuilding the International.

Taking the initiative in the creation of a revolutionary International, an International against the social-chauvinists and against the " centre."[3]

A NAME FOR OUR PARTY WHICH WOULD BE SCIENTIFICALLY SOUND AND CONDUCIVE TO PROLETARIAN CLASS THINKING

I am coming to the last point, the name of our party. We must call ourselves the Communist Party—just as Marx and Engels called themselves Communists.

We must insist that we are Marxists and that we have as a basis *The Communist Manifesto*, which has been perverted and betrayed by the Social-Democracy on two important points : (1) The workers have no country ; " national defence " in an imperialist war is a betrayal of Socialism ; (2) Marx's teaching about the state has been perverted by the Second International.

The term " Social-Democracy " is unscientific, as Marx showed repeatedly, particularly in the *Critique of the Gotha Programme*, in 1875, and as Engels restated in a more popular form, in 1894. Mankind can pass directly from capitalism only into Socialism, i.e., into social ownership

---

[1] A state the model for which was given by the Paris Commune.

[2] Instead of " Social-Democracy," whose official leaders throughout the world have betrayed Socialism by going over to the bourgeoisie (defencists and vacillating Kautskians), we must call ourselves the *Communist Party*.

[3] The " centre " in the international Social-Democracy is the tendency vacillating between chauvinists (" defencists ") and internationalists, i.e. Kautsky and Co. in Germany, Longuet and Co. in France, Chkheidze and Co. in Russia, Turati and Co. in Italy, MacDonald and Co. in England, etc.

of the means of production and the distribution of products according to the work of the individual. Our party looks farther ahead than that : Socialism is bound sooner or later to ripen into Communism, whose banner bears the motto : " From each according to his ability, to each according to his needs."

That is the first reason.

Here is my second : The second part of the term " Social-*Democracy* " is scientifically wrong. Democracy is only a form of state, while we Marxists are opposed to every form of state.

The leaders of the Second International (1889–1914), Messrs. Plekhanov, Kautsky and their ilk, perverted and debased Marxism.

The difference between Marxism and Anarchism is that Marxism admits the necessity of the state during the transition from capitalism to Socialism ; but (and here is where we differ from Kautsky and Co.) not the kind of state found in the usual, parliamentary, bourgeois, democratic republic, but rather something like the Paris Commune of 1871 and the Soviets of Workers' Deputies of 1905 and 1917.

There is a third reason : Life and the revolution have already established here in a concrete way (although in a form which is still weak and embryonic), this new type of " state," though it is not really a state in the proper sense of the word.

It is now a question of the action of the masses and not merely the theories of leaders.

Essentially the state is the power exercised over the masses by a group of armed men separated from the people.

Our new state, which is now in process of being born, is also a real state, for we, too, need detachments of armed men ; we, too, need the strictest order, and the ruthless crushing of all attempts at a tsarist as well as a Guchkov-bourgeois counter-revolution.

But our forming, new state is not yet a state in the proper sense of the word, for detachments of armed men found in many parts of Russia are really the masses themselves, the people, and not simply privileged individuals, practically unremovable, placed above and separated from the people.

We ought to look forward, not backward ; we ought to look away from the usual bourgeois type of democracy which has been strengthening the domination of the bourgeoisie by the means of the old, monarchistic organs of government—the police, the army, and the bureaucracy.

We must look forward to the advent of the newly born democracy, which is already ceasing to be a democracy, for democracy means the people's rule, while, obviously, an armed people could not rule over itself.

The word democracy is not only not scientific when applied to the Communist Party, but, since March 1917, it has simply become a blinker placed upon the eyes of the revolutionary people, preventing the latter from establishing boldly, freely, and on its own initiative a new form of power : the Soviets of Workers', Soldiers', etc., Deputies, as the sole power in the state and as the harbinger of the " withering away " of the state as such.

There is a fourth reason : We must take into account the objective international condition of Socialism.

Its condition is no longer what it was between the years 1871 and 1914, when Marx and Engels consciously allowed the inaccurate, opportunist term " Social-Democracy." For history proved that what was most needed in those days, i.e., right after the defeat of the Paris Commune, was slow work of organisation and enlightenment. Nothing else was possible. The Anarchists were then, as they are now, theoretically, economically, and politically wrong. The Anarchists made a wrong estimate of the time, for they did not understand the world situation : the worker of England corrupted by imperialist profits ; the Paris Commune destroyed ; the bourgeois-national movement in Germany flushed with recent victory ; and semi-feudal Russia still sleeping the sleep of centuries.

Marx and Engels gauged the hour accurately ; they understood the international situation ; they realised the need of a slow approach toward the beginning of the Social Revolution.

We, in turn, must understand the peculiarities and the tasks of the new epoch. Let us not imitate the woe-Marxians of whom Marx himself said : " I sowed dragons and I reaped fleas."

The objective needs of capitalism which has grown into imperialism have brought forth the imperialist war. This war has brought mankind to the brink of a precipice, to the destruction of civilisation, the ruin and brutalisation of countless millions of human beings.

There is no other way out, except a proletarian revolution.

And just when that revolution is beginning, when it is taking its first awkward, timid, weak, unconscious steps, when it is still trusting the bourgeoisie, at that moment the majority (it is the truth, it is a fact) of the Social-Democratic leaders, of the Social-Democratic parliamentarians, of the Social-Democratic papers, in a word, all those who could spur the masses to action, or at least the majority of them, are betraying Socialism, are selling Socialism, are going to fight the battles of their national bourgeoisie.

The masses are distracted, baffled, deceived by their leaders.

And should we aid and abet that deception by retaining the old and worn-out party name, which is as decayed as the Second International ?

It may be that many workers understand the meaning of Social-Democracy honestly. It is high time that we learn to distinguish between the objective and the subjective.

Subjectively, these workers, who are Social-Democrats, are the most loyal leaders of the proletarian masses.

Objectively, however, the world situation is such that the old name of our party helps to fool the masses and retard their onward march. Every day, in every paper, in every parliamentary group, the masses see leaders, i.e., people whose voice carries far, whose acts are very much in evidence, who also call themselves Social-Democrats, who are " for unity " with the betrayers of Socialism, the social-chauvinists, and who are trying to collect on the notes issued by Social-Democracy. . . .

Are there any reasons against the new name ? We are told that one may confuse us with Anarchists-Communists.

Why are we not afraid of being confused with the Social-Nationalists, the Social-Liberals, the Radical-Socialists, the foremost, the most adroit bourgeois party in the French Republic at deceiving the masses ? We are told : " The masses have grown used to the name, the workers have learned to love their Social-Democratic Party."

That is the only reason, but this reason goes counter to the teachings of Marxism, disregards the revolutionary tasks of to-morrow, the objective position of Socialism the world over, the shameful breakdown of the Second International, and the injury done to the cause by the pack of " also Social-Democrats " surrounding the proletarians.

This reason is based solely on laziness, somnolence, and love of routine.

We want to rebuild the world. We want to end this imperialist World War in which hundreds of millions of people are involved and billions of dollars are invested, a war which cannot be ended in a truly democratic way without the greatest proletarian revolution in history.

And here we are, afraid of our own shadow. Here we are, keeping on our backs the same old soiled shirt. . . .

It is high time to cast off the soiled shirt, it is high time to put on clean linen.

N. Lenin.

J. Stalin

REPORT ON THE POLITICAL
SITUATION, AUGUST 1917

*English translation contained in " Preparing for October " (the
Minutes of the VIth Congress of the Bolshevik Party), Modern
Books Ltd., 1931.*

[At the Sixth Congress of the Bolshevik Party in August
1917, Stalin made the political report on behalf of the
Central Committee. This report on the political situation,
midway between the March and November revolutions,
is an analysis of all the circumstances driving the revolution
forward to its completion.]

REPORT ON THE POLITICAL SITUATION,
AUGUST 1917

THE question of the moment is the question of the fate
of our revolution, of the forces moving the revolution
forward and of the forces undermining it.

Who made the revolution ? A coalition of four forces :
the proletariat, the peasantry, the liberal bourgeoisie and
capitalists of the Allied countries. Why did the proletariat
take part in the revolution ? Because it is the mortal foe
of Tsarism. Why did the peasantry take part in it ? Because
it trusted the proletariat and was hungry for land. Why
did the liberal bourgeoisie take part in the revolution ?
Because during the war it had become disillusioned with
Tsarism. It thought Tsarism would enable it to conquer
fresh lands. Having lost hope in the expansion of the home
market, it chose the path of least resistance : the expansion
of the foreign market. But it made a mistake. Tsarism

and its forces were unable even to protect the frontiers and gave up fifteen provinces to the enemy. Hence, the betrayal of Tsarism by the liberal bourgeoisie. But what of Allied capital ? It regarded Russia as an auxiliary means for attaining its imperialist aims. Meanwhile, Tsarism, which during the first two years offered some hopes for maintaining a united front, began to incline toward a separate peace. Hence, the betrayal of Tsarism by Allied capital.

Tsarism proved to be isolated and quietly and peacefully passed away.

These four forces, which jointly made the February Revolution, had various aims in view. The liberal bourgeoisie and Allied capital wanted a little revolution for the sake of a big war. But it was not for this that the mass of workers and peasants participated in the revolution. They had other aims in view :. (1) to put an end to the war, and (2) to overthrow the big landlords and the bourgeoisie.

These are the fundamental contradictions of the revolution. The crisis of May 3rd–4th was the first manifestation of these contradictions. Miliukov tried to transform passive imperialism into active imperialism. As a result of the mass movement, a coalition government was formed. As experience has shown, the principle of coalition is the most effective means the bourgeoisie possesses for deceiving the masses and sweeping them along with it. From the moment the coalition government was formed the mobilisation of the counter-revolution from above and from below was begun. Meanwhile, the war continued, economic ruin was intensified, the revolution continued to develop and to assume more and more a socialist character. The revolution invades the sphere of production, it raises the question of control of industry. The revolution invades the sphere of agriculture, the question arises, not only of confiscating the land, but also of confiscating livestock and implements. The Bolsheviks, in so far as they were the harbingers of the proletarian revolution, correctly analysed its character. Those who proposed to confine themselves to consolidating the conquests of the revolution were not revolutionaries. The path of compromise, which has been chosen by the Socialist-Revolutionaries and Mensheviks, meant condemning themselves to impotence. There was no power, there was no possibility of stopping the revolution half-way. Thus, the fact that the revolution has been developing and moving forward has brought us up against the necessity of passing over the bourgeois revolution to the socialist revolution.

Several comrades have said that since capitalism is only feebly developed here, it is Utopian to raise the question of a socialist revolution. They would be right if it were not for the war, if it were not for the devastation, if the foundations of national economy had not been shaken. But these questions of interfering in the economic sphere are being raised in all countries as vital questions. In Germany this question has been raised and settled without the direct and active participation of the masses. It is quite otherwise here in Russia. Here economic collapse has assumed more ominous dimensions. On the other hand, in no other country has there ever been such freedom in time of war as here in Russia. Then, there is the high degree of organisation of the workers : for example, in Petrograd 66 per cent of the metal workers are organised. Finally, in no other country has the proletariat such an extensive organisation as the Soviets of Workers' and Soldiers' Deputies. Under these circumstances it was impossible for the workers to refrain from interfering in economic life. This is the real reason why the question of the socialist revolution could arise here in Russia.

In so far as the workers have begun actively to intervene in the process of organising control of production and exchange, the question of the socialist revolution has become a practical issue. Therefore the comrades who object to this are in the wrong.

Inasmuch as the revolution has gone so far ahead, it could not help arousing the vigilance of the counter-revolutionaries ; it was bound to give birth to the counter-revolution ; that is the first factor which is mobilising the counter-revolution.

The second factor is the wild adventure begun by the policy of the offensive at the front, and a whole series of breaches of the line at the front, which have robbed the government of all prestige and have lent wings to the counter-revolution, which has launched its attack on this government. Rumours are afloat to the effect that the period of provocation on a large scale has begun. The delegates from the front consider that both the offensive and the retreat, in a word, all that has taken place at the front, was prepared in order to dishonour the revolution and overthrow the " revolutionary " ministry. I do not know whether they are right or not, but it is remarkable that on July 15th the Cadets retired from the government, that the July events began on July 16th and that on July 17th news was received of the collapse at the front. It is impossible to argue that the Cadets retired because of the decision on the Ukrainian question : the Cadets had declared that the Ukrainian question must be solved. But there is a second fact showing that the period of provocation had actually begun. I refer to the skirmish in the Ukraine. In connection with these facts it must be plain to the comrades that the collapse at the front was one of the facts which helped to discredit the revolution in the eyes of the broad petty-bourgeois masses.

There is yet a third factor which reinforces the strength of the counter-revolution in Russia : that is Allied capital. If Allied capital could betray the government of Nicholas II when it saw that Tsarism was heading for a separate peace, nothing will prevent it from breaking with the present government if the latter proves incapable of maintaining a " united " front.

At one of the meetings of the cabinet Miliukov stated that

the international Exchange regarded Russia as a supplier of men and that she gets money for that. And if it becomes obvious that the new power, represented by the Provisional Government, is incapable of maintaining the united front in the offensive against Germany, then it will not be worth while subsidising such a government. But a government without money and without credit was bound to fail. This explains the secret why the Cadets, in the period of crisis, gained such tremendous force. However, Kerensky and all the ministers proved to be mere puppets in the hands of the Cadets. Wherein lies the strength of the Cadets? It lies in the support given them by Allied capital.

Russia has two paths before her :

Either the war is brought to an end, all financial bonds with imperialism are torn asunder, the revolution moves forward, the foundations of the bourgeois world are shaken and the era of the working-class revolution begins—

Or else the other path, the path of continuing the war, the continuation of the offensive, submission to all the orders of Allied capital and of the Cadets—and in that case, complete financial dependence upon Allied capital (in the Taurida Palace there have been definite rumours that America would give eight billions, would furnish means to restore the national economy) and the triumph of the counter-revolution.

There can be no third path, it does not exist.

The attempt made by the Socialist-Revolutionaries and Mensheviks to describe the demonstration of July 16th–17th—the demonstration of the workers who could no longer tolerate the policy of capitalism—as an armed insurrection, is simply ridiculous. If we are to speak of culprits, we must keep in mind the objective conditions: (1) the development of the revolution into a socialist revolution, (2) the collapse at the front which has shown the petty-bourgeoisie the uselessness of the coalition government, and (3) Allied capital, which is unwilling to subsidise the revolution. As compared with these forces the workers' demonstration is of such small importance as to be scarcely noticeable. The only thing really to blame for the demonstration is that the counter-revolution has become insolvent.

The Mensheviks and Socialist-Revolutionaries set about striking at the left, at the Bolsheviks, and by that very fact they opened the revolutionary front to the enemy and betrayed both themselves and us to the counter-revolutionaries. On July 16th we proposed the unity of the revolutionary front against the counter-revolution. Our slogan was " All Power to the Soviets," which meant, form a united revolutionary front. But fearing to break with the bourgeoisie, they turned their backs on us, and that broke the revolutionary front, to the advantage of the counter-revolution. If we are going to speak of who is to blame for the counter-revolution, then the ones to blame are the Socialist-Revolutionaries and Mensheviks, the traitors to the revolution. If we ask wherein lies the strength of the Cadets, who are able to sit in their office and give instructions to the Central Executive Committee, if we ask whence they draw their strength, then there can only be one answer : from Allied capital, from the fact that Russia needs money, needs an internal loan, which the bourgeoisie is unwilling to give, or a guaranteed foreign loan, which Allied capital will not give because it does not like the policy of the coalition government. The counter-revolutionary bourgeoisie, Allied capital and the upper ranks of the officers form the three mainstays of the counter-revolution. Our misfortune is that Russia is a petty-bourgeois country, which follows the lead of the Socialist-Revolutionaries and Mensheviks, who are compromising with the Cadets, so that until the peasantry is disillusioned with the idea of compromise between the upper and lower classes we shall suffer and the revolution will fail.

But the hidden forces of the revolution are not slumber-img : inasmuch as the war is continuing, inasmuch as the collapse of economic life is continuing, no repressions, no executions, no Moscow Conferences will save the government from fresh outbreaks. The peasantry will not get the land, the worker will not secure control over production, the soldier will be sent back to his former slavery. The delegates from the front report that among the soldiers the idea of bloody revenge is ripening and as the counter-revolution triumphs, new battles and new explosions are absolutely inevitable. And if the counter-revolutionaries succeed in keeping the power for another month or two, it will be only because the principle of coalition is not yet discredited.

What is the Provisional Government ? It is a puppet, it is a wretched screen behind which stand the Cadets, the military clique and Allied capital, the three mainstays of the counter-revolution. If the " Socialist " ministers were not in the government, the counter-revolutionaries might already have been overthrown. But the character-istic feature of the present situation is the fact that the measures of the counter-revolutionaries are being carried out by the " Socialists." It is only because such a screen has been put up that the counter-revolution can go on existing for another month or two. But since the forces of the revolution are developing, there will be explosions, and the moment will come when the workers will arouse and rally around them the poorer strata of the peasantry, will unfurl the banner of the workers' revolution and open the era of the socialist revolution in Western Europe.

I should like to explain one passage in the resolution : Until July 16th a peaceful victory was possible, the peace-ful transfer of power to the Soviets. If the Congress of Soviets had made up its mind to take power into its hands, the Cadets, I believe, would not have dared to act openly against the Soviets, for such an action would have been doomed to failure. But at the present time, since the counter-revolution has become organised and strong, to say that the Soviets can peacefully take power into their hands is to talk nonsense. The peaceful period of the revolution is over, the storm period has begun, the period of battle and explosions. . . .

V. I. Lenin

ON THE EVE OF OCTOBER

Articles and letters written in the weeks preceding November 7, 1917; some only published after the Revolution. English edition, Martin Lawrence Ltd., 1932.

[First from Finland, and then after his return to Petrograd, Lenin urged on the Central Committee of the Bolsheviks that the situation was ripe for revolution—" armed uprising is inevitable and has fully matured." The Central Committee hesitated, and even after a majority decision in favour of an uprising, the two dissentients, Kamenev and Zinoviev, published a declaration against it. The letters printed below show Lenin's application of the Marxist theory of revolution, and his insistence on action at " the *crucial point* of the maturing revolution."]

ON THE EVE OF OCTOBER

MARXISM AND UPRISING

Among the most vicious and perhaps most widespread distortions of Marxism practised by the prevailing " Socialist " parties, is to be found the opportunist lie which says that preparations for an uprising, and generally the treatment of an uprising as an art, is " Blanquism."

Bernstein, the leader of opportunism, long since gained sad notoriety by accusing Marxism of Blanquism ; and our present opportunists, by shouting about Blanquism, in reality do not in any way improve or " enrich " the meagre " ideas " of Bernstein.

To accuse Marxists of Blanquism for treating uprising as an art ! Can there be a more flagrant distortion of the truth, when there is not a single Marxist who denies that it was Marx who expressed himself in the most definite, precise and categorical manner on this score ; that it was Marx who called uprising nothing but an *art*, who said that uprising must be treated as an art, that one must *gain* the first success and then proceed from success to success without stopping the *offensive* against the enemy and making use of his confusion, etc., etc.

To be successful, the uprising must be based not on a conspiracy, not on a party, but on the advanced class. This is the first point. The uprising must be based on the revolutionary upsurge of the people. This is the second point. The uprising must be based on the *crucial point* in the history of the maturing revolution, when the activity of the vanguard of the people is at its height, when the *vacillations* in the ranks of the enemies, and *in the ranks of the weak, half-hearted, undecided friends of the revolution are at their highest point*. This is the third point. It is in pointing out these three conditions as the way of approaching the question of an uprising, that Marxism differs from Blanquism.

But once these conditions exist, then to refuse to treat the uprising *as an art* means to betray Marxism and the revolution.

To show why this very moment must be recognised as the one when it is obligatory for the party to recognise the uprising as placed on the order of the day by the course of objective events, and to treat uprising as an art—to show this, it will perhaps be best to use the method of comparison and to draw a parallel between July 16–17 and the September days.

On July 16–17 it was possible, without trespassing against the truth, to put the question thus : it would have been more proper to take power, since our enemies would anyway accuse us of revolt and treat us as rebels. This, however, did not warrant a decision to take power at that time, because there were still lacking the objective conditions for a victorious uprising.

1. We did not yet have behind us the class that is the vanguard of the revolution. We did not yet have a majority among the workers and soldiers of the capitals. Now we have a majority in both Soviets. It was created *only* by the history of July and August, by the experience of ruthless punishment meted out to the Bolsheviks, and by the experience of the Kornilov affair.

2. At that time there was no general revolutionary upsurge of the people. Now there is, after the Kornilov affair. This is proven by the situation in the provinces and by the seizure of power by the Soviets in many localities.

3. At that time there were no *vacillations* on a serious, general, political scale among our enemies and among the undecided petty bourgeoisie. Now the vacillations are enormous ; our main enemy, the imperialism of the Allies and of the world (for the " Allies " are at the head of world imperialism), has begun to vacillate between war to a victory and a separate peace against Russia. Our petty-bourgeois democrats, having obviously lost their majority among the people, have begun to vacillate enormously, rejecting a bloc, i.e., a coalition with the Cadets.

4. This is why an uprising on July 16–17 would have been an error : we would not have retained power either physically or politically. Not physically, in spite of the fact that at certain moments Petrograd was in our hands, because our workers and soldiers would not have *fought and died* at that time for the sake of holding Petrograd ; at that time people had not yet become so " brutalised " ; there was not in existence such a burning hatred both towards the Kerenskys and towards the Tseretelis and Chernovs ; and

BBM

our own people were not yet hardened by the experience of the Bolsheviks being persecuted, while the Socialist-Revolutionaries and Mensheviks took part in the persecuting.

We could not have retained power July 16–17 politically, for, *before the Kornilov affair*, the army and the provinces could and would have marched against Petrograd.

Now the picture is entirely different.

We have back of us the majority of a *class* that is the vanguard of the revolution, the vanguard of the people, and is capable of drawing the masses along.

We have back of us a *majority* of the people, for Chernov's resignation, far from being the only sign, is only the most striking, the most outstanding sign showing that the peasantry *will not receive land* from a bloc with the S.-R.'s, or from the S.-R.'s themselves. And in this lies the essence of the popular character of the revolution.

We are in the advantageous position of a party which knows its road perfectly well, while *imperialism as a whole*, as well as the entire bloc of the Mensheviks and the S.-R.'s, is vacillating in an extraordinary manner.

Victory is assured to us, for the people are now very close to desperation, and we are showing the whole people a sure way out, having demonstrated to the whole people the significance of our leadership during the " Kornilov days," and then having *offered* the bloc politicians a compromise which they *rejected* at a time when their vacillations continued uninterruptedly.

It would be a very great error to think that our compromise offer has *not yet* been rejected, that the " *Democratic Conference* " *still* may accept it. The compromise was offered from *party to parties*. It could not have been offered otherwise. The *parties* have rejected it. The Democratic Conference is nothing but a *conference*. One must not forget one thing, namely, that this conference does not represent the *majority* of the revolutionary people, the poorest and most embittered peasantry. One must not forget the self-evident truth that this conference represents a *minority of the people*.

It would be a very great error, a very great parliamentary idiocy on our part, if we were to treat the Democratic Conference as a parliament, for even *if* it were to proclaim itself a parliament, the sovereign parliament of the revolution, it would not be able to *decide* anything. The decision lies *outside* of it, in the workers' sections of Petrograd and Moscow.

We have before us all the objective prerequisites for a successful uprising. We have the advantages of a situation where *only* our victory in an uprising will put an end to the most painful thing on earth, the vacillations that have sickened the people ; a situation where *only our* victory in an uprising will *put an end* to the game of a separate peace against the revolution by openly offering a more complete, more just, more immediate peace *in favour of* the revolution.

Only our party, having won a victory in an uprising, *can* save Petrograd, for if our offer of peace is rejected, and we obtain not even a truce, then *we* shall become " defensists," then we shall place ourselves *at the head of the war parties*, we shall be the most " warring " party, and we shall carry on a war in a truly revolutionary manner. We shall take away from the capitalists all the bread and all the shoes. We shall leave them crumbs. We shall dress them in bast shoes. We shall send all the bread and all the shoes to the front.

And then we shall save Petrograd.

The resources, both material and spiritual, of a truly revolutionary war are still immense in Russia ; there are ninety-nine chances in a hundred that the Germans will at least grant us a truce. And to secure a truce at present means to conquer the *whole world*.

Having recognised the absolute necessity of an uprising of the workers of Petrograd and Moscow for the sake of saving the revolution and of saving Russia from being " separately " divided among the imperialists of both coalitions, we must first adapt our political tactics at the conference to the conditions of the maturing uprising ; secondly, we must prove that we accept, and not only in words, the idea of Marx about the necessity of treating uprising as an art.

At the conference, we must immediately consolidate the Bolshevik fraction without worrying about numbers, without being afraid of leaving the vacillators in the camp of the vacillating : they are more useful *there* to the cause of revolution than in the camp of the resolute and courageous fighters.

We must compose a brief declaration in the name of the Bolsheviks in which we sharply emphasise the irrelevance of long speeches, the irrelevance of " speeches " generally, the necessity of quick action to save the revolution, the absolute necessity of breaking completely with the bourgeoisie, of completely ousting the whole present government, of completely severing relations with the Anglo-French imperialists who are preparing a " separate " partition of Russia, the necessity of all power immediately passing into the hands of *revolutionary democracy headed by the revolutionary proletariat.*

Our declaration must be the briefest and sharpest formulation of this conclusion ; it must connect up with the points in the programme of peace to the people, land to the peasants, confiscation of scandalous profits, and a halt to the scandalous damage to production done by the capitalists.

The briefer, the sharper the declaration, the better. Only two more important points must be clearly indicated in it, namely, that the people are tired of vacillations, that they are tortured by the lack of decisiveness on the part of the S.-R.'s and Mensheviks ; and that we are definitely severing relations with these *parties* because they have betrayed the revolution.

The other point. In offering an immediate peace without annexations, in breaking at once with the Allied imperialists and with all imperialists, we obtain either an immediate truce or a going over of the entire revolutionary proletariat to the side of defence, and a truly just, truly revolutionary war will then be waged by revolutionary democracy under the leadership of the proletariat.

Having made this declaration, having appealed for *decisions* and not talk ; for *actions*, not writing resolutions, we must *push* our whole fraction *into the factories and barracks* : its place is there ; the pulse of life is there ; the source of saving the revolution is there ; the moving force of the Democratic Conference is there.

In heated, impassioned speeches we must make our programme clear and we must put the question this way : either the conference accepts it *fully*, or an uprising follows. There is no middle course. Delay is impossible. The revolution is perishing.

Having put the question this way, having concentrated our entire fraction in the factories and barracks, *we shall correctly estimate the best moment to begin the uprising.*

And in order to treat uprising in a Marxist way, i.e., as an art, we must at the same time, without losing a single moment, organise the staff of the insurrectionary detachments ; designate the forces ; move the loyal regiments to the most important points ; surround the Alexander theatre; occupy Peter and Paul Fortress ; arrest the general staff and the government ; move against the military cadets, the Wild Division, etc., such detachments as will die rather than allow the enemy to move to the centre of the city ; we must mobilise the armed workers, call them to a last desperate battle, occupy at once the telegraph and telephone stations, place *our* staff of the uprising at the central telephone station, connect it by wire with all the factories, the regiments, the points of armed fighting, etc.

Of course, this is all by way of an example, to *illustrate* the idea that at the present moment it is impossible to remain loyal to the revolution *without treating uprising as an art.*

Written September 26–27, 1917.

THE CRISIS HAS MATURED

. . . What, then, is to be done ? We must *aussprechen, was ist*, " say what is," admit the truth, that in our Central

Committee and at the top of our party there is a tendency in favour of *awaiting* the Congress of Soviets, *against* the immediate seizure of power, *against* an immediate uprising. We must *overcome* this tendency or opinion.

Otherwise the Bolsheviks would *cover themselves with shame for ever* ; they would be *reduced to nothing* as a party.

For to miss such a moment and to " await " the Congress of Soviets is either *absolute idiocy* or *complete betrayal*.

It is a complete betrayal of the German workers. Indeed, we must not wait for the *beginning* of their revolution ! ! When it begins, even the Liberdans will be in favour of " supporting " it. But it *cannot* begin as long as Kerensky, Kishkin and Co. are in power.

It is a complete betrayal of the peasantry. To have the Soviets of *both capitals* and to allow the uprising of the peasants to be suppressed means *to lose, and justly so,* all the confidence of the peasant ; it means to become in the eyes of the peasants equal to the Liberdans and other scoundrels.

To " await " the Congress of Soviets is absolute idiocy, for this means losing *weeks*, whereas weeks and even days now decide *everything*. It means timidly to *refuse* the seizure of power, for on November 14–15 it will be impossible (both politically and technically, since the Cossacks will be mobilised for the day of the foolishly " appointed "[1] uprising).

To " await " the Congress of Soviets is idiocy, for the Congress *will give nothing, it can give nothing* !

The " moral " importance ? Strange indeed ! The " importance " of resolutions and negotiations with the Liberdans when we know that the Soviets are *in favour* of the peasants and that the peasant uprising *is being suppressed* ! ! Thus, we will reduce the *Soviets* to the rôle of miserable chatterers. First vanquish Kerensky, then call the Congress.

The victory of the uprising is now *secure* for the Bolsheviks:

[1] To "call" the Congress of Soviets for November 2, in order to decide upon the seizure of power—is there any difference between this and a foolishly "appointed" uprising? Now we can seize power, whereas November 2–11 you will not be allowed to seize it.

(1) we can[1] (if we do not " await " the Soviet Congress) launch a *sudden* attack from three points, from Petrograd, from Moscow, from the Baltic fleet ; (2) we have slogans whose support is guaranteed : down with the government that suppresses the uprising of the peasants against the landowners ! (3) we have a majority *in the country* ; (4) complete disorganisation of the Mensheviks and S.-R.'s ; (5) we are technically in a position to seize power in Moscow (which might even be the one to start, so as to deal the enemy a surprise blow) ; (6) we have *thousands* of armed workers and soldiers in Petrograd who can seize *at once* the Winter Palace, the General Staff Building, the telephone exchange and all the largest printing establishments. They will not be able to drive us out from there, whereas there will be such propaganda *in the army* that it will be *impossible* to fight against this government of peace, of land for the peasants, etc.

If we were to attack at once, suddenly, from three points, in Petrograd, Moscow, and the Baltic fleet, there are ninety-nine out of a hundred chances that we would gain a victory with fewer victims than on July 16–18, because *the troops will not advance* against the government of peace. Even if Kerensky has *already* " loyal " cavalry, etc., in Petrograd, when we attack from two sides and when the army is in sympathy *with us*, Kerensky will be compelled to *surrender*. If, with chances like the present, we do not seize power, then all talk of Soviet rule becomes a *lie*.

To refrain from seizing power at present, to " wait," to " chatter " in the Central Committee, to confine ourselves to " fighting for the organ " (of the Soviet), to " fighting for the Congress," means to *ruin the revolution*.

Seeing that the Central Committee has left *even without an answer* my writings insisting on such a policy since the beginning of the Democratic Conference, that the Central Organ *is deleting* from my articles references to such

---

[1] What has the party done by way of *studying* the location of the troops, etc.? What has it done for the carrying out of the uprising as " an art " ? Only talk in the Central Committee, etc. ! !

glaring errors of the Bolsheviks as the shameful decision to participate in the pre-parliament, as giving seats to the Mensheviks in the Presidium of the Soviets, etc., etc.—seeing all that, I am compelled to recognise here a " gentle " hint as to the unwillingness of the Central Committee even to consider this question, a gentle hint at gagging me and at suggesting that I retire.

I am compelled to *tender my resignation from the Central Committee,* which I hereby do, leaving myself the freedom of propaganda *in the lower ranks* of the party and at the Party Congress.

For it is my deepest conviction that if we " await " the Congress of Soviets and let the present moment pass, we *ruin* the revolution.

P.S. A whole series of facts has proven that even the Cossack troops will not move against the government of peace ! And how many are they ? Where are they ? And will not the entire army delegate units in *our favour* ?

LETTER TO THE MEMBERS OF THE CENTRAL COMMITTEE

COMRADES !

I am writing these lines on the evening of the 6th. The situation is extremely critical. It is as clear as can be that delaying the uprising now really means death.

With all my power I wish to persuade the comrades that now everything hangs on a hair, that on the order of the day are questions that are not solved by conferences, by congresses (even by Congresses of Soviets), but only by the people, by the masses, by the struggle of armed masses.

The bourgeois onslaught of the Kornilovists, the removal of Verkhovsky show that we must not wait. We must at any price, this evening, to-night, arrest the Ministers, having disarmed (defeated if they offer resistance) the military cadets, etc.

We must not wait ! We may lose everything !

The immediate gain from the seizure of power at present

is : defence of *the people* (not the congress, but the people, in the first place, the army and the peasants) against the Kornilovist government which has driven out Verkhovsky and has hatched a second Kornilov plot.

Who should seize power ?

At present this is not important. Let the Military Revolutionary Committee seize it, or " some other institution " which declares that it will relinquish the power only to the real representatives of the interests of the people, the interests of the Army (immediate offer of peace), the interests of the peasants (take the land immediately, abolish private property), the interests of the hungry.

It is necessary that all the boroughs, all regiments, all forces should be mobilised and should immediately send delegations to the Military Revolutionary Committee, to the Central Committee of the Bolsheviks, insistently demanding that under no circumstances is power to be left in the hands of Kerensky and Co. until the 7th, by no means !—but that the matter must absolutely be decided this evening or to-night.

History will not forgive delay by revolutionists who could be victorious to-day (and will surely be victorious to-day), while they risk losing much to-morrow, they risk losing all.

If we seize power to-day, we seize it not against the Soviets but for them.

Seizure of power is the point of the uprising ; its political task will be clarified after the seizure.

It would be a disaster or formalism to wait for the uncertain voting of November 7. The people have a right and a duty to decide such questions not by voting but by force ; the people have a right and duty in critical moments of a revolution to give directions to their representatives, even their best representatives, and not to wait for them.

This has been proven by the history of all revolutions, and the crime of revolutionists would be limitless if they let go the proper moment, knowing that upon them depends the *saving of the revolution,* the offer of peace, the saving of

Petrograd, the saving from starvation, the transfer of the land to the peasants.

The government is tottering. We must *deal it the death blow* at any cost.

To delay action is the same as death.

Written November 6, 1917.

J. Stalin

THE OCTOBER REVOLUTION

Articles and speeches on the Soviet Revolution, published in various Soviet journals between 1918 and 1927. English edition, Martin Lawrence Ltd., 1934.

[Two of these articles are reprinted below. The first, on the National Question, was published in *Pravda*, November 6 and 19, 1918. It shows the Marxist attitude to the national question—this " is only part of the general question of the transformation of the existing order of society " ; and that the Russian Revolution has changed the content of the national question " into a general question of liberating the oppressed nations, colonies and semi-colonies from imperialism." The second article, on the " middle strata," brings out the importance to the revolution of its " reserves," possible allies—in Russia, chiefly the peasantry. This was published in *Pravda*, Nov. 7, 1923.]

THE OCTOBER REVOLUTION

THE OCTOBER REVOLUTION AND THE NATIONAL QUESTION

THE NATIONAL QUESTION is not something that is self-sufficient, fixed once for all time. Being only part of the general question of the transformation of the existing order of society, the national question is wholly determined by the conditions of the social environment, the character of the government of the country and, generally, by the whole course of social development. This is particularly noticeable during revolutionary epochs, when the national question and the national movement rapidly change their content in full view of everyone, according to the course and outcome of the revolution.

I. The February Revolution and the National Question

In the epoch of the bourgeois revolution in Russia (dating from February 1917) the national movement in the borderlands bore the character of a bourgeois emancipatory movement. The nationalities of Russia, for ages oppressed and exploited by the " old régime," now for the first time felt that they possessed strength and hurled themselves into the combat with their oppressors. " Liquidate national oppression " was the slogan of the movement. The borderlands of Russia were instantly covered with " all-national " institutions. The movement was headed by the national bourgeois-democratic intelligentsia. " National Councils " in Latvia, in the Esthonian region, in Lithuania, Georgia, Armenia, Azerbaijan, in the cities of the Caucasus, in Kirghizstan and the Middle Volga region ; the " Rada " in the Ukraine and in White Russia ; " Sfatul Tarei " in Bessarabia ; " Kurultai " in the Crimea and in Bashkiria ; the " Autonomous Government " in Turkestan—such were the " all-national " institutions around which the national bourgeoisie was gathering strength. The question at issue was emancipation from tsarism as the " basic cause " of national oppression, and the formation of national bourgeois States. The right of nations to self-determination was interpreted to mean the right of the national bourgeoisie in the borderlands to take power into its own hands and make use of the February Revolution for the purpose of forming its " own " national state. The above-mentioned bourgeois institutions did not contemplate and could not contemplate developing the revolution further. At the same time it was overlooked that naked, barefaced, imperialism was coming to take the place of tsarism, and that this imperialism was a stronger and more dangerous enemy of nationalities, was the basis of a new national oppression.

The abolition of tsarism and the coming into power of the bourgeoisie did not, however, lead to the abolition of national oppression. The old, coarse form of national oppression gave way to a new, refined, yet more dangerous, form of oppression. The government of Lvov-Miliukov-Kerensky not only did not break with the policy of national oppression but organised a new campaign against Finland (dispersion of the Sejm in the summer of 1917) and the Ukraine (destruction of the cultural institutions of the Ukraine). More than that. This government, imperialist by nature, called on the population to continue the war in order to subjugate new lands, new colonies and nationalities. It was impelled to take this course not only by its intrinsic imperialist character but also by the existence of the old imperialist States in Western Europe which were irresistibly endeavouring to subjugate new lands and nationalities and threatened to constrict its sphere of influence. A struggle by the imperialist States to subjugate the small nationalities as a condition of the existence of these States was the picture revealed in the course of the imperialist war. The annihilation of tsarism and the appearance on the scene of the Miliukov-Kerensky government wrought virtually no improvement in this ungainly picture. Naturally, in so far as the " all-national " institutions in the borderlands displayed a tendency towards political independence, they encountered the irresistible opposition of the imperialist government of Russia. However, in so far as they consolidated the power of the national bourgeoisie and remained deaf to the vital interests of " their own "

workers and peasants, they evoked grumbling and discontent among the latter. The so-called " national regiments " only poured oil on the flames ; they were powerless
as against the danger from above, and merely intensified
and aggravated the danger from below. The " all-national "
institutions were left without defence against the blows
dealt from without as well as against an explosion within.
The budding bourgeois national States began to fade before
blossom-time.

Thus the old bourgeois-democratic interpretation of the
principle of self-determination became a fiction and lost its
revolutionary meaning. In such conditions there could
clearly be no question of the abolition of national oppression and of the independence of small and national States.
It was becoming obvious that the liberation of the toiling
masses of the oppressed nationalities and the abolition of
national oppression were inconceivable without a break
with imperialism, without overthrowing " one's own "
national bourgeoisie and without the seizure of power by
the toiling masses themselves.

This became especially apparent after the October
Revolution.

II. The October Revolution and the National Question

The February Revolution concealed in its bosom irreconcilable inner contradictions. The revolution was accomplished through the efforts of workers and peasants
(soldiers), whereas, as a result of the revolution, power
passed, not to the workers and peasants, but to the bourgeoisie. By making the revolution the workers and peasants
wanted to put an end to the war, wanted to secure peace,
whereas the bourgeoisie, which assumed power, strove to
use the revolutionary ardour of the masses to continue the
war, was against peace. The economic ruin of the country
and the food crisis demanded the expropriation of capital
and of the industrial enterprises for the benefit of the

workers, the confiscation of the landlord estates for the benefit of the peasants, whereas the bourgeois Miliukov-Kerensky government was standing guard over the interests of the landlords and capitalists, resolutely protecting the latter against attack by workers or peasants. That was a bourgeois revolution, effected at the hands of the workers and peasants for the benefit of " their own " exploiters.

Meanwhile the country continued to groan under the burden of the imperialist war, of economic disintegration and of the collapse of the food supply. The front was falling to pieces and was fast melting away. Factories and mills were stopping work. Famine was on the increase in the country. The February Revolution with its inner contradictions proved obviously inadequate to " save the country." The Miliukov-Kerensky government proved obviously incapable of solving the basic problems of the revolution.

A new, *socialist* revolution was necessary to lead the country out of the impasse of imperialist war and economic ruin.

This revolution came about as a result of the October insurrection.

By overthrowing the power of the landlords and the bourgeoisie and placing a government of the workers and peasants in its stead, the October Revolution at one blow solved the contradictions of the February Revolution. The abolition of landlord-kulak omnipotence and the transfer of the use of the land to the toiling masses of the villages ; the expropriation of the factories and mills, and their transfer to the management of the workers ; the break with imperialism and the termination of the predatory war ; the publication of the secret treaties and the exposure of the policy of foreign territorial annexations ; finally the proclamation of self-determination for the toiling masses of the oppressed nations and the recognition of the independence of Finland constitute the principal measures carried into effect by the Soviet government in the course of the revolution.

This was a truly *socialist* revolution.

The revolution which started at the centre could not be long confined to the narrow territory of the central area. After being victorious at the centre, it was absolutely bound to spread to the border regions. And, indeed, the revolutionary wave, from the very first days of the revolution spread from the North throughout the whole of Russia, engulfing one borderland after another. However, here it struck a rampart in the form of the " national councils " and regional " governments " (Don, Kuban, Siberia) which had been formed prior to October. The fact of the matter was that these " national governments " would not hear of a socialist revolution. Bourgeois by nature, they had no intention whatever of destroying the old bourgeois world ; on the contrary, they considered it their duty to exert all their energy to preserve and consolidate it. Imperialist in essence, they had not the slightest intention of breaking with imperialism ; on the contrary, they were never averse to capturing and subjugating bits and morsels of " foreign " nationalities, whenever an opportunity to do so presented itself. No wonder then that these " national governments " in the borderlands declared war on the socialist government at the centre. Once they had declared war, they naturally became hotbeds of reaction, to which everything counter-revolutionary in Russia gravitated. It is no secret to anyone that all the counter-revolutionaries cast out of Russia rushed to these hotbeds, and that there, around these hotbeds, they formed white guard " national " regiments.

However, in addition to " national " governments, the borderlands also have national workers and peasants. Even before the October Revolution they were organised in their own revolutionary Soviets of Deputies, after the model of the Soviet of Deputies obtaining in the central parts of Russia, and never severed their connections with their brothers in the North. They, too, strove for victory over the bourgeoisie ; they, too, fought for the triumph of socialism. No wonder the conflict between them and

" their own " national governments increased from day to day. The October Revolution only consolidated the alliance between the workers and peasants of the borderlands and the workers and peasants of Russia, inspiring them with faith in the triumph of socialism. And the war of the " national governments " against the Soviet government brought their conflict with these " governments " to a complete break with them, brought them to open rebellion against them.

Thus was formed the socialist alliance between the workers and peasants of all Russia against the counter-revolutionary alliance of the national-bourgeois " governments " of Russia's borderlands.

Some people depict the struggle of the borderland " governments " as a struggle for national liberation and against the " soulless centralism " of the Soviet government. This, however, is wrong. No government in the world ever granted such extensive decentralisation, no government in the world ever afforded its peoples such plenary national freedom as does the Soviet government of Russia. The struggle of the borderland " governments " was and remains a struggle of the bourgeois counter-revolution against socialism. The national flag is tacked on to the cause only to deceive the masses, only as a popular flag which conveniently covers up the counter-revolutionary designs of the national bourgeoisie.

However, the struggle of the " national " and regional " governments " proved to be an unequal struggle. Attacked from two quarters—from without by the Soviet government, and from within by " their own " workers and peasants—the " national governments " had to retreat after the very first battles. The uprising of the Finnish workers and agricultural labourers and the flight of the bourgeois " Senate " ; the uprising of the Ukrainian workers and peasants and the flight of the bourgeois " Rada " ; the uprising of the workers and peasants in the Don region, in Kuban, in Siberia and the downfall of

Kaledin, of Kornilov and of the Siberian " government " ; the uprising of the poor of Turkestan and the flight of the " autonomous government " ; the agrarian revolution in the Caucasus and the utter helplessness of the " national councils " of Georgia, Armenia and Azerbaijan—these are facts of common knowledge demonstrating the complete isolation of the borderland " governments " from " their own " masses. Having been completely defeated, the " national governments " were " forced " to appeal to the imperialists of Western Europe, to the age-long oppressors and exploiters of the small nations of the whole world, for aid against " their own " workers and peasants.

Such was the beginning of the period of foreign intervention in, and occupation of, the borderlands—a period revealing once more the counter-revolutionary nature of the " national " and regional " governments."

Only now has it become obvious to all that the national bourgeoisie is striving not for the liberation of " its own people " from national oppression but for the liberty of wringing profits from it, for the liberty of preserving its own privileges and capital.

Only now has it become obvious that the liberation of the oppressed nationalities is inconceivable without breaking with imperialism, without overthrowing the bourgeoisie of the oppressed nations, without power passing into the hands of the toiling masses of those nationalities.

Thus the old bourgeois conception of the principle of self-determination with the slogan " All Power to the National Bourgeoisie " was exposed and rejected by the very course of the revolution. The socialist conception of self-determination with the slogan " All Power to the Toiling Masses of the Oppressed Nations " obtained full recognition and opportunity of application.

Thus the October Revolution, after putting an end to the old bourgeois emancipatory national movement, inaugurated the era of a new socialist movement of the workers and peasants of the oppressed nations, directed against all—which signifies also national—oppression, against the rule of the bourgeoisie, whether " its own " or foreign, against imperialism in general.

III. The International Importance of the October Revolution

After being victorious in the central part of Russia and taking possession of a number of borderlands, the October Revolution could not stop short at the territorial boundaries of Russia. In the atmosphere of imperialist world war and general discontent among the lower classes, it could not but spread to the neighbouring countries. The break with imperialism and the liberation of Russia from the predatory war, the publication of the secret treaties and the solemn abrogation of the policy of seizing foreign soil, the proclamation of national freedom and the recognition of the independence of Finland, the declaration of Russia as a " Federation of Soviet National Republics " and the militant battle-cry of a resolute struggle against imperialism broadcast all over the world by the Soviet government in millions of pamphlets, newspapers and leaflets in the mother tongues of the peoples of the East and West—all this could not fail to have its effect on the enslaved East and the bleeding West.

And, in truth, the October Revolution is the first revolution in the history of the world that has broken the sleep of centuries of the toiling masses of the oppressed nations of the East and drawn them into the struggle against world imperialism. The formation of workers' and peasants' soviets in Persia, China and India, modelled after the soviets in Russia, is sufficiently convincing proof of this.

The October Revolution is the first revolution in the world that provided the workers and peasants of the West with a living and salutary example and urged them on to the path of real liberation from the yoke of war and imperialism. The uprising of the workers and soldiers in Austria-Hungary and Germany, the formation of Soviets of Workers' and Soldiers' Deputies, the revolutionary struggle of the nations of Austria-Hungary against national oppression are quite eloquent proofs of this.

That the struggle in the East and even in the West has not yet succeeded in shedding the bourgeois-nationalist features is not at all the point at issue—the point is that the struggle against imperialism *has begun*, that it goes on and is inevitably bound to reach its logical termination.

Foreign intervention and the policy of occupation pursued by the " foreign " imperialists only intensify the revolutionary crisis, drawing new nations into the struggle and extending the area of revolutionary clashes with imperialism.

Thus the October Revolution, by establishing ties between the nations of the backward East and the advanced West, draws them together into the joint camp of the struggle against imperialism.

The national question thus grows from the partial question of struggling against national oppression to the general question of liberating the nations, colonies and semi-colonies from imperialism.

The mortal sin of the Second International and its leader Kautsky consists incidentally in this : that they were always deviating towards a bourgeois conception of national self-determination, that they did not understand the revolutionary meaning of the latter, that they did not know how, or did not want, to put the national question on the revolutionary basis of an open struggle against imperialism, that they did not know how, or did not want, to link the national question to the question of liberating the colonies.

The thick-headedness of the Austrian Social-Democrats of the type of Bauer and Renner consists indeed in that they failed to understand the indissoluble bond between the national question and the question of power, and tried to separate the national question from politics and confine it within the scope of cultural and educational questions, oblivious of the existence of such " trifles " as imperialism and the colonies enslaved by it.

It is said that the principles of self-determination and of the " defence of the fatherland " have been abrogated by the very course of events in the conditions of an ascendent socialist revolution. In fact it is not self-determination and the " defence of the fatherland " that have been abrogated, but their bourgeois interpretation. It is sufficient to cast a glance at the occupied regions, languishing under the yoke of imperialism and yearning for liberation ; sufficient to cast a glance at Russia conducting a revolutionary war for the defence of the socialist fatherland against the pirates of imperialism ; sufficient to ponder the events that are now transpiring in Austria-Hungary ; sufficient to glance at the enslaved colonies and semi-colonies, that have already organised soviets in their respective countries (India, Persia, China)—one need but cast a glance at all this to realise the full revolutionary significance of the principle of self-determination in its socialist interpretation.

Indeed the great international importance of the October Revolution consists mainly in that this revolution :

(1) has widened the scope of the national question, transforming it from a partial question of struggling against national oppression into a general question of liberating the oppressed nations, colonies and semi-colonies from imperialism ;

(2) has ushered in vast opportunities and disclosed the actual means for this liberation, thus considerably facilitating the task of the oppressed nations of the West and East to accomplish their liberation and drawing them into the common channel of a victorious struggle against imperialism ;

(3) has thereby erected a bridge between the socialist West and the enslaved East, by setting up a new front of revolutions extending from the proletarians of the West on

through the Russian Revolution to the oppressed nations of the East *against* world imperialism.

This, in effect, explains the indescribable enthusiasm now displayed by the toiling and exploited masses of the East and West with regard to the Russian proletariat.

This largely explains the brutal fury with which the imperialist robbers of the whole world have hurled themselves against Soviet Russia.

THE OCTOBER REVOLUTION AND THE QUESTION OF THE MIDDLE STRATA

The question of the middle strata undoubtedly presents one of the fundamental questions of the workers' revolution. The middle strata are the peasantry and the petty labouring populace of the cities. In this category must also be classified the oppressed nationalities, which consist nine-tenths of middle strata. As you see, these are precisely the strata which, by their economic position, are situated between the proletariat and the capitalist class. The relative importance of these strata is determined by two circumstances : in the first place, these strata represent the majority, or, at any rate, a considerable minority of the population of the existing States ; second, they represent the important reserves from among which the capitalist class recruits its army against the proletariat. The proletariat cannot maintain power without the sympathy and support of the middle strata, primarily of the peasantry, especially in a country like our union of republics. The proletariat cannot even seriously think of seizing power unless these strata have at least been neutralised, unless these strata have already had time to divorce themselves from the capitalist class, if they still constitute, in their mass, an army of the capitalists. Hence the struggle for the middle strata, the struggle for the peasantry, which passes like a coloured thread through the whole fabric of our revolution, from 1905 to 1917, a struggle which is far from over and which will go on in the future as well.

The Revolution of 1848 in France suffered defeat because, among other things, it failed to evoke sympathetic response among the French peasants. The Paris Commune fell because, among other things, it encountered the opposition of the middle strata, especially of the peasantry. The same must be said of the Russian Revolution of 1905. Some of the vulgar Marxists, with Kautsky at their head, basing themselves on the experience of the European revolutions, arrived at the conclusion that the middle strata, especially of the peasantry, were well-nigh born enemies of the workers' revolution, and that it was necessary on that account to steer towards a more lengthy period of development, as a result of which the proletariat would become the majority of the nation whereby the actual conditions prerequisite to a victory of the workers' revolution would be created. On the basis of this conclusion, these vulgar Marxists warned the proletariat against a " premature " revolution. On the basis of this conclusion, they, for " considerations of principle," placed these middle strata at the complete disposal of the capitalists. On the basis of this conclusion, they prophesied to us the doom of the Russian October Revolution, referring to the fact that the proletariat constituted a minority in Russia, that Russia was a peasant country and that on that account a victorious workers' revolution was impossible in Russia.

It is characteristic that Marx himself evaluated the middle strata, especially the peasantry, quite differently. Whereas the vulgar Marxists, after giving up the peasantry and placing it at the complete disposal of capital, vociferously swaggered about their " unswerving adherence to principles "—Marx, most consistent of all Marxists in questions of principle, insistently advised the party of the Communists not to lose sight of the peasantry, to win it over to the side of the proletariat and to make sure of its support in the coming proletarian revolution. It is well known that in the 'fifties, after the defeat of the February Revolution in France and in Germany, Marx wrote to Engels, and through him to the Communist Party of Germany, as follows :

> The whole thing in Germany will depend on the possibility to back the proletarian revolution by some second edition of the Peasant War.

This was written about the Germany of the 'fifties, a peasant country, in which the proletariat formed an insignificant minority, in which the proletariat was less organised than in the Russia of 1917, and in which the peasantry, owing to its position, was less disposed to support a proletarian revolution than was the case in the Russia of 1917.

The October Revolution undoubtedly presented the happy combination of a " peasant war " and a " proletarian revolution " of which Marx wrote, all the chatterboxes and their " principles " notwithstanding. The October Revolution proved that such a combination is both possible and feasible. The October Revolution proved that the proletariat can seize power and maintain it, provided it is able to wrest the middle strata, especially the peasantry, from the capitalist classes, provided it knows how to transform these strata from reserves of capitalism into reserves of the proletariat.

In brief : the October Revolution was the first of all the revolutions of the world to advance to the forefront the question of the middle strata, primarily the peasantry, and to settle it victoriously, all the " theories " and lamentations of the heroes of the Second International notwithstanding.

This constitutes the first service of the October Revolution, if one may speak altogether of services in this case.

However, matters did not rest there. The October Revolution went further, trying to rally the oppressed nationalities round the proletariat. It was stated above that these nationalities consist nine-tenths of peasants and the petty labouring populace of the cities. However, this does not fully characterise the concept " oppressed nationality." The oppressed nationalities are usually oppressed not only as peasantry and the labouring populace of the cities but also as nationalities, i.e., as workers of a definite statehood, language, culture, manner of life, customs and habits. The double weight of oppression cannot but revolutionise the toiling masses of the oppressed nationalities, cannot but urge them on to the struggle against the principal force of oppression—to the struggle against capital. This circumstance served as the base on which the proletariat succeeded in realising the combination of a " proletarian revolution " and not only a " peasant war " but also a " national war." All this could not fail to extend the field of action of the proletarian revolution far beyond the confines of Russia, could not fail to jeopardise the most deep-seated reserves of capitalism. If the struggle for the middle strata of a given dominating nationality means the struggle for the immediate reserves of capitalism, the struggle for the liberation of the oppressed nationalities could not but be transformed into a struggle for the conquest of the separate, most deep-seated reserves of capitalism, into a struggle for the liberation of the colonial and partly disfranchised nations from the yoke of capitalism. This latter struggle is not over by far—besides, it has not yet had time to yield even the first decisive successes. However, this struggle for the deep-seated reserves owes its commencement to the October Revolution, and it will undoubtedly develop step by step, commensurate with the development of imperialism, commensurate with the increase in power of our union of republics, commensurate with the development of the proletarian revolution in the West.

In brief : the October Revolution has actually initiated the struggle of the proletariat for the deep-seated reserves of capitalism from among the masses of the people in the oppressed and partly disfranchised countries ; it was the first to raise the standard of struggle for winning these reserves—this constitutes its second service.

Winning the peasantry proceeded in our country under the banner of socialism. The peasantry, which had received land at the hands of the proletariat, which had defeated the landlords with the aid of the proletariat, and which had risen to power under the leadership of the proletariat, could not but feel, could not but understand that the process of its liberation proceeded, and would proceed in the future, under the banner of the proletariat, under its Red Banner. This circumstance could not fail to transform the banner of socialism, which was formerly a bogey to the peasantry, into a standard attracting its attention and facilitating its liberation from wretchedness, destitution and oppression. The same must be said with even more emphasis in regard to the oppressed nationalities. The call to struggle for the liberation of the nationalities, a call re-enforced by facts such as the liberation of Finland, the evacuation of troops from Persia and China, the formation of the Union of Republics, open moral support to the peoples of Turkey, China, Hindustan, Egypt—this call was first sounded by the people who were the victors in the October Revolution. The fact that Russia, which formerly served as the symbol of oppression in the eyes of the oppressed nationalities, has now, after it has become socialist, been transformed into a symbol of liberation, cannot be described as a mere chance. Nor is it accidental that the name of Comrade Lenin, the leader of the October Revolution, is now the most cherished name of the downtrodden, browbeaten peasants and revolutionary intelligentsia of the colonial and semi-enfranchised countries. If formerly Christianity was considered an anchor of salvation among the oppressed and downtrodden slaves of the vast Roman Empire, now things are heading towards a point where socialism can serve (and is already beginning to serve !) as a banner of liberation for the many millions in the vast colonial States of imperialism. It is hardly susceptible of doubt that this circumstance considerably facilitated the struggle to combat the prejudices against socialism and opened the road to the ideas of socialism in the most remote corners of the oppressed countries. If formerly it was difficult for a socialist to show himself with open visor among the non-proletarian middle strata of the oppressed or oppressing countries, to-day he can openly propagate the idea of socialism among these strata and expect to be listened to and perhaps even followed, for he possesses so cogent an argument as the October Revolution. This is also a result of the October Revolution.

In brief : the October Revolution cleared the path to the ideas of socialism for the middle non-proletarian peasant strata of all nationalities and tribes ; it popularised the banner of socialism among them—which constitutes the third service of the October Revolution.

V. I. Lenin

THE PROLETARIAN REVOLUTION AND KAUTSKY THE RENEGADE

Published 1919. English Edition, Modern Books Ltd., 1929.

[After the Soviet Government had been in existence over a year, and when many parts of Central Europe were approaching revolutionary crisis, a large section of Social Democracy in Western Europe began to carry on active propaganda against the " dictatorship of the proletariat," on the same general grounds as the more recent statement of the British Labour Party and the Second International— " we are for democracy and against dictatorship." Not only Vandervelde (*Socialism versus the State*), but also Karl Kautsky, once a Marxist, entered the campaign against the Soviets. In his pamphlet *Dictatorship of the Proletariat* Kautsky attacked the dictatorship in Russia, partly distorting the facts, but more particularly advancing the theory of " pure democracy " as essential in the advance to Socialism. Lenin replied in *The Proletarian Revolution and Kautsky the Renegade*, bringing out the theories of Marx and Engels on the State (see also Lenin's *The State and Revolution*), and showing the Soviets as the highest form of democracy yet seen, proletarian democracy. Parts of the chapters dealing with democracy and dictatorship are reprinted here.]

THE PROLETARIAN REVOLUTION AND KAUTSKY THE RENEGADE

BOURGEOIS AND PROLETARIAN DEMOCRACY

(Ch. II)

. . . Proletarian democracy, of which the Soviet régime constitutes one of the forms, has given to the world a hitherto unknown expansion and development of democracy for the gigantic majority of the population, for the exploited and labouring masses. To have written a whole pamphlet about democracy, as Kautsky has done (who devotes two pages to the question of dictatorship and scores of pages to that of " pure democracy ") and *not* to have noticed this fact, means simply that he has distorted the facts, after the approved Liberal manner.

Or take foreign policy. In no bourgeois State, not even in the most democratic one, is it carried out openly. Everywhere the masses are deceived—in democratic France, Switzerland, America, or England in an incomparably more refined and wholesale manner than in other countries. It was the Soviet Government which by a revolutionary act has torn off the veil of mystery from foreign policy. But Kautsky has not noticed this, and passes it over in silence, although in the present era of predatory wars and secret treaties about spheres of influence (that is, about the partition of the world between the capitalist bandits), the subject is one of cardinal importance, on which the happiness and the life and death of millions depend.

Or take the organisation of the State. Kautsky seizes upon all manner of petty things, including the system of " indirect " elections under the Soviet constitution, but the essence of things wholly escapes him. He does not see the *class* nature of the State machinery. By a thousand-and-one tricks the capitalists, in a bourgeois democracy —and these tricks are the more skilful and the more effective the further " pure " democracy has developed—keep the masses out of the administration and frustrate the freedom of the Press, the right of meeting, etc. The Soviet régime, on the contrary, is the first in the world (or strictly speaking, the second, because the Commune of Paris attempted to do the same thing) to *attract* the masses, that is, the *exploited* masses, to the work of administration. The labouring masses are kept away from the bourgeois parliament (which *never* decides the most important questions in a bourgeois democracy, as they are decided by the Stock Exchange and the banks) by a thousand-and-one barriers, in consequence of which the working class perfectly well realises that the bourgeois parliaments are institutions *foreign* to them, are an *instrument of oppression* of the proletariat by the bourgeoisie, are an institution of the hostile class of the exploiting minority.

As against this, the Soviets are the direct organisation of the labouring and exploited masses themselves, which enables them to organise and to administer the State by their own efforts and their own manner. The urban proletariat, the advance guard of the toiling and exploited, enjoys under this arrangement a position of advantage, due to its being best organised by the large industrial concerns, which enables it best to hold elections and to control the elected. The Soviet system automatically facilitates the rally of all those who work and are exploited round their advance guard, the proletariat. The old bourgeois apparatus, the bureaucracy, the privileges of wealth, of bourgeois education, of social connections, etc., which are the more varied, the more highly bourgeois democracy has developed—all this disappears under the Soviet system. Freedom of the Press ceases to be an hypocrisy, because the printing presses and the paper are taken away from the bourgeoisie. It is the same with the best buildings, the palaces, the villas, and the country houses. Thousands and thousands of these best buildings have been taken away from the exploiters by the Soviet authority, which has thereby made the right of meeting for the masses a thousand times more " democratic " than before, since without this right all democracy is a fraud and a delusion. The indirect elections of the non-local Soviets make it easier to arrange for congresses of the Soviets, render the entire apparatus cheaper, more elastic, more accessible to the workers and peasants at the time when life is overflowing and it is necessary to be able rapidly to recall a delegate or to send him to the General Congress of Soviets. Proletarian democracy is a million times more democratic than any bourgeois democracy, and the Soviet régime is a million times more democratic than the most democratic régime in a bourgeois republic.

This could only have remained unnoticed by a person who is either the deliberate henchman of the bourgeoisie or is politically dead, does not see life except from behind the dusty pages of bourgeois books, is permeated through and through by bourgeois democratic prejudices, and thereby, objectively speaking, becomes the lackey of the bourgeoisie.

This could only have remained unnoticed by a man who is incapable of putting the question from the point of view of the exploited classes : is there one single country in the world, even among the most democratic bourgeois countries, in which the ordinary rank-and-file worker, the ordinary rank-and-file village labourer or village semi-proletarian (that is, the overwhelming majority of the population), enjoys anything approaching such *liberty* of holding meetings in the best buildings, such *liberty* of giving utterance to his ideas and of protecting his interests in print by means of the best printing works and largest stocks of paper, such liberty of appointing men and women of his own class to administer and to organise the State, as in Soviet Russia ?

The mere thought is absurd that Mr. Kautsky could find in any country one single worker or agricultural labourer in a thousand who, on being informed of the facts, would hesitate in replying to this question. Instinctively, through reading the bare fragments of truth in the bourgeois press, the workers of the entire world sympathise with the Soviet Republic, just because they see in it *proletarian* democracy, a democracy *for the poor*, and not a democracy for the rich, as is the case with every bourgeois democracy, even the best. "We are ruled, and our State is run, by bourgeois bureaucrats, by capitalist parliaments, by capitalist judges "—such is the simple, indisputable, and obvious truth, which is known and felt, through their own daily experience, by tens and hundreds of millions of the exploited classes in all bourgeois countries, including the most democratic. In Russia, on the other hand, the bureaucratic apparatus has been completely smashed up, the old judges have all been driven from their seats, the bourgeois parliament has been dispersed, and instead the workers and peasants have received a much more *popular* representation, their Soviets have replaced the bureaucrats, or are controlling them, and their Soviets have become the authorities who elect the judges. This fact alone is enough to justifiy all the oppressed classes in regarding the Soviet régime, that is, the Soviet form of the dictatorship of the proletariat, as a million times more democratic than the most democratic bourgeois republic.

But Kautsky does not understand this truth, so obvious to every worker, because he has forgotten how to put the question : democracy for what class ? If he starts from " pure " (does it mean non-class ? or above-class ?) democracy and simply says : Without equality of all citizens there can be no democracy, one has to ask the learned Mr. Kautsky, the " Marxist " and the " Socialist," the following question : Can there be any equality between the exploited and the exploiters ? It is monstrous, it is incredible, that one should have to ask such a question in discussing a book by the leading thinker of the Second International. But there is no way of escaping from this necessity. In writing about Kautsky one has to explain to him, learned man that he is, why there can be no equality between the exploiters and the exploited.

Can there be Equality between the Exploiters and the Exploited ?

Kautsky says " The exploiters always formed but a small minority of the population " (p. 14).

This is certainly true. Taking it as the starting point, what should be the argument ? One may argue in a Marxist, in a Socialist way, taking as a basis the relation between the exploited and the exploiter, or one may argue in a Liberal, in a bourgeois-democratic way, taking as a basis the relation of the majority to the minority.

If we argue in the Marxist way we must say : The exploiters must inevitably turn the State (we are speaking of a democracy, that is, one of the forms of State) into an instrument of domination of their class over the class of exploited. Hence, so long as there are exploiters ruling the majority of exploited, the democratic State must inevitably be a democracy for the exploiters. The State of the exploited must fundamentally differ from such a State ; it must be a democracy for the exploited, a political order of suppression of the exploiters. But the suppression of a class means inequality in so far as this class is concerned, and its exemption from the privileges of " democracy."

If, on the other hand, we argue in a bougeois-Liberal way, we have to say : The majority decides and the minority obeys. Those who do not obey are punished. And this is all. There is no need of talking about the class character of the State in general, or about " pure democracy " in particular, since it would not be relevant. The majority is the majority and the minority is the minority. That ends the matter. And this is just Kautsky's way of reasoning. He says :

" Why should the rule of the proletariat necessarily receive a form which is incompatible with democracy ? " (p. 21). There follows a very detailed and a very verbose explanation, garnished with a quotation from Marx and the figures of the elections to the Paris Commune, of the fact that the proletariat is always in a majority. The conclusion is : " A régime which is so strongly rooted in the masses has not the slightest reason for infringing democracy. It cannot, it is true, always do without violence, as, for instance, in cases when violence is employed to put down democracy. Force is the only reply to force. But a régime which is aware of the support of the masses will only employ force and violence for the *protection*, and not for the *destruction*, of democracy. It would simply commit suicide if it wanted to destroy its own most secure basis—universal suffrage, that deep source of mighty moral authority." (p. 22).

You see that the relation between the exploited and the

exploiters has entirely vanished in Kautsky's arguments, and all that remains is a majority in general, a minority in general, a democracy in general, that is, the " pure democracy " which is already familiar to us. And all this, mark you, is said à *propos* of the Commune of Paris ! Let us quote, by the way of illustration, how Marx and Engels discuss the subject of dictatorship, also à *propos* of the Commune : *Marx :* " When the workers put in the place of the dictatorship of the bourgeoisie . . . their revolutionary dictatorship . . . in order to break down the resistance of the bourgeoisie . . . the workers invest the State with a revolutionary and temporary form . . ." *Engels :* " The party which has triumphed in the revolution is necessarily compelled to maintain its rule by means of that fear with which its arms inspire the reactionaries. If the Commune of Paris had not based itself on the authority of the armed people against the bourgeoisie, would it have maintained itself more than twenty-four hours ? Are we not, on the contrary, justified in blaming the Commune for having made too little use of its authority ? "

Engels : " As the State is only a temporary institution which is to be made use of in the revolution, in order forcibly to suppress the opponents, it is a perfect absurdity to speak about the free popular State ; so long as the proletariat still needs the State, it needs it, not in the interest of freedom but in order to suppress its opponents, and when it becomes possible to speak of freedom, the State as such ceases to exist."

The distance between Kautsky, on the one hand, and Marx and Engels, on the other, is as great as between heaven and earth, as between the bourgeois Liberal and the proletarian revolutionary. Pure democracy, or simple " democracy," of which Kautsky speaks, is but a paraphrase of the " free popular State," that is, a perfect *absurdity*. Kautsky, with the learned air of a most learned arm-chair fool, or else with the innocent air of a ten-year-old girl, is asking : Why do we need a dictatorship when we have

Ccm

a majority ? And Marx and Engels explain : In order to break down the resistance of the bourgeoisie ; in order to inspire the reactionaries with fear ; in order to maintain the authority of the armed people against the bourgeoisie ; in order that the proletariat may forcibly suppress its enemies !

But Kautsky does not understand these explanations. He is infatuated with the " pure democracy," he does not see its bourgeois character, and " consistently " urges that the majority, once it is the majority, has no need " to break down the resistance " of the minority, has no need " forcibly to suppress " it : it is sufficient to suppress cases of *infraction* of the democracy infatuated with the "purity" of democracy. Kautsky unwittingly commits the same little error which is committed by all bourgeois democrats, namely, he accepts the formal equality, which under capitalism is only a fraud and a piece of hypocrisy, at its face value as a *de facto* equality. Quite a bagatelle !

But the exploiter cannot be equal to the exploited. This is a truth which, however disgraceful to Kautsky, is nevertheless of the essence of Socialism. Another truth is that there can be, in reality, no *de facto* equality, unless and until the possibility of exploitation of one class by another has been abolished.

It is possible, by means of a successful insurrection in the centre or of a mutiny in the army, to defeat the exploiters at one blow, but except in very rare and particular cases, the exploiters cannot be destroyed at once. It is impossible to expropriate at one blow all the landlords and capitalists of a large country. In addition, expropriation alone, as a legal or political act, does not by far settle the matter, since it is necessary practically to replace the landlords and capitalists, to substitute for theirs another, a *working class*, management of the factories and estates. There can be no equality between the exploiters, who, for many generations have enjoyed education and the advantages and habits of prosperity, and the exploited, the majority of whom, even in the most advanced and the most democratic bourgeois republics, are cowed, frightened, ignorant, unorganised. It is inevitable that the exploiters should still enjoy a large number of great practical advantages for a considerable period after the revolution. They still have money (since it is impossible to abolish money at once), some moveable property (often of a considerable extent), social connections, habits of organisation and management, knowledge of all the secrets (customs, methods, means, and possibilities) of administration, higher education, closeness to the higher personnel of technical experts (who live and think after the bourgeois style), and incomparably higher knowledge and experience in military affairs (which is very important), and so forth, and so forth. If the exploiters are defeated in one country only—and this, of course, is the rule, since a simultaneous revolution in a number of countries is a rare exception— they still remain stronger than the exploited, because the international connections of the exploiters are enormous. And that a portion of the exploited from among the least intelligent section of the " middle " peasant and artisan class may and, indeed, do follow the exploiters has been shown hitherto by all revolutions, including the Commune of Paris (since there were proletarians also among the troops of Versailles, which the most learned Kautsky seems to have forgotten).

In these circumstances to suppose that in any serious revolution the issue is decided by the simple relation between majority and minority is the acme of stupidity, a typical delusion of an ordinary bourgeois Liberal, as well as a *deception of the masses* from whom a well-established historical truth is concealed. This truth is that in any and every serious revolution *a long, obstinate, desperate* resistance of the exploiters, who for many years will yet enjoy great advantages over the exploited, constitutes the rule. Never, except in the sentimental Utopia of the sentimental Mr. Kautsky, will the exploiters submit to the decision of the exploited majority without making use of their advantages in a last desperate battle, or in a series of battles.

The transition from capitalism to Communism forms a whole historical epoch. Until it is complete, the exploiters will still retain the hope of a restoration, and this hope will inevitably express itself in *attempts* at restoration. After the first serious defeat, the overthrown exploiters who did not expect their overthrow, did not believe in it, did not admit even the thought of it, will with tenfold energy, with mad passion, and with a hate intensified to an extreme degree, throw themselves into the fray in order to get back their lost paradise for themselves and their families, who formerly led such a pleasant life, and who are now condemned by the " rascals," the " mob," to ruin or penury (or " ordinary " labour). And these capitalist exploiters will necessarily be followed by a wide stream of the petty bourgeoisie, as to whom decades of historical experience of all countries bear witness that they are constantly oscillating and hesitating, to-day following the proletariat, and to-morrow taking fright at the difficulties of the revolution, succumbing with panic after the first defeat or semi-defeat of the workers, giving way to " nerves," whining, running hither and thither, deserting from one camp to another—just like our Mensheviks and Socialist revolutionaries !

And in face of this condition of things, at the time of a most desperate war, when history is placing on the order of the day the question of the life and death of age-long privileges—at this time to talk about majority and minority, about pure democracy, about the superfluity of the dictatorship, and equality between the exploiter and the exploited—what bottomless stupidity and philistinism are needed to do it ! But, of course, the decades of comparatively " peaceful " capitalism between 1871 and 1914 had accumulated in the opportunist-minded Socialist parties whole Augean stables of Philistinism, imbecility, and mockery.

The reader will have noticed that Kautsky, in the above-quoted passage from his pamphlet, speaks of an attempt against universal suffrage (extolling it, by the way, as a deep source of mighty moral authority, as against Engels who *à propos* of the same Commune and of the same question of dictatorship spoke of the authority of the armed people against the bourgeoisie—a very characteristic difference between the Philistine's and the revolutionist's view of " authority "). One may say in this connection that the question about the suppression of the franchise of the exploiter is *entirely a Russian question*, and not at all one of the dictatorship of the proletariat in general. If Kautsky, without hypocrisy, had entitled his pamphlet : " Against the Bolsheviks," the title would have corresponded to the contents of this pamphlet, and Kautsky would have been justified in speaking of the question of franchise. But Kautsky wanted to write as a " theoretician." He called his pamphlet *The Dictatorship of the Proletariat.* He speaks about the Soviets and about Russia in the second part of the pamphlet only, beginning with its fifth section. In its first part, from which I quoted, the subject matter is democracy and dictatorship in general. Kautsky, by raising the question of the franchise, has given himself away as a literary opponent of the Bolsheviks, who cares not a brass farthing for theory. For a theoretical discussion of the *general* (in contradiction to national and particular) class-basis of democracy and dictatorship ought to deal not with a *special* question, such as that of the franchise, but with the general question whether democracy can be preserved for the rich and the exploiters as well as for the exploited, at the historical moment of the overthrow of the former, and the substitution, in the place of *their* State, of the State of the exploited ? This is the only form in which the question can be put by a theoretical inquirer.

We all know the example of the Commune, we all know what the founders of Marxism said in connection with it. On the strength of their pronouncement I examined the question of democracy and dictatorship in my book, *The State and Revolution*, which I wrote before the November revolution. The restriction of the franchise was not touched by me at all. At present it might be added that the question of the restriction of the franchise is a specific national question, and not one relating to dictatorship in general. One must study the question of the restriction of the franchise in the light of the *specific* conditions of the *Russian* revolution and the specific course of its development. This will be done in subsequent pages. But it would be rash to guarantee in advance that the impending proletarian revolution in Europe will all, or for the most part, be accompanied by a restriction of the franchise in the case of the bourgeoisie. This may be so. In fact, after the war and after the experience of the Russian revolution it will propably be so. But it is not absolutely necessary for the establishment of a dictatorship. It is not necessarily implied in the idea of dictatorship, it does not enter as a necessary condition into the historical or class conception of dictatorship. What forms a necessary aspect, or a necessary condition of dictatorship, is the forcible suppression of the exploiters as a class, and consequently an infringement of " pure democracy," that is, of equality and freedom, *in respect of that class*.

In this way alone can the question be theoretically discussed ; and, by not doing so, Kautsky has proved that he came forward against the Bolsheviks not as a theoretical inquirer, but as a sycophant of the opportunists and of the bourgeoisie.

The question : In what countries and under what national peculiarities of this or that Capitalism a wholesale or partial restriction of democracy will be applied to the exploiters, is the question of just those national peculiarities of capitalism and of this or that revolution, and has nothing to do with the theoretical question at issue, which is this : Is a dictatorship of the proletariat possible without an infringement of democracy in respect of the class of exploiters ? Kautsky has evaded this, the only theoretically important, question. He has quoted all sorts of passages from Marx and Engels, except the one relating to the subject, and quoted by me. He talks about everything that may be pleasant to bourgeois Liberals and democrats and does not go beyond their system of ideas. As for the main thing, namely, that the proletariat cannot triumph without breaking the resistance of the bourgeoisie, without forcibly suppressing its enemies, and that where there is forcible suppression there is, of course, no " freedom," no democracy—this Kautsky did not understand. . . .

J. Stalin

FOUNDATIONS OF LENINISM

A lecture delivered in April 1924 ; published in a collection of Stalin's works, 1926. English edition, " Leninism," Allen & Unwin, Ltd., 1928. A better translation was published by the Co-operative Publishing Society of Foreign Workers in the U.S.S.R., 1935 ; the section given below is from this edition.

[This was a lecture delivered by Stalin at Sverdlov University, in April, 1924. In the introduction, Stalin defines Leninism as " the Marxism of the epoch of imperialism and of the proletarian revolution." The lecture covers the Historical Roots of Leninism ; Method ; Theory ; the Dictatorship of the Proletariat ; the Peasant Problem ; the National Question ; Strategy and Tactics ; the Party, and Style in the Work. It is the most important study of Leninism that exists, bringing out the development of Marxism made by Lenin " in a period of fully developed imperialism ; in a period when the proletarian revolution was already under way . . ." The section reprinted below, on The Party, shows the development of the revolutionary party of the proletariat under Lenin's guidance, and the part played by the Party both before and after the revolution.]

FOUNDATIONS OF LENINISM

THE PARTY

In the pre-revolutionary period, in the period of more or less peaceful development, when the parties of the Second International were the predominant force in the labour movement and parliamentary forms of struggle were regarded as the principal forms, the Party neither had nor could have that great and decisive importance which it acquired afterwards in the midst of open revolutionary battles. In defending the Second International against the attacks that were made upon it, Kautsky says that the parties of the Second International are instruments of peace and not of war, that for that very reason they were powerless to take any far-reaching steps during the war, during the period of revolutionary action by the proletariat. That is absolutely true. But what does it prove? It proves that the parties of the Second International are not suitable for the revolutionary struggle of the proletariat, that they are not militant parties of the proletariat leading the workers to power, but an election apparatus suitable for parliamentary elections and parliamentary struggle. This, properly speaking, explains why, in the days when the opportunists of the Second International were dominant, it was not the Party but the parliamentary fraction that was the fundamental political organisation of the proletariat. It is well known that the Party at that time was really an appendage or an auxiliary of the parliamentary fraction. It is superfluous to add that under such circumstances and with such a Party at its head, it was utterly impossible to prepare the proletariat for revolution.

With the dawn of the new period, however, matters

changed radically. The new period is a period of open collisions between the classes, a period of revolutionary action by the proletariat, a period of proletarian revolution ; it is the period of the immediate mustering of forces for the overthrow of imperialism, for the seizure of power by the proletariat. This period confronts the proletariat with new tasks of reorganising al! Party work on new, revolutionary lines ; of educating the workers in the spirit of the revolutionary struggle for power ; of preparing and moving up the reserves ; of establishing an alliance with the prolatarians of neighbouring countries ; of establishing durable contact with the liberation movement in the colonies and dependent countries, etc., etc. To imagine that these new tasks can be fulfilled by the old Social-Democratic parties, brought up as they were in the peaceful atmosphere of parliamentarism, can lead only to hopeless despair and to inevitable defeat. To have such tasks to shoulder under the leadership of the old parties is tantamount to being left completely disarmed. It goes without saying that the proletariat could not accept such a position.

Hence the necessity for a new party, a militant party, a revolutionary party, bold enough to lead the proletarians to the struggle for power, with sufficient experience to be able to orientate itself in the complicated problems that arise in a revolutionary situation, and sufficiently flexible to steer clear of any submerged rocks on the way to its goal.

Without such a party it is futile to think of overthrowing imperialism and achieving the dictatorship of the proletariat.

This new party is the party of Leninism.

What are the special features of this new party ?

(1) *The Party as the Vanguard of the Working Class*

The Party must first of all constitute the *vanguard* of the working class. The Party must absorb all the best elements of the working class, their experience, their revolutionary spirit and their unbounded devotion to the cause of the proletariat. But in order that it may really be the vanguard, the Party must be armed with a revolutionary theory, with a knowledge of the laws of the movement, with a knowledge of the laws of revolution. Without this it will be impotent to guide the struggle of the proletariat and to lead the proletariat. The Party cannot be a real Party if it limits itself to registering what the masses of the working class think or experience, if it drags along at the tail of the spontaneous movement, if it does not know how to overcome the inertness and the political indifference of the spontaneous movement, or if it cannot rise above the transient interests of the proletariat, if it cannot raise the masses to the level of the class interests of the proletariat. The Party must take its stand at the head of the working class, it must see ahead of the working class, lead the proletariat and not trail behind the spontaneous movement. The parties of the Second International which preach " tailism " are the exponents of bourgeois politics which condemn the proletariat to being a tool in the hands of the bourgeoisie. Only a party which adopts the point of view of the vanguard of the proletariat, which is capable of raising the masses to the level of the class interests of the proletariat, is capable of diverting the working class from the path of craft unionism and converting it into an independent political force. The Party is the political leader of the working class.

I have spoken above of the difficulties encountered in the struggle of the working class, of the complicated nature of this struggle, of strategy and tactics, of reserves and manœuvring operations, of attack and defence. These conditions are no less complicated, perhaps more so, than war operations. Who can understand these conditions, who can give correct guidance to the vast masses of the proletariat ? Every army at war must have an experienced General Staff if it is to avoid certain defeat. All the more reason therefore why the proletariat must have such a

General Staff if it is to prevent itself from being routed by its mortal enemies. But where is this General Staff? Only the revolutionary party of the proletariat can serve as this General Staff. A working class without a revolutionary party is like an army without a General Staff. The Party is the Military Staff of the proletariat.

But the Party cannot be merely a *vanguard*. It must at the same time be a unit of the *class*, be part of that class, intimately bound to it with every fibre of its being. The distinction between the vanguard and the main body of the working class, between Party members and non-Party workers, will continue as long as classes exist, as long as the proletariat continues replenishing its ranks with newcomers from other classes, as long as the working class as a whole lacks the opportunity of raising itself to the level of the vanguard. But the Party would cease to be a party if this distinction were widened into a rupture : if it were to isolate itself and break away from the non-Party masses. The Party cannot lead the class if it is not connected with the non-Party masses, if there is no close union between the Party and the non-Party masses, if these masses do not accept its leadership, if the Party does not enjoy moral and political authority among the masses. Recently, two hundred thousand new workers joined our Party. The remarkable thing about this is that these workers did not *come* into the Party, but were rather *sent* there by the mass of other non-Party workers who took an active part in the acceptance of the new members and without whose approval no new member was accepted. This fact proves that the broad masses of non-Party workers regard our Party as *their* Party, as a Party near *and dear* to them, in the expansion and consolidation of which they are vitally interested and to whose leadership they willingly entrust their destinies. It goes without saying that without these intangible moral ties connecting the Party with the non-Party masses, the Party could never become the decisive force of its class. The Party is an inseparable part of the working class.

We are the party of a class—says Lenin—and therefore *almost the entire class* (and in times of war, during the period of civil war, the entire class) must act under the leadership of our Party, must link itself up with our Party as closely as possible. But we would be guilty of Manilovism and "khvostism" if we believed that at any time under capitalism nearly the whole class, or the whole class, would be able to rise to the level of the class consciousness and degree of activity of its vanguard, of its socialist party. No sensible Socialist has ever yet doubted that under capitalism even the trade union organisations (which are more primitive and more accesible to the intelligence of the undeveloped strata) are unable to embrace nearly the whole, or the whole, working class. To forget the distinction between the vanguard and the whole of the masses gravitating towards it, to forget the constant duty of the vanguard to *raise* these increasingly widening strata to this advanced level, only means deceiving oneself, shutting one's eyes to the immensity of our tasks and narrowing them. (*Collected Works*, Russian edition, Vol. VI, pp. 205–206.)

(2) *The Party as the Organised Detachment of the Working Class*

The Party is not only the *vanguard* of the working class. If it desires really to lead the struggle of the class it must at the same time be the *organised* detachment of its class. Under the capitalist system the Party's tasks are huge and varied. The Party must lead the struggle of the proletariat under the exceptionally difficult circumstances of inner as well as outer development ; it must lead the proletariat in its attack when the situation calls for an attack, it must withdraw the proletariat from the blows of a powerful opponent when the situation calls for retreat ; it must imbue the millions of unorganised non-Party workers with the spirit of discipline and system in fighting, with the spirit of organisation and perseverance. But the Party can acquit itself of these tasks only if it itself is the embodiment of discipline and organisation, if it itself is the *organised* detachment of the proletariat. Unless these conditions are fulfilled it is idle to talk about the Party really leading the vast masses of the proletariat. The Party is the organised detachment of the working class.

The conception of the Party as an organised whole has become firmly fixed in Lenin's well-known formulation of the first point of our Party rules in which the Party is regarded as the *sum total* of the organisations and the Party member as a member of one of the organisations of the Party. The Mensheviks, who had objected to this formulation as early as 1903, proposed to substitute for it a " system " of self-enrolment in the Party, a " system " of conferring the " title " Party member upon every "professor" and " high school student," upon every " sympathiser " and " striker " who gave support to the Party in one way or another, but who did not belong and had no inclination to belong to any one of the Party organisations. We need not stop to prove that had this odd " system " become firmly entrenched in our Party it would have been inundated with professors and students, it would have degenerated into a widely diffused, amorphous, disorganised " body " lost in a sea of " sympathisers," that would have obliterated the line of demarcation between the Party and the class and would have frustrated the aim of the Party to raise the unorganised masses to the level of the vanguard. It goes without saying that under such an opportunist " system " our Party would not have been able to accomplish its mission as the organising nucleus of the working class during the course of our revolution.

> From Martov's point of view—says Lenin—the boundary line of the Party remains absolutely unfixed inasmuch as " every striker could declare himself a member of the Party." What advantage is there in this diffuseness? Spreading wide a " title." The harmfulness of it lies in that it introduces the *disruptive* idea of identifying the class with the Party. (*Collected Works*, Russian edition, Vol. VI, p. 211.)

But the Party is not merely the *sum total* of Party organisations. The Party at the same time represents a single system of these organisations, their formal unification into a single whole, possessing higher and lower organs of leadership, with submission of the minority to the majority, where decisions on questions of practice are obligatory upon all members of the Party. Unless these conditions are fulfilled the Party is unable to form a single organised whole capable of exercising systematic and organised leadership of the struggle of the working class.

> *Formerly*—says Lenin—our Party was not a formally organised whole, but only the sum total of separate groups. Therefore, no other relations except that of ideological influence were possible between these groups. *Now*, we have become an organised Party, and this implies the creation of a power, the conversion of the authority of ideas into the authority of power, the subordination of the lower Party bodies to the higher Party bodies. (*Ibid.*, p. 291.)

The principle of the minority submitting to the majority, the principle of leading Party work from a centre, has been a subject of repeated attacks by wavering elements who accuse us of " bureaucracy," " formalism," etc. It hardly needs to be proved that systematic work of the Party, as one whole, and the leadership of the struggle of the working class would have been impossible without the enforcement of these principles. On the organisational question, Leninism stands for the strict enforcement of these principles. Lenin terms the fight against these principles " Russian nihilism " and " gentleman's anarchism " which deserve only to be ridiculed and thrown aside.

This is what Lenin has to say about these wavering elements in his book entitled *One Step Forward, Two Steps Backward* :

> The Russian nihilist is especially addicted to this gentleman's anarchism. To him the Party organisation appears to be a monstrous " factory," the subordination of the part to the whole and the submission of the minority to the majority appears to him to be " serfdom " . . . the division of labour under the

leadership of a centre evolves tragi-comical lamentations about people being reduced to mere " cogs and screws " . . . the bare mention of the Party rules on organisation calls forth a contemptuous grimace and some disdainful . . . remark to the effect that we could get along without rules. . . . It seems clear, however, that these outcries against the alleged bureaucracy are an attempt to conceal the dissatisfaction with the personnel of these centres, a fig leaf. . . . " You are a bureaucrat because you were appointed by the Congress without my consent and against my wishes : you are a formalist because you seek support in the formal decisions of the Congress and not in my approval : you act in a crudely mechanical way, because your authority is the ' mechanical ' majority of the Party Congress and you do not consult my desire to be co-opted ; you are an autocrat because you do not want to deliver power into the hands of the old gang."[1] (*Collected Works*, Russian edition, Vol. VI, pp. 310 and 287.)

(3) *The Party as the Highest Form of Class Organisation of the Proletariat*

The Party is the organised detachment of the working class. But the Party is not the only organisation of the working class. The proletariat has in addition a great number of other organisations which are indispensable in its correct struggle against the capitalist system—trade unions, co-operative societies, factory and shop organisations, parliamentary fractions, non-Party women's associations, the press, cultural and educational organisations, youth leagues, military revolutionary organisations (in times of direct revolutionary action), soviets of deputies as the State form of organisation (where the proletariat is in power), etc. Most of these organisations are non-Party and only a certain part of these adhere directly to the Party, or represent its offshoots. All these organisations, under certain conditions, are absolutely necessary for the working class, as without them it is impossible to consolidate the

[1] The " old gang " here referred to is that of Axelrod, Martov, Potresov and others who would not submit to the decisions of the Second Congress and who accused Lenin of being a " bureaucrat."—J. S.

class position of the proletariat in the diversified spheres of struggle, and without them it is impossible to steel the proletariat as the force whose mission it is to replace the bourgeois order by the socialist order. But how can unity of leadership become a reality in the face of such a multiplicity of organisations ? What guarantee is there that this multiplicity of organisations will not lead to discord in leadership ? It might be argued that each of these organisations carries on its work in its own field in which it specialises and cannot, therefore, interfere with the others. That, of course, is true. But it is likewise true that the activities of all these organisations ought to be directed into a single channel, as they serve *one* class, the class of the proletariat. The question then arises : who is to determine the line, the general direction along which the work of all these organisations is to be conducted ? Where is that central organisation which is not only able, having the necessary experience, to work out such a general line, but also capable, because of its authority, of prevailing upon all these organisations to carry out this line, in order to attain unity of direction and preclude the possibility of working at cross purposes ?

This organisation is the party of the proletariat.

The Party possesses all the necessary qualifications for this purpose because, in the first place, it is the common meeting ground of the best elements in the working class that have direct connections with the non-Party organisations of the proletariat and very frequently lead them ; because, secondly, the Party, as the meeting ground of the best members of the working class, is the best school for training leaders of the working class, capable of directing every form of organisation of their class ; because, thirdly, the Party, as the best school for training leaders of the working class, is, by reason of its experience and authority, the only organisation capable of centralising the leadership of the struggle of the proletariat and in this way of transforming each and every non-Party organisation of the working class into an auxiliary body, a transmission belt linking it with the class. The Party is the highest form of class organisation of the proletariat.

This does not mean, of course, that non-Party organisations like trade unions, co-operative societies, etc., must be formally subordinated to Party leadership. It means simply that the members of the Party who belong to these organisations and doubtless exercise influence in them should do all they can to persuade these non-Party organisations to draw nearer to the Party of the proletariat in their work and voluntarily accept its political guidance.

That is why Lenin says that " the Party is the *highest* form of class association of proletarians " whose political leadership ought to extend to every other form of organisation of the proletariat. (" *Left-Wing* " *Communism, etc.,* Chap. VI.)

That is why the opportunist theory of the " independence " and " neutrality " of the non-Party organisations, which theory is the progenitor of *independent* parliamentarians and publicists who are *isolated* from the Party, and of *narrow-minded* trade unionists and co-operative society officials who have become petty bourgeois, is wholly incompatible with the theory and practice of Leninism.

(4) *The Party as the Weapon of the Dictatorship of the Proletariat*

The Party is the highest form of organisation of the proletariat. The Party is the fundamental leading element within the class of the proletariat and within the organisations of that class. But it does not follow by any means that the Party can be regarded as an end in itself, as a self-sufficing force. The Party is not only the highest form of class association of the proletarians ; it is at the same time a *weapon* in the hands of the proletariat *for* the achievement of the dictatorship where that has not yet been achieved ; *for* the consolidation and extension of the dictatorship

where it has already been achieved. The Party would not
rank so high in importance and it could not overshadow all
other forms of organisation of the proletariat if the latter
were not face to face with the question of power, if the
conditions of imperialism, the inevitability of wars and the
presence of a crisis did not demand the concentration of
all the forces of the proletariat on one point and the
gathering together of all the threads of the revolutionary
movement in one spot, to overthrow the bourgeoisie and
to establish the dictatorship of the proletariat. The proletariat needs the Party first of all as its General Staff, which
it must have for the successful seizure of power. Needless to
say, the Russian proletariat could never have established
its revolutionary dictatorship without a Party capable of
rallying around itself the mass organisations of the prola-
tariat and of centralising the leadership of the entire movement during the progress of the struggle.

But the proletariat needs the Party not only to achieve
the dictatorship, it needs it still more to maintain, consolidate and extend its dictatorship in order to attain complete victory for socialism.

> Certainly almost everyone now realises—says Lenin—that
> the Bolsheviks could not have maintained themselves in power
> for two and a half years, and not even for two and a half months,
> without the strictest discipline, the truly iron discipline, in our
> Party, and without the fullest and unreserved support rendered
> it by the whole mass of the working class, that is, by all those
> belonging to this class who think, who are honest, self-sacrific-
> ing, influential, and capable of leading and attracting the back-
> ward masses. (" Left-Wing " Communism, etc., Chap. II.)

Now what is meant by " maintaining " and " extending "
the dictatorship? It means imbuing these millions of proletarians with the spirit of discipline and organisation : it means
creating among the proletarian masses a bulwark against
the corrosive influences of petty-bourgeois spontaneity and
petty-bourgeois habits ; it means that the organising work
of the proletarians in re-educating and remoulding the

petty-bourgeois strata must be reinforced ; it means that assistance must be given to the masses of the proletarians in educating themselves so that they may become a force capable of abolishing classes and of preparing the ground for the organisation of socialist production. But it is impossible to accomplish all this without a Party, which is strong by reason of its cohesion and discipline.

The dictatorship of the proletariat—says Lenin—is a persistent struggle—sanguinary and bloodless, violent and peaceful, military and economic, educational and administrative—against the forces and traditions of the old society. The force of habit of millions and of tens of millions is a terrible force. Without an iron party steeled in the struggle, without a party enjoying the confidence of all that is honest in the given class, without a party capable of keeping track of and influencing the mood of the masses, it is impossible to conduct such a struggle successfully. (" Left-Wing " Communism, etc., Chap. V.)

The proletariat needs the Party for the purpose of achieving and maintaining the dictatorship. The Party is the instrument of the dictatorship of the proletariat.

From this it follows that when classes disappear and the dictatorship of the proletariat dies out, the Party will also die out.

(5) The Party as the Expression of Unity of Will, Which is Incompatible With the Existence of Factions

The achievement and maintenance of the dictatorship of the proletariat are impossible without a party strong in its cohesion and iron discipline. But iron discipline in the Party is impossible without unity of will and without absolute and complete unity of action on the part of all members of the Party. This does not mean, of course, that the possibility of a conflict of opinion within the Party is thus excluded. On the contrary, iron discipline does not preclude but presupposes criticism and conflicts of opinion within the Party. Least of all does it mean that this discipline must be " blind " discipline. On the contrary, iron discipline does not preclude but presupposes conscious and voluntary submission, for only conscious discipline can be truly iron discipline. But after a discussion has been closed, after criticism has run its course and a decision has been made, unity of will and unity of action of all Party members become indispensable conditions without which Party unity and iron discipline in the Party are inconceivable.

> In the present epoch of intensified civil war—says Lenin—the Communist Party can discharge its duty only if it is organised with the highest degree of centralisation, ruled by iron discipline bordering on military discipline, and if its Party centre proves to be a potent authoritative body invested with broad powers and enjoying the general confidence of the Party members. (*Conditions of Affiliation to the Communist International.*)

This is the position in regard to discipline in the Party in the period of struggle preceding the establishment of the dictatorship.

The same thing applies, but to a greater degree, to discipline in the Party after the establishment of the dictatorship.

In this connection, Lenin said :

> Whoever in the least weakens the iron discipline of the party of the proletariat (especially during its dictatorship) actually aids the bourgeoisie against the proletariat. ("*Left-Wing*" *Communism, etc.,* Chap. V.)

It follows that the existence of factions is incompatible with Party unity and with its iron discipline. It need hardly be emphasised that the existence of factions leads to the creation of a number of centres, and the existence of a number of centres connotes the absence of a common centre in the Party, a breach in the unity of will, the weakening and disintegration of discipline, the weakening and disintegration of the dictatorship. It is true that the parties of the Second International, which are fighting against the dictatorship of the proletariat and have no desire to lead the proletariat to power can permit themselves the luxury of such liberalism as freedom for factions, for they have no need whatever of iron discipline. But the parties of the

Communist International, which organise their activities on the basis of the task of achieving and strengthening the dictatorship of the proletariat, cannot afford to be "liberal" or to permit the formation of factions. The Party is synonymous with unity of will, which leaves no room for any factionalism or division of authority in the Party.

Hence Lenin's warning on the " danger of factionalism from the point of view of Party unity and of the realisation of unity of will in the vanguard of the proletariat as the primary prerequisite for the success of the dictatorship of the proletariat," which is embodied in a special resolution of the Tenth Congress of our Party, *On Party Unity.*

Hence Lenin's demand for the " complete extermination of all factionalism " and the " immediate dissolution of all groups, without exception, that had been formed on the basis of this or that platform " on pain of " unconditional and immediate expulsion from the Party." (*Cf.* the resolution, *On Party Unity.*)

(6) *The Party Is Strengthened by Purging Itself of Opportunist Elements*

The opportunist elements in the Party are the source of Party factionalism. The proletariat is not an isolated class. A steady stream of peasants, small tradesmen and intellectuals, who have become proletarianised by the development of capitalism, flows into the ranks of the proletariat. At the same time the upper strata of the proletariat— principally the trade union leaders and labour members of parliament—who have been fed by the bourgeoisie out of the super-profits extracted from the colonies, are undergoing a process of decay.

> This stratum of the labour aristocracy or of workers who have become bourgeois—says Lenin—who have become quite pettybourgeois in their mode of life, in their earnings, and in their outlook, serve as the principal bulwark of the Second International, and, in our days, the principal *social* (not military)

support of the bourgeoisie. They are the real *agents of the bourgeoisie in the labour movement,* the labour lieutenants of the capitalist class, channels of reformism and chauvinism. (*Imperialism,* Preface to the French and German editions.)

All these petty-bourgeois groups somehow or other penetrate into the Party into which they introduce an element of hesitancy and opportunism, of disintegration and lack of self-confidence. Factionalism and splits, disorganisation and the undermining of the Party from within are principally due to them. Fighting imperialism with such " allies " in one's rear is as bad as being caught between two fires, coming both from the front and rear. Therefore, no quarter should be given in fighting such elements, and their relentless expulsion from the Party is a condition precedent for the successful struggle against imperialism.

The theory of " overcoming " opportunist elements by ideological struggle within the Party ; the theory of " living down " these elements within the confines of a single Party are rotten and dangerous theories that threaten to reduce the Party to paralysis and chronic infirmity, that threaten to abandon the Party to opportunism, that threaten to leave the proletariat without a revolutionary party, that threaten to deprive the proletariat of its main weapon in the fight against imperialism. Our Party could not have come out on to the high road, it could not have seized power and organised the dictatorship of the proletariat, it could not have emerged victorious from the civil war, if it had had within its ranks people like Martov and Dan, Potresov and Axelrod. Our Party succeeded in creating true unity and greater cohesion in its ranks than ever before, mainly because it undertook in time to purge itself of opportunist pollution and expelled the liquidators and Mensheviks from its ranks. The proletarian parties develop and become strong by purging themselves of opportunists and reformists, social-imperialists and social-chauvinists, social-patriots and social-pacifists. The Party becomes strong by ridding itself of opportunist elements.

With reformists and Mensheviks in our ranks—says Lenin—*we cannot* be victorious in the proletarian revolution *nor can* we defend it against attack. This is clearly so in principle. It is strikingly confirmed by the experiences of Russia and Hungary. . . . Russia found itself in a tight corner *many* a time, when the Soviet régime would certainly have been overthrown had the Mensheviks, reformists or petty-bourgeois democrats remained within our Party. . . . It is generally admitted that in Italy events are heading towards decisive battles of the proletariat with the bourgeoisie for the capture of State power. At such a time not only does the removal of the Mensheviks, reformists and Turatists from the Party become absolutely necessary, but it may even prove useful to remove certain excellent Communists who might and who do waver in the direction of desiring to maintain " unity " with the reformists—to remove these from all responsible positions. . . . On the eve of the revolution and in the midst of the desperate struggle for victory, the slightest hesitancy within the Party is apt to *ruin* everything, to disrupt the revolution and to snatch the power out of the hands of the proletariat, since that power is as yet insecure and the attacks upon it are still too violent. The retirement of wavering leaders at such a time does not weaken but strengthens the Party, the labour movement and the revolution. (*Collected Works*, Russian edition, Vol. XXV, pp. 462–4.)

V. I. Lenin

" LEFT-WING " COMMUNISM : AN INFANTILE DISORDER

First published, June 1920. English edition, Martin Lawrence, Ltd., 1934.

[After the end of the world war and the formation of the Third International, Lenin was continually discussing with representatives of revolutionary groups in other countries the practical problems of Marxist strategy and tactics in their own countries. He found particularly strong tendencies of an ultra-left character, as well as a general misunderstanding of the international significance of the Russian revolution and the strategy and tactics of the Bolshevik Party. Before the Second Congress of the Third International (August 1920) he wrote this book as a general guide to the revolutionary movements outside Russia. It was of great importance in helping the consolidation of the sections of the Third International on a Marxist basis. The passages reprinted here deal with the need for a revolutionary Party, work in the Trade Unions, the use of Parliament, and the general conditions for a successful revolution.]

"LEFT-WING" COMMUNISM: AN INFANTILE DISORDER

IN WHAT SENSE CAN WE SPEAK OF THE INTERNATIONAL SIGNIFICANCE OF THE RUSSIAN REVOLUTION?

(Ch. I)

DURING the first months after the conquest of political power by the proletariat in Russia (November 7, [October 25] 1917) it might have appeared that the tremendous difference between backward Russia and the advanced countries of western Europe will cause the proletarian revolution in these latter countries to have very little resemblance to ours. Now we already have very considerable international experience which very definitely establishes the fact that some of the fundamental features of our revolution have a significance which is not local, not peculiarly national, not Russian only, but international. I speak here of international significance not in the broad sense of the term : Not some but all fundamental and many secondary features of our revolution are of international significance in the sense of the influence it has upon all countries. I speak of it in the narrower sense, i.e., by international significance I mean the international significance or the historical inevitability of a repetition on an international scale of what has taken place here, and it must be admitted that some of the fundamental features of our revolution possess such international significance.

Of course, it would be a very great mistake to exaggerate this truth and to apply it to more than some of the fundamental features of our revolution. It would also be a mistake to lose sight of the fact that, after the victory of the proletarian revolution in at least one of the advanced countries, things will, in all probability, take a sharp turn, viz., Russia will cease to be the model country and once again become a backward (in the "Soviet" and in the socialist sense) country.

But at the present historical moment the situation is precisely that the Russian model reveals to *all* countries something that is very essential in their near and inevitable future. The advanced workers in every land have long understood this, although in most cases they did not so much understand it as grasp it, sense it, by their revolutionary class instinct. Herein lies the international " significance " (in the narrow sense of the term) of the Soviet power as well as of the fundamentals of Bolshevik theory and tactics. . . .

SHOULD REVOLUTIONARIES WORK IN REACTIONARY
TRADE UNIONS?

(Ch. VI)

. . . Capitalism inevitably leaves to Socialism a heritage of old trade and craft distinctions among the workers created in the course of centuries, and trade unions which only very slowly and in the course of years can and will develop into broader, industrial unions having much less of the craft union about them (embracing whole industries, not merely crafts and trades). Later these industrial unions will, in their turn, lead to the abolition of division of labour among people, to the education, training and preparation of people who will have an *all-round* development, an *all-round* training, people who *will be able to do everything*. Towards this goal communism is marching, and must march, and it must reach it—but only after very many years. To attempt in practice to-day to anticipate this future result of a fully developed, fully stabilised and formed, fully expanded and mature communism would be like trying to teach higher mathematics to a four-year-old child.

We can (and must) begin to build up socialism not with the fantastic human material especially created by our imagination but with the material bequeathed us by capitalism. This, no doubt, is very " difficult," but any other approach to this task is not serious enough to deserve discussion.

Trade unions represented a gigantic step forward for the working class at the beginning of the development of capitalism, as the transition from the disintegration and helplessness of the workers to the *rudiments* of a class organisation. When the *highest* form of proletarian class organisation began to arise, viz., the *revolutionary Party of the proletariat* (which does not deserve the name until it learns to bind the leaders with the class and with the masses into one single indissoluble whole), the trade unions inevitably began to reveal *certain* reactionary traits, a certain craft narrowness, a certain tendency towards becoming non-political, a certain inertness, etc. But the development of the proletariat did not and could not, anywhere in the world, proceed otherwise than through the trade unions, through their inter-action with the Party of the working class. The conquest of political power by the proletariat is a gigantic step forward for the proletariat as a class, and the Party must more and more than ever, and in a new way, not merely in the old way, educate and guide the trade unions ; at the same time it must not forget that they are, and will long remain, a necessary " school of communism," a preparatory school for training the proletariat to exercise its dictatorship, an indispensable organisation of the workers for gradually transferring the management of the whole economy of the country to the hands of the working *class* (and not of the separate trades) and later to the hands of all the toiling masses.

A *certain* " reactionism " in the trade unions, in the sense mentioned, is *inevitable* under the dictatorship of the proletariat. Not to understand this means to fail completely to understand the fundamental conditions of the *transition* from capitalism to socialism. To fear *this* " reactionism," to try to *avoid* it or skip it, is the greatest folly, for it means fearing to assume the rôle of proletarian vanguard which implies training, educating, enlightening and attracting into the new life the most backward strata and masses of the working class and the peasantry. On the other hand, to postpone the realisation of the dictatorship of the proletariat until such time as not a single worker with narrow craft interests, not a single worker with guild and trade union prejudices is left, would be a still greater mistake. The art of statesmanship (and the correct understanding by a Communist of his tasks) lies in correctly gauging the conditions and the moment when the vanguard of the proletariat can successfully seize power, when it will be able during and after this seizure of power to obtain adequate support from sufficiently broad strata of the working class and of the non-proletarian toiling masses, and when, thereafter, it will be able to maintain, consolidate and extend its rule, educating, training and attracting ever broader masses of the toilers.

Further : in countries more advanced than Russia a certain reactionism in the trade unions has been revealed, and was unquestionably bound to be revealed, much more strongly than in our country. Our Mensheviks found (and in a very few trade unions still find some) support in trade unions precisely because of their craft narrowness, craft egoism, and opportunism. In the West the Mensheviks have acquired a much firmer " footing " in the trade unions. There the *trade union* " labour aristocracy " constitutes a much thicker stratum of *narrow-minded, selfish, hard-hearted, covetous, petty-bourgeois elements—imperialistically-minded, bribed and corrupted by imperialism.* This is incontestable. The struggle against the Gomperses and Hendersons, against Jouhaux, Merrheim, Legien and Co. in western Europe, is much more difficult than the struggle against our Mensheviks, who represent an *absolutely similar* social and political type. This struggle must be waged ruthlessly to the very end, as we waged it, until all the incorrigible leaders of opportunism and social-chauvinism have been completely discredited and expelled from the trade unions. It is impossible to capture political power (and the attempt to capture it should not be made) until this struggle has reached a *certain* stage. Moreover, in different countries and under different circumstances this " certain stage " will not be the same ; it can be correctly gauged only by thoughtful, experienced, and well-informed political leaders of the proletariat in each separate country. (In Russia, the measure of success in the struggle was gauged by the elections to the Constituent Assembly in November 1917, a few days after the proletarian revolution of November 7, 1917. In these elections the Mensheviks were utterly defeated ; they obtained 700,000 votes—1,400,000, if the vote of Transcaucasia be added—as against 9,000,000 votes obtained by the Bolsheviks. See my article, " Elections to the Constituent Assembly and the Dictatorship of the Proletariat," No. 7–8 of the *Communist International*.)

But we wage the struggle against the " labour aristocracy " in the name of the working masses and in order to attract the latter to our side ; we wage the struggle against the opportunist and social-chauvinist leaders in order to attract the working class to our side. To forget this most elementary and self-evident truth would be stupid. But the German " Left " Communists are guilty of just this stupidity when, because of the reactionary and counter-revolutionary character of the *heads* of the trade unions, they jump to the conclusion that it is necessary to leave the trade unions, to refuse to work in them, to create new, *fantastic* forms of labour organisations ! ! This is an unpardonable blunder that would equal the greatest service the Communists could render the bourgeoisie. Our Mensheviks, like all opportunist, social-chauvinist, Kautskyist trade union leaders, are nothing more nor less than " agents of the bourgeoisie in the labour movement " (as we have always characterised the Mensheviks) or " labour lieutenants of the capitalist class " (to use the excellent and profoundly true expression of the followers of Daniel De Leon in America). To refuse to work in the reactionary trade unions means leaving the insufficiently developed or backward working masses under the influence of reactionary leaders, agents of the bourgeoisie, labour aristocrats, or " bourgeoisified workers." (See Engels's letter to Marx in 1852 concerning the British workers.)

It is just this absurd " theory " that Communists must not belong to reactionary trade unions that demonstrates most clearly how frivolously these " Left " Communists regard the question of influence over " the masses," how they misuse their outcries about " the masses." In order to be able to help " the masses " and to win the sympathy, confidence, and support of " the masses," it is necessary to brave all difficulties and to be unafraid of the pinpricks, obstacles, insults, and persecution of the " leaders " (who, being opportunists and social-chauvinists, are, in most cases, directly or indirectly connected with the bourgeoisie and the police), and it is imperatively necessary to *work wherever the masses are to be found.* Every sacrifice must be made, the greatest obstacles must be overcome, in order to carry on agitation and propaganda systematically, stubbornly, insistently, and patiently, precisely in all those institutions, societies, and associations to which proletarian or semi-proletarian masses belong, however ultra-reactionary they may be. And the trade unions and workers' co-operatives (the latter, at least sometimes), are precisely the organisations in which the masses are to be found. In England, according to figures quoted in the Swedish paper, *Folkets Dagblad Politiken* of March 10, 1919, the membership of the trade unions increased from 5,500,000 at the end of 1917 to 6,600,000 at the end of 1918, i.e., an increase of 19 per cent. At the end of 1919 the membership was 7,500,000. I have not at hand the corresponding figures for France and Germany, but the facts testifying to the rapid growth in membership of the trade unions in these countries as well are absolutely incontestable and generally known.

These facts very clearly indicate what is confirmed by thousands of other symptoms : the growth of class consciousness and of the desire for organisation precisely among the proletarian masses, among the " rank and file," among the backward elements. Millions of workers in England, France, and Germany are *for the first time* passing from complete lack of organisation to the lowest, most elementary, most simple, and (for those still thoroughly imbued with bourgeois-democratic prejudices) most easily accessible form of organisation, namely, the trade unions. And the revolutionary but foolish Left Communists stand by, shouting, " the masses, the masses ! "—and *refuse to work within the trade unions*, refuse on the pretext that they are " reactionary," and invent a brand-new, pure " Workers' Union," guiltless of bourgeois-democratic prejudices, innocent of craft or narrow trade sins ! ! and which they claim, will be (will be !) a wide organisation, and the only (only !) condition of membership of which will be " recognition of the Soviet system and the dictatorship ! ! " (See the citation above.)

Greater stupidity, and greater damage to the revolution than that caused by the " Left " revolutionaries cannot be imagined ! If, in Russia to-day, after two and a half years of unprecedented victories over the bourgeoisie of Russia and the Entente, we were to make the " recognition of the dictatorship " a condition of membership in the trade unions, we should be doing a stupid thing, we should damage our influence over the masses, we should be helping the Mensheviks. For the whole task of the Communists is to be able to *convince* the backward elements, to be able to work *among* them, and not to *fence themselves off* from them by artificial and childishly " Left-wing " slogans.

There can be no doubt that Messieurs the Gomperses, Hendersons, Jouhaux, Legiens, and the like, are very grateful to such " Left " revolutionaries, who, like the German opposition " on principle " (heaven preserve us from such " principles ! ") or like some revolutionaries in the American Industrial Workers of the World, advocate leaving the reactionary trade unions and refusing to work in them. Undoubtedly, Messieurs the " leaders " of opportunism will resort to every trick of bourgeois diplomacy, to the aid of bourgeois governments, the priests, the police, and the courts, in order to prevent Communists from getting into the trade unions, to force them out by every means, to make their work in the trade unions as unpleasant as possible, to insult, to hound, and persecute them. It is necessary to be able to withstand all this, to agree to any and every sacrifice, and even—if need be—to resort to all sorts of devices, manœuvres, and illegal methods, to evasion and subterfuge, in order to penetrate into the trade unions, to remain in them, and to carry on Communist work in them at all costs. Under Tsarism, until 1905, we had no " legal possibilities," but when Zubatov, the secret service agent, organised Black Hundred workers' meetings and workmen's societies for the purpose of trapping revolutionaries and combating them, we sent members of our Party to these meetings and into these societies. (I personally remember one such comrade, Babushkin, a prominent St. Petersburg workman, who was shot by the Tsar's generals in 1906.) They established contacts with the masses, managed to carry on their propaganda, and succeeded in wresting the workers from the influence of Zubatov's

agents. Of course, in western Europe, which is particularly
saturated with inveterate legalist, constitutionalist, bourgeois-democratic prejudices, it is more difficult to carry on
such work. But it can and must be carried on and carried
on systematically.

The Executive Committee of the Third International
must, in my opinion, directly condemn, and should call
upon the next Congress of the Communist International
to condemn, the policy of refusing to join reactionary trade
unions in general (stating in detail why this refusal to join
is unreasonable and pointing out the extreme harm it does
to the cause of the proletarian revolution) and, in particular,
the line of conduct of the Dutch Tribunists, who, either
directly or indirectly, openly or covertly, wholly or parti-
ally, supported this erroneous policy. The Third International must break with the tactics of the Second International and not evade or cover up sore points, but raise
them bluntly. The whole truth has been put squarely to the
" Independents " (Independent Social-Democratic Party
of Germany) ; the whole truth must likewise be told to the
" Left " Communists.

SHOULD WE PARTICIPATE IN BOURGEOIS PARLIAMENTS?
(Ch. VII)

. . . The surest way of discrediting a new political (and
not only political) idea, and to damage it, is to reduce
it to an absurdity while ostensibly defending it. For every
truth, if carried to " excess " (as Dietzgen Senior said), if
it is exaggerated, if it is carried beyond the limits within
which it can be actually applied, can be reduced to absurdity, and, under the conditions mentioned, is even inevitably
converted into an absurdity. This is just the kind of back-
handed service the Dutch and German Lefts are rendering
the new truth about the superiority of the Soviet form of
government over bourgeois-democratic parliaments. Of

course, any one who would say in the old way and in general that refusal to participate in bourgeois parliaments is under no circumstances permissible would be wrong. I cannot attempt to formulate here the conditions under which a boycott is useful, for the task of this treatise is far more modest, namely, to study Russian experience in connection with certain topical questions of international Communist tactics. Russian experience has given us one successful and correct (1905) and one incorrect (1906) example of the application of the boycott by the Bolsheviks. Analysing the first case, we see that we succeeded in *preventing the convocation* of a reactionary parliament by a reactionary government in a situation in which extra-parliamentary, revolutionary mass action (strikes in particular) was growing with exceptional rapidity, when not a single stratum of the proletariat or of the peasantry could support the reactionary government, when the revolutionary proletariat was acquiring influence over the broad, backward masses by means of the strike struggle and the agrarian movement. It is quite obvious that *this* experience is not applicable to present-day European conditions. It is also quite obvious, on the strength of the foregoing arguments, that even a conditional defence of the refusal to participate in parliaments by the Dutch and other " Lefts," is fundamentally wrong and harmful to the cause of the revolutionary proletariat.

In western Europe and America parliament has become an object of special hatred to the advanced revolutionaries of the working class. This is incontestable and quite comprehensible, for it is difficult to imagine anything more base, abominable and treacherous than the behaviour of the overwhelming majority of Socialist and Social-Democratic deputies in parliament during and after the war. But it would be not only unreasonable but actually criminal to yield to this mood when deciding the question of *how* to fight against this generally recognised evil. In many countries of western Europe the revolutionary mood is at

DDM

present, we might say, a " novelty," a " rarity," for which
we have been vainly and impatiently waiting for a long
time, and perhaps that is why we so easily give way to
moods. Of course, without a revolutionary mood among
the masses, and without conditions favouring the growth
of this mood, revolutionary tactics will never be converted
into action ; but we in Russia have been convinced by long,
painful and bloody experience of the truth that revolutionary tactics cannot be built up on revolutionary moods
alone. Tactics must be based on a sober and strictly objective estimation of *all* the class forces in a given State (in
neighbouring states and in all states, i.e., on a world scale),
as well as on an evaluation of the experience of revolutionary movements. To express one's " revolutionism " solely
by hurling abuse at parliamentary opportunism, solely
by refusing to participate in parliaments, is very easy ;
but, just because it is too easy, it is not the solution of a
difficult, a very difficult problem. It is much more difficult
to create a really revolutionary parliamentary fraction in a
European parliament than it was in Russia. Of course. But
this is only a particular expression of the general truth that
it was easy for Russia, in the concrete, historically exceed-
ingly unique, situation of 1917, *to start* a Socialist revolution,
but that it will be more difficult for Russia to *continue*
and bring it to its consummation than for the European
countries. Even in the beginning of 1918 I had occasion to
point this out, and our experience of the last two years has
entirely confirmed the correctness of this argument. Certain
specific conditions existed in Russia which do not at present
exist in western Europe, and a repetition of these or similar
conditions is not very probable. These specific conditions
were : (1) the possibility of linking up the Soviet Revolution
with the ending (as a consequence of this revolution) of the
imperialist war, which had exhausted the workers and
peasants to an incredible degree ; (2) the possibility of
taking advantage, for a certain time, of the mortal conflict between two world-powerful groups of imperialist

plunderers, who were unable to unite against their Soviet enemy : (3) the possibility of holding out in a comparatively lengthy civil war, owing partly to the gigantic dimensions of the country and the poor means of communication ; (4) the existence of such a profound bourgeois-democratic revolutionary movement among the peasantry that the Party of the proletariat was able to adopt the revolutionary demands of the peasant party (the Socialist-Revolutionary Party, a party which, in the main, was very hostile to Bolshevism) and at once realise them, thanks to the conquest of political power by the proletariat. The absence of these specific conditions—not to mention a number of other causes—accounts for the fact that it will be more difficult *to start* a socialist revolution in western Europe than it was in Russia. To attempt to " circumvent " this difficulty by " skipping " the difficult task of utilising reactionary parliaments for revolutionary purposes is absolutely childish. You wish to create a new society, and yet you fear the difficulties involved in forming in a reactionary parliament a good parliamentary fraction consisting of convinced, devoted, heroic Communists ! Is not this childish ? If Karl Liebknecht in Germany and Z. Höglund in Sweden were able, even without the support of the masses from below, to give examples of a truly revolutionary utilisation of reactionary parliaments, why, then, should a rapidly growing revolutionary mass party, under the conditions of the post-war disillusionment and exasperation of the masses, be unable to *forge* for itself a Communist fraction in the worst of parliaments ? It is just because the backward masses of the workers and, to a still greater degree, of the small peasants in western Europe are much more strongly imbued with bourgeois-democratic and parliamentary prejudices than they are in Russia that it is *only* within such institutions as bourgeois parliaments that Communists can (and must) wage a long and stubborn struggle— undaunted by difficulties—to expose, dispel and overcome these prejudices. . . .

"LEFT-WING" COMMUNISM IN ENGLAND
(Ch. IX)

In England there is not yet a Communist Party, but there is a fresh, broad, powerful and rapidly growing Communist movement among the workers which justifies the brightest hopes. There are several political parties and organisations (British Socialist Party, the Socialist Labour Party, the South Wales Socialist Society, the Workers' Socialist Federation) which desire to form a Communist Party and are already carrying on negotiations towards this end. The *Workers' Dreadnought*, the weekly organ of the last-mentioned organisation, in its issue of February 21, 1920 (No. 48, Vol. VI), contains an article by the editor, Comrade Sylvia Pankhurst, entitled : "Towards a Communist Party." In this article she outlines the progress of the negotiations taking place between the four organisations mentioned for the formation of a united Communist Party on the basis of affiliation to the Third International, the recognition of the Soviet system instead of parliament-arism and the dictatorship of the proletariat. It appears that one of the greatest obstacles to the immediate formation of a united Communist Party is the disagreement on the question of parliamentary action and the question of whether the new Communist Party should affiliate to the old, trade unionist, opportunist and social-chauvinist Labour Party. The Workers' Socialist Federation and the Socialist Labour Party[1] are opposed to taking part in parliamentary elections and in Parliament and are opposed to affiliation to the Labour Party, and in this disagree with all, or with the majority, of the members of the British Socialist Party, which they regard as the " Right wing of the Communist Parties " in England. (P. 5, Sylvia Pank-hurst's article.)

Thus, the main division is the same as that in Germany,

---

[1] I believe this party is opposed to affiliation to the Labour Party, but is not altogether opposed to parliamentary action.

notwithstanding the enormous difference in the form in which the disagreement manifests itself (in Germany the form is more analogous to the Russian than to the English) and in a number of other things. Let us examine the arguments of the " Lefts."

On the question of parliamentary action, Comrade Sylvia Pankhurst refers to an article in the same issue of her paper by Comrade W. Gallacher, who, in the name of the Scottish Workers' Council in Glasgow, writes :

> The above " Council " is definitely anti-parliamentarian, and has behind it the Left wing of the various political bodies.
>
> We represent the revolutionary movement in Scotland, striving continually to build up a revolutionary organisation within the industries, and a Communist Party, based on social committees, throughout the country. For a considerable time we have been sparring with the official parliamentarians. We have not considered it necessary to declare open warfare on them, *and they are afraid* to open attacks on us.
>
> But this state of affairs cannot long continue. We are winning all along the line.
>
> The rank and file of the I.L.P. in Scotland is becoming more and more disgusted with the thought of Parliament, and soviets or workers' councils are being supported by almost every branch.
>
> This is very serious, of course, for the gentlemen who look to politics for a profession, and they are using any and every means to persuade their members to come back into the parliamentary fold.
>
> Revolutionary comrades *must not* give any support to this gang. Our fight here is going to be a difficult one. One of the worst features of it will be the treachery of those whose personal ambition is a more impelling force than their regard for the revolution.
>
> Any support given to parliamentarism is simply assisting to put power into the hands of our British Scheidemanns and Noskes. Hendersons, Clynes and Co. are hopelessly reactionary. The official I.L.P. is more and more coming under the control of middle class Liberals, who, since the rout of the Liberal Party, have found their spiritual home in the camp of Messrs. Mac-Donald, Snowden and Co. The official I.L.P. is bitterly hostile to the Third International, the rank and file is for it. Any support to the parliamentary opportunists is simply playing into the hands of the former.

The B.S.P. doesn't count at all here. . . .

What is wanted here is a sound, revolutionary, industrial organisation and Communist Party working along clear, well-defined, scientific lines. If our comrades can assist us in building these, we will take their help gladly ; if they cannot, for God's sake let them keep out altogether, lest they betray the revolution by lending their support to the reactionaries, who are so eagerly clamouring for parliamentary honours (?) [the query belongs to the author of the letter], and who are anxious to prove that they *can rule* as effectively as the boss class politicians themselves.

In my opinion this letter excellently expresses the temper and point of view of the young Communists, or rank and file workers, who are only just coming over to communism. This temper is very gratifying and valuable ; we must learn to prize it and to support it, because without it, it is hopeless to expect the victory of the proletarian revolution in England, or in any other country for that matter. People who can give expression to this temper of the masses, who can rouse such temper (very often dormant, not realised, not roused) among the masses, must be prized and every assistance must be given them. At the same time we must openly and frankly tell them that temper *alone* is not sufficient to lead the masses in the great revolutionary struggle, and that the mistakes that these very loyal adherents of the cause of the revolution are about to make, or are making, can damage the cause of the revolution. Comrade Gallacher's letter undoubtedly betrays the embryos of *all* the mistakes committed by the German " Left " Communists and which were committed by the " Left " Bolsheviks in 1908 and 1918.

The writer of the letter is imbued with noble, proletarian (intelligible and near, not only to the proletarians but also to all toilers, to all " small men," to use a German expression) hatred for the bourgeois " class politicians." The hatred felt by this representative of the oppressed and exploited masses is in truth the " beginning of all wisdom," the very basis of every socialist and communist movement, and of its success. But the author apparently fails to take into account the fact that politics is a science and an art that does not drop from the skies, is not acquired for nothing, and that if it wants to conquer the bourgeoisie, the proletariat must train *its own* proletarian " class policitians " who shall be as skilled as the bourgeois politicians.

The writer of the letter understands excellently that it is not parliament but workers' Soviets that alone can serve as instruments for achieving the aims of the proletariat, and, of course, those who have failed to understand this up to now are hopeless reactionaries, no matter whether they are the most highly educated people in the world, the most experienced politicians, the most sincere socialists, the most erudite Marxists, the most honest citizens and family men. But the writer of the letter does not raise the question, does not think of raising the question, as to whether it is possible to bring about the victory of the Soviets over Parliament without getting our " Soviet " politicians *into* Parliament, without disrupting parliamentarism from *within*, without preparing the ground within Parliament for the success of the Soviets' forthcoming task of dispersing Parliament. And yet the writer of the letter expresses the correct idea that the Communist Party in England must operate on the basis of *scientific* principles. Science demands, first, the calculation of the experience of other countries, especially if these other countries, also capitalist countries, are undergoing, or have recently undergone, a very similar experience ; second, science demands the calculation of *all* the forces, groups, parties, classes and masses operating in the given country, and does not demand that policy be determined by mere desires and views, degree of class consciousness and readiness for battle of only one group or party.

It is true that the Hendersons, the Clynes, the Mac-Donalds and the Snowdens are hopelessly reactionary. It is also true that they want to take power in their own hands (although they prefer a coalition with the bourgeoisie), that they want to govern according to the old bourgeois rules, and that when they do get into power they will certainly act in the same way as the Scheidemanns and Noskes. All this is true. But the logical conclusion to be drawn from this is not that to support them is treachery to the revolution, but that in the interests of the revolution the revolutionaries in the working class should give these gentlemen a certain amount of parliamentary support. In order to explain this idea I will take two contemporary English political documents : (1) the speech delivered by the Prime Minister, Lloyd George, on March 18, 1920 (reported in the *Manchester Guardian* of March 19, 1920) and (2) the arguments of the " Left " Communist, Comrade Sylvia Pankhurst, in the article mentioned above.

Arguing against Asquith (who was especially invited to attend this meeting, but declined) and against those Liberals who do not want a coalition with the Conservatives but a *rapprochement* with the Labour Party (Comrade Gallacher in his letter also points to the fact that Liberals have joined the Independent Labour Party), Lloyd George said that a coalition, and a *close* coalition, with the Conservatives was essential because otherwise there would be a victory of the Labour Party, which Lloyd George " prefers to call " the Socialist Party and which is striving to " collectivise " the means of production.

In France this is called communism, the leader of the British bourgeoisie explained to his hearers (members of the Liberal Party who probably up to that time had been unaware of it). " In Germany it is called socialism, and in Russia it is called Bolshevism." This is opposed to Liberal principles, explained Lloyd George, because Liberalism stands for private property. " Civilisation is in danger," declared the orator, and, therefore, the Liberals and Conservatives must unite. . . .

. . . If you go to the agricultural areas—said Lloyd George —I agree that you have the old party divisions as strong as ever, they are far removed from the danger. It does not walk their lanes. But when they see it, they will be as strong as some of these industrial constituencies now are. Four-fifths of this country is industrial and commercial ; hardly one-fifth is agricultural. It is one of the things I have constantly in mind when I think of the dangers of the future here. In France the population is agricultural, and you have a solid body of opinions which does not move very rapidly, and which is not very easily excited by revolutionary movements. That is not the case here. This country is more top-heavy than any country in the world, and if it begins to rock, the crash here, for that reason, will be greater than in any land.

From this the reader will see that Lloyd George is not only a clever man, but that he has also learned a great deal from the Marxists. It would not be a sin to learn from Lloyd George.

It is interesting to note the following episode that occurred in the course of the discussion which followed Lloyd George's speech :

Mr. Wallace, M.P. : I should like to ask what the Prime Minister considers the effect might be in the industrial con-stituencies upon the industrial workers, so many of whom are Liberals at the present time and from whom we get so much support. Would not a possible result be to cause an immediate overwhelming accession of strength to the Labour Party from men who are at present our cordial supporters ?

The Prime Minister : I take a totally different view. The fact that Liberals are fighting among themselves undoubtedly drives a very considerable number of Liberals in despair to the Labour Party, where you get a considerable body of Liberals, very able men, whose business it is to discredit the Government. The result is undoubtedly to bring a good accession of public sentiment to the Labour Party. It does not go to the Liberals who are outside, it goes to the Labour Party, the by-elections show that.

Incidentally, I would like to say that this argument shows especially how even the cleverest people among the bourgeoisie have got themselves entangled and cannot avoid committing irreparable acts of stupidity. This will bring about their downfall. But our people may do stupid things (provided they are not very serious and are rectified in time) and yet, in the last resort, they will prove the victors.

The second political document is the following argument advanced by the " Left " Communist, Comrade Sylvia Pankhurst :

> . . . Comrade Inkpin (the General Secretary of the British Socialist Party) refers to the Labour Party as " the main body of the working class movement." Another comrade of the British Socialist Party, at the conference of the Third International just held, put the British Socialist Party view more strongly. He said : " We regard the Labour Party as the organised working class."
>
> But we do not take this view of the Labour Party. The Labour Party is very large numerically, though its membership is to a great extent quiescent and apathetic, consisting of many workers who have joined the trade unions because their workmates are trade unionists, and to share the friendly benefits.
>
> But we recognise that the great size of the Labour Party is also due to the fact that it is the creation of a school of thought beyond which the majority of the British working class has not yet emerged, though great changes are at work in the mind of the people which will presently alter this state of affairs. . . .
>
> The British Labour Party, like the social-patriotic organisations of other countries, will, in the natural development of society, inevitably come into power. It is for the Communists to build up the forces which will overthrow the social-patriots, and in this country we must not delay or falter in that work.
>
> We must not dissipate our energy in adding to the strength of the Labour Party ; its rise to power is inevitable. We must concentrate on making a Communist movement that will vanquish it.
>
> The Labour Party will soon be forming a government ; the revolutionary opposition must make ready to attack it.

Thus, the liberal bourgeoisie is abandoning the historical " two-party " (exploiters') system which has been sanctified by age-long experience and which has been extremely advantageous to the exploiters, and considers it necessary to unite their forces to fight the Labour Party. A section of the Liberals are deserting the Liberal Party, like rats leaving a sinking ship, and are joining the Labour Party. The Left Communists are of the opinion that the Labour

Party's rise to power is inevitable and they admit that at present it has the support of the majority of the workers. From this they draw the strange conclusion which Comrade Sylvia Pankhurst formulates as follows :

> The Communist Party must not enter into compromises. . . . The Communist Party must keep its doctrine pure, and its independence of reformism inviolate ; its mission is to lead the way, without stopping or turning, by the direct road to the communist revolution.

On the contrary, from the fact that the majority of the workers in England still follow the lead of the English Kerenskys or Scheidemanns and that they have not yet had the experience of a government composed of these people, which experience was necessary in Russia and in Germany in order to secure the mass transition of workers to Communism, from this fact it undoubtedly follows that the British Communists *should* participate in parliament, should from *within* Parliament help the masses of the workers see the results of a Henderson and Snowden government, should help the Hendersons and Snowdens to defeat the combined Lloyd Georges and Churchills. To act in a different way would mean to place difficulties in the way of the cause of the revolution, because, revolution is impossible without a change in the views of the majority of the working class, and this change is brought about by the political experience of the masses, never by propaganda alone. " To march forward without compromise, without turning from the path "—if this is said by an obviously impotent minority of the workers who know (or at all events should know) that very soon, when the Hendersons and Snowdens will have gained the victory over the Lloyd Georges and Churchills, the majority will be disappointed in their leaders and will begin to support Communism (or at all events will adopt an attitude of neutrality, and largely an attitude of friendly neutrality towards the Communists), then this slogan is obviously mistaken. It is like 10,000 soldiers going into battle against 50,000 enemy soldiers, when it would be wise to " halt," to " turn from the path " and even enter into a " compromise " in order to gain time until the arrival of the reinforcements of 100,000 which are bound to come, but which cannot go into action immediately. This is intellectual childishness and not the serious tactics of a revolutionary class.

The fundamental law of revolution, confirmed by all revolutions and particularly by all three Russian revolutions in the twentieth century, is as follows : it is not sufficient for revolution that the exploited and oppressed masses understand the impossibility of living in the old way and demand changes ; for revolution it is necessary that the exploiters should not be able to live and rule in the old way. Only when the " lower classes " *do not want* the old and when the " upper classes " cannot *continue in the old way* then only can the revolution be victorious. This truth may be expressed in other words : revolution is impossible without a national crisis affecting both the exploited and the exploiters. It follows that for revolution it is essential, first, that a majority of the workers (or at least a majority of the class-conscious, thinking, politically active workers) should fully understand the necessity for revolution and be ready to sacrifice their lives for it ; secondly, that the ruling classes be in a state of governmental crisis which draws even the most backward masses into politics (a symptom of every real revolution is : the rapid tenfold and even hundredfold increase in the number of hitherto apathetic representatives of the toiling and oppressed masses capable of waging the political struggle), weakens the government and makes it possible for the revolutionaries to overthrow it rapidly.

In England, as can be seen incidentally from Lloyd George's speech, both conditions for the successful proletarian revolution are obviously maturing. And the mistakes the Left Communists are making are particularly dangerous at the present time precisely because certain revolutionaries are not displaying a sufficiently thoughtful, attentive, intelligent and calculating attitude towards either of these conditions. If we—not a revolutionary group, but the Party of the revolutionary *class*—if we want the *masses* to follow us (and unless they do, we stand the risk of remaining mere talkers) we must, first, help Henderson or Snowden beat Lloyd George and Churchill (or to be more correct : compel the former to beat the latter, because the former are *afraid to win*) ; secondly, help the majority of the working class to become convinced by their own experience that we are right, i.e., that the Hendersons and Snowdens are utterly worthless, that they are petty-bourgeois and treacherous and that their bankruptcy is inevitable ; thirdly, bring nearer the moment when, on the basis of the disappointment of the majority of the workers in the Hendersons, it will be possible with good chances of success to overthrow the government of the Hendersons at once, because if the very clever and solid, not petty bourgeois but big bourgeois, Lloyd George, betrays utter consternation and weakens himself (and the whole of the bourgeoisie) more and more by his " friction " with Churchill one day and his " friction " with Asquith the next day, how much more so will this be the case with the Henderson government !

I will speak more concretely. In my opinion, the British Communists should unite their four (all very weak and some of them very, very weak) parties and groups into a single Communist Party on the basis of the principles of the Third International and of *obligatory* participation in Parliament. The Communist Party should propose to the Hendersons and Snowdens that they enter into a " compromise " election agreement, viz., march together against the alliance of Lloyd George and the Conservatives, divide the seats in Parliament in proportion to the number of votes cast for the Labour Party and Communist Party respectively (not at parliamentary elections, but in a special ballot), while the Communist Party retains *complete liberty* to carry on agitation, propaganda and political activity. Without the latter condition, of course, no such *bloc* could be concluded, for that would be an act of betrayal : the British Communists must insist on **and** secure complete liberty to expose the Hendersons and the Snowdens in the same way as (*for fifteen years*—1903–17) the Russian Bolsheviks insisted on and secured it in relation to the Russian Hendersons and Snowdens, i.e., the Mensheviks.

If the Hendersons and the Snowdens accept the *bloc* on these terms, then we gain, because the number of seats in Parliament is not a matter of importance to us ; we are not chasing after seats, therefore we can yield on this point (the Hendersons and particularly their new friends—or is it their new masters ?—the Liberals, who have joined the Independent Labour Party, are particularly eager to get seats). We will gain, because we will carry *our* agitation among the *masses* at a moment when Lloyd George *himself* has " incensed " them, and we will not only help the Labour Party establish its government more quickly, but also help the masses understand more quickly the Communist propaganda that we will carry on against the Hendersons without curtailment and without evasions.

If the Hendersons and the Snowdens reject the *bloc* with us on these terms we will gain still more, because we will have at once shown the *masses* (note that even in the purely Menshevik and utterly opportunist Independent Labour Party the *rank and file* is in favour of Soviets) that the Hendersons prefer *their* closeness with the capitalists to the unity of all the workers. We will immediately gain in the eyes of the *masses* who, particularly after the brilliant, very correct and very useful (for communism) explanations given by Lloyd George, will sympathise with the idea of uniting all the workers against the Lloyd George-Conservative alliance. We will gain immediately because we will demonstrate to the masses that the Hendersons and the Snowdens are afraid to beat Lloyd George, afraid to take power themselves and are *secretly* striving to get the support of Lloyd George, who is *openly* stretching out his hand to the

Conservatives against the Labour Party. It should be noted that in Russia, after the Revolution of March 12 [February 27], 1917, the propaganda of the Bolsheviks against the Mensheviks and Socialist-Revolutionaries (i.e., the Russian Hendersons and Snowdens) gained a great deal precisely because of a circumstance like this. We said to the Mensheviks and the Socialist-Revolutionaries : take complete power without the bourgeoisie, because you have the majority in the Soviets (at the First All-Russian Congress of Soviets in June 1917, the Bolsheviks had only 13 per cent of the votes). But the Russian Hendersons and Snowdens feared to take power without the bourgeoisie, and when the bourgeoisie delayed the convocation of the Constituent Assembly because they knew perfectly well that the Mensheviks and the Socialist-Revolutionaries would have the majority in it[1] (the latter had entered into a close political *bloc* and both really represented *nothing but* pettybourgeois democracy), the Mensheviks and Socialist-Revolutionaries were not able to put up a consistent and strenuous struggle against these delays.

If the Hendersons and the Snowdens reject the *bloc* with the Communists, the Communists will gain immediately in regard to winning the sympathy of the masses and in discrediting the Hendersons and Snowdens, and if, as a result, we do lose a few parliamentary seats it is not a matter of importance. We would put up candidates in a very few, but absolutely safe constituencies, i.e., where our candidate would not let the Liberal in, in opposition to the Labour candidate. We would take part in the election campaign, distribute leaflets advocating communism, and in *all* constituencies where we have no candidates urge the electors *to vote for the Labour candidate against the bourgeois*

[1] The elections to the constituent Assembly in November 1917 resulted in the following (based on returns covering over 36,000,000 votes : the Bolsheviks obtained 25 per cent of the votes cast ; the various parties of the landlords and capitalists obtained 13 per cent and the petty bourgeois democratic parties, i.e., the Socialist-Revolutionaries, Mensheviks and a number of kindred groups, obtained 62 per cent.

candidate. Comrades Sylvia Pankhurst and Gallacher are mistaken in thinking that this is the betrayal of communism, the abandonment of the struggle against the social-traitors. On the contrary, the communist revolution undoubtedly stands to gain by it.

At the present time the British Communists very often find it hard to approach the masses and even to get them to listen to them. If I as a Communist come out and call upon the workers to vote for the Hendersons against Lloyd George, they will certainly listen to me. And I will be able to explain in a popular manner not only why Soviets are better than Parliament and why the dictatorship of the proletariat is better than the dictatorship of Churchill (which is concealed behind the signboard of bourgeois " democracy "), but I will also be able to explain that I want to support Henderson with my vote in the same way as a rope supports one who is hanged—that the establishment of a Henderson government will prove that I am right, will bring the masses over to my side, and will accelerate the political death of the Hendersons and the Snowdens as was the case with their friends in Russia and Germany.

And if the objection is raised : these tactics are too " subtle " or too complicated, the masses will not understand them, they will split up and scatter our forces, will prevent us from concentrating our forces in the Soviet revolution, etc.—I will reply to the " Left " who raise this objection : don't put the blame for your dogmatism upon the masses ! In all probability the masses in Russia are not more educated than the masses in England ; if anything they are less so. And yet the masses understood the Bolsheviks ; and the fact that on the *eve* of the Soviet revolution, in September 1917, the Bolsheviks put up their candidates for a bourgeois parliament (the Constituent Assembly) and on the *morrow* of the Soviet revolution, in November, 1917, took part in the election of this Constituent Assembly which they dispersed on January 18 [5],

1918—this fact did not hamper the Bolsheviks, but on the contrary, it helped them.

I cannot deal here with the second point of disagreement among the British Communists, viz., the question of affiliation to the Labour Party. I have too little material at my disposal on this question, which is a particularly complicated one in view of the peculiar character of the Labour Party, the very structure of which is so unlike the ordinary political party on the Continent. It is beyond doubt, however, first, that on this question also, those who think that they will be able to deduce the tactics of the revolutionary proletariat from principles like : " A Comcomunist Party must keep its doctrine pure and its independence of reformism inviolate ; its mission is to lead the way, without stopping or turning, by the direct road to the communist revolution "—will fall into error. For such principles are merely a repetition of the mistakes committed by the French Communard-Blanquists, who, in 1874, " repudiated " all compromises and all the intermediary stations. Secondly, it is beyond doubt that in this question, too, the task is to apply the general and main principles of communism to the *peculiar* relations between classes and parties, to the *peculiar features* in the objective development towards communism which are observed in every country and which one must know, study, seek, divine.

But this must be discussed not only in connection with British communism alone but in connection with the general conclusions concerning the development of communism in all capitalist countries. We shall now proceed to deal with this theme.

SOME CONCLUSIONS
(Ch. X)

The Russian bourgeois revolution of 1905 marked a very peculiar turn in world history : on one of the most backward capitalist countries the strike movement attained a breadth and power unprecedented in the world. In the *first month of* 1905 *alone* the number of strikers was ten times the average yearly number of the previous ten years (1895–1904) ; and from January to October 1905, strikes grew continuously and on an enormous scale. Under the influence of a number of entirely unique historical conditions, backward Russia was the first to show to the world not only a spasmodic growth of independent activity on the part of the oppressed masses during revolution (this happened in all great revolutions), but also a proletariat whose significance was infinitely greater than its numerical proportion to the total population, the combination of the economic and political strike, the transformation of the latter into an armed uprising, and the birth of a new form of mass struggle and mass organisation of the classes oppressed by capitalism, viz., the Soviets.

The February and October Revolutions of 1917 resulted in the all-round development of the Soviets on a national scale, and in their victory in the proletarian, socialist revolution. And in less than two years the international character of the Soviets, the spread of this method of struggle and form of organisation to the working class movement of the whole world, and the historical mission of the Soviets to be the grave-digger, the heir, and the successor of bourgeois parliamentarism, of bourgeois democracy in general, became revealed.

More than that, the history of the working class movement now shows that in all countries it is about to experience (and it has already begun to experience) the struggle of nascent communism—which is becoming strong and is marching towards victory—with, first and foremost, *its own* (of each particular country) " Menshevism," i.e., opportunism and social-chauvinism, and, second, as a sort of supplement, with " Left-wing " Communism. The first struggle has developed in all countries, apparently without a single exception, as a struggle between the Second International already virtually dead and the Third

International. The second struggle can be observed in Germany, in England, in Italy, in America (at least a certain *section* of the Industrial Workers of the World and the anarcho-syndicalist elements in America defend the errors of " Left " Communism while simultaneously there is an almost universal, almost unanimous acceptance of the Soviet system), and in France (the attitude of a section of the former syndicalists towards the political party and parliamentarism, and here, too, while at the same time accepting the Soviet system), i.e., the struggle, undoubtedly, is being waged not only on a national but also on an international scale.

But, while the working class movement is everywhere passing through what is practically a similar preparatory school for victory over the bourgeoisie, it is in each country achieving this development in *its own way*. The big, advanced capitalist countries are marching along this road *much more rapidly* than did Bolshevism, which history granted a period of fifteen years to prepare itself for victory as an organised political trend. The Third International has already scored a decisive victory in the short space of one year ; it has defeated the yellow, social-chauvinist Second International, which only a few months ago was incomparably stronger than the Third International and which seemed to be firm and strong, enjoying the all-round support—direct and indirect, material (ministerial posts, passports, the press) and ideological—of the world bourgeoisie.

The main thing now is that the Communists of every country should quite consciously take into account the fundamental tasks of the struggle against opportunism and " Left " doctrinairism as well as the concrete *peculiar features* which this struggle assumes and inevitably must assume in each separate country in accordance with the peculiar features of its economics, politics, culture, national composition (Ireland, etc.), its colonies, religious divisions, etc. Everywhere we observe widening and growing dissatisfaction with the Second International because of its opportunism, its inability or incapability, to create a really centralised, really leading centre which would be capable of guiding the international tactics of the revolutionary proletariat in its struggle for the world Soviet republic. We must clearly realise that such a leading centre cannot under any circumstances be built up on stereotyped, mechanically equalised, identical tactical rules of the struggle. As long as national and state differences exist among peoples and countries—and these differences will continue to exist for a very long time, even after the dictatorship of the proletariat has been established on a world scale—the unity of international tactics of the communist working class movement of all countries demands not the elimination of variety, not the abolition of national differences (this is a foolish dream at the present moment), but such an application of the *fundamental* principles of communism (Soviet power and the dictatorship of the proletariat) as will *correctly modify* these principles in *certain particulars*, will properly adapt them to the national and national-state differences. To investigate, study, seek out, divine, grasp that which is specifically national in the *concrete manner* in which each country *approaches* the fulfilment of the *single* international task, the victory over opportunism and " Left " doctrinairism in the working class movement, the overthrow of the bourgeoisie, the establishment of a Soviet republic and a proletarian dictatorship—this is the main task of the historical period through which all the advanced (and not only the advanced) countries are now passing. The main thing—not everything, by a very long way—but the main thing has already been achieved in that the vanguard of the working class has been won over, in that it has gone over to the side of the Soviet power against parliamentarism, to the side of the dictatorship of the proletariat against bourgeois democracy. Now all efforts, all attention must be concentrated on the *next* step—which seems, and from a certain standpoint really is, less fundamental, but which in

fact is much closer to the practical carrying out of the task
—namely, on seeking out the forms of *transition or approach*
to the proletarian revolution.

The proletarian vanguard has been ideologically won
over. This is the most important thing. Without this, we
cannot take even the first step towards victory. But from
this first step it is still a long way to victory. With the
vanguard alone victory is impossible. To throw the vanguard alone into the decisive battle when the whole class,
when the broad masses have not yet taken up a position
either of direct support of the vanguard, or at least of
benevolent neutrality towards it and one in which they
cannot possibly support the enemy, would not merely be
folly, but a crime. And in order that actually the whole
class, that actually the broad masses of toilers and those
oppressed by capital may take up such a position, propaganda and agitation alone are not sufficient. For this the
masses must have their own political experience. Such is
the fundamental law of all great revolutions, confirmed
now with astonishing force and vividness not only in Russia
but also in Germany. It has been necessary—not only for
the uncultured, often illiterate, masses of Russia, but for the
highly cultured, entirely literate masses of Germany—to
realise through their own painful experience the absolute
impotence and characterlessness, the absolute helplessness
and servility before the bourgeoisie, the absolute baseness
of the government of the knights of the Second International,
the absolute inevitability of a dictatorship of the extreme
reactionaries (Kornilov in Russia, Kapp and Co. in Germany) as the only alternative to a dictatorship of the
proletariat, in order to turn them resolutely toward
communism.

The immediate task that confronts the class conscious
vanguard of the international labour movement, i.e., the
Communist Parties, groups and trends, is to be able to *lead*
the broad masses (now, for the most part, slumbering,
apathetic, hidebound, inert, and dormant) to their new

position, or, rather, to be able to lead *not only* their own Party but also the masses during the course of their approach, their transition to the new position. While the first historical task (viz., that of winning over the class conscious vanguard of the proletariat to the side of the Soviet power and the dictatorship of the working class) could not be accomplished without a complete ideological and political victory over opportunism and social-chauvinism, the second task, which now becomes the immediate task, and which is to lead *the masses* to the new position that will assure the victory of the vanguard in the revolution, this immediate task cannot be accomplished without the liquidation of Left doctrinairism, without completely overcoming and getting rid of its mistakes.

As long as the question was (and in so far as it still is) one of winning over the vanguard of the proletariat to the side of communism, so long and to that extent propaganda took first place ; even propaganda circles, with all the imperfections that circles suffer from, are useful under these conditions and produce fruitful results. But if it is a question of the practical activities of the masses, a question of the disposition, if one may so express it, of vast armies, of the alignment of all the class forces of the given society *for the final and decisive battle*, then propaganda alone, the mere repetition of the truths of " pure " communism are of no avail. In these circumstances one must count, not up to a thousand—as is really done by the propagandist who belongs to a small group which does not yet lead the masses ; but one must count in millions and tens of millions. In these circumstances one must not only ask oneself whether the vanguard of the revolutionary class has been convinced but also whether the historically effective forces of *all* classes —positively of all the classes in the given society without exception—are aligned in such a way that the decisive battle is fully matured, in such a way that (1) all the class forces hostile to us have become sufficiently confused, are sufficiently at loggerheads with each other, have sufficiently weakened themselves in a struggle beyond their capacities ; that (2) all the vacillating, wavering, unstable, intermediate elements—the petty bourgeoisie and the petty-bourgeois democracy as distinct from the bourgeoisie—have sufficiently exposed themselves before the people and have sufficiently disgraced themselves through their practical bankruptcy ; and that (3) among the proletariat a mass mood in favour of supporting the most determined, unreservedly bold, revolutionary action against the bourgeoisie has arisen and begins to grow powerfully. Then, indeed, revolution is ripe ; then, indeed, if we have correctly gauged all the conditions outlined above, and if we have chosen the moment rightly, our victory is assured.

The disagreements between the Churchills and the Lloyd Georges—with insignificant national differences, these types exist in *all* countries—on the one hand, and between the Hendersons and the Lloyd Georges on the other, are quite unimportant and petty from the point of view of pure, i.e., abstract communism, i.e., communism that has not yet matured to the stage of practical, mass, political action. But from the point of view of this practical mass action, these differences are very, very important. It is the very important business and task of the Communist who wants to be not merely a class conscious, convinced and ideological propagandist, but a practical leader of the *masses* in the revolution to take them into account, to determine the moment when the inevitable conflicts between these " friends," which will weaken *all the " friends " taken together* and render them impotent, will have completely matured. It is necessary to combine the strictest loyalty to the ideas of communism with the ability to make all necessary practical compromises, to " tack," to make agreements, zig-zags, retreats and so on, in order to accelerate the coming into political power of the Hendersons (the heroes of the Second International, if we are not to speak of individuals who represent petty-bourgeois democracy but who call themselves socialists) and then their loss of power ; to accelerate their inevitable practical bankruptcy which will enlighten the masses in the spirit of our ideas, in the direction of communism ; to accelerate the inevitable friction, quarrels, conflicts and complete disunity between the Hendersons, the Lloyd Georges and Churchills (Mensheviks, Socialist-Revolutionaries, Constitutional Democrats, Monarchists, Scheidemanns, the bourgeoisie, the Kappists, etc.) and to select the moment when the disunity among these " pillars of the sacred right of property" is at its highest, in order to defeat them all by a determined attack of the proletariat and capture political power.

History generally, and the history of revolutions in particular, is always richer in content, more varied, more many-sided, more lively and " subtle " than the best parties and the most class-conscious vanguards of the most advanced class imagine. This is understandable, because the best vanguards express the class consciousness, the will, the passion, the fantasy of tens of thousands, while the revolution is made, at the moment of its climax and the exertion of all human capabilities, by the class consciousness, the will, the passion and the fantasy of tens of millions who are urged on by the very acutest class struggle. From this follow two very important practical conclusions : first, that the revolutionary class, in order to fulfil its task, must be able to master *all* forms or sides of social activity without exception (and complete after the capture of political power, sometimes at great risk and amidst very great dangers, what it did not complete before the capture of power) ; second, that the revolutionary class must be ready to pass from one form to another in the quickest and most unexpected manner.

Everyone will agree that an army which does not train itself to wield all arms, all means and methods of warfare that the enemy possesses or may possess, is behaving in an unwise or even in a criminal manner. This applies to politics to a greater degree than it does to war. In politics it is harder to forecast what methods of warfare will be applied and be considered useful for us under certain future conditions. Unless we are able to master all methods of warfare we stand the risk of suffering great and sometimes decisive defeat if the changes in the position of the other classes, which we cannot determine, will bring to the front forms of activity in which we are particularly weak. If, however, we are able to master all methods of warfare, we shall certainly be victorious, because we represent the interests of the really advanced, of the really revolutionary class, even if circumstances do not permit us to use weapons that are most dangerous for the enemy, weapons that are most quickly death-dealing. Inexperienced revolutionaries often think that legal methods of struggle are opportunist because in this field the bourgeoisie very frequently (especially in "peaceful," non-revolutionary times) deceived and fooled the workers, and they think that illegal methods of struggle are revolutionary. But this is not true. What is true is that the opportunists and the traitors to the working class are those parties and leaders who are not able or who do not want (don't say : you cannot ; say : you won't ; *wer will, kann*) to apply illegal methods of struggle in conditions such as, for example, prevailed during the imperialist war of 1914–18, when the bourgeoisie of the freest democratic countries deceived the workers in the most impudent and brutal manner and prohibited everyone from speaking the truth about the predatory character of the war. But revolutionaries who are unable to combine illegal forms of struggle with every form of legal struggle are very bad revolutionaries. It is not difficult to be a revolutionary when the revolution has already flared up, when everybody joins the revolution simply because they are carried away by it, because it is the fashion and sometimes even because it might open a career. After the victory the proletariat has to exert extreme effort, to suffer pains and one might say martyrdom to "liberate" itself from such alleged revolutionaries. It is much more difficult—and much more useful—to be a revolutionary when the conditions for direct, open, really mass and really revolutionary struggle have *not yet* matured, to be able to defend the interests of the revolution (by propaganda, agitation and organisation) in non-revolutionary bodies and even in reactionary bodies, in non-revolutionary circumstances, among the masses who are incapable of immediately appreciating the necessity for revolutionary methods of action. The main task of contemporary Communism in western Europe and America is to acquire the ability to seek, to find, to determine correctly the concrete path, or the particular turn of events that will *bring* the masses *right up* to the real, decisive, last and great revolutionary struggle.

Take England, for example : We cannot say, and no one is in a position to say beforehand, how soon the real proletarian revolution will flare up there and *what* will serve as the *cause* to rouse it, to kindle it and move into the struggle very wide masses who are at present dormant. Hence, it is our duty to carry on our preparatory work in such a manner as to be " well shod on all four legs," as the late Plekhanov was fond of saying when he was a Marxist and revolutionary. It is possible that a parliamentary crisis will cause the " breach," will " break the ice " ; perhaps it will be a crisis caused by the hopelessly entangled and increasingly painful and acute colonial and imperialist contradictions, perhaps some third cause, etc. We are not discussing the kind of struggle that will *determine* the fate of the proletarian revolution in England (not a single Communist has any doubts on that score ; as far as we are concerned, this question is settled and definitely settled). What we are discussing is the *immediate cause* that will rouse the proletarian masses, at present dormant, and bring them right up to the revolution.

Let us not forget that in the bourgeois French Republic for example, in a situation which from both the international and national aspect was a hundred times less revolutionary than the present one, one out of the thousands and thousands of dishonest tricks the reactionary military caste play (the Dreyfuss case) was enough to serve as the "unexpected" and "petty" cause which brought the people to the verge of civil war !

In England the Communists should uninterruptedly, unfalteringly and undeviatingly utilise the parliamentary struggle and all the perturbations of the Irish, colonial and world imperialist policy of the British government and all other spheres and sides of social life and work in all of them in a new way, in a communist way, in the spirit not of the Second but of the Third International. I have neither the time nor the space here to describe the methods of " Russian," " Bolshevik " participation in parliamentary elections and in the parliamentary struggle, but I can assure the foreign Communists that this was not anything like the usual West-European parliamentary campaign. From this the conclusion is usually drawn : " Well, that was in Russia, but in our country parliamentarism is something different." This conclusion is wrong. The very purpose of the existence of Communists in the world, adherents of the Third International in all countries, is to *change* all along the line, in all spheres of life, the old socialist, trade unionist, syndicalist parliamentary work into *new* communist work. In Russia, too, we had a great deal of opportunist and purely bourgeois, money-making and capitalist swindling during elections. The Communists in western Europe and America must learn to create a new, unusual, non-opportunist, non-careerist parliamentarism ; the Communist Parties must issue their slogans, real proletarians with the help of the unorganised and very poorest people should scatter and distribute leaflets, canvass the workers' houses and the cottages of the rural proletarians and peasants in the remote villages (fortunately there are not nearly so many remote villages in Europe as there are in Russia, and in England there are very few), they should go into the most common inns, penetrate into the unions, societies and casual meetings where the common people gather and talk to the people, not in scientific (and not very parliamentary) language, not in the least to strive to " get seats " in Parliament, but everywhere to rouse the thoughts of the masses and draw them into the struggle, to take the bourgeoisie at their word, to utilise the apparatus they have set up, the elections they have called for, the appeal to the country that they have made and to tell the people what Bolshevism is in a way that has not been possible (under bourgeois rule) outside of election times (not counting, of course, times of big strikes, when in Russia a *similar* apparatus for widespread popular agitation worked even more intensively). It is very difficult to do this in western Europe and America—very, very difficult—but it can and must be done, because generally speaking the tasks of communism cannot be fulfilled without effort, and every effort must be made to fulfil the *practical* tasks, ever more varied, ever more connected with all branches of social life, *winning* branch after branch from the *bourgeoisie*.

In England, also, it is necessary to organise in a new way (not in a socialist manner but in a communist manner, not in a reformist manner but in a revolutionary manner) the work of propaganda, agitation and organisation among the armed forces and among the oppressed and disfranchised nationalities in " one's own " state (Ireland, the colonies). Because in all these spheres of social life, in the epoch of imperialism generally, and particularly now, after the war which tortured nationalities and quickly opened their eyes to the truth (viz., tens of millions killed and maimed only for the purpose of deciding whether the British or German pirates shall plunder the largest number of countries)—all these spheres of social life are becoming particularly filled with inflammable material and create numerous causes of conflict, crises and the intensification of the class struggle. We do not know and we cannot know which spark—out of the innumerable sparks that are flying around in all countries as a result of the political and economic world crises—will kindle the conflagration, in the sense of specially rousing the masses, and we must, therefore, with the aid of our new, communist principles, set to work to "stir up" all, even the oldest, mustiest and seemingly hopeless spheres, for otherwise we shall not be able to cope with our tasks, we will not be all-sided, we will not be able to master all weapons and we will not be prepared either for victory over the bourgeoisie (which arranged all sides of social life, and has now disarranged all sides of social life in a bourgeois way) nor for the forthcoming communist reorganisation of the whole of social life after the victory. . . . . . .

J. Stalin

THE INTERNATIONAL SITUATION, AUGUST 1927

English translation published in " The Communist International," October 15, 1927.

[This was a speech delivered at a meeting of the Central Committee of the Communist Party of the Soviet Union, on August 1st, 1927. At this time the Trotskyist Opposition was making attacks on the policy of the Communist International, especially in connection with the situation in China. The section of Stalin's speech reprinted below, dealing with the situation in China, is of great importance not only as an answer to the Trotskyist criticisms, but as a positive statement of Marxist tactics in the development of the national revolutionary movements.]

THE INTERNATIONAL SITUATION, AUGUST 1927

ABOUT CHINA

LET US TURN to the question of China. I am not going to enlarge upon the mistakes of the Opposition on the question of the character and the outlook of the Chinese revolution. I am not going to do so, because there has been said a good deal, and with sufficient conviction, so that it is not worth while to repeat all that has been said. Neither am I going to enlarge upon the fact that the Chinese revolution at its present stage appears to be a revolution for tariff autonomy (Trotsky). Nor is it worth while enlarging upon the fact that in China there appear to exist no survivals of feudalism, and that if they do exist, they are not of any serious importance, so that the agrarian revolution in China thus becomes quite incomprehensible (Trotsky and Radek). With these and similar errors of the Opposition on the Chinese question, you are probably familiar from our Party press.

Let us pass on to the question of the fundamental starting points of Leninism in the solution of questions relating to the revolutionary movement in the colonial and subject countries ?

What is the starting point of the Comintern, and generally of the Communist Parties, in settling the questions relating to the revolutionary movement in the colonial and subject countries ?

It consists in drawing a rigid distinction between the revolution in the imperialist countries, in the countries which oppress other peoples, and the revolution in the colonial and subject countries, in the countries which suffer from the imperialist yoke of other countries. The revolution is one thing in the imperialist countries : there the bourgeoisie is the oppressor of other nations ; there the bourgeoisie is counter-revolutionary through all the stages of the revolution ; there the national aspect is lacking as a factor in the struggle for freedom. Quite a different thing is the revolution in the colonial and subject countries : there the imperialist yoke of other countries constitutes one of the factors of the revolution ; there the yoke is bound to affect also the national bourgeoisie ; there the national bourgeoisie may, at a certain stage and for a certain length of time, support the revolutionary movement of their country against imperialism ; there the national aspect, as a factor in the struggle for freedom, becomes a factor of revolution. To ignore this distinction, to fail to see the difference, to identify the revolution in the imperialist countries with the revolution in the colonial countries, is to stray from the path of Marxism, from the path of Leninism, and to follow the path of the adherents of the Second International.

Here is what Lenin said on this subject in his report on the national and colonial question at the Second Congress of the Comintern :

> What constitutes the *most important, the fundamental* idea of our theses ? The *distinction* between the *oppressed* and the *oppressing* nations. We lay stress on this distinction, as against the position of the Second International and the bourgeois democracy.

The fundamental error of the Opposition is that it fails to *appreciate* and to *recognise* this distinction between the revolution of one type and that of another type.

The fundamental mistake of the Opposition is that it *identifies* the revolution of 1905 in Russia, an imperialist country oppressing other nations, with the revolution in China, an oppressed, semi-colonial country, compelled to fight against the imperialistic oppression of other countries.

Here, in Russia, the revolution in 1905 went against the bourgeoisie, against the liberal bourgeoisie, despite the fact that it was a bourgeois-democratic revolution. Why ? Because the liberal bourgeoisie of an imperialist country cannot help being counter-revolutionary. It was for this very reason that the Bolsheviks then could not even talk about temporary blocs and understandings with the liberal bourgeoisie. On these grounds it is asserted by the Opposition that the same policy should be pursued in China through all the stages of the revolutionary movement, that never and under no circumstances are temporary understandings and blocs with the national bourgeoisie admissible in China. But the Opposition forgets that such assertions can be made only by people who fail to understand and to recognise the difference between a revolution in the oppressed countries, and a revolution in the oppressing countries, by people who break away from Leninism, drifting into the fold of the Second International.

Here is what Lenin said about the admissibility of temporary understandings and blocs with the bourgeois emancipation movement in the colonial countries :

> The Communist International should form *temporary understandings*, even *alliances*, with the bourgeois democracy of the colonies and the backward countries, but not merge with it, unconditionally preserving the independence of the proletarian movement, even in its most embryonic form. . . . We, as Communists, must and will *support bourgeois emancipation* movements in the colonial countries only in those cases when these movements are really revolutionary, when their representatives will not hinder us in educating and organising the peasantry and the large masses of the exploited in the revolutionary spirit.

But could it " happen " that Lenin, who thundered against any understandings with the bourgeoisie in Russia, admitted such understandings and blocs in China ? Perhaps Lenin made a mistake ? Perhaps he turned from revolutionary tactics to those of opportunism ? Of course not. It " happened " because Lenin understood the difference between a revolution in an oppressed country and a revolution in an oppressing country. It " happened " because Lenin understood that at a certain stage of development the national bourgeoisie in the colonial countries may support the revolutionary movement of their country against foreign imperialism. This the Opposition refuses to understand, and it does so because it breaks with the revolutionary tactics of Lenin, and with the revolutionary tactics of Leninism.

Did you notice that the Opposition leaders in their speeches have carefully evaded these points made by Lenin, although Bukharin in his report has confronted them with these points? Why do they evade these well-known points of policy given by Lenin in regard to colonial and subject countries? Why are they afraid of the truth? Because the policy of Lenin upset the whole political ideology of Trotskyism on questions of the Chinese revolution.

As to the stages of the Chinese revolution. The Opposition has become so entangled that it now denies the existence of any stages whatsoever in the development of the Chinese revolution. But can there be a revolution without certain stages of development? Was our own revolution without its stages? Take the April theses of Lenin and you will see that Lenin recognised in our revolution two stages : the first stage, the bourgeois-democratic revolution with the agrarian movement as its principal axis, and the second stage, the October revolution with the capture of power by the proletariat as its principal axis. What are the stages of the Chinese revolution? To my mind, there ought to be three : the first stage, the revolution of the common national united front, the Canton period, when the revolution levelled its chief blow against foreign imperialism, whilst the national bourgeoisie supported the revolutionary movement ; the second stage, the bourgeois-democratic revolution, after the emergence of the national troops on the Yangtse river, when the national bourgeoisie turned its back on the revolution, whilst the agrarian movement grew into a mighty upheaval involving the teeming millions of the peasantry (just now the Chinese revolution is in the second stage of its development) ; the third stage, the Soviet.

EEM

revolution, which has not yet arrived, but which will come. He who fails to see that a revolution cannot but be without certain stages of development, he who fails to see the existence of three stages in the development of the Chinese revolution, is perfectly ignorant both of Marxism and of the Chinese question.

What is the characteristic feature of the first stage in the Chinese revolution? The characteristic feature of the first stage in the Chinese revolution is that, firstly, it was the revolution of the common national united front, and secondly, that it was chiefly directed against the yoke of foreign imperialism (the Hong Kong strike, etc.). Was Canton then the centre of the revolutionary movement in China? Decidedly, it was. This can now be denied only by the blind.

Is it true that the first stage of the colonial revolution must be precisely of such character? I believe it is. In the "Supplementary Theses" of the Second Congress of the Comintern dealing with the revolution in China and in India, it is explicitly stated that in those countries, "the foreign aggression has been obstructing the development of social life all along," that "therefore the *first step* of the revolution in the colonies should be the overthrow of foreign capitalism."

The outstanding feature of the Chinese revolution consists in the fact that it has gone through this "first step," through the first stage of its development, that it has passed through the period of the revolution of the common national united front, and has entered into the second stage of development—into the period of agrarian revolution.

On the other hand, the outstanding feature, say, of the Turkish revolution (the Kemalists) consists in the fact that it got stranded on the "first step," on the first stage of the bourgeois liberation movement, making no attempt even to pass on to the second stage of its development, to that of the agrarian revolution.

What did the Kuomintang and its government represent

in the first stage of the revolution, during the Canton period? They represented then a bloc of workers, peasants, bourgeois intellectuals, and the national bourgeoisie. Was Canton then the centre of the revolutionary movement? Was it then the proper policy to support the Canton Kuomintang, as the government of the fight of emancipation against imperialism? Were we right then in extending aid to Canton in China, and, let us say, to Angora in Turkey, when Canton and Angora were waging a fight against imperialism? Yes, we were. We were right, and we followed then in the footsteps of Lenin, for the struggle of Canton and Angora were scattering the forces of imperialism, weakening and depriving imperialism of its glory, thereby facilitating the cause of the development of the centre of world revolution, the U.S.S.R. Is it true that the present Opposition leaders supported then, together with us, both Canton and Angora, rendering them a certain amount of assistance? Yes, it is. Let anybody try to question this.

But how is the united front with the national bourgeoisie during the first stage of the colonial revolution to be understood? Does it mean that the Communists should not accentuate the fight of the workers and peasants against the landowners and the national bourgeoisie, that the proletariat should sacrifice its independence in the least degree, even for a single instant? No, it does not mean that. The united front can have a revolutionary meaning only on condition that it does not hinder the Communist Party in conducting its own independent political and organisational activity, in organising the proletariat into an independent political force, in arousing the peasantry against the landlords, and in openly organising the workers' and peasants' revolution, thus creating the conditions for the proletarian hegemony. I believe the case has been proved up to the hilt by comrade Bukharin in his report, on the basis of documents with which everyone is familiar, that it was precisely such an understanding of the united front that was suggested to the Chinese Communist Party by the Comintern.

Comrades Kamenev and Zinoviev alluded here to one single telegram sent to Shanghai on October 26, 1926, which advised for the time being, until the capture of Shanghai, not to accentuate the agrarian movement. Far be it from me to consider that telegram as right and proper. I never thought, nor do I think, our Central Committee to be infallible. Mistakes do happen now and then, and that telegram was incontestably a mistake. But, firstly, that very telegram was retracted by ourselves a few weeks afterwards (in November 1926) without any advice on the part of the Opposition. Secondly, why has the Opposition recollected the telegram now, after a lapse of nine months, and why does it conceal from the Party that the telegram was retracted by us nine months ago ? It would, therefore be a malicious calumny to assert that the telegram in question determined the line of our leadership. As a matter of fact, it was an incidental, isolated telegram which was in no way characteristic of the line of the Comintern, and the line of our leadership. This, I repeat, is already clear from the fact that it was retracted a few weeks afterwards in a series of documents which were absolutely characteristic of the line of our leadership.

Permit me to refer to those documents.

Here, for instance, is a passage from the resolution of the Seventh Plenum of the Comintern in November, 1926, that is, one month after the date of the afore-mentioned telegram :

> The unique feature of the present situation is its transitional character, when the proletariat has to choose between the prospect of a bloc with considerable strata of the bourgeoisie, and the prospect of further consolidating its alliance with the peasantry. *If the proletariat fails to launch a radical agrarian programme, it will not be able to draw the peasantry into the revolutionary struggle and will lose the leadership in the national emancipation movement.*

And further ;

The National Government of Canton will not be able to retain power, the revolution will not advance towards the complete victory over foreign imperialism and native reaction, unless national liberation is identified with agrarian revolution.

Here you have a document which really defines the line of the Comintern leadership.

It is very strange that the Opposition leaders avoid mentioning this well-known Comintern document.

Perhaps I shall not sin against modesty if I refer to my own speech in the Chinese Commission of the Comintern, which in the same November, 1926, was working out—of course, not without my participation—the resolution of the Seventh Enlarged Plenum on the Chinese question. That speech has since been published in pamphlet form, under the title of " Perspectives of the Chinese Revolution." Here are a few quotations from that speech :

I know that among the Kuomintang people, and even among the Chinese Communists, there are people who do not believe it possible to develop the revolution in the village, fearing that by having the peasantry drawn into the revolutionary movement, the united anti-imperialist front would be broken. This is a profound error, comrades. The anti-imperialist front in China will become stronger and more powerful the quicker and the more thoroughly the Chinese peasantry are drawn into the revolution.

And further :

I know that among the Chinese Communists there are comrades who believe workers' strikes for better material and legal conditions undesirable, and dissuade the workers from striking.

This is a great mistake, comrades. It implies a grave under-estimation of the rôle and specific weight of the proletariat in China. This should be put down in the theses as an absolutely negative phenomenon. It would be a great mistake for the Chinese Communists not to take advantage of the present favourable situation to help the workers improve their material and legal conditions, even if by means of strikes. What good is, then, the revolution in China ?

And here is a third document, *dated December* 1926, at a moment when the C.I. was bombarded with declarations from all the cities of China, to the effect that the development of the workers' struggle was leading to a crisis, to unemployment, and to the closing down of factories and workshops :

> The general policy of retreat in the cities, and of ceasing the struggle of the workers for better conditions, *is incorrect*. In the villages the struggle should be developed, but at the same time the favourable moment should be utilised to improve the material and legal status of the workers, endeavouring in every way to give an organised character to the workers' struggle, so as to prevent excesses and premature action. Particular care should be taken to get the struggle in the cities directed against the big imperialists, so as to retain the petty and middle bourgeoisie of China as far as possible in the united front against the common foe. The system of conciliation boards, arbitration courts, etc., we consider expedient, providing that a proper labour policy be secured in these institutions. At the same time we deem it necessary to say that it is absolutely inadmissible to issue decrees prohibiting strikes, workers' meetings, etc. In view of the importance of this question, we ask you to send regular information.

A fourth document, issued six weeks prior to Chiang Kai Shek's *coup d'état* :

> It is necessary to increase the activity of the Kuomintang and Communist nuclei in the army, and to organise them where none exist, but where it is possible to organise them. Where the organisation of Communist nuclei is impossible, it is necessary to carry on increased activity with the aid of secret Communists.
>
> It is necessary to steer our course towards the arming of the workers and the peasants, the transformation of the local peasant committees into actual organs of authority, with the organisation of self-defence, and so on.
>
> It is necessary that everywhere the Communist Party shall act as such : the policy of voluntary semi-legality is inadmissible ; *the Communist Party may not act as a brake on the mass movement ; the Communist Party should not shield the treacherous and reactionary policy of the Kuomintang right wingers : in order to expose them, it is*

necessary to mobilise the masses around the Kuomintang and the Chinese Communist Party.

" It is necessary to draw the attention of workers who are faithful to the revolution to the fact that at the present time the Chinese revolution, in view of the re-grouping of the class forces and the concentration of the imperialist armies, is passing through a critical period, and that further victories will be possible only if a determined course will be taken to develop the mass movement. Otherwise the revolution is menaced with grave peril. For this reason following the policy laid down is just now more essential than ever.

And at a still earlier date, in April 1926, a whole year prior to the *coup d'état* by the Kuomintang right wing and Chiang Kai Shek, the Comintern had warned the Chinese Communist Party, urging that it was " essential to work either for the withdrawal or expulsion of the right wingers from the Kuomintang."

This is how the Comintern understood, and continues to understand the tactics of the united front against imperialism during the first stage of the colonial revolution.

Does the Opposition know about these documents ? Of course it does. Why, then, does it hold its tongue about them ? Because it wants a quarrel, and not the truth.

And yet there was a time when the present Opposition leaders, particularly comrades Zinoviev and Kamenev, did understand something about Leninism, and, in the main, they advocated the same policy in regard to the Chinese revolutionary movement as was carried out by the Comintern, and which had been outlined to us by comrade Lenin in his theses. I have in mind the Sixth Plenum of the Communist International in February–March 1926, when comrade Zinoviev was the president of the Comintern, when he was still a Leninist and had not yet gone over to the Trotsky camp. I refer to the Sixth Plenum of the Communist International because there exists a resolution of that Plenum on the Chinese revolution, unanimously adopted in February–March 1926, containing approximately the same evaluation of the first stage of the Chinese revolution, of the Canton Kuomintang and the Canton Government, as is given by the Comintern and the Soviet C.P., and which is now disowned by the Opposition : I refer to that resolution because comrade Zinoviev voted for it, whilst no one of the C.C. members raised any objection to it, including comrades Trotsky, Kamenev and other leaders of the present Opposition.

Permit me to quote a few passages from that resolution. Here is what the resolution has to say on the Kuomintang :

> The Shanghai and Hong Kong political strikes of the Chinese workers (June–September 1925), have brought about a momentous departure in the fight for liberation of the Chinese people against the foreign imperialists. . . . The political action of the proletariat has given a wonderful impulse to the further development and consolidation of all the revolutionary-democratic organisations of the country, and in the first place, of the national-revolutionary Kuomintang Party and the revolutionary government at Canton. The Kuomintang Party, whose main body has acted in alliance with the Chinese Communists, represents a *revolutionary bloc of workers, peasants, intellectuals and urban democracy* on the grounds of the common class interests of these elements in the fight against the foreign imperialists and the whole of the militarist and feudal system, for the independence of the country, and for a united revolutionary-democratic national authority.

Here, then, we have the Canton Kuomintang as the alliance of four classes. Here, as you see, we get something near to the " Martynov doctrine " sanctioned by none other than the then president of the Comintern, comrade Zinoviev.

> *The revolutionary government at Canton formed by the Kuomintang Party* has already established contact with the largest masses of the workers, the peasants and the urban democracy, and, relying on them, it has smashed the counter-revolutionary bands supported by the imperialists and is now working on the radical democratisation of the whole political life of the Kwantung Province. Constituting thus the vanguard in the struggle of the Chinese people for independence, *the Canton Government constitutes a model for the future revolutionary-democratic building of the country.*

Thus we find that the Canton Kuomintang government, representing a bloc of four classes, was a revolutionary government, and not only that, but even a model for the future revolutionary-democratic government in China.

In the face of the new dangers the Chinese Communist Party and the Kuomintang should develop the most extensive political activity, organising mass action in support of the fight of the people's army, taking advantage of internal friction in the imperialist camp, and opposing to them the *united national-revolutionary front of the widest elements of the population* (workers, peasants and the *bourgeoisie*) under the guidance of the revolutionary-democratic organisations.

Thus we find that temporary blocs and understandings with the bourgeoisie in the colonial countries at a certain stage in the colonial revolution are not only admissible, but even necessary.

Don't you think that this resembles very closely what Lenin told us in his famous thesis on the tactics of Communists in the colonial and subject countries ? It is only a pity that comrade Zinoviev has already managed to forget all about it.

Individual strata of the upper bourgeoisie of China, who temporarily grouped themselves around the Kuomintang Party, have deserted it during the last year, which has caused the formation of a little group of the right wing of the Kuomintang who are openly opposed to the close alliance of the Kuomintang with the toiling masses, who want the Communists expelled from the Kuomintang, and who oppose the revolutionary policy of the Canton Government. *The denunciation of this right wing at the Second Congress of the Kuomintang (January 1926) and the confirmation of the need of the militant alliance of the Kuomintang with the Communists consolidates the revolutionary trend of the activities of the Kuomintang and the Canton Government, and ensures to the Kuomintang the revolutionary backing of the proletariat.*

Thus we find that the withdrawal of the Communists from the Kuomintang during the first stage of the Chinese revolution would have constituted a serious mistake. It was only a pity that comrade Zinoviev, who voted for this revolution, has managed to forget all about it a month or so afterwards. For we find that in April 1926 (one month after) Zinoviev demanded the immediate withdrawal of the Communists from the Kuomintang.

> The political self-determination of the Chinese Communists will grow in the course of combating two equally harmful deviations : the right wing liquidators which ignore the independent class tasks of the Chinese proletariat and which leads to a formless fusion with the general democratic national movement, and the extreme left tendencies which are trying to *jump over the revolutionary-democratic stage of the movement* directly to the tasks of the proletarian dictatorship and Soviet rule, *forgetting about the peasantry*, this fundamental and deciding factor of the Chinese national emancipation movement.

Here, as you see, there is everything to show up the present Opposition in regard to jumping over the Kuomintang stage of development in China, under-estimating the peasant movement, and leaping in the direction of Soviets. What a give-away this is.

Are comrades Zinoviev, Kamenev and Trotsky aware of this resolution ?

Presumably they are. At any rate, it ought to be known to comrade Zinoviev, who was President of the Comintern when it was adopted by the Sixth Plenum, and he himself voted for it. Why is it that the Opposition leaders now avoid mentioning this resolution carried by the supreme organ of the International Communist movement ? Why do they keep quiet about it ? Because it turns against them on all questions relating to the present Trotskyist argument of the Opposition. Because they have gone astray from the Comintern, astray from Leninism, and now, afraid of their own past, afraid of their own shadow, they are constrained to resort to cowardly evasion of the resolution of the Sixth Plenum of the Comintern.

This much in regard to the first stage of the Chinese revolution.

Let us now turn to the second stage of the Chinese revolution.

If the essential feature of the first stage consisted in the fact that the edge of the revolution was directed mainly against foreign imperialism, the characteristic feature of the second stage consists in the fact that the edge of the revolution is directed chiefly against the internal enemies, and above all, against the feudal landlords and the feudal régime. Has the first stage accomplished its tasks of overthrowing foreign imperialism ? No, it has not. It has left the accomplishment of this task as a legacy to the second stage of the Chinese revolutionary masses to rise against imperialism, to call a halt and to leave this work for the future. It should be presumed that the second stage of the revolution too will fail in the complete achievement of the task of chasing out the imperialists. It will give a further impetus to the fight of the masses of the Chinese workers and peasants against imperialism ; but whilst doing this, it will leave the final achievement of the task to the next stage of the Chinese revolution, to the Soviet stage.

And in this, there is nothing to be wondered at. Do we not recollect similar facts in the history of our own revolution, if under different circumstances ? Do we not know that the first stage of our own revolution did not completely fulfil its task of accomplishing the agrarian revolution, leaving this task to the next stage of the revolution, the October revolution, which has completely and entirely accomplished the task of stamping out the survivals of feudalism ? Therefore, it will be no surprise if the second stage of the Chinese revolution does not succeed in bringing about the agrarian revolution in full, and if the second stage of the revolution, after having aroused the teeming millions of the peasantry to the fight against the survivals of feudalism, leaves the final accomplishment of this task to the next stage of the revolution, to the Soviet stage. And this will constitute another task for the future Soviet revolution in China.

What was the essential task of the Communists at the second stage of the revolution in China, when the centre of the revolutionary movement had been clearly transferred from Canton to Wuhan, and as a counterpoise to the revolutionary government of Wuhan a counter-revolutionary centre was formed at Nanking ? Their task was to take full advantage of the possibility of open organisation of the Party, the proletariat (the trade unions), the peasantry (the peasant unions), and the revolution in general. Their task was to drive the Wuhan Kuomintang people towards the left, towards the agrarian revolution. Their task was to turn the Wuhan Kuomintang into the centre of the fight against the counter-revolution, and into the nucleus of the future revolutionary-democratic dictatorship of the proletariat and the peasantry.

Was this policy the correct one ? The facts have shown it to have been the only correct policy, capable of educating the wide masses of the workers and peasants in the spirit of the further development of the revolution.

The Opposition demanded at that time immediate formation of Soviets of workers' and peasants' deputies. But this was adventurism, an adventurous leap forward ; for the immediate formation of Soviets would have meant them jumping over the left Kuomintang phase of development. Why ? Because the Kuomintang at Wuhan, which was allied with the Communists, had not yet discredited and exposed itself before the wide masses of the workers and peasants, had not yet spent itself as a bourgeois revolutionary organisation. Because to launch the slogan of Soviets and the overthrow of the Wuhan government at a moment when the masses had not yet become convinced from their own experience about the rottenness of that government, and about the need to overthrow it, was to leap forward, to break away from the masses, to lose the support of the masses, and thus leap to defeat. The Opposition thinks that if it could see the hopelessness, the instability, and the lack of revolutionary principle on the part of the Wuhan Kuomintang (and this could easily be seen by any politically qualified worker) the situation was equally clear to the masses, so much so that the masses could be induced to form Soviets instead of the Kuomintang. But this is the usual ultra-left error of the Opposition, which takes its own consciousness and understanding for the consciousness and understanding of the millions of workers and peasants.

The Opposition is right in saying that the Party should move onward. This is the usual Marxian rule, and no real Communist Party can exist without abiding by it. But this is only part of the truth. The whole truth is that the Party should not only move onward, but should also lead the masses behind it. To move onward without the masses following is really to lag behind, to stay in the tail of the movement. To move onward while breaking away from the rearguard, failing to get the rearguard to follow, is to take a headlong leap which may have the result of arresting the onward movement of the masses for some time to come. It is the essence of Leninist leadership that the vanguard should get the rearguard to follow, that the vanguard should move onward without breaking away from the masses. But in order that the vanguard might not break away from the masses, that the vanguard should lead behind it the millions, there is one essential condition that is of decisive import, namely, that the masses themselves should become convinced from their own experience of the correctness of the instructions, policy and slogans of the vanguard. It is precisely the trouble with the Opposition that it fails to recognise this simple Leninist rule of leading the masses, that a single party, a single advanced group, without the support of the teeming millions of the masses, is unable to bring about a revolution, that the revolution is " made " in the long run by the teeming millions of the toiling masses.

J. Stalin

REPORT AT SEVENTEENTH CONGRESS OF THE COMMUNIST PARTY OF THE SOVIET UNION,

1934

English edition, Stalin Reports on the Soviet Union, Martin Lawrence Ltd., 1934

[Stalin's report on the work of the Central Committee of the Communist Party of the Soviet Union is not only a record of facts ; it is a theoretical statement of the first importance. The report is in three main sections : The Continuing Crisis of World Capitalism and the Foreign Relations of the Soviet Union ; The Continued Progress of the National Economy and the Internal Position of the U.S.S.R. ; and The Party. Parts of the first and third sections are reprinted here. The first is an analysis of " the *general* crisis of capitalism in the midst of which the *economic* crisis is proceeding." The third section raises theoretical questions of great practical interest in the Soviet Union, questions on which there has been considerable misunderstanding among socialists in other countries : the stages in the building of classless society ; the question of equality ; the national question ; organisational leadership as against bureaucracy.]

REPORT AT SEVENTEENTH CONGRESS OF THE COMMUNIST PARTY OF THE SOVIET UNION, 1934

THE CONTINUING CRISIS OF WORLD CAPITALISM AND THE FOREIGN RELATIONS OF THE SOVIET UNION

COMRADES, more than three years have passed since the Sixteenth Congress. The period is not a very long one. But it has been fuller in content than any other period. I do not think a single period in the last decade has been so rich in events as this.

In the *economic* sphere these years have been years of continuing world economic crisis. The crisis has affected not only industry but even agriculture as a whole. The crisis has not only raged in the sphere of production and trade, but has also swept into the sphere of credit and the circulation of money, and has overturned the established credit and currency relationships between countries. Formerly, there were disputes here and there as to whether there was a world economic crisis or not, but now nobody argues about this because the existence of the crisis and its devastating effects are only too obvious. Now the controversy centres around another question, viz., is there a way out of the crisis or not ? And if there is a way out, where is it to be found ?

In the *political* sphere these years have been years of growing acuteness in relations both as between capitalist countries as well as within the respective countries. The war between Japan and China and the occupation of Manchuria which have strained relations in the Far East ; the victory of fascism in Germany and the triumph of the idea of *revanche* which have strained relations in Europe ; the withdrawal of Japan and Germany from the League of Nations which has given a new impetus to the growth of armaments and to the preparations for an imperialist war ; the defeat of fascism in Spain, which once again showed that the revolutionary crisis is maturing and that fascism is not long lived by a long way—such are the most important facts of the period under review. It is not surprising that bourgeois pacifism is living its last hours and that the trend towards disarmament is openly and directly being replaced by a trend towards arming and re-arming.

Amidst the surging waves of economic shocks and military-political catastrophes, the U.S.S.R. stands out alone, like a rock, continuing its work of socialist construction and its fight to preserve peace. While in capitalist countries the economic crisis is still raging, in the U.S.S.R. progress is continuing both in the sphere of industry as well as in the sphere of agriculture. While in capitalist countries feverish preparations are in progress for a new war, for a new redistribution of the world and spheres of influence, the U.S.S.R. is continuing its systematic and stubborn struggle against the menace of war and for peace ; and it cannot be said that the efforts of the U.S.S.R. in this sphere have been quite unsuccessful.

Such is a general picture of the international situation at the present moment.

Let us pass on to examine the main data on the economic and political position of the capitalist countries.

1. The Movement of the Economic Crisis in Capitalist Countries

The present economic crisis in capitalist countries differs from all analogous crises, among other things, by the fact that it is the longest and most protracted crisis. Formerly, crises lasted one or two years ; the present crisis, however, is now in its fifth year and from year to year has devastated the economy of capitalist countries and has wasted the fat it accumulated in previous years. It is not surprising that this crisis is the severest of all crises.

How is the unprecedentedly protracted character of the present industrial crisis to be explained ?

It is to be explained first of all by the fact that the industrial crisis affected every capitalist country without exception and made it difficult for some countries to manœuvre at the expense of others.

Secondly, it is to be explained by the fact that the industrial crisis became interwoven with the agrarian crisis which affected all the agrarian and semi-agrarian countries without exception, and this could not but make the industrial crisis more complicated and profound.

Thirdly, it is to be explained by the fact that the agrarian crisis became more acute in this period and affected all branches of agriculture, including cattle-raising, degrading it to the level of passing from machine labour to hand labour, to the substitution of the horse for the tractor, to the sharp diminution in the use, and sometimes to the complete abandonment of, artificial fertilisers, which caused the industrial crisis to become still more protracted.

Fourthly, it is to be explained by the fact that the monopolist cartels which dominate industry strive to maintain the high prices of goods, and this circumstance makes the crisis particularly painful and hinders the absorption of stocks of commodities.

Lastly, and what is most important, it is to be explained by the fact that the industrial crisis broke out amidst the conditions of the *general* crisis of capitalism, when capitalism no longer has, nor can have, either in the home states or in the colonial and dependent countries, the strength and stability it had before the war and the October revolution, when industry in the capitalist countries is suffering from the heritage it received from the imperialist war in the shape of the chronic working of enterprises under capacity, and of an army of unemployed numbering millions from which it is no longer able to release itself.

Such are the circumstances which determine the extremely protracted character of the present industrial crisis. It is these circumstances, too, that explain the fact that the crisis has not been restricted to the sphere of production and trade, but has also affected the credit system, currency, the sphere of debt obligations, etc., and has broken down the traditionally established relations both between separate countries as well as between social groups in the separate countries.

An important rôle in this was played by the drop in the price of commodities. Notwithstanding the resistance of the monopolist cartels, the drop in prices increased with elemental force, and the drop in prices occurred primarily and mostly in regard to the commodities of the unorganised commodity owners, viz., peasants, artisans, small capitalists; the drop was gradual and smaller in degree in regard to the prices of commodities offered by the organised commodity owners, viz., the capitalists united in cartels. The drop in price made the position of debtors (manufacturers, artisans, peasants, etc.) intolerable, while on the other hand it placed the creditors in an unprecedentedly privileged position. Such a situation had to lead, and really did lead, to the colossal bankruptcy of firms and of separate *entrepreneurs*. During the past three years tens of thousands of joint stock companies were ruined in this way in the United States, in Germany, in England and in France. The bankruptcy of joint stock companies was followed by the depreciation of the currency, which to some extent eased the position of the debtors. Depreciation of currency was followed by the legalised non-payment of debts, both foreign and internal. The collapse of such banks as the Darmstadt and Dresden Banks in Germany, the Kredit Anstalt in Austria and also concerns like the Kreuger concern in Sweden, the Insull Company in the United States, etc., is well known to all.

It goes without saying that these phenomena which shook the foundations of the credit system had to bring in their train, and did bring in their train, the cessation of payments on credits and foreign loans, the cessation of payments of inter-Allied debts, the cessation of the export of capital, the further diminution of foreign trade, the further diminution of the export of commodities, the intensification of the struggle for foreign markets, trade war between countries and—dumping. Yes, comrades, dumping. I do not mean the alleged Soviet dumping, about which only very recently certain noble deputies in the noble parliaments of Europe and America were shouting until they were hoarse. I mean the real dumping that is now being practised by nearly all the " civilised " states, about which the gallant and noble deputies maintain a prudent silence.

It goes without saying also that these destructive phenomena accompanying the industrial crisis which operated outside the sphere of production could not but in their turn influence the course of the industrial crisis and make it more intense and more complicated.

Such is the general picture of the movement of the industrial crisis.

Here are a few figures taken from official materials which illustrate the movement of the industrial crisis in the period under review.

VOLUME OF INDUSTRIAL PRODUCTION

(Per cent. of 1929)

	1929	1930	1931	1932	1933
U.S.S.R.	100·0	129·7	161·9	184·7	201·6
U.S.A.	100·0	80·7	68·1	53·8	64·9
England	100·0	92·4	83·8	83·8	86·1
Germany	100·0	88·3	71·7	59·8	66·8
France	100·0	100·7	89·2	69·1	77·4

As you see, this table speaks for itself.

While industry in the principal capitalist countries declined from year to year compared with 1929 and began to recover somewhat only in 1933—although it has not reached the level of 1929 by a long way yet—industry in the U.S.S.R. increased from year to year and experienced a process of uninterrupted rise.

While industry in the principal capitalist countries shows

on the average a *reduction* of 25 per cent and more in the volume of production at the end of 1933 compared with the level of 1929, the industry of the U.S.S.R. during this period *grew* more than twice its size, i.e., increased more than 100 per cent.

Judging by this table it may seem that of the four capitalist countries England occupies the most favourable position. But that is not quite so. If we take the industry of these countries and compare it with the pre-war level, we shall get a somewhat different picture.

Here is the corresponding table:

VOLUME OF INDUSTRIAL PRODUCTION

(Per cent. of pre-war level)

	1913	1929	1930	1931	1932	1933
U.S.S.R.	100·0	194·3	252·1	314·7	359·0	391·9
U.S.A.	100·0	170·2	137·3	115·9	91·4	110·2
England	100·0	99·1	91·5	83·0	82·5	85·2
Germany	100·0	113·0	99·8	81·0	67·6	75·4
France	100·0	139·0	140·0	124·0	96·1	107·6

As you see, the industry of England and Germany has not yet reached the pre-war level, while that of the United States and France has exceeded it by several per cent and the U.S.S.R. has increased its industrial production during this period by 290 per cent compared with the pre-war level.

But there is still another conclusion that must be drawn from these tables.

While industry in the principal capitalist countries has been steadily declining since 1930, and particularly since 1931, and reached its lowest point in 1932, it began slightly to recover and rise in 1933. If we take the monthly returns for 1932 and 1933 we will find that they still further confirm this conclusion because they show that, in spite of fluctuations of production in the course of 1933, industry in these countries has not revealed any tendency for these fluctuations to drop to the level of the lowest point reached in the summer of 1932.

What does that mean ?

It means that, apparently, industry in the principal capitalist countries had already passed the lowest point of decline and did not return to it in the course of 1933.

Some people are inclined to ascribe this phenomenon to the influence of exclusively artificial factors, such as a war-inflation boom. There cannot be any doubt that the war-inflation boom plays a not unimportant rôle here. It is particularly true in regard to Japan, where this artificial factor is the principal and decisive force in some revival, principally in the munition branches of industry. But it would be a crude mistake to attempt to explain everything by the war-inflation boom. Such an explanation is wrong, if only for the reason that the changes in industry which I have described are observed, not in separate and chance districts, but in all, or nearly all, industrial countries, including those countries which have a stable currency. Apparently, side by side with the war-inflation boom the operation of the internal economic forces of capitalism also has effect here.

Capitalism has succeeded in somewhat easing the position of industry *at the expense of the workers*—increasing their exploitation by increasing the intensity of their labour ; *at the expense of the farmers*—by pursuing a policy of paying the lowest prices for the product of their labour, for foodstuffs and partly for raw materials ; *at the expense of the peasants in the colonies and in the economically weak countries*—by still further forcing down the prices of the products of their labour, principally of raw materials, and also of foodstuffs.

Does this mean that we are witnessing a transition from a crisis to an ordinary depression which brings in its train a new boom and flourishing industry ? No, it does not mean that. At all events at the present time there are no data, direct or indirect, that indicate the approach of an industrial boom in capitalist countries. More than that, judging by all things, there cannot be such data, at least in the near future. There cannot be, because all the unfavourable conditions which prevent industry in the capitalist countries from rising to any serious extent still continue to operate. I have in mind the continuing *general* crisis of capitalism in the midst of which the *economic* crisis is proceeding, the chronic working of the enterprises under capacity, the chronic mass unemployment, the interweaving of the industrial crisis with the agricultural crisis, the absence of tendencies towards any serious renewal of fixed capital which usually heralds the approach of a boom, etc.

Apparently, what we are witnessing is the transition from the lowest point of decline of industry, from the lowest depth of the industrial crisis to a depression, not an ordinary depression, but to a depression of a special kind which does not lead to a new boom and flourishing industry, but which, on the other hand, does not force it back to the lowest point of decline.

2. The Growing Acuteness of the Political Situation in Capitalist Countries

A result of the protracted economic crisis was the hitherto unprecedented acuteness of the political situation in capitalist countries, both within the respective countries as well as between them.

The intensified struggle for foreign markets, the abolition of the last vestiges of free trade, prohibitive tariffs, trade war, currency war, dumping and many other analogous measures which demonstrate extreme *nationalism* in economic policy, have caused the relations between the countries to become extremely acute, have created the soil for military conflicts, and have brought war to the front as a means for a new redistribution of the world and spheres of influence in favour of the strongest states.

Japan's war against China, the occupation of Manchuria, Japan's withdrawal from the League of Nations and her advance in North China have served to make the situation still more acute. The intensified struggle for the Pacific and the growth of the naval armaments of Japan, United States, England and France, represent the results of this increased acuteness.

Germany's withdrawal from the League of Nations and the spectre of *revanche* have given a fresh impetus to the acuteness of the situation and to the growth of armaments in Europe.

It is not surprising that bourgeois pacifism is now dragging out a miserable existence, and that idle talk about disarmament is being replaced by " business-like " talk about arming and re-arming.

Again as in 1914 the parties of bellicose imperialism, the parties of war and *revanche* are coming into the foreground.

Quite clearly things are moving towards a new war.

In view of the operation of these same factors the internal situation of the capitalist countries is becoming still more acute. Four years of industrial crisis have exhausted the working class and reduced it to despair. Four years of agricultural crisis have finally ruined the poorer strata of the peasantry, not only in the principal capitalist countries but also—and particularly—in the dependent and colonial countries. It is a fact that notwithstanding all the attempts to manipulate statistics in order to show a diminution in the number of unemployed, the number of unemployed according to the official returns of bourgeois institutions reaches 3,000,000 in England, 5,000,000 in Germany and 10,000,000 in the United States, not to speak of other countries in Europe. Add to this the number of workers employed part-time, which exceeds 10,000,000, add the millions of ruined peasants—and you will get an approximate picture of the poverty and despair of the toiling masses. The masses of the people have not yet reached the stage when they are ready to storm the citadel of capitalism, but the idea of storming it is maturing in the minds of the masses—there can hardly be any doubt about that. This is eloquently testified to by such facts as, say, the Spanish revolution which overthrew the fascist régime, and the expansion of the Soviet regions in China which the united counter-revolution of the Chinese and foreign bourgeoisie is unable to stop.

This, as a matter of fact, explains the fact that the ruling classes in the capitalist countries are zealously destroying, or nullifying, the last vestiges of parliamentarism and bourgeois democracy which might be used by the working class in its struggle against the oppressors, the fact that they are driving the Communist parties underground and resorting to open terrorist methods in order to maintain their dictatorship.

Chauvinism and preparation for war as the main elements of foreign policy, bridling the working class and terror in the sphere of home policy as a necessary means for strengthening the rear of future war fronts—this is what is particularly engaging the minds of contemporary imperialist politicians.

It is not surprising that fascism has now become the most fashionable commodity among bellicose bourgeois politicians. I do not mean fascism in general, I mean, primarily, fascism of the German type, which is incorrectly called National-Socialism, for the most searching examination will fail to reveal even an atom of socialism in it.

In this connection the victory of fascism in Germany must be regarded not only as a symptom of the weakness of the working class and as a result of the betrayal of the working class by Social-Democracy, which paved the way for fascism ; it must also be regarded as a symptom of the weakness of the bourgeoisie, as a symptom of the fact that the bourgeoisie is already unable to rule by the old methods of parliamentarism and bourgeois democracy, and, as a consequence, is compelled in its home policy to resort to terroristic methods of administration—it must be taken as a symptom of the fact that it is no longer able to find a way out of the present situation on the basis of a peaceful foreign policy, as a consequence of which it is compelled to resort to a policy of war.

That is the position.

Thus, you see that things are moving towards a new imperialist war as a way out of the present situation.

Of course there are no grounds for assuming that the war can provide a real way out. On the contrary, it must confuse the situation still more. More than that, it will certainly unleash revolution and put in question the very existence of capitalism in a number of countries, as was the case in the course of the first imperialist war. And if, notwithstanding the experience of the first imperialist war, the bourgeois politicians clutch at war as a drowning man clutches at a straw, it shows that they have become utterly confused, have reached an impasse, and are ready to rush headlong over the precipice.

It will not be amiss, therefore, to briefly examine the plans for the organisation of war which are now being hatched in the circles of bourgeois politicians.

Some think that war must be organised against one of the Great Powers. They think of imposing a crushing defeat upon it and of improving their own affairs at its expense. Let us assume that they organise such a war. What can come of it ? As is well known, during the first imperialist war it was intended to destroy one of the Great Powers, viz., Germany, and to profit at her expense. And what came of it ? They did not destroy Germany, but in Germany they sowed such a hatred for the victors and created such a rich soil for *revanche* that they have not been able to clear up the revolting mess they have made even to this day, and will not, perhaps, be able to do so for some time. But instead, they got the smash-up of capitalism in Russia, the victory of the proletarian revolution in Russia and—of course—the Soviet Union. What guarantee is there that the second imperialist war will produce " better " results for

them than the first ? Would it not be more correct to assume
that the opposite will be the case ?

Others think that war should be organised against a
country that is militarily weak, but which represents an
extensive market—for example, against China, which moreover, they have discovered, cannot be described as a state
in the strict sense of the word, but which merely represents
" unorganised territory " which needs to be seized by
strong states. Apparently, they want to divide it up completely and improve their affairs at its expense. Let us
assume that they organise such a war. What will come of
it ? It is well known that in the beginning of the nineteenth
century the same opinion was held in regard to Italy and
Germany as is now held in regard to China, viz., they were
regarded as " unorganised territories " and not states, and
they were enslaved. But what came of it ? As is well known,
it resulted in wars of independence waged by Germany
and Italy and their unification into independent states. It
resulted in increased hatred in the hearts of the peoples of
these countries for the oppressors, the results of which
have not been liquidated to this day and will not, perhaps,
be liquidated for some time. The question arises : What
guarantee is there that the same thing will not happen as
a result of an imperialist war against China ?

Still others think that war should be organised by a
" superior race," say, the German " race," against an
" inferior race," primarily against the Slavs, that only such
a war can provide a way out of the situation because it is
the mission of the " superior race " to fertilise the " inferior race " and rule over it. Let us assume that this queer
theory, which is as far removed from science as heaven is
from earth, is put into practice. What will come of it ? It
is well known that ancient Rome regarded the ancestors
of the present-day Germans and French in the same way as
the representatives of the " superior race " now regard the
Slavonic tribes. It is well known that ancient Rome treated
them as an " inferior race," as " barbarians " whose destiny

it was to be eternally subordinated to the " superior race," to " great Rome," and, between ourselves let it be said, ancient Rome had some grounds for this, which cannot be said about the representatives of the present " superior race." But what came of it ? The result was that the non-Romans, i.e., all the " barbarians " united against the common enemy, hurled themselves against Rome and overthrew it. The question arises : what guarantee is there that the claims of the representatives of the present " superior race " will not lead to the same deplorable results ? What guarantee is there that the fascist-literary politicians in Berlin will be more fortunate than the ancient and experienced conquerors in Rome ? Would it not be more correct to assume that the opposite will be the case ?

Still others, again, think that war should be organised against the U.S.S.R. Their plan is to smash the U.S.S.R., divide up its territory and profit at its expense. It would be a mistake to believe that it is only certain military circles in Japan who think in this way. We know that similar plans are being hatched in the circles of political leaders of certain states of Europe. Let us assume that these gentlemen pass from words to deeds. What can come of it ? There can hardly be any doubt that such a war would be a very dangerous war for the bourgeoisie. It would be a very dangerous war, not only because the peoples of the U.S.S.R. would fight to the very death to preserve the gains of the revolution ; it would be a very dangerous war for the bourgeoisie also because such a war will be waged not only at the fronts but also in the rear of the enemy. The bourgeoisie need have no doubt that the numerous friends of the working class of the U.S.S.R. in Europe and in Asia will be sure to strike a blow in the rear at their oppressors who commenced a criminal war against the fatherland of the working class of all countries. And let not Messieurs the bourgeoisie blame us if on the morrow of the outbreak of such a war they will miss certain of the governments that are near and dear to them and who are to-day happily ruling " by the grace of God." One such war against the U.S.S.R. has been waged, already, if you remember, fifteen years ago. As is well known, the universally esteemed Churchill clothed this war in a poetic formula—" the invasion of fourteen states." You remember of course that this war rallied the toilers of our country in a single camp of heroic warriors who defended their workers' and peasants' homeland against the foreign foe tooth and nail. You know how it ended. It ended with the invaders being driven from our country and the establishment of revolutionary Councils of Action in Europe. It can hardly be doubted that a second war against the U.S.S.R. will lead to the complete defeat of the aggressors, to revolution in a number of countries in Europe and in Asia, and to the overthrow of the bourgeois-landlord governments in these countries.

Such are the war plans of the perplexed bourgeois politicians.

As you see, they are not distinguished either for their brilliance or valour.

But if the bourgeoisie chooses the path of war, then the working class in the capitalist countries, who have been reduced to despair by four years of crisis and unemployment, takes the path of revolution. That means that a revolutionary crisis is maturing and will continue to mature. And the more the bourgeoisie becomes entangled in its war combinations, the more frequently it resorts to terroristic methods in the struggle against the working class and the toiling peasantry, the sooner will the revolutionary crisis mature.

Some comrades think that as soon as a revolutionary crisis occurs the bourgeoisie must drop into a hopeless position, that its end is predetermined, that the victory of the revolution is assured, and that all they have to do is to wait for the bourgeoisie to fall, and to draw up victorious resolutions. This is a profound mistake. The victory of revolution never comes by itself. It has to be prepared for and won. And only a strong proletarian revolutionary party can prepare for and win victory. Moments occur when the situation is revolutionary, when the rule of the bourgeoisie is shaken to its very foundations, and yet the victory of the revolution does not come, because there is no revolutionary party of the proletarian sufficiently strong and authoritative to lead the masses and take power. It would be unwise to believe that such " cases " cannot occur.

In this connection, it will not be amiss to recall Lenin's prophetic words on a revolutionary crisis, uttered at the Second Congress of the Communist International :

> We have now come to the question of the revolutionary crisis as the basis of our revolutionary action. And here we must first of all note two widespread errors. On the one hand, the bourgeois economists depict this crisis simply as " unrest," to use the elegant expression of the English. On the other hand, revolutionaries sometimes try to prove that there is absolutely no way out of the crisis. That is a mistake. There is no such thing as absolutely hopeless positions. The bourgeoisie behaves like an arrogant brigand who has lost his head, it commits blunder after blunder, thus making the position more acute and hastening its own doom. All this is true. But it cannot be " proved " that there are absolutely no possibilities whatever for it to lull a certain minority of the exploited with certain concessions, for it to suppress a certain movement or uprising of a certain section of the oppressed and exploited. To try to " prove " beforehand that a position is " absolutely " hopeless would be sheer pedantry or playing with concepts and catchwords. Practice alone can serve as real " proof " in this and similar questions. The bourgeois system all over the world is experiencing a great revolutionary crisis. And the revolutionary parties must now " prove " by their practice that they are sufficiently intelligent and organised, have contacts with the exploited masses, are sufficiently determined and skilful to utilise this crisis for a successful and victorious revolution. (Lenin, *Collected Works*, Vol. XXV, 1920, Russian edition.)

3. The Relations Between The U.S.S.R. and the Capitalist States

It is quite easy to understand how difficult it has been for the U.S.S.R. to pursue its peace policy in this atmosphere poisoned with the miasma of war combinations.

In the midst of this eve-of-the-war hullabaloo which is going on in a number of countries, the U.S.S.R. during these years has stood firmly and indomitably by its position of peace, fighting against the menace of war, fighting to preserve peace, going out to meet those countries which in one way or another stand for the preservation of peace, exposing and tearing the masks from those who are preparing for and provoking war.

What did the U.S.S.R. rely on in this difficult and complex struggle for peace ?

(*a*) On its growing economic and political might.

(*b*) On the moral support of millions of the working class in every country who are vitally interested in the preservation of peace.

(*c*) On the common sense of those countries which for this or that motive are not interested in disturbing the peace, and which want to develop commercial relations with such a punctual client as the U.S.S.R.

(*d*) Finally—on our glorious army, which is ready to defend our country against attack from without.

On this basis arose our campaign for the conclusion of pacts of non-aggression and of pacts defining the aggressor with our neighbouring states. You know that this campaign has been successful. As is known, pacts of non-aggression have been concluded not only with the majority of our neighbours in the west and in the south, including Finland and Poland, but also with such countries as France and Italy ; and pacts defining the aggressor have been concluded with these same neighbouring states, including the Little Entente.

On this basis also the friendship between the U.S.S.R. and Turkey was consolidated, relations between the U.S.S.R. and Italy have improved and have become indisputably satisfactory, relations with France, Poland and other Baltic states have improved, relations have been restored with the U.S.A., China, etc.

Of these facts reflecting the successes of the peace policy of the U.S.S.R. two of indisputably serious significance should be noted and singled out.

1. I have in mind, first, the change for the better that has taken place recently in the relations between the U.S.S.R. and Poland, between the U.S.S.R. and France. As is well known, our relations with Poland in the past were not at all good. Representatives of our state were assassinated in Poland. Poland regarded herself as the barrier of the Western states, against the U.S.S.R. All and sundry imperialists looked upon Poland as the vanguard in the event of a military attack upon the U.S.S.R. The relations between the U.S.S.R. and France were not much better. It is sufficient to recall the facts in the history of the trial of The Ramzin wreckers' group in Moscow in order to restore in one's mind the picture of the relations between the U.S.S.R. and France. But now these undesirable relations are gradually beginning to disappear. They are being replaced by other relations, which cannot be otherwise described than relations of *rapprochement*. It is not only that we have concluded pacts of non-aggression with these countries, although these pacts in themselves are of very serious importance. The most important thing first of all is that the atmosphere charged with mutual distrust is beginning to be dissipated. This does not mean, of course, that the incipient process of *rapprochement* can be regarded as sufficiently stable and as guaranteeing ultimate success. Surprises and zigzags in policy, for example in Poland, where anti-Soviet moods are still strong, cannot be regarded as being excluded by a long way. But a change for the better in our relations, irrespective of its results in the future, is a fact worthy of being noted and put in the fore-front as a factor in the advancement of the cause of peace.

What is the cause of this change ? What stimulates it ?

First of all, the growth of the strength and might of the U.S.S.R. In our times it is not the custom to give any consideration to the weak—consideration is only given to the strong. Then there have been certain changes in the policy of Germany which reflect the growth of *revanche*-ist and imperialist moods in Germany.

In this connection certain German politicians say that now the U.S.S.R. has taken an orientation towards France and Poland, that from being an opponent of the Versailles Treaty it has become a supporter of it and that this change is to be explained by the establishment of a fascist régime in Germany. This is not true. Of course, we are far from being enthusiastic about the fascist régime in Germany. But fascism is not the issue here, if only for the reason that fascism, for example in Italy, did not prevent the U.S.S.R. establishing very good relations with that country. Nor are the alleged changes in our attitude towards the Versailles Treaty the point of issue. It is not for us, who have experienced the shame of the Brest-Litovsk Peace, to sing the praises of the Versailles Treaty. We merely do not agree to the world being flung into the throes of a new war for the sake of this treaty. The same thing must be said in regard to the alleged new orientation taken by the U.S.S.R. We never had any orientation towards Germany nor have we any orientation towards Poland and France. Our orientation in the past and our orientation at the present time is towards the U.S.S.R. and towards the U.S.S.R. alone. And if the interests of the U.S.S.R. demand *rapprochement* with this or that country which is not interested in disturbing peace, we shall take this step without hesitation.

No, that is not the point. The point is that the policy of Germany has changed. The point is that even before the present German politicians came into power, and particularly after they came into power, a fight between two political lines broke out in Germany, between the old policy which found expression in the well-known treaties between the U.S.S.R. and Germany and the " new " policy which in the main recalls the policy of the ex-Kaiser of Germany who at one time occupied the Ukraine, undertook a march against Leningrad and transformed the Baltic countries into a *place d'armes* for this march ; and this " new " policy is obviously gaining the upper hand over the old policy. The fact that the supporters of the " new " policy are gaining supremacy in all things while the supporters of the old policy are in disgrace cannot be regarded as an accident. Nor can the well-known action of Hugenberg in London, nor the equally well-known declarations of Rosenberg, the director of the foreign pclicy of the ruling party in Germany, be regarded as accidents. That is the point, comrades.

2. Secondly, I have in mind the restoration of normal relations between the U.S.S.R. and the United States. There cannot be any doubt that this act has very serious significance for the whole system of international relations. It is not only that it improves the chances of preserving peace, that it improves the relations between the two countries, strengthens commercial intercourse between them and creates a base for mutual co-operation ; it is a landmark between the old, when the United States in various countries was regarded as the bulwark for all sorts of anti-Soviet tendencies, and the new, when this bulwark was voluntarily removed, to the mutual advantage of both countries.

Such are the two main facts which reflect the successes of the Soviet peace policy.

It would be wrong, however, to think that everything went smoothly in the period under review. No, not everything went smoothly by a long way.

Recall, say, the pressure that was brought to bear upon us by England, the embargo on our exports, the attempt to interfere in our internal affairs and to put out feelers to test our power of resistance. It is true that nothing came of this attempt and that later the embargo was removed ; but the aftermath of these attacks is still felt in all things that affect the relations between England and the U.S.S.R., including the negotiations for a commercial treaty. And

Ffm

these attacks upon the U.S.S.R. must not be regarded as accidental. It is well known that one section of the English conservatives cannot live without such attacks. And precisely because they are not accidental we must bear in mind that attacks on the U.S.S.R. will be made in the future, that all sorts of menaces will be created, attempts to damage it will be made, etc.

Nor can we lose sight of the relations between the U.S.S.R. and Japan which stand in need of very considerable improvement. Japan's refusal to conclude a pact of non-aggression, of which Japan stands in need no less than the U.S.S.R., once again emphasises the fact that all is not well in the sphere of our relations. The same thing must be said in regard to the rupture of negotiations concerning the Chinese Eastern Railway due to no fault of the U.S.S.R., and also in regard to the outrageous deeds the Japanese agents are committing on the C.E.R., the illegal arrests of Soviet employees on the C.E.R., etc. This is quite apart from the fact that one section of the military men in Japan are openly advocating in the Press the necessity for a war against the U.S.S.R. and the seizure of the Maritime Province with the avowed approval of another section of the military, while the government of Japan, instead of calling these instigators of war to order, is pretending that this is not a matter that concerns it. It is not difficult to understand that such circumstances cannot but create an atmosphere of uneasiness and uncertainty. Of course, we will continue persistently to pursue the policy of peace and strive for an improvement in our relations with Japan because we want to improve these relations. But it does not entirely depend upon us. That is why we must at the same time adopt all measures for the purpose of guarding our country against surprises and be prepared to defend it in the event of attack.

As you see, besides successes in our peace policy we also have a number of negative phenomena.

Such are the foreign relations of the U.S.S.R.

Our foreign policy is clear. It is a policy of preserving peace and strengthening commercial relations with all countries. The U.S.S.R. does not think of threatening anybody—let alone of attacking anybody. We stand for peace and champion the cause of peace. But we are not afraid of threats and are prepared to answer blow for blow against the instigators of war. Those who want peace and are striving for business intercourse with us will always receive our support. And those who try to attack our country— will receive a stunning rebuff to teach them not to poke their pig's snout into our Soviet garden again.

Such is our foreign policy.

The task is to continue to pursue this policy with all persistence and consistency. . . .

THE PARTY

I come now to the question of the Party.

The present Congress is taking place under the flag of the complete victory of Leninism, under the flag of the liquidation of the remnants of anti-Leninist groups.

The anti-Leninist-Trotskyist group has been defeated and scattered. Its organisers are now hanging around the backyards of the bourgeois parties abroad.

The anti-Leninist Right deviationist group has been defeated and scattered. Its organisers long ago renounced their views and are now trying very hard to expiate the sins they committed against the Party.

The national deviationist groups have been defeated and scattered. Their organisers long ago became finally merged with the interventionist *émigrés*, or else have recanted.

The majority of the adherents of these anti-revolutionary groups have been compelled to admit that the line of the Party was right and have capitulated before the Party.

At the Fifteenth Party Congress it was still necessary to prove that the Party line was right and to wage a struggle against certain anti-Leninist groups ; and at the Sixteenth

Party Congress the last adherents of these groups had to be despatched. At this Congress, however, there is nothing to prove and, perhaps, no one to beat. Everyone now sees that the line of the Party has conquered.

The policy of industrialising the country has conquered. Its results are obvious to everyone. What argument can be advanced against this fact?

The policy of liquidating the kulaks and of mass collectivisation has conquered. Its results also are obvious to everyone. What argument can be advanced against that fact?

The experience of our country has shown that it is quite possible to build socialism in a single country taken separately. What argument can be advanced against that fact?

Evidently, all these successes, and primarily the victory of the Five-Year Plan, have utterly demoralised and smashed to atoms all and sundry anti-Leninist groups.

It must be admitted that the Party to-day is as united as it never has been before.

1. Problems of Ideological-Political Leadership

Does this mean, however, that the fight is ended and that the further offensive of socialism is to be abandoned as something superfluous?

No, it does not mean that.

Does this mean that all is well in the Party, that there will be no more deviations and that we can now rest on our laurels?

No, it does not mean that.

The enemies of the Party, the opportunists of all shades, the national-deviationists of all types, have been defeated. But remnants of their ideologies still live in the minds of individual members of the Party, and not infrequently they find expression. The Party must not be regarded as something isolated from the people who surround it. It lives and works in its environment. It is not surprising that not infrequently unhealthy moods penetrate the Party from without. And the soil for such moods undoubtedly still exists in our country, if only for the reason that certain intermediary strata of the population still exist in town and country and represent the medium which fosters such moods.

The Seventeenth Conference of our Party declared that one of the fundamental political tasks in connection with the fulfilment of the Second Five-Year Plan is " to overcome the survivals of capitalism in economy and in the minds of men." This is an absolutely correct idea. But can we say that we have already overcome all the survivals of capitalism in economy ? No, we cannot say that. Still less reason would there be for saying that we have overcome the survivals of capitalism in the minds of men. This cannot be said, not only because the development of the mind of man lags behind his economic position but also because the capitalist environment exists, which tries to revive and support the survivals of capitalism in economy and in the minds of the people of the U.S.S.R., and against which we Bolsheviks must always keep our powder dry.

It goes without saying that these survivals cannot but create a favourable soil for the revival of the ideology of the defeated anti-Leninist groups in the minds of individual members of our Party. Add to this the not very high theoretical level of the majority of the members of our Party, the weak ideological work of the Party organs and the fact that our Party workers are overburdened with purely practical work, which deprives them of the opportunity of augmenting their theoretical knowledge, and you will understand whence comes the confusion on a number of problems of Leninism that exists in the minds of individual members of the Party, which not infrequently penetrates our Press, and which helps to revive the survivals of the ideology of the defeated anti-Leninist groups.

That is why we cannot say that the fight is ended, and that there is no longer any need for the policy of the socialist offensive.

A number of problems of Leninism could be taken to demonstrate how tenacious the survivals of the ideology of the defeated anti-Leninist groups are in the minds of certain Party members.

Take, for example, the question of building *classless socialist society*. The Seventeenth Party Conference declared that we are marching towards classless socialist society. It goes without saying that classless society cannot come by itself. It has to be won and built by the efforts of all the toilers, by strengthening the organs of the dictatorship of the proletariat, by extending the class struggle, by abolishing classes, by liquidating the remnants of the capitalist classes in battles with the enemy, both internal and external.

The thing is clear, one would think.

And yet, who does not know that the promulgation of this clear and elementary thesis of Leninism has given rise to not a little confusion and unhealthy moods among a certain section of Party members ? The thesis—advanced as a slogan—about our advancing towards classless society is interpreted by them as a spontaneous process. And they begin to reason in the following way : if it is classless society then we can relax the class struggle, we can relax the dictatorship of the proletariat and generally abolish the state, which in any case has got to die out soon. And they dropped into a state of moon-calf ecstasy in the expectation that soon there will be no classes and therefore no class struggle, and therefore no cares and worries, and therefore it is possible to lay down our arms and retire—to sleep and to wait for the advent of classless society.

There can be no doubt that this confusion of mind and these moods are as like as two peas to the well-known views of the Right deviationists who believed that the old must automatically grow into the new, and that one fine day we shall wake up and find ourselves in socialist society.

As you see, the remnants of the ideology of the defeated anti-Leninist groups can be revived, and have not lost their tenacity by a long way.

It goes without saying that if this confusion of mind and these non-Bolshevik moods overcame the majority of our Party, the Party would find itself demobilised and disarmed.

Now take the question of the agricultural artel and the agricultural commune. Everybody admits now that under present conditions the artel is the only proper form of the collective farm movement. And that is quite understandable :

(a) The artel properly combines the personal, everyday interests of the collective farmers with their public interests.

(b) The artel successfully adapts the personal everyday interest to public interests, and thereby helps to educate the individual farmer of yesterday in the spirit of collectivism.

Unlike the artel, where only the means of production are socialised, in the communes, until recently, not only were the means of production socialised, but so also was the everyday life of every member of the commune. That is to say, the members of the commune, unlike the members of an artel, did not personally own domestic poultry, small livestock, a cow, some grain or a kitchen garden. This means that in the commune the personal everyday interests of the members are not so much taken into account and combined with the public interests as eclipsed by the latter in the pursuit of petty bourgeois equalitarianism. It goes without saying that this is the weakest side of the commune. This, properly speaking, explains why the commune is not widespread, and why there are so few of them. For the same reason, in order to preserve their existence and prevent their collapse, the communes were compelled to abandon the system of socialised everyday life and are beginning to work on the work-day principle, have begun to distribute grain among the members, to permit their members to own their own poultry, small livestock, a cow, etc. But from this it follows that, actually, the commune has passed over to the position of the artel. And there is nothing bad in this because the sound development of the mass collective farm movement demands this.

This does not mean, of course, that the commune is not needed at all, that it does not represent the highest form of the collective farm movement. No, the commune is needed, and, of course, it is the highest form of the collective farm movement. But this applies, not to the present commune, which arose on the basis of undeveloped technique and of a shortage of products, and which is itself passing to the position of the artel, but to the commune of the future which will arise on the basis of a more developed technique and of an abundance of products. The present agricultural commune arose on the basis of an under-developed technique and shortage of products. This, properly speaking, explains why it practised equalitarianism and showed little concern for the personal everyday interests of its members, as a result of which it is now being compelled to pass to the position of the artel, in which the personal and public interests of the collective farmers are sensibly combined. The future commune will arise out of the developed and well-to-do artels. The future agricultural commune will arise when the fields and farms of the artel will be replete with grain, with cattle, with poultry, with vegetables, and all other produce ; when the artels will have their mechanised laundries, modern dining-rooms, bakeries, etc. ; when the collective farmer will see that it is more to his advantage to receive his meat and milk from the farm than to have his own cow and small livestock ; when the woman collective farmer will see that it is more to her advantage to take her meals in a dining-room, to get her bread from the public bakery and to get her linen washed in the public laundry than to prepare all these things herself. The future commune will arise on the basis of a more developed technique and of a more developed artel, on the basis of an abundance of products. When will that be ? Not soon, of course. But it will be. It would be a crime to accelerate the process of transition from the artel to the commune artificially. That would confuse the whole issue, and would facilitate the task of our enemies. The process of transition from the artel to the future commune must be gradual and to the extent that *all* the collective farmers are convinced that such a transition is necessary.

That is the position in regard to the question of the artel and the commune.

One would think that it was clear and almost elementary.

And yet, among a section of the members of the Party there is a fair amount of confusion on this question. They are of the opinion that by declaring the artel to be the fundamental form of the collective farm movement, the Party had removed itself from socialism, had retreated from the commune, from the higher form of the collective farm movement, to the lower form. The question arises—why ? Because, it appears, there is no equality in the artel, because differences in the requirements and in the personal life of the members of the artel are preserved, whereas in the commune there is equality, in the commune the requirements and the personal position of all the members are equal. But in the first place, there are no longer any communes in which there is equality, equalitarianism in requirements and in personal life. Practice has shown that the communes would certainly have died out had they not abandoned equality and had they not actually passed to the position of an artel. Hence, it is useless talking about what no longer exists. Secondly, every Leninist knows, if he is a real Leninist, that equality in the sphere of requirements and personal life is a piece of reactionary petty-bourgeois stupidity worthy of a primitive sect of ascetics, but not of socialist society organised on Marxian lines, because we cannot demand that all people should have the same requirements and tastes, that all people shall live their individual lives in the same way. And finally, are not differences in requirements and in personal life preserved among the workers ? Does that mean that the workers are more remote from socialism than the members of an agricultural commune ?

These people evidently think that socialism calls for equality, for levelling the requirements and the personal lives of the members of society. Needless to say, such an assumption has nothing in common with Marxism, with Leninism. By equality Marxism means, not equality in personal requirements and personal life, but the abolition of classes, i.e., (a) the equal emancipation of all toilers from exploitation after the capitalists have been overthrown and expropriated ; (b) the equal abolition for all of private property in the means of production after they have been transformed into the property of the whole of society ; (c) the equal duty of all to work according to their ability and the equal right of all toilers to receive according to the amount of work they have done (*socialist* society) ; (d) the equal duty of all to work according to their ability and the equal right of all toilers to receive according to their requirements (*communist* society). And Marxism starts out with the assumption that people's tastes and requirements are not, and cannot be, equal in quality or in quantity, either in the period of socialism or in the period of communism.

That is the Marxian conception of equality.

Marxism has not recognised, nor does it recognise, any other equality.

To draw from this the conclusion that socialism calls for equality, for the levelling of the requirements of the members of society, for the levelling of their tastes and of their personal lives, that according to Marxism all should wear the same clothes, and eat the same dishes and in the same quantity—means talking banalities and slandering Marxism.

It is time it was understood that Marxism is opposed to levelling. Even in *The Communist Manifesto* Marx and Engels scourged primitive Utopian socialism and described it as reactionary because it preached " universal asceticism and social levelling in its crudest form." In his *Mr. Dühring Revolutionises Science*, Engels devotes a whole chapter to the withering criticism of the " radical equalitarian socialism " proposed by Dühring to counteract Marxian socialism. And Engels wrote :

> . . . the real content of the proletarian demand for equality is the demand for the abolition of classes. Any demand for equality which goes beyond that of necessity passes into absurdity.

Lenin said the same thing :

> Engels was a thousand times right when he wrote : any demand for equality which goes beyond the demand for the abolition of classes is a stupid and absurd prejudice. Bourgeois professors tried to use the argument about equality in order to expose us by saying that we wanted to make all men equal. They tried to accuse the Socialists of an absurdity that they themselves invented. But owing to their ignorance they did not know that the Socialists—and precisely the founders of modern scientific socialism, Marx and Engels—said : equality is an empty phrase unless by equality is meant the abolition of classes. We want to abolish classes, and in that respect we are in favour of equality. But the claim that we want to make all men equal to each other is an empty phrase and a stupid invention of the intellectuals. (Lenin's speech, *On Deceiving the People with Slogans about Liberty and Equality*.)

Clear, one would think.

Bourgeois writers are fond of depicting Marxian socialism like the old Tsarist barracks, where everything was subordinated to the " principle " of equality. Marxists cannot be responsible for the ignorance and stupidity of bourgeois writers.

There cannot be any doubt that the confusion in the minds of individual members of the Party concerning Marxian socialism and their infatuation with the equalitarian tendencies of agricultural communes are as like as two peas to the petty-bourgeois views of our " Leftist " blockheads who at one time idealised the agricultural commune to such an extent that they even tried to implant the commune in the factories where skilled and unskilled workers, each working at his trade, had to put his wages into the common fund which was then shared out equally. We know what harm these infantile equalitarian exercises of our " Leftist " blockheads caused our industry.

As you see, the remnants of the ideology of the defeated anti-Party groups still display rather considerable tenacity.

It goes without saying that if these " Leftist " views were to triumph in the Party, the Party would cease to be Marxian, and the collective farm movement would finally be disorganised.

Or take for example the question of the slogan : " *make every collective farmer well-to-do.*" This slogan not only affects collective farmers ; it affects the workers to a far larger extent, because we want to make all the workers well-to-do, to enable them to lead a well-to-do and cultured existence.

One would think the point was clear. There would have been no use overthrowing capitalism in October 1917, and building socialism for a number of years if we are not going to secure a life of plenty for our people. Socialism means, not poverty and privation, but the abolition of poverty and privation, the organisation of a well-to-do and cultured life for all members of society.

And yet, this clear and essentially elementary slogan has caused perplexity, muddle and confusion among a certain section of our Party members. Is not this slogan, they ask, a reversion to the old slogan " enrich yourselves " that was rejected by the Party ? If everyone becomes well-to-do, they continue to argue, and the poor cease to be with us, whom can we Bolsheviks rely upon in our work ? How shall we be able to work without the poor ?

This may sound funny, but the existence of such naïve and anti-Leninist views among a section of the members of the Party is an undoubted fact, which we must take note of.

Apparently, these people do not understand that a wide

gulf lies between the slogan " enrich yourselves " and the slogan " make the collective farmers well-to-do." In the first place only *individual* persons or groups can enrich themselves, whereas the slogan concerning a well-to-do existence affects, not individual persons or groups, but *all* collective farmers. Secondly, *individual* persons or groups enrich themselves for the purpose of subjecting other people, and of *exploiting* them, whereas the slogan concerning the well-to-do existence of *all* collective farmers—with the means of production in the collective farms socialised— *excludes* all possibility of the exploitation of some persons by others. Thirdly, the slogan, " enrich youselves," was issued in the period of the initial stage of the New Economic Policy, when capitalism was partly restored, when the kulak was strong, when individual peasant farming predominated in the country, and collective farming was in a rudimentary state, whereas the slogan, " make every collective farmer well-to-do," was issued in the last stage of N.E.P., when the capitalist elements in industry had been destroyed, the kulaks in the countryside crushed, individual peasant farming forced into the background and the collective farms transformed into the predominant form of agriculture. I need not mention that the slogan, " make every collective farmer well-to-do," is not isolated, but is inseparably connected with the slogan, " make all collective farms Bolshevik farms."

Is it not clear that in essence the slogan, " enrich yourselves," was a call for the *restoration* of capitalism, whereas the slogan, " make every collective farmer well-to-do," is a call to *finally crush* the last remnants of capitalism by increasing the economic power of the collective farms and by transforming all collective farmers into well-to-do toilers ?

Is it not clear that there is not, nor can there be, anything in common between these two slogans ?

The argument that Bolshevik work and socialism are inconceivable without the existence of the poor is so stupid that one finds it embarrassing to talk about it. The Leninists rely upon the poor when there are capitalist elements and the poor who are exploited by the capitalists. But when the capitalist elements are crushed and the poor are emancipated from exploitation, the task of the Leninists is not to perpetuate and preserve poverty and the poor—the premises of whose existence have already been destroyed—but to abolish poverty and to raise the poor to a well-to-do standard of living. It would be absurd to think that socialism can be built on the basis of poverty and privation, on the basis of reducing personal requirements and the standard of living to the level of the poor, who, moreover, refuse to remain poor any longer and are pushing their way upward to a well-to-do standard of living. Who wants this sort of socialism ? This would not be socialism, but a caricature of socialism. Socialism can only be built up on the basis of a rapid growth of the productive forces of society, on the basis of an abundance of products and goods, on the basis of a well-to-do standard of living of the toilers, and on the basis of the rapid growth of culture. For socialism, Marxian socialism, means not the cutting down of personal requirements, but their universal expansion ; not the restriction or the abstention from satisfying these requirements, but the all-sided and full satisfaction of all the requirements of culturally developed working people.

There cannot be any doubt that this confusion in the minds of certain members of the Party concerning poverty and prosperity is a reflection of the views of our " Leftist " blockheads, who idealise the poor as the eternal bulwark of Bolshevism under all conditions, and who regard the collective farms as the arena of fierce class struggle.

As you see, here, too, on this question, the remnants of the ideology of the defeated anti-Party groups have not yet lost their tenacity.

It goes without saying that had such blockheaded view achieved victory in our Party, the collective farms would not have achieved the successes they have achieved during the

past two years, and they would have fallen to pieces in a
very short time.

Or take, for example, the *national question*. Here too, in the
sphere of the national question as in other questions, there is
confusion in the minds of a certain section of the Party,
which creates a certain danger. I have spoken of the tenacity
of the survivals of capitalism. It should be observed that the
survivals of capitalism in the minds of men are much more
tenacious in the sphere of the national question than in any
other sphere. They are more tenacious because they are
able to disguise themselves in national costumes. Many
think that Skrypnik's fall was an individual case, an exception to the rule. That is not true. The fall of Skrypnik and
his group in the Ukraine is not an exception. Similar
" dislocations " are observed among certain comrades in
other national republics.

What does a deviation towards nationalism mean—
irrespective of whether it is a deviation towards Great
Russian nationalism or towards local nationalism ? The
deviation towards nationalism is the adaptation of the
internationalist policy of the working class to the nationalist
policy of the bourgeoisie. The deviation towards nationalism
reflects the attempts of " one's own " " national " bourgeoisie to undermine the Soviet system and to restore
capitalism. As you see, both these deviations have a common source. This source is a *departure* from Leninist internationalism. If you want to keep both these deviations under
fire, then aim primarily against this source, against those
who depart from internationalism—irrespective of whether
the deviation is towards local nationalism or towards Great
Russian nationalism.

There is a controversy as to which deviation represents
the major danger, the deviation towards Great Russian
nationalism or the deviation towards local nationalism ?
Under present conditions this is a formal and therefore a
purposeless controversy. It would be absurd to attempt to
give ready-made recipes for the major and minor dangers

that would be suitable for all times and for all conditions. Such recipes do not exist. The major danger is the deviation against which we have ceased to fight and thereby enabled it to grow into a danger to the state.

Only very recently, in the Ukraine, the deviation towards Ukrainian nationalism did not represent the major danger ; but when we ceased to fight against it and enabled it to grow to the extent that it joined up with the interventionists, this deviation became the major danger. The question as to which is the major danger in the sphere of the national question is determined not by futile and formal controversies but by a Marxian analysis of the situation at the given moment, and by the study of the mistakes that have been committed in this sphere.

The same thing must be said about the *Right* and " *Left* " *deviation* in the sphere of general policy. Here too, as in other spheres, there is no little confusion in the minds of certain members of the Party. Sometimes while fighting against the Right deviation they take their hands away from the " Left " deviation and relax the fight against it on the assumption that it is not dangerous, or only slightly dangerous. This is a very serious and dangerous mistake. This is a concession to the " Left " deviation, which is impermissible for a member of the Party. It is all the more impermissible for the reason that recently the " Lefts " have completely slipped to the positions of the Rights, so that there is no longer any essential difference between them.

We have always said that the " Lefts " are the Rights who mask their Right-ness with Left phrases. Now the " Lefts " themselves confirm the correctness of our statement. Take last year's issues of the Trotskyist *Bulletin*. What do Messieurs the Trotskyists demand, what do they write about, in what does their " Left " programme express itself ? They demand : *the dissolution of the Soviet farms* because they are unprofitable ; *the dissolution of the majority of the collective farms* because they are fictitious ; *the abandonment of the policy of liquidating the kulaks* ; *reversion to the policy of concessions,* and *the leasing of a number of our industrial enterprises to concessionaires* because they are unprofitable.

Such is the programme of the contemptible cowards and capitulators, a counter-revolutionary programme of restoring capitalism, in the U.S.S.R.

In what way does it differ from the programme of the extreme Rights ? Clearly, it differs in no way. It follows, then, that the " Lefts " have openly associated themselves with the counter-revolutionary programme of the Rights in order to enter into a *bloc* with them and to wage a joint struggle against the Party.

After this, how can anyone say that the " Lefts " are not dangerous, or are only slightly dangerous ? Is it not clear that those who talk such rubbish bring grist to the mill of the bitter enemies of Leninism ?

As you see, here too, in the sphere of deviations from the line of the Party—irrespective of whether they are deviations on general policy, or deviations on the national question—the survivals of capitalism in the minds of men, including the minds of certain members of our Party, are sufficiently tenacious.

These, then, are a few serious and urgent questions concerning our ideological and political work on which lack of clarity, confusion and even direct deviation from Leninism exist among certain strata of the Party. And these are not the only questions which could serve to demonstrate the confusion of mind among certain members of the Party.

After this, can it be said that all is well in the Party ?

Clearly, it cannot.

Our tasks in the sphere of ideological and political work are :

1. To raise the theoretical level of the Party to its proper plane.

2. To intensify ideological work in all the links of the Party.

3. To carry on unceasing propaganda of Leninism in the ranks of the Party.

4. To train the Party organisations and the non-Party *active* which surrounds them in the spirit of Leninist internationalism.

5. Not to gloss over but boldly to criticise the deviations of certain comrades from Marxism-Leninism.

6. Systematically to expose the ideology and remnants of the ideology of trends that are hostile to Leninism.

2. *Problems of Organisational Leadership*

I have spoken about our successes. I have spoken about the victory of the Party line in the sphere of national economy and culture as well as in the sphere of overcoming anti-Leninist groups in the Party. I have spoken of the world-historical significance of our victories. But this does not mean that victory has been achieved in all things, and that all problems have been solved. Such successes and such victories never occur in real life. Not a few unsolved problems and defects have remained. We are confronted by a heap of problems demanding solution. But it does undoubtedly mean that the major part of the urgent problems are already solved, and, in this sense, the great victory of our Party is beyond question.

But here the question arises : how were these victories achieved, how were they obtained ; in fact, what fight was put up for them, what efforts were exerted for them ?

Some people think that it is sufficient to draw up a correct Party line, proclaim it from the housetops, enunciate it in the form of general theses and resolutions and carry them unanimously in order to make victory come of itself, automatically, so to speak. This, of course, is wrong. Those who think like that are greatly mistaken. Only incorrigible bureaucrats and office rats can think that. As a matter of fact, these successes and victories were obtained not automatically but as a result of a fierce struggle to carry out the Party line. Victory never comes by itself—it has to be dragged by the hand. Good resolutions and declarations in favour of the general line of the Party are only a beginning, they merely express the desire to win, but it is not victory. After the correct line has been given, after a correct solution of the problem has been found, success depends on the manner in which the work is organised, on the organisation of the struggle for the application of the line of the Party, on the proper selection of workers, on supervising the fulfilment of the decisions of the leading organs. Without this the correct line of the Party and the correct solutions are in danger of being severely damaged. More than that, after the correct political line has been given, the organisational work decides everything, including the fate of the political line itself, i.e., its success or failure.

As a matter of fact, victory was achieved and won by a systematic and stern struggle against all sorts of difficulties that lay in the path of carrying out the Party line, by overcoming these difficulties, by mobilising the Party and the working class for the purpose of overcoming these difficulties, by organising the struggle to overcome these difficulties, by removing inefficient workers and selecting better ones capable of waging the struggle against difficulties.

What are these difficulties, and where are they concealed?

These difficulties are difficulties of our organisational work, difficulties of our organisational leadership. They are concealed within ourselves, in our leading workers, in our organisation, in the apparatus of our Party, of our Soviets, our economic, trade union, Young Communist League, and all other organisations.

It must be understood that the power and authority of our Party, Soviet, economic and all other organisations, and of their leaders, have grown to an unprecedented degree. And precisely because their power and authority have grown to an unprecedented degree it is their work that now determines everything, or nearly everything. Reference to so-called objective conditions cannot be justified. After the correctness of the political line of the Party has been confirmed by the experience of a number of years, and after the readiness of the workers and peasants to support this line no longer calls for any doubt, the rôle of so-called objective conditions has been reduced to a minimum, whereas the rôle of our organisations and of their leaders has become decisive, exceptional. What does that mean ? It means that from now on nine-tenths of the responsibility for the failure and defects in our work rests not on " objective " conditions but on ourselves, and on ourselves alone.

We have in our Party more than two million members and candidates. In the Young Communist League we have more than four million members and candidates. We have over three million worker and peasant correspondents. The Aviation, Chemical and Defence League has more than twelve million members. The trade unions have a membership of over seventeen millions. It is to these organisations that we are obliged for our successes. And if, notwithstanding the existence of such organisations and of such possibilities which facilitate the achievement of success, we still suffer from a number of defects and not a few failures in our work, then the responsibility for this rests only upon ourselves, upon our organisational work, our bad organisational leadership.

Bureaucracy in the administration departments ; idle chatter about " leadership in general " instead of real and concrete leadership ; the functional system of organisation and the absence of personal responsibility ; depersonalisation in work and equalitarianism in the wages system ; the absence of systematic supervision over the fulfilment of decisions ; fear of self-criticism—these are the sources of our difficulties, that is where our difficulties now lie concealed.

It would be naïve to think that it is possible to combat these difficulties by means of resolutions and orders. The bureaucrats have long become past masters in the art of demonstrating their loyalty to the decisions of the Party and of the government in words and pigeon-holing them in deed. In order to combat these difficulties it was necessary to abolish the lag between our organisational work and the requirements of the political line of the Party, it was necessary to raise the level of organisational leadership in all spheres of national economy to the level of political leadership, it was necessary to secure that our organisational work guaranteed the practical application of the political slogans and decisions of the Party.

In order to combat these difficulties and achieve success it was necessary to *organise* the struggle to overcome these difficulties, it was necessary to draw the masses of the workers and peasants into this struggle, it was necessary to mobilise the Party itself, it was necessary to purge the Party and the business organisations of unreliable, unstable and demoralised elements.

What was required for that ?

We had to organise :

1. Extensive self-criticism and the exposure of the defects in our work.

2. The mobilisation of the Party, Soviet, business, trade union and Young Communist League organisations for the struggle against difficulties.

3. The mobilisation of the masses of the workers and peasants for the fight to apply the slogans and decisions of the Party and of the government.

4. The extension of competition and shock-brigade work among the toilers.

5. A wide network of political departments of machine and tractor stations and Soviet farms and the bringing of the Party Soviet leadership nearer to the villages.

6. The splitting up of the commissariats, the chief boards and trusts, and bringing the business leadership nearer to the enterprises.

7. The abolition of depersonalisation in work and the liquidation of equalitarianism in the wages system.

8. The abolition of the " functional " system, increasing personal responsibility and taking the line towards liquidating collegiates.

9. Increase supervision of fulfilment of decisions and taking the line towards the reorganisation of the Central Control Commission and Workers' and Peasants' Inspection in the direction of still further increasing supervision of the fulfilment of decisions.

10. The transferring of skilled workers from the offices to bring them nearer to production.

11. The exposure and expulsion from the management departments of incorrigible bureaucrats and office rats.

12. Removal from their posts of those who violate the decisions of the Party and the government, of " window-dressers " and idle chatterers and the promotion to their place of new people—business-like people, people capable of securing concrete leadership of the work entrusted to them and the tightening of Party Soviet discipline.

13. The purging of Soviet and business organisations and reduction of their staffs.

14. Lastly, the purging of the Party of unreliable and demoralised persons.

These, in the main, are the means which the Party had to adopt in order to combat difficulties, to raise our organisational work to the level of political leadership and in this way to secure the application of the Party line.

You know that this is exactly the way the Central Committee of the Party carried on its organisational work during the period under review.

In this, the Central Committee was guided by the great thought uttered by Lenin, namely that the main thing in organisational work is *the selection of people and supervision of fulfilment of decisions.*

In regard to the selection of people and the dismissal of those who failed to justify the confidence placed in them, I would like to say a few words.

Apart from incorrigible bureaucrats and office rats, about

the removal of whom there are no differences of opinion among us, there are two other types of workers who retard our work, hinder our work, and prevent us from advancing.

One of these types of workers are those who have rendered certain services in the past, people who have become " aristocrats," as it were, who consider that the laws of the Party and Soviets were not written for them but for fools. These are the people who do not think it is their duty to fulfil the decisions of the Party and of the government, and who thus destroy the foundations of Party and state discipline. What do they base their calculations on when they violate Party and Soviet laws ? They hope that the Soviet government will not dare touch them because of the services they have rendered in the past. These swelled-headed aristocrats think that they are irreplaceable, and that they can flaunt the decisions of the leading bodies with impunity. What is to be done with workers like that ? They must without hesitation be removed from their leading posts, irrespective of the services they have rendered in the past. They must be degraded to lower positions, and this must be announced in the Press. This must be done in order to knock the pride out of these swelled-headed aristocrat-bureaucrats, and to put them in their proper place. This must be done in order to tighten up Party and Soviet discipline in the whole of our work.

And now about the second type of workers. I have in mind the chatterboxes, I would say, honest chatterboxes—people who are honest and loyal to the Soviet government, but who are incapable leaders, who are incapable of organising anything. Last year I had a conversation with one such comrade, a very respected comrade, but an incorrigible chatterbox, who was capable of submerging any living cause in a flood of talk. Well, here is the conversation :

I : How are you getting on with the sowing ?

He : With the sowing, Comrade Stalin ? We have mobilised ourselves.

I : Well, and what then ?

He : We have put the question bluntly.

I : And what next ?

He : There is a turn, Comrade Stalin ; soon there will be a turn.

I : But still ?

He : We can observe some progress.

I : But for all that, how are you getting on with the sowing ?

He : Nothing has come of the sowing as yet, Comrade Stalin.

Here you have the physiognomy of the chatterbox. They have mobilised themselves, they have put the question bluntly, they have a turn and some progress, but things remain as they were.

This is exactly the way in which a Ukrainian worker once described the state of a certain organisation when he was asked whether this organisation had any definite line : " Well," he said, " they have a line all right, but they do not seem to be doing any work." Evidently there are honest chatterboxes in that organisation as well.

And when such chatterboxes are dismissed from their posts and are given jobs far removed from operative work, they shrug their shoulders in perplexity and ask : " Why have we been dismissed ? Have we not done all that was necessary for the cause ? Have we not organised a rally of shock-brigade workers ? Did we not at conferences of shock-brigade workers proclaim the slogans of the Party and of the government ? Did we not elect the whole of the Political Bureau of the Central Committee to the honorary Presidium ? Did we not send greetings to Comrade Stalin— what else do they expect us to do ? "

What is to be done with these incorrigible chatterboxes ? If they were allowed to remain on operative work they would submerge every living cause in a flood of watery and endless speeches. Obviously, they must be dismissed from leading posts and given work other than operative work. There is no place for chatterboxes in operative work.

Everybody now admits that our successes are great and extraordinary. In a relatively short period of time our country has been transferred to the rails of industrialisation and collectivisation. The First Five-Year Plan has been successfully carried out. This rouses a sense of pride and increases the confidence of our workers in their own strength. This is all very good, of course. But successes sometimes have their dark side. They sometimes give rise to certain dangers which, if allowed to develop, may wreck the whole cause. There is, for example, the danger that some of our comrades may have their heads turned by these successes. There have been cases like that, as you know. There is the danger that certain of our comrades, having become intoxicated with success, will get swelled-headed and begin to soothe themselves with boastful songs, such as " We care for nobody," " We'll knock everybody into a cocked hat," etc. This is by no means excluded, comrades. There is nothing more dangerous than moods of this kind, because they disarm the Party and demobilise its ranks. If such moods were to predominate in our Party we would be faced with the danger of all our successes being wrecked. Of course, the First Five-Year Plan has been successfully carried out. This is true. But this does not, and cannot, end the matter, comrades. Before us is the Second Five-Year Plan, which we must also carry out, and also successfully. You know that plans are carried out in the struggle against difficulties, in the process of overcoming difficulties. That means that there will be difficulties and there will be a struggle against them. Comrades Molotov and Kuibyshev will tell you about the Second Five-Year Plan. From their reports you will see what great difficulties we will have to overcome in order to carry out this great plan. That means that we must not lull the Party but rouse its vigilance, we must not lull it to sleep but keep it in a state of fighting preparedness, not disarm but arm it, not demobilise it but keep it in a state of mobilisation for the purpose of fulfilling the Second Five-Year Plan.

Hence, the first conclusion : *we must not allow ourselves to be carried away by the successes achieved, and must not get swelled-headed.*

We achieved successes because we had the correct guiding-line of the Party, and because we were able to organise the masses for the purpose of applying this line. Needless to say, without these conditions we would not have achieved the successes we have achieved, and of which we are justly proud. But it is a very rare thing for ruling parties to have a correct line and to be able to apply it. Look at the countries which surround us : are there many ruling parties there that have a correct line and are able to apply it ? Strictly speaking, there are no longer any such parties in the world, because they are all living without prospects, are wallowing in the chaos of crises, and see no road to lead them out of the swamp. Our Party alone knows where to lead the cause, and it is leading it forward successfully. What is our Party's superiority due to ? It is due to the fact that it is a Marxian Party, a Leninist Party. It is due to the fact that it is guided in its work by the tenets of Marx, Engels and Lenin. There cannot be any doubt that as long as we remain true to these tenets, as long as we have this compass, we will achieve successes in our work.

It is said that in the West, in some countries, Marxism has already been destroyed. It is said that it was destroyed by the bourgeois-nationalist trend known as Fascism. That is nonsense, of course. Only those who are ignorant of history can talk like that. Marxism is the scientific expression of the fundamental interests of the working class. In order to destroy Marxism the working class must be destroyed. And it is impossible to destroy the working class. More than eighty years have passed since Marxism stepped into the arena. During this time scores and hundreds of bourgeois governments have tried to destroy Marxism. And what happened ? Bourgeois governments have come and gone, but Marxism still goes on.

More than that, Marxism has achieved complete victory

on one-sixth of the globe and achieved victory in the very country in which Marxism was considered to have been utterly destroyed.

It is not an accident that the country in which Marxism achieved complete victory is now the only country in the world which knows no crisis and no unemployment, whereas in all other countries, including the Fascist countries, crisis and unemployment have been reigning for four years. No, comrades, it is not an accident.

Yes, comrades, our successes are due to the fact that we worked and fought under the banner of Marx, Engels and Lenin.

Hence the second conclusion : *to remain loyal to the end to the great banner of Marx, Engels and Lenin.*

The working class of the U.S.S.R. is strong, not only because it has a Leninist Party that has been tried in battle ; it is strong not only because it enjoys the support of millions of toiling peasants ; it is strong also because it is supported and assisted by the world proletariat. The working class of the U.S.S.R. is part of the world proletariat, its vanguard; and our republic is the offspring of the world proletariat. There can be no doubt that if it had not been supported by the working class in the capitalist countries it would not have been able to retain power, it would not have secured for itself the conditions for socialist construction, and hence it would not have achieved the successes that it did achieve. International ties between the working class of the U.S.S.R. and the workers of the capitalist countries, the fraternal alliance between the workers of the U.S.S.R. and the workers of all countries—this is one of the cornerstones of the strength and might of the Republic of Soviets. The workers in the West say that the working class of the U.S.S.R. is the shock brigade of the world proletariat. That is very good. It shows that the world proletariat is prepared to continue to render all the support it can to the working class of the U.S.S.R. But this imposes a very serious duty upon us. It means that we must prove worthy

of the honourable title of the shock brigade of the proletarians of all countries. It imposes upon us the duty to
work better, and to fight better, for the final victory of
socialism in our country, for the victory of socialism in all
countries.

Hence the third conclusion : *to remain loyal to the end to the
cause of proletarian internationalism, to the cause of the fraternal
alliance of the proletarians of all countries.*

Such are the conclusions.

*Long live the great and invincible banner of Marx, Engels and
Lenin.*

J. Stalin

ADDRESS TO THE GRADUATES FROM THE RED ARMY ACADEMY

Delivered May 14, 1935.

[This speech is in effect a summary of the stages through
which the Soviet Union has passed in the process of
economic reconstruction. Its special importance lies in its
insistence on the development of " cadres "—technically
efficient leaders—" cadres decide everything " after the
stage has been passed through in which " technique
decides everything."]

ADDRESS TO THE GRADUATES FROM THE RED ARMY ACADEMY

COMRADES, it cannot be denied that we have recently
achieved important successes both in the sphere of construction and in the sphere of administration. In this

connection there is too much talk about the merits of chiefs, about the merits of leaders. All or nearly all our achievements are ascribed to them. That, of course, is wrong, it is incorrect. It is not merely a matter of leaders. But it is not of this I wanted to speak to-day. I should like to say a few words about cadres, about our cadres in general and about the cadres of our Red Army in particular.

You know that we inherited from the olden days a technically backward, impoverished and ruined country. Ruined by four years of imperialist war, and ruined again by three years of civil war, a country with a semi-literate population, with a low technical level, with isolated industrial oases lost in a welter of minute peasant farms—such was the country we inherited from the past. The problem was to transfer this country from the lines of mediæval darkness to the lines of modern industry and mechanised agriculture. The problem, as you see, was a serious and difficult one. The question that confronted us was that *either* we solve this problem in the shortest possible time and consolidate socialism in our country, *or* we do not solve it, in which case our country—technically weak and culturally unenlightened—would lose its independence and become a stake in the game of the imperialist powers.

At that time our country was passing through a period of acute famine in technical resources. There were not enough machines for industry. There were no machines for agriculture. There were no machines for transport. There was not that elementary technical base without which the industrial transformation of a country is inconceivable. All that existed were isolated preliminary requisites for the creation of such a base. A first-class industry had to be created. This industry had to be so directed as to be capable of technically reorganising not only industry, but also our agriculture and our railway transport. And for this it was necessary to make sacrifices and to impose the most rigorous economy in everything ; it was necessary to economise on food, on schools and on textiles, in order to accumulate the funds required for the creation of industry. There was no other way of overcoming the famine in technical resources. So Lenin taught us, and in this matter we followed in the footsteps of Lenin.

Naturally, in so great and difficult a matter unvarying and rapid success could not be expected. In a matter like this success comes only after several years. We had therefore to arm ourselves with strong nerves, Bolshevik grit and stubborn patience in order to counteract the first failures and to march unswervingly towards the great goal, without permitting any wavering or uncertainty in our ranks.

You know that we set about this task in precisely this way. But not all our comrades had the necessary spirit, patience and grit. Among our comrades there proved to be people who at the first difficulties began to call for a retreat. Let bygones be bygones, it is said. That, of course, is true. But man is endowed with memory, and when summing up the results of our work one involuntarily recalls the past. Well then, there were comrades among us who were scared by the difficulties and began to call on the Party to retreat. They said : " What is the good of your industrialisation and collectivisation, your machines, iron and steel industry, tractors, combines, automobiles ? It would be better if you gave us more textiles, if you bought more raw materials for the production of consumers' goods and gave the population more of the small things which adorn the life of man. The creation of industry, and a first-class industry at that, when we are so backward, is a dangerous dream."

Of course, we could have used the three billion rubles of foreign currency obtained as a result of the severest economy and spent on the creation of our industry, for the importation of raw materials and for increasing the production of articles in general consumption. That is also a kind of " plan." But with such a " plan " we should not have had a metallurgical industry, or a machine-building industry, or tractors and automobiles, or aeroplanes and tanks. We should have found ourselves unarmed in face of the external

foe. We should have undermined the foundations of socialism in our country. We should have found ourselves in
captivity to the bourgeoisie, home and foreign.

It is evident that a choice had to be made between two
plans : between the plan of retreat, leading, and bound to
lead, to the defeat of socialism, and the plan of advance,
which led and, as you know, has already led to the victory
of socialism in our country.

We chose the plan of advance and moved forward along
the Leninist road, brushing those comrades aside, as being
people who saw something only when it was under their
noses, but who closed their eyes to the immediate future of
our country, to the future of socialism in our country.

But these comrades did not always confine themselves to
criticism and passive resistance. They threatened to raise a
revolt in the Party against the Central Committee. More,
they threatened some of us with bullets. Evidently, they
reckoned on frightening us and compelling us to leave the
Leninist road. These people, apparently, forgot that we
Bolsheviks are people of a special cut. They forgot that you
cannot frighten Bolsheviks by difficulties or by threats.
They forgot that we were forged by the great Lenin, our
leader, our teacher, our father, who did not know fear in
the fight and did not recognise it. They forgot that the more
the enemies rage and the more hysterical the foes within
the Party become, the more red-hot the Bolsheviks become
for fresh struggles and the more vigorously they push
forward.

Of course, it never even occurred to us to leave the
Leninist road. More, having established ourselves on this
road, we pushed forward still more vigorously, brushing
every obstacle from our path. It is true that in our course
we were obliged to handle some of these comrades roughly.
But you cannot help that. I must confess that I too took a
hand in this business.

Yes, comrades, we proceeded confidently and vigorously
along the road of industrialising and collectivising our

country. And now we may consider that the road has been traversed.

Everybody now admits that we have achieved tremendous successes along this road. Everybody now admits that we already have a powerful, a first-class industry, a powerful mechanised agriculture, a growing and improving transport system, an organised and excellently equipped Red Army.

This means that we have in the main outlived the period of famine in technical resources.

But, having outlived the period of famine in technical resources, we have entered a new period, a period, I would say, of famine in the matter of people, in the matter of cadres, in the matter of workers capable of harnessing technique and advancing it. The point is that we have factories, mills, collective farms, Soviet farms, an army; we have technique for all this; but we lack people with sufficient experience to squeeze out of technique all that can be squeezed out of it. Formerly, we used to say that " technique decides everything." This slogan helped us in this respect, that we put an end to the famine in technical resources and created an extensive technical base in every branch of activity for the equipment of our people with first-class technique. That is very good. But it is very, very far from enough. In order to set technique going and to utilize it to the full, we need people who have mastered technique, we need cadres capable of mastering and utilizing this technique according to all the rules of the art. Without people who have mastered technique, technique is dead. Technique in the charge of people who have mastered technique can and should perform miracles. If in our first-class mills and factories, in our Soviet farms and collective farms and in our Red Army we had sufficient cadres capable of harnessing this technique, our country would secure results three times and four times greater than at present. That is why emphasis must now be laid on people, on cadres, on workers who have mastered technique. That is why the old slogan, "Technique decides everything," which is a reflection of a period we have already passed through, a period in which we suffered from a famine in technical resources, must now be replaced by a new slogan, the slogan " Cadres decide everything." That is the main thing now.

Can it be said that our people have fully understood and realised the great significance of this new slogan ? I would not say that. Otherwise, there would not have been the outrageous attitude towards people, towards cadres, towards workers, which we not infrequently observe in practice. The slogan " Cadres decide everything " demands that our leaders should display the most solicitous attitude towards our workers, " little " and " big," no matter in what sphere they are engaged, cultivating them assiduously, assisting them when they need support, encouraging them when they display their first successes, advancing them, and so forth. Yet in practice we meet in a number of cases with a soulless, bureaucratic and positively outrageous attitude towards workers. This, indeed, explains why instead of being studied, and placed at their posts only after being studied, people are frequently flung about like pawns. People have learnt how to value machinery and to make reports of how many machines we have in our mills and factories. But I do not know of one instance when a report was made with equal zest of the number of people we have developed in a given period, how we assisted people to grow and become tempered in their work. How is this to be explained ? It is to be explained by the fact that we have not yet learnt to value people, to value workers, to value cadres.

I recall an incident in Siberia, where I was at one time in exile. It was in the spring, at the time of the spring floods. About thirty men went to the river to pull out timber which had been carried away by the vast, swollen river. Towards evening they returned to the village, but with one comrade missing. When asked where the thirtieth man was, they unconcernedly replied that the thirtieth man had

GGM

" remained there." To my question, " How do you mean, remained there ? " they replied with the same unconcern, " Why ask—drowned, of course." And thereupon one of them began to hurry away, saying, " I have got to go and water the mare." When I reproached them for having more concern for animals than for men, one of them, amid the general approval of the rest, said, " Why should we be concerned about men ? We can always make men. But a mare . . . just try and make a mare." Here you have a case, not very significant perhaps, but very characteristic. It seems to me that the indifference shown by certain of our leaders to people, to cadres, and their inability to value people, is a survival of that strange attitude of man to man displayed in the episode in far-off Siberia just related.

And so, comrades, if we want successfully to overcome the famine in the matter of people and to provide our country with sufficient cadres capable of advancing technique and setting it going, we must first of all learn to value people, to value cadres, to value every worker capable of benefiting our common cause. It is time to realise that of all the valuable capital the world possesses, the most valuable and most decisive is people, cadres. It must be realised that under our present conditions " cadres decide everything." If we have good and numerous cadres in industry, agriculture, transport and the army—our country will be invincible. If we do not have such cadres—we shall be lame on both feet.

In concluding my speech, permit me to offer a toast to the health and success of our graduates from the Red Army Academy. I wish them success in the cause of organising and leading the defence of our country.

Comrades, you have graduated from the academy, a school in which you received your first steeling. But school is only a preparatory stage. Cadres receive their real steeling in actual work, outside school, in fighting difficulties, in over-coming difficulties. Remember, comrades, that only those cadres are any good who do not fear difficulties, who do not hide from difficulties, but who, on the contrary, go out to meet difficulties, in order to overcome them and eliminate them. It is only in combating difficulties that real cadres are forged. And if our army possesses genuinely steeled cadres in sufficient numbers it will be invincible.

THE PROGRAMME OF THE COMMUNIST INTERNATIONAL

English edition, Modern Books Ltd., 1929.

[The Third (Communist) International was founded in March 1919. At the Fifth Congress of the Communist International, in 1924, a draft programme was adopted, and after considerable discussion by all national sections of the International, the programme was adopted in its final form at the Sixth Congress, in 1928. It is, in a sense, a restatement of *The Communist Manifesto* of 1848, in relation to the imperialist stage of capitalism. The first and second sections deal with the The World System of Capitalism, and The General Crisis of Capitalism. The third section states the ultimate aim of the Communist International—World Communism. The fourth section deals with the period of transition from Capitalism to Socialism and the Dictatorship of the Proletariat ; this includes a number of economic and social transitional aims, besides an outline of the transitional form of the State and a statement of national and colonial policy. The fifth section deals with the stages of development in the Soviet Union. The sixth and last section states the strategy and tactics of the Communist International : the struggle against distortions of Marxism, and the work of the Party in each country to win the most important sections of the proletariat for the revolutionary overthrow of capitalism, together with winning the support of the middle strata of the town and country population and the nationalities oppressed by imperialism.]

THE PROGRAMME OF THE COMMUNIST INTERNATIONAL

I. THE WORLD SYSTEM OF CAPITALISM, ITS DEVELOPMENT AND INEVITABLE DOWNFALL

1. The Dynamic Laws of Capitalism and the Epoch of Industrial Capital

THE CHARACTERISTIC features of capitalist society which arose on the basis of commodity production are the monopoly of the most important and vital means of production by the capitalist class and big landlords ; the exploitation of the wage labour of the proletariat, which, being deprived of the means of production, is compelled to sell its labour power ; the production of commodities for profit ; and, linked up with all this, the planless and anarchic character of the process of production as a whole. Exploitation relationships and the economic domination of the bourgeoisie find their political expression in the organised capitalist State—the instrument for the suppression of the proletariat.

The history of capitalism has entirely confirmed the theories of Marx and Engels concerning the laws of development of capitalist society and concerning the contradictions of this development that must inevitably lead to the downfall of the whole capitalist system.

In its quest for profits the bourgeoisie was compelled to develop the productive forces on an ever-increasing scale and to strengthen and expand the domination of capitalist relationships of production. Thus, the development of capitalism constantly reproduces on a wider scale all the inherent contradictions of the capitalist system—primarily, the vital contradiction between the social character of labour and private acquisition, between the growth of the productive forces and the property relations of capitalism. The predominance of private property in the means of production and the anarchy prevailing in the process of production have disturbed the equilibrium between the various branches of production ; for a growing contradiction developed between the tendency towards unlimited expansion of production and the restricted consumption of the masses of the proletariat (general over-production), and this resulted in periodical devastating crises and mass unemployment among the proletariat. The predominance of private property also found expression in the competition that prevailed in each separate capitalist country as well as in the constantly expanding world market. This latter form of capitalist rivalry resulted in a number of wars, which are the inevitable accompaniment of capitalist development.

On the other hand, the technical and economic advantages of mass production have resulted in the squeezing out and destruction in the competitive struggle of the pre-capitalist economic forms and in the ever-increasing concentration and centralisation of capital. In the sphere of industry this law of concentration and centralisation of capital manifested itself primarily in the direct ruin of small enterprises or alternatively in their being reduced to the position of auxiliary units of large enterprises. In the domain of agriculture which, owing to the existence of the monopoly in land and in absolute rent, must inevitably lag behind the general rate of development, this law not only found expression in the process of differentiation that took place among the peasantry and in the proletarianisation of broad strata of them, but also and mainly in the open and concealed subordination of small peasant economy to the domination of big capital. Small farming has been able to maintain a nominal independence only at the price of extreme intensification of labour and systematic under-consumption.

The ever-growing application of machinery, the constant improvement in technique and, consequently, the uninterrupted rise in the organic composition of capital, accompanied by still further division, increased productivity and intensity of labour, meant also increased employment of female and child labour, the formation of enormous industrial reserve armies which are constantly replenished by the proletarianised peasantry who are forced to leave their villages as well as by the ruined small and middle urban bourgeoisie. The collection of a handful of capitalist magnates at one pole of social relationships and of a gigantic mass of the proletariat at the other ; the constantly increasing rate of exploitation of the working class, the reproduction on a wider scale of the deepest contradictions of capitalism and their consequences (crises, wars, etc.) ; the constant growth of social inequality, the rising discontent of the proletariat united and schooled by the mechanism of capitalist production itself—all this has inevitably undermined the foundations of capitalism and has brought nearer the day of its collapse.

Simultaneously, a profound change has taken place in the social and cultural life of capitalist society ; the parasitical decadence of the rentier group of the bourgeoisie ; the breakup of the family, which expresses the growing contradiction between the mass participation of women in social production and the forms of family and domestic life largely inherited from previous economic epochs ; the growing shallowness and degeneracy of cultural and ideological life resulting from the minute specialisation of labour, the monstrous forms of urban life and the restrictedness of rural life ; the incapability of the bourgeoisie, notwithstanding the enormous achievements of the natural sciences, to create a synthetically scientific philosophy, and the growth of ideological, mystical and religious superstition, are all phenomena signalising the approach of the historical end of the capitalist system.

2. *The Era of Finance Capitalism (Imperialism)*

The period of industrial capitalism was, in the main, a period of " free competition " ; a period of a relatively smooth evolution and expansion of capitalism throughout the whole world, when the as yet unoccupied colonies were being divided up and conquered by armed force ; a period of continuous growth of the inherent contradictions of capitalism, the burden of which fell mainly upon the systematically plundered, crushed and oppressed colonial periphery.

Towards the beginning of the twentieth century, this period was replaced by the period of imperialism, during which capitalism developed spasmodically and conflictingly ; free competition rapidly gave way to monopoly, the previously " available " colonial lands were all divided up, and the struggle for a redistribution of colonies and spheres of influence inevitably began to assume primarily the form of a struggle by force of arms.

Thus, the full intensity and the truly world-wide extent of the contradictions of capitalism became most glaringly revealed in the epoch of imperialism (finance capitalism), which, from the historical standpoint is a new form of capitalism, a new system of relationships between the various parts of world capitalist economy and a change in the relationship between the principal classes of capitalist society.

The new historical period set in as a result of the operation of the principal dynamic laws of capitalist society. It grew out of the development of industrial capitalism, and is the historical continuation of the latter. It sharpened the manifestations of all the fundamental tendencies and dynamic laws of capitalist development, of all its fundamental contradictions and antagonisms. The law of the concentration and centralisation of capital led to the formation of powerful combines (cartels, syndicates, trusts), to new forms of gigantic combinations of enterprises, linked up into one system by the banks. The merging of industrial capital with bank capital, the absorption of big land ownership into the general system of capital organisation, and the monopolist character of this form of capitalism transferred the epoch of industrial capital into the epoch of finance capital. " Free competition " of the period of industrial capitalism, which replaced feudal monopoly and the monopoly of merchant capital, became itself transformed into finance capital monopoly. At the same time, although capitalist monopolist organisations grow out of free competition, they do not eliminate competition, but exist side by side with it and hover over it, thus giving rise to a series of exceptionally great and acute contradictions, frictions and conflicts.

The growing use of complex machinery, of chemical processes and of electrical energy ; the resulting higher organic composition of capital ; and the consequent decline in the rate of profit, which only the biggest monopolist combines are able to counteract for a time by their policy of high cartel prices, still further stimulate the quest for colonial super-profits and the struggle for a new division of the world. Standardised mass production creates a demand for more foreign markets. The growing demand for raw materials and fuel intensifies the race for their sources. Lastly, the system of high protection, which hinders the export of merchandise and secures additional profit for exported capital, creates additional stimuli to the export of capital. Export of capital becomes, therefore, the decisive and specific form of economic contact between the various parts of world capitalist economy. The total effect of all this is that the monopolist ownership of colonial markets, of sources of raw materials and of spheres of investment of capital extremely accentuates the general unevenness of capitalist development and sharpens the conflicts between the " great powers " of finance capital over the re-allocation of colonies and spheres of influence.

The growth of the productive forces of world economy

thus leads to the further internationalisation of economic life and simultaneously leads to a struggle for a redistribution of the world, already divided up among the biggest finance capital States, to a change in, and sharpening of, the forms of this struggle and to the older method of bringing down prices being superseded to an increasing degree by the method of direct force (boycott, high protection, tariff wars, wars proper, etc.). Consequently, the monopolist form of capitalism is inevitably accompanied by imperialist wars, which, by the area they embrace and the destructiveness of their technique, have no parallel in world history.

3. The Forces of Imperialism and the Forces of Revolution

Expressing the tendency for unification of the various sections of the dominant class, the imperialist form of capitalism places the broad masses of the proletariat in opposition, not to a single employer, but, to an increasing degree, to the capitalist class as a whole and to the capitalist State. On the other hand, this form of capitalism breaks down the national barriers that have become too restricted for it, widens the scope of the capitalist State power of the dominant Great Powers and brings them into opposition to vast masses of nationally oppressed peoples in the so-called small nations as well as in the colonies. Finally, this form of capitalism brings the imperialist States most sharply into opposition to each other.

This being the case, State power, which is becoming the dictatorship of the finance-capitalist oligarchy and the expression of its concentrated might, acquires special significance for the bourgeoisie. The functions of this multi-national imperialist State grow in all directions. The development of State capitalist forms, which facilitate the struggle in foreign markets (mobilisation of industry for war purposes) as well as the struggle against the working class ;

the monstrous growth of militarism (armies, naval and air fleets, and the employment of chemistry and bacteriology) ; the increasing pressure of the imperialist State upon the working class (the growth of exploitation and direct suppression of the workers on the one hand and the systematic policy of bribing the bureaucratic reformist leadership on the other), all this expresses the enormous growth of the power of the State. Under these circumstances, every more or less important action of the proletariat becomes transformed into an action against the State power, i.e., into political action.

Hence the development of capitalism, and particularly the imperialist epoch of its development, reproduces the fundamental contradictions of capitalism on an increasingly magnified scale. Competition among small capitalists ceases, only to make way for competition among big capitalists ; where competition among big capitalists subsides, it flares up between gigantic combinations of capitalist magnates and their governments ; local and national crises become transformed into crises affecting a number of countries and, subsequently, into world crises ; local wars give way to wars between coalitions of States and to world wars ; the class struggle changes from isolated actions by single groups of workers into nation-wide conflicts and, subsequently, into an international struggle of the world proletariat against the world bourgeoisie. Finally, two main revolutionary forces are organising against the organised might of finance capital—on the one hand *the workers in the capitalist States*, on the other hand the victims of the oppression of foreign capital, *the masses of the people in the colonies*, marching under the leadership and the hegemony of the international revolutionary proletarian movement.

However, this fundamental revolutionary tendency is temporarily paralysed by the fact that certain sections of the European, North American and Japanese proletariat are bribed by the imperialist bourgeoisie, and by the treachery of the national bourgeoisie in the semi-colonial and colonial countries who are scared by the revolutionary mass movement. The bourgeoisie in imperialist countries, able to secure additional surplus profits from the position it holds in the world market (more developed technique, export of capital to countries with a higher rate of profit, etc.), and from the proceeds of its plunder of the colonies and semi-colonies, was able to raise the wages of its " own " workers out of these surplus profits, thus giving these workers an interest in the development of " home " capitalism, in the plunder of the colonies and in being loyal to the imperialist State.

This systematic bribery was and is being very widely practised in the most powerful imperialist countries and finds most striking expression in the ideology and practice of the labour aristocracy and the bureaucratic strata of the working class, i.e., the social-democratic and trade union leaders, who proved to be direct agents of bourgeois influence among the proletariat and stalwart pillars of the capitalist system.

By stimulating the growth of the corrupt upper stratum of the working class, however, imperialism in the end destroys its influence upon the working class, because the growing contradictions of imperialism, the worsening of the conditions of the broad masses of the workers, the mass unemployment among the proletariat, the enormous cost of military conflicts and the burdens they entail, the fact that certain Powers have lost their monopolist position in the world market, the break-away of the colonies, etc., serve to undermine the basis of social-democracy among the masses. Similarly, the systematic bribery of the various sections of the bourgeoisie in the colonies and semi-colonies, their betrayal of the national-revolutionary movement and their rapprochement with the imperialist Powers can paralyse the development of the revolutionary crisis only for a time. In the final analysis, this leads to the intensification of imperialist oppression, to the decline of the influence of the national bourgeoisie upon the masses of the people, to the sharpening of the revolutionary crisis, to the unleashing of the agrarian revolution of the broad masses of the peasantry and to the creation of conditions favourable for the establishment of the leaders of the proletariat in the popular mass struggle in the colonies and dependencies for independence and complete national liberation.

4. Imperialism and the Downfall of Capitalism

Imperialism has greatly developed the productive forces of world capitalism. It has completed the preparation of all the material prerequisites for the socialist organisation of society. By its wars it has demonstrated that the productive forces of world economy, which have outgrown the restricted boundaries of imperialist States, demand the organisation of economy on a world, or international scale. Imperialism tries to remove this contradiction by hacking a road with fire and sword towards a single world State-capitalist trust, which is to organise the whole world economy. This sanguinary Utopia is being extolled by the social-democratic ideologists as a peaceful method of newly " organised " capitalism. In reality, this Utopia encounters insurmountable objective obstacles of such magnitude that capitalism must inevitably fall beneath the weight of its own contradictions. The law of uneven development of capitalism, which becomes intensified in the epoch of imperialism, renders firm and durable international combinations of imperialist powers impossible. On the other hand, imperialist wars, which are developing into world wars, and through which the law of the centralisation of capitalism strives to reach its world limit—a single world trust—are accompanied by so much destruction and place such burdens upon the shoulders of the working class and of the millions of colonial proletarians and peasants, that capitalism must inevitably perish beneath the blows of the proletarian revolution long before this goal is reached.

Being the highest phase of capitalist development, imperialism, expanding the productive forces of world economy to enormous dimensions and re-fashioning the whole world after its own image, draws within the orbit of finance capitalist exploitation all colonies, all races and all nations. At the same time, however, the monopolist form of capital develops increasingly the elements of parasitical degeneration, decay and decline within capitalism. In destroying, to some extent, the driving force of competition, by conducting a policy of cartel prices, and by having undivided mastery of the market, monopoly capital reveals a tendency to retard the further development of the forces of production. In squeezing enormous sums of surplus profit out of the millions of colonial workers and peasants and in accumulating colossal incomes from this exploitation, imperialism is creating a type of decaying and parasitically degenerate rentier-class, as well as whole strata of parasites who live by clipping coupons. In completing the process of creating the material prerequisites for socialism (the concentration of means of production, the enormous socialisation of labour, the growth of labour organisations), the epoch of imperialism intensifies the antagonisms among the " Great Powers " and gives rise to wars which cause the break-up of its single world economy. Imperialism is therefore capitalism moribund and decaying. It is the final stage of development of the capitalist system. It is the threshold of world social revolution.

Hence, international proletarian revolution logically emerges out of the conditions of development of capitalism generally, and out of its imperialist phase in particular. The capitalist system as a whole is approaching its final collapse. The dictatorship of finance capital is perishing to give way to the dictatorship of the proletariat.

II. THE GENERAL CRISIS OF CAPITALISM AND THE FIRST PHASE OF WORLD REVOLUTION

1. *The World War and the Progress of the Revolutionary Crisis*

The imperialist struggle among the largest capitalist States for the redistribution of the globe led to the first imperialist world war (1914–18). This war shook the whole system of world capitalism and marked the beginning of an epoch of general crisis. The war bent to its service the entire national economies of the belligerent countries, thus creating the mailed fist of State capitalism. It increased unproductive expenditures to enormous dimensions, destroyed enormous quantities of the means of production and human labour power, ruined large masses of the population and imposed incalculable burdens upon the industrial workers, the peasants and the colonial peoples. It inevitably led to the intensification of the class struggle, which grew into open, revolutionary mass action and civil war. The imperialist front was broken at its weakest link, in Tsarist Russia. The February revolution of 1917 overthrew the domination of the autocracy of the big land-owning class. The October revolution overthrew the rule of the bourgeoisie. This victorious proletarian revolution expropriated the expropriators, took the means of production from the landlords and the capitalists, and for the first time in human history set up and consolidated the dictatorship of the proletariat in an enormous country. It brought into being a new, Soviet type of State and laid the foundations for the international proletarian revolution.

The powerful shock to which the whole of world capitalism was subjected, the sharpening of the class struggle and the direct influence of the October proletarian revolution gave rise to a series of revolutions and revolutionary actions on the Continent of Europe as well as in the colonial and semi-colonial countries : January, 1918, the proletarian revolution in Finland ; August, 1918, the so-called " rice riots " in Japan ; November, 1918, the revolutions in Austria and Germany, which overthrew the semi-feudal monarchist régime ; March, 1919, the proletarian revolution in Hungary and the uprising in Korea ; April, 1919, the Soviet Government in Bavaria ; January, 1920, the bourgeois-national revolution in Turkey ; September, 1920, the seizure of the factories by the workers in Italy ; March, 1921, the rising of the advanced workers of Germany ; September, 1923, the uprising in Bulgaria ; Autumn, 1923, the revolutionary crisis in Germany ; December, 1924, the uprising in Esthonia ; April, 1923, the uprising in Morocco ; August, 1925, uprising in Syria ; May, 1926, the general strike in England ; July, 1927, the proletarian uprising in Vienna. These events, as well as events like the uprising in Indonesia, the deep ferment in India, and the great Chinese revolution, which shook the whole Asiatic continent, are links in one and the same international revolutionary chain, constituent parts of the profound general crisis of capitalism. This international revolutionary process embraced the immediate struggle for the dictatorship of the proletariat, as well as national wars of liberation and colonial uprisings against imperialism, which go together with the agrarian mass-movement of millions of peasants. Thus, an enormous mass of humanity was swept into the revolutionary torrent. World history entered a new phase of development—a phase of prolonged general crisis of the capitalist system. In this process, the unity of world economy found expression in the international character of the revolution, while the uneven development of its separate parts was expressed in the different times of the outbreak of revolution in the different countries.

The first attempts at revolutionary overthrow, which sprang from the acute crisis of capitalism (1918–21) ended in the victory and consolidation of the dictatorship of the proletariat in the U.S.S.R. and in the defeat of the proletariat in a number of other countries. These defeats were primarily due to the treacherous tactics of the social-democratic and reformist trade union leaders, but they were also due to the fact that the majority of the working class had not yet accepted the lead of the Communists and that in a number of important countries Communist Parties had not yet been established at all. As a result of these defeats, which created the opportunity for intensifying the exploitation of the mass of the proletariat and the colonial peoples, and for severely depressing their standard of living, the bourgeoisie was able to achieve a partial stabilisation of capitalist relations.

2. The Revolutionary Crisis and Counter-Revolutionary Social-Democracy

During the progress of the international revolution, the leading cadres of the social-democratic parties and of the reformist trade unions on the one hand, and the militant capitalist organisations of the Fascist type on the other, acquired special significance as a powerful counter-revolutionary force actively fighting against the revolution and actively supporting the partial stabilisation of capitalism.

The war crisis of 1914–18 was accompanied by the disgraceful collapse of the social-democratic Second International. Acting in complete violation of the thesis of *The Communist Manifesto* written by Marx-Engels, that the proletariat has no fatherland under capitalism and in complete violation of the anti-war resolutions passed by the Stuttgart and Basle Congresses, the leaders of the social-democratic parties in the various countries, with a few exceptions, voted for the war credits, came out definitely in defence of the imperialist " fatherland " (i.e., the State organisations of the imperialist bourgeoisie) and instead of combating the imperialist war, became its loyal soldiers, bards and propagandists (social-patriotism, which grew into social-imperialism). In the subsequent period, social-democracy supported the predatory treaties (Brest-Litovsk, Versailles) ; it actively aligned itself with the militarists in the bloody suppression of proletarian uprisings (Noske) ; it conducted armed warfare against the first proletarian republic (Soviet Russia) ; it despicably betrayed the victorious proletariat (Hungary) ; it joined the imperialist League of Nations (Albert Thomas, Paul Boncour, Vandervelde) ; it openly supported the imperialist slave-owners against the colonial slaves (the British Labour Party) ; it actively supported the most reactionary executioners of the working class (Bulgaria, Poland) ; it took upon itself the initiative in securing the passage of imperialist " military laws " (France) ; it betrayed the general strike of the British proletariat ; it helped and is still helping to strangle China and India (the MacDonald Government) ; it acts as the propagandist for the imperialist League of Nations ; it is capital's herald and organiser in its struggle against the dictatorship of the proletariat in the U.S.S.R. (Kautsky, Hilferding).

In its systematic conduct of this counter-revolutionary policy, social-democracy operates on two flanks. The right wing of social-democracy, avowedly counter-revolutionary, is essential for negotiating and maintaining direct contact with the bourgeoisie ; the left wing is essential for the subtle deception of the workers. While playing with pacifist and at times even with revolutionary phrases, " left " social-democracy in practice acts against the workers, particularly in acute and critical situations (the British I.L.P. and the " left " leaders of the General Council during the general strike in 1926 ; Otto Bauer and Co., at the time of the Vienna uprising), and is therefore the most dangerous faction in the social-democratic parties. While serving the interests of the bourgeoisie in the working class and being wholly in favour of class co-operation and coalition with the bourgeoisie, social-democracy, at certain periods, is compelled to play the part of an opposition party and even to pretend that it is defending the class interests of the proletariat in its industrial struggle. It tries thereby to win the confidence of a section of the working class and to be in a position more shamefully to betray the lasting interests of the working class, particularly in the midst of decisive class battles.

The principal function of social democracy at the present time is to disrupt the essential militant unity of the proletariat in its struggle against imperialism. In splitting and disrupting the united front of the proletarian struggle against capital, social democracy serves as the mainstay of imperialism in the working class. International social democracy of all shades ; the Second International and its trade union branch, the Amsterdam Federation of Trade Unions, have thus become the last reserve of bourgeois society and its most reliable pillar of support.

3. The Crisis of Capitalism and Fascism

Side by side with social democracy, with whose aid the bourgeoisie suppresses the workers or lulls their class vigilance, stands Fascism.

The epoch of imperialism, the sharpening of the class struggle and the growth of the elements of civil war—particularly after the imperialist war—led to the bankruptcy of parliamentarism. Hence, the adoption of " new " methods and forms of administration (for example, the system of inner cabinets, the formation of oligarchical groups, acting behind the scenes, the deterioration and falsification of the function of " popular representation," the restriction and annulment of " democratic liberties," etc.). Under certain special historical conditions, the progress of this bourgeois, imperialist, reactionary offensive assumes the form of Fascism. These conditions are : instability of capitalist relationships ; the existence of considerable declassed social elements, the pauperisation of broad strata of the urban petty-bourgeoisie and of the intelligentsia ; discontent among the rural petty-bourgeoisie and, finally, the constant menace of mass proletarian action. In order to stabilise and perpetuate its rule, the bourgeoisie is compelled to an increasing degree to abandon the parliamentary system in favour of the Fascist system, which is independent of inter-party arrangements and combinations. The Fascist system is a system of direct dictatorship, ideologically marked by the " national idea " and by representation of the " professions " (in reality, representation of the various groups of the ruling class). It is a system that resorts to a peculiar form of social demagogy (anti-semitism, occasional sorties against usurers' capital and gestures of impatience with the parliamentary " talking shop ") in order to utilise the discontent of the petty bourgeois, the intellectuals and other strata of society, and to corruption—the creation of a compact and well paid hierarchy of Fascist units, a party apparatus and a bureaucracy. At the same time, Fascism strives to permeate the working class by recruiting the most backward strata of workers to its ranks—by playing upon their discontent, by taking advantage of the inaction of social-democracy, etc. The principal aim of Fascism is to destroy the revolutionary labour vanguard, i.e., the Communist Sections and leading units of the proletariat. The combination of social-demagogy, corruption and active white terror, in conjunction with extreme imperialist aggression in the sphere of foreign politics, are the characteristic features of Fascism. In periods of acute crisis for the bourgeoisie, Fascism resorts to anti-capitalist phraseology, but, after it has established itself at the helm of State, it casts aside its anti-capitalist prattle and discloses itself as a terrorist dictatorship of big capital.

The bourgeoisie resorts either to the method of Fascism or to the method of coalition with social-democracy according to the changes in the political situation ; while social-democracy itself, often plays a Fascist rôle in periods when the situation is critical for capitalism.

In the process of development social-democracy reveals

Fascist tendencies which, however, do not prevent it, in other political situations, from acting as a sort of *Fronde* against the bourgeois government in the capacity of an opposition party. The Fascist method and the method of coalition with social-democracy are not the methods usually employed in " normal capitalist conditions ; they are the symptoms of the general capitalist crisis, and are employed by the bourgeoisie in order to stem the advance of the revolution.

4. The Contradictions of Capitalist Stabilisation and the Inevitability of the Revolutionary Collapse of Capitalism

Experience throughout the post-war historical period has shown that the stabilisation achieved by the repression of the working class and the systematic depression of its standard of living can be only a partial, transient and decaying stabilisation.

The spasmodic and feverish development of technique, bordering in some countries on a new technical revolution, the accelerated process of concentration and centralisation of capital, the formation of giant trusts and of " national " and " international " monopolies, the merging of trusts with the State power and the growth of world capitalist economy cannot, however, eliminate the general crisis of the capitalist system. The break-up of world economy into a capitalist and a socialist sector, the shrinking of markets and the anti-imperialist movement in the colonies intensify all the contradictions of capitalism, which is developing on a new, post-war basis. This very technical progress and rationalisation of industry, the reverse side of which is the closing down and liquidation of numerous enterprises, the restriction of production, and the ruthless and destructive exploitation of labour power, leads to chronic unemployment on a scale never before experienced. The absolute deterioration of the conditions of the working class becomes a fact even in certain highly developed capitalist countries. The growing competition between imperialist countries, the constant menace of war and the growing intensity of class conflicts prepare the ground for a new and higher stage of development of the general crisis of capitalism and of the world proletarian revolution.

As a result of the first round of imperialist wars (the world war of 1914–18) and of the October victory of the working class in the former Russian Tsarist Empire, world economy has been split into two fundamentally hostile camps : the camp of the imperialist States and the camp of the dictatorship of the proletariat in the U.S.S.R. The difference in structure and in the class character of the government in the two camps, the fundamental differences in the aims each pursues in internal, foreign, economic and cultural policy, the fundamentally different courses of their development, brings the capitalist world into sharp conflict with the victorious proletarian State. Within the framework of a formerly uniform world economy two antagonistic systems are now contesting against each other : the system of capitalism and the system of socialism. The class struggle, which hitherto was conducted in circumstances when the proletariat was not in possession of State power, is now being conducted on an enormous and really world scale ; the working class of the world has now its own State—the one and only fatherland of the international proletariat. The existence of the Soviet Union and the influence it exercises upon the toiling and oppressed masses all over the world is in itself a most striking expression of the profound crisis of the world capitalist system and of the expansion and intensification of the class struggle to a degree hitherto without parallel in history.

The capitalist world, powerless to eliminate its inherent contradictions, strives to establish international associations (the League of Nations) the main purpose of which is to retard the irresistible growth of the revolutionary crisis and to strangle the Soviet Proletarian Republics by war or blockade. At the same time, all the forces of the revolutionary proletariat and of the oppressed colonial masses are rallying around the U.S.S.R. The world coalition of *Capital*, unstable, internally corroded, but armed to the teeth, is confronted by a single world coalition of *Labour*. Thus, as a result of the first round of imperialist wars a new, fundamental antagonism has arisen of world historical scope and significance ; the antagonism between the U.S.S.R. and the capitalist world.

Meanwhile, the inherent antagonisms within the capitalist sector of world economy itself have become intensified. The shifting of the economic centre of the world to the United States of America and the fact that the " Dollar Republic " has become a world exploiter have caused the relations between United States and European capitalism, particularly British capitalism, to become strained. The conflict between Great Britain—the most powerful of the old, conservative imperialist States and the United States—the greatest of the young imperialist States, which has already won world hegemony for itself—is becoming the pivot of the world conflicts among the finance capitalist States. Germany, though plundered by the Versailles Peace, is now economically recovered ; she is resuming the path of imperialist politics, and once again she stands out as a serious competitor on the world market. The Pacific is becoming involved in a tangle of contradictions which centre mainly around the antagonism between America and Japan. Simultaneously, the antagonism of interests among the unstable and constantly changing groupings of powers is increasing, while the minor powers serve as auxiliary instruments in the hands of the imperialist giants and their coalitions.

The growth of the productive capacity of the industrial apparatus of world capitalism, at a time when the European home markets have shrunk as a result of the war, of the Soviet Union's dropping out of the system of purely capitalist intercourse, and of the close monopoly of the most important sources of raw material and fuel, leads to ever-widening conflicts between the capitalist States. The "peaceful" struggle for oil, rubber, cotton, coal and metals and for a redistribution of markets and spheres for the export of capital is inexorably leading to *another world war*, the destructiveness of which will increase proportionately to the progress achieved in the furiously developing technique of war.

Simultaneously, the antagonisms between the *imperialist home countries and the semi-colonial countries are growing*. The relative weakening of European imperialism as a result of the war, of the development of capitalism in the colonies, of the influence of the Soviet revolution and the centrifugal tendencies revealed in the premier maritime and colonial Empire—Great Britain (Canada, Australia, South Africa) —has helped to stimulate the movement of rebellion in the colonies and semi-colonies. The great Chinese revolution, which roused hundreds of millions of the Chinese people to action, caused an enormous breach in the imperialist system. The unceasing revolutionary ferment among hundreds of millions of Indian workers and peasants is threatening to break the domination of the world citadel of imperialism, Great Britain. The growth of tendencies directed against the powerful imperialism of the United States in the Latin-American countries threatens to undermine the expansion of North American capital. Thus, the revolutionary process in the colonies, which is drawing into the struggle against imperialism the overwhelming majority of the world's population that is subjected to the rule of the finance capitalist oligarchy of a few " Great Powers " of imperialism, also expresses the profound general crisis of capitalism. Even in Europe itself, where imperialism has put a number of small nations under its heel, the national question is a factor that intensifies the inherent contradictions of capitalism.

Finally, the revolutionary crisis is inexorably maturing in the very centres of imperialism : the capitalist offensive against the working class, the attack upon the workers' standard of living, upon their organisations and their political rights, with the growth of white terror, rouses increasing resistance on the part of the broad masses of the proletariat and intensifies the class struggle between the working class and trustified capital. The great battles fought between Labour and Capital, the accelerated swing to the left of the masses, the growth in the influence and authority of the Communist Parties ; the enormous growth of sympathy among the broad masses of workers for the land of the proletarian dictatorship—all this is a clear symptom of the rise of a new tide in the centres of imperialism.

Thus, the system of world imperialism, and with it the partial stabilisation of capitalism, is being corroded from various causes : First, the antagonisms and conflicts between the imperialist States ; second, the rise of the struggle of vast masses in the colonial countries ; third, the action of the revolutionary proletariat in the imperialist home countries ; and, lastly, the leadership exercised over the whole world revolutionary movement by the proletarian dictatorship in the U.S.S.R. The international revolution is developing.

Against this revolution, imperialism is gathering its forces. Expeditions against the colonies, a new world war, a campaign against the U.S.S.R., are matters which now figure prominently in the politics of imperialism. This must lead to the release of all the forces of international revolution and to the inevitable doom of capitalism.

III. THE ULTIMATE AIM OF THE COMMUNIST INTERNATIONAL—WORLD COMMUNISM

The ultimate aim of the Communist International is to replace world capitalist economy by a world system of Communism. Communist society, the basis for which has been prepared by the whole course of historical development, is mankind's only way out, for it alone can abolish the contradictions of the capitalist system which threaten to degrade and destroy the human race.

Communist society will abolish the class division of society, i.e., simultaneously with the abolition of anarchy in production, it will abolish all forms of exploitation and oppression of man by man. Society will no longer consist of antagonistic classes in conflict with each other, but will present a united commonwealth of labour. For the first time in its history mankind will take its fate into its own hands. Instead of destroying innumerable human lives and incalculable wealth in struggles between classes and nations, mankind will devote all its energy to the struggle against the forces of nature, to the development and strengthening of its own collective might.

After abolishing private ownership of the means of production and converting these means into social property, the world system of Communism will replace the elemental forces of the world market, competitive and blind processes of social production, by consciously organised and planned production for the purpose of satisfying rapidly growing social needs. With the abolition of competition and anarchy in production, devastating crises and still more devastating wars will disappear. Instead of colossal waste of productive forces and spasmodic development of society there will be a planned utilisation of all material resources and a painless economic development on the basis of unrestricted, smooth and rapid development of productive forces.

The abolition of private property and the disappearance of classes will do away with the exploitation of man by man. Work will cease to be toiling for the benefit of a class enemy : instead of being merely a means of livelihood it will become a necessity of life : want and economic inequality, the misery of enslaved classes, and a wretched standard of life generally will disappear ; the hierarchy created in the division of labour system will be abolished together with the antagonism between mental and manual labour ; and the last vestige of the social inequality of the sexes will be removed. At the same time, the organs of class domination, and the State in the first place, will disappear also. The State, being the embodiment of class domination, will die out in so far as classes die out, and with it all measures of coercion will expire.

With the disappearance of classes the monopoly of education in every form will be abolished. Culture will become the acquirement of all and the class ideologies of the past will give place to scientific materialist philosophy. Under such circumstances, the domination of man over man, in any form, becomes impossible, and a great field will be opened for the social selection and the harmonious development of all the talents inherent in humanity.

In Communist society no social restrictions will be imposed upon the growth of the forces of production. Private ownership in the means of production, the selfish lust for profits, the artificial retention of the masses in a state of ignorance, poverty—which retards technical progress in capitalist society—and unproductive expenditures will have no place in a Communist society. The most expedient utilisation of the forces of nature and of the natural conditions of production in the various parts of the world, the removal of the antagonism between town and country, that under capitalism results from the low technical level of agriculture and its systematic lagging behind industry ; the closest possible co-operation between science and technique, the utmost encouragement of research work and the practical application of its results on the widest possible social scale ; planned organisation of scientific work ; the application of the most perfect methods of statistical accounting and planned regulation of economy ; the rapid growth of social needs, which is the most powerful internal driving force of the whole system—all these will secure the maximum productivity of social labour, which in turn will release human energy for the powerful development of science and art.

The development of the productive forces of world

Communist society will make it possible to raise the well-being of the whole of humanity and to reduce to a minimum the time devoted to material production and, consequently, will enable culture to flourish as never before in history. This new culture of a humanity that is united for the first time in history, and has abolished all State boundaries, will, unlike capitalist culture, be based upon clear and transparent human relationships. Hence, it will bury for ever all mysticism, religion, prejudice and superstition, and will give a powerful impetus to the development of all-conquering, scientific knowledge.

This higher stage of Communism—the stage in which Communist society will have developed on its own foundation, in which an enormous growth of social productive forces has accompanied the manifold development of man, in which humanity has already inscribed on its banner : " From each according to his abilities to each according to his needs ! "—presupposes, as an historical condition precedent, a lower stage of development, the stage of socialism. At this lower stage, Communist society only just emerges from capitalist society and bears all the economic, ethical and intellectual birthmarks it has inherited from the society from whose womb it is just emerging. The productive forces of socialism are not yet sufficiently developed to assure a distribution of the products of labour according to needs : these are distributed according to the amount of labour expended. Division of labour, i.e., the system whereby certain groups perform certain labour functions, and especially the distinction between mental and manual labour, still exists. Although classes are abolished, traces of the old class division of society and, consequently, remnants of the proletarian State power, coercion, laws, still exist. Consequently, certain traces of inequality, which have not yet managed to die out altogether, still remain. The antagonism between town and country has not yet been entirely removed. But none of these survivals of former society is protected or defended by any social force. Being the product of a definite level of development of productive forces, they will disappear as rapidly as mankind, freed from the fetters of the capitalist system, subjugates the forces of nature, re-educates itself in the spirit of Communism, and passes from socialism to complete Communism.

IV. THE PERIOD OF TRANSITION FROM CAPITALISM TO SOCIALISM AND THE DICTATORSHIP OF THE PROLETARIAT

1. The Transition Period and the Conquest of Power by the Proletariat

Between capitalist society and Communist society a period of revolutionary transformation intervenes, during which the one changes into the other. Correspondingly, there is also an intervening period of political transition, in which the essential State form is the revolutionary dictatorship of the proletariat. The transition from the world dictatorship of imperialism to the world dictatorship of the proletariat extends over a long period of proletarian struggles with defeats as well as victories ; a period of continuous general crisis in capitalist relationships and growth of social revolutions, i.e., of proletarian civil wars against the bourgeoisie ; a period of national wars and colonial rebellions which, although not in themselves revolutionary proletarian socialist movements, are nevertheless, objectively, in so far as they undermine the domination of imperialism, constituent parts of the world proletarian revolution ; a period in which capitalist and socialist economic and social systems exist side by side in " peaceful " relationships as well as in armed conflict ; a period of formation of a Union of Soviet Republics ; a period of wars of imperialist States against Soviet States ; a period in which the ties between the Soviet States and colonial peoples become more and more closely established, etc.

Uneven economic and political development is an absolute law of capitalism. This unevenness is still more pronounced and acute in the epoch of imperialism. Hence, it follows that the international proletarian revolution cannot be conceived as a single event occurring simultaneously all over the world. At first socialism may be victorious in a few, or even in one single capitalist country. Every such proletarian victory, however, broadens the basis of the world revolution and consequently, still further intensifies the general crisis of capitalism. Thus, the capitalist system as a whole reaches the point of its final collapse ; the dictatorship of finance capital perishes and gives place to the dictatorship of the proletariat.

Bourgeois revolutions brought about the political liberation of a system of productive relationships which had already established itself and become economically dominant by transferring political power from the hands of one class of exploiters to the hands of another. Proletarian revolution, however, signifies the forcible invasion of the proletariat into the domain of property relationships of bourgeois society, the expropriation of the expropriating classes, and the transference of power to a class that aims at the radical reconstruction of the economic foundations of society and the abolition of all exploitation of man by man. The political domination of the feudal barons all over the world was broken in a series of separate bourgeois revolutions that extended over a period of centuries. The international proletarian revolution, however, although it will not be a single simultaneous act, but one extending over a whole epoch, nevertheless—thanks to the closer ties that now exist between the countries of the world—will accomplish its mission in a much shorter period of time. Only after the proletariat has achieved victory and consolidated its power all over the world will a prolonged period of the intensive construction of socialist world economy set in.

The conquest of power by the proletariat is a necessary condition precedent to the growth of socialist forms of economy and to the cultural growth of the proletariat, which changes its own nature, perfects itself for the leadership of society in all spheres of life, and draws into this process of transformation all other classes ; this preparing the ground for the abolition of classes altogether.

In the struggle for the dictatorship of the proletariat, and later for the transformation of the social system, as against the alliance of capitalists and landlords, an alliance of workers and peasants is formed, under the intellectual and political leadership of the former, an alliance which serves as the basis for the dictatorship of the proletariat.

The characteristic features of this transition period as a whole are the ruthless suppression of the resistance of the exploiters, the organisation of socialist construction, the mass training of men and women in the spirit of socialism and the gradual disappearance of classes. Only to the extent that these great historical tasks are fulfilled will society of the transition period become transformed into Communist society.

Thus, the dictatorship of the world proletariat is an essential and vital condition precedent to the transformation of world capitalist economy into socialist economy. This world dictatorship can be established only when the victory of socialism has been achieved in certain countries or groups of countries, when the newly established proletarian republics enter into a federal union with the already existing proletarian republics, when the number of such federations has grown and extended also to the colonies which have emancipated themselves from the yoke of imperialism, and when these federations of republics have grown finally into a World Union of Soviet Socialist Republics uniting the whole of mankind under the hegemony of the international proletariat organised as a State.

The conquest of power by the proletariat does not mean peacefully " capturing " the ready-made bourgeois State machinery by means of a parliamentary majority. The bourgeoisie resorts to every means of violence and terror to safeguard and strengthen its predatory property and its political domination. Like the feudal nobility of the past, the bourgeoisie cannot abandon its historical position to the new class without a desperate and frantic struggle. Hence, the violence of the bourgeoisie can be suppressed only by the stern violence of the proletariat. The conquest of power by the proletariat is the violent overthrow of bourgeois power, the destruction of the capitalist State apparatus (bourgeois armies, police, bureaucratic hierarchy, the judiciary, parliaments, etc.), and the substitution in its place of new organs of proletarian power, to serve primarily as instruments for the suppression of the exploiters.

2. The Dictatorship of the Proletariat and its Soviet Form

As has been shown by the experience of the October revolution of 1917 and by the Hungarian revolution, which immeasurably enlarged the experience of the Paris Commune of 1871, the most suitable form of proletarian State is the Soviet State—a new type of State, which differs in principle from the bourgeois State, not only in its class content, but also in its internal structure. This is precisely the type of State which, emerging as it does directly out of the broadest possible mass movement of the toilers, secures the maximum of mass activity and is, consequently, the surest guarantee of final victory.

The Soviet form of State, being the highest form of democracy, namely, proletarian-democracy, is the very opposite of bourgeois-democracy, which is bourgeois-dictatorship in a masked form. The Soviet State is the dictatorship of the proletariat, the rule of a single class—the proletariat. Unlike bourgeois democracy, proletarian-democracy openly admits its class character and aims avowedly at the suppression of the exploiters in the interests of the overwhelming majority of the population. It deprives its class enemies of political rights and, under special historical conditions, may grant the proletariat a number of temporary advantages over the diffused petty bourgeois peasantry in order to strengthen its rôle of leader. While disarming and suppressing its class enemies, the proletarian State at the same time regards this deprivation of political rights and partial restriction of liberty as temporary measures in the struggle against the attempts on the part of the exploiters to defend or restore their privileges. It inscribes on its banner the motto : the proletariat holds power not for the purpose of perpetuating it, not for the purpose of protecting narrow craft and professional interests, but for the purpose of uniting the backward and scattered rural proletariat, the semi-proletariat and the toiling peasants still more closely with the more progressive strata of the workers, for the purpose of gradually and systematically overcoming class divisions altogether. Being an all-embracing form of the unity and organisation of the masses under the leadership of the proletariat, the Soviets, in actual fact, draw the broad masses of the proletariat, the peasants and all toilers into the struggle for socialism, into the work of building up socialism, and into the practical administration of the State. In the whole of their work they rely upon the working-class organisations and practise the principles of broad democracy among the toilers to an extent far greater and immeasurably more close to the masses than does any other form of government. The right of electing and recalling delegates, the combination of the executive with the legislative power, the electoral system based on a productive and not on a residential qualification (election by workshops, factories, etc.)—all this secures for the working class and for the broad masses of the toilers who march under its leadership, systematic, continuous and active participation in all public affairs—economic, social, political, military and cultural—and marks the sharp difference that exists between the bourgeois-parliamentary republic and the Soviet dictatorship of the proletariat.

Bourgeois-democracy, with its formal equality of all citizens before the law, is in reality based on a glaring material and economic inequality of classes. By leaving inviolable, defending and strengthening the monopoly of the capitalist and landlord classes in the vital means of production, bourgeois-democracy, as far as the exploited classes (especially the proletariat) is concerned, converts this formal equality before the law and these democratic rights and liberties—which in practice are curtailed systematically, into a juridical fiction and, consequently, into a means for deceiving and enslaving the masses. Being the expression of the political domination of the bourgeoisie, so-called democracy is therefore capitalist-democracy. By depriving the exploiting classes of the means of production, by placing the monopoly of these means of production in the hands of the proletariat as the dominant class in society, the Soviet State, first and foremost, guarantees to the working class and to the toilers generally the material conditions for the exercise of these rights by providing them with premises, public buildings, printing plants, travelling facilities, etc.

In the domain of general political rights the Soviet State, while depriving the exploiters and the enemies of the people of political rights, completely abolishes for the first time all inequalities of citizenship, which under systems of exploitation are based on distinctions of sex, religion and nationality ; in this sphere it establishes an equality that is not to be found in any bourgeois country. In this respect also, the dictatorship of the proletariat steadily lays down the material basis upon which this equality may be truly exercised by introducing measures for the emancipation of women, the industrialisation of former colonies, etc.

Soviet-democracy, therefore, is proletarian-democracy, democracy of the toiling masses, democracy directed against the exploiters.

The Soviet State completely disarms the bourgeoisie and concentrates all arms in the hands of the proletariat ; it is the armed proletarian State. The armed forces under the Soviet State are organised on a class basis, which corresponds to the general structure of the proletarian

Hʜᴍ

dictatorship, and guarantees the rôle of leadership to the industrial proletariat. This organisation, while maintaining revolutionary discipline, ensures to the warriors of the Red Army and Navy close and constant contacts with the masses of the toilers, participation in the administration of the country and in the work of building up socialism.

3. The Dictatorship of the Proletariat and the Expropriation of the Expropriators

The victorious proletariat utilises the conquest of power as a lever of economic revolution, i.e., the revolutionary transformation of the property relations of capitalism into relationships of the socialist mode of production. The starting point of this great economic revolution is the expropriation of the landlords and capitalists, i.e., the conversion of the monopolist property of the bourgeoisie into the property of the proletarian State.

In this sphere the Communist International advances the following fundamental tasks of the proletarian dictatorship :

(A) *Industry, Transport and Communication Services*

(a) The confiscation and proletarian nationalisation of all large private capitalist undertakings (factories, works, mines and electric power stations), and the transference of all State and municipal enterprises to the Soviets.

(b) The confiscation and proletarian nationalisation of private capitalist railway, waterway, automobile and air transport services (commercial and passenger air fleet) and the transference of all State and municipal transport services to the Soviets.

(c) The confiscation and proletarian nationalisation of private capitalist communication services (telegraph, telephones and radio) and the transference of State and municipal communication services to the Soviets.

(d) The organisation of workers' management of industry. The establishment of State organs for the management of industry with provision for the close participation of the trade unions in this work of management. Appropriate functions to be guaranteed for the factory and works councils.

(e) Industrial activity to be directed towards the satisfaction of the needs of the broad masses of the toilers. The reorganisation of the branches of industry that formerly served the needs of the ruling class (luxury trades, etc.). The strengthening of the branches of industry that will facilitate the development of agriculture, with the object of strengthening the ties between industry and peasant economy, of facilitating the development of State farms, and of accelerating the rate of development of national economy as a whole.

(B) *Agriculture*

(a) The confiscation and proletarian nationalisation of all large landed estates in town and country (private, church, monastery and other lands) and the transference of State and municipal landed property including forests, minerals, lakes, rivers, etc., to the Soviets with subsequent nationalisation of the whole of the land.

(b) The confiscation of all property utilised in production belonging to large landed estates, such as : buildings, machinery, etc., cattle, enterprises for the manufacture of agricultural products (large flour mills, cheese plants, dairy farms, fruit and vegetable drying plants, etc.).

(c) The transfer of large estates, particularly model estates and those of considerable economic importance to the management of the organs of the proletarian dictatorship and of the Soviet farm organisations.

(d) Part of the land confiscated from the landlords and others—particularly where the land was cultivated by the peasants on a tenant basis and served as a means of holding the peasantry in economic bondage—to be transferred to the use of the peasantry (to the poor and partly also to the middle strata of the peasantry). The amount of land to be so transferred to be determined by economic expediency as well as by the degree of necessity to neutralise the peasantry and to win them over to the side of the proletariat ; this amount must necessarily vary according to the different circumstances.

(e) Prohibition of buying and selling of land, as a means of preserving the land for the peasantry and preventing its passing into the hands of capitalists, land speculators, etc. Offenders against this law to be severely prosecuted.

(f) To combat usury. All transactions entailing terms of bondage to be annulled. All debts of the exploited strata of the peasantry to be annulled. The poorest stratum of the peasantry to be relieved from taxation, etc.

(g) Comprehensive State measures for developing the productive forces of agriculture ; the development of rural electrification ; the manufacture of tractors ; the production of artificial fertilisers ; the production of pure quality seeds and raising throughbred stock on Soviet farms ; the extensive organisation of agricultural credits for land reclamation, etc.

(h) Financial and other support for agricultural co-operation and for all forms of collective production in the rural districts (co-operative societies, communes, etc.). Systematic propaganda in favour of peasant co-operation (selling, credit and supply co-operative societies) to be based on the mass activity of the peasants themselves ; propaganda in favour of the transition to large-scale agricultural production which—owing to the undoubted technical and economic advantages of large-scale production—provide the greatest immediate economic gain and also a method of transition to socialism most accessible to the broad masses of the toiling peasants.

(c) *Trade and Credit*

(a) The proletarian nationalisation of private banks (the entire gold reserve, all securities, deposits, etc., to be transferred to the proletarian State) ; the proletarian State to take over State, municipal, etc., banks.

(b) The centralisation of banking ; all nationalised big banks to be subordinated to the central State bank.

(c) The nationalisation of wholesale trade and large retail trading enterprises (warehouses, elevators, stores, stocks of goods, etc.), and their transfer to the organs of the Soviet State.

(d) Every encouragement to be given to consumers' co-operatives as representing an integral part of the distributing apparatus, while preserving uniformity in their system of work and securing the active participation of the masses themselves in their work.

(e) The monopoly of foreign trade.

(f) The repudiation of State debts to foreign and home capitalists.

(D) *Conditions of Life, Labour, etc.*

(a) Reduction of the working day to seven hours, and to six hours in industries particularly harmful to the health of the workers. Further reduction of the working day and transition to a five-day week in countries with developed productive forces. The regulation of the working day to correspond to the increase of the productivity of labour.

(b) Prohibition, as a rule, of night work and employment in harmful trades for all females. Prohibition of child labour. Prohibition of overtime.

(c) Special reduction of the working day for the youth (a maximum six-hour day for young persons up to 18 years of age). Socialist reorganisation of the labour of young persons so as to combine employment in industry with general and political education.

(d) Social insurance in all forms (sickness, old age, accident, unemployment, etc.), at State expense (and at the expense of the owners of private enterprises where they still exist), insurance affairs to be managed by the insured themselves.

(e) Comprehensive measures of hygiene ; the organisation of free medical service. To combat social diseases (alcoholism, venereal diseases, tuberculosis).

(f) Complete equality between men and women before the law and in social life : a radical reform of marriage and family laws ; recognition of maternity as a social function ; protection of mothers and infants. Initiation of social care and upbringing of infants and children (crèches, kindergarten, children's homes, etc.). The establishment of institutions that will gradually relieve the burden of house drudgery (public kitchens and laundries), and systematic cultural struggle against the ideology and traditions of female bondage.

(E) *Housing*

(a) The confiscation of big house property.

(b) The transfer of confiscated houses to the administration of the local Soviets.

(c) Workers to be removed to bourgeois residential districts.

(d) Palaces and large private and public buildings to be placed at the disposal of labour organisations.

(e) The carrying out of an extensive programme of house construction.

(F) *National and Colonial Questions*

(a) The recognition of the right of all nations, irrespective of race, to complete self-determination, that is, self-determination inclusive of the right to State separation.

(b) The voluntary unification and centralisation of the military and economic forces of all nations liberated from capitalism for the purpose of fighting against imperialism and for building up socialist economy.

(c) Wide and determined struggle against the imposition of any kind of limitation and restriction upon any nationality, nation or race. Complete equality for all nations and races.

(d) The Soviet State to guarantee and support with all the resources at its command the national cultures of nations liberated from capitalism, at the same time to carry out a consistent proletarian policy directed towards the development of the content of such cultures.

(e) Every assistance to be rendered to the economic, political and cultural growth of the formerly oppressed " territories," " dominions " and " colonies," with the object of transferring them to socialist lines, so that a durable basis may be laid for complete national equality.

(f) To combat all remnants of chauvinism, national hatred, race prejudices and other ideological products of feudal and capitalist barbarism.

(G) *Means of Ideological Influence*

(a) The nationalisation of printing plants.

(b) The monopoly of newspapers and book-publishing.

(c) The nationalisation of big cinema enterprises, theatres, etc.

(d) The utilisation of the nationalised means of " intellectual production " for the most extensive political and general education of the toilers and for the building up of a new socialist culture on a proletarian class basis.

4. *The Basis for the Economic Policy of the Proletarian Dictatorship*

In carrying out all these tasks of the dictatorship of the proletariat, the following postulates must be borne in mind :

(1) The complete abolition of private property in land, and the nationalisation of the land, cannot be brought about immediately in the more developed capitalist countries, where the principle of private property is deep-rooted among a broad strata of the peasantry. In such countries, the nationalisation of all land can only be brought about

gradually, by means of a series of transitional measures.

(2) Nationalisation of production should not, as a rule, be applied to small and middle-sized enterprises (peasants, small artisans, handicrafts, small and medium shops, small manufacturers, etc.). Firstly, because the proletariat must draw a strict distinction between the property of the small commodity producer working for himself, who can and must be gradually brought into the groove of socialist construction, and the property of the capitalist exploiter, the liquidation of which is an essential condition precedent for socialist construction.

Secondly, because the proletariat, after seizing power, may not have sufficient organising forces at its disposal, particularly in the first phases of the dictatorship, for the purpose of destroying capitalism and at the same time to organise with the smaller and medium individual units of production on a socialist basis. These small individual enterprises (primarily peasant enterprises) will be drawn into the general socialist organisation of production and distribution only gradually, with the powerful and systematic aid which the proletarian State will render to organise them in all the various forms of collective enterprises. Any attempt to break up their economic system violently and to complete them to adopt collective methods by force will only lead to harmful results.

(3) Owing to the prevalence of a large number of small units of production (primarily peasant farms, farmers' enterprises, small artisans, small shopkeepers, etc.) in colonies, semi-colonies and economically backward countries, where the petty-bourgeois masses represent the overwhelming majority of the population, and even in centres of capitalist world industry (the United States of America, Germany, and to some degree also England), it is necessary, in the first stage of development, to preserve to some extent market forms of economic contacts, the money system, etc. The variety of prevailing economic forms (ranging from socialist large-scale industry to small

peasant and artisan enterprises), which unavoidably come into conflict with each other ; the variety of classes and class groups corresponding to this variety of economic forms, each having different stimuli for economic activity and conflicting class interests ; and finally, the prevalence in all spheres of economic life, of habits and traditions inherited from bourgeois society, which cannot be removed all at once—all this demands that the proletariat, in exercising its economic leadership, shall properly combine, on the basis of market relationships, large-scale socialist industry with the small enterprises of the simple commodity producers, i.e., it must combine them in such a way as to guarantee the leading rôle to socialist industry and at the same time bring about the greatest possible development of the mass of peasant enterprises. Hence, the greater the importance of scattered, small peasant labour in the general economy of the country, the greater will be the volume of market relations, the smaller will be the significance of directly planned management, and the greater will be the degree to which the general economic plan will depend upon forecasts of uncontrollable economic relations. On the other hand, the smaller the importance of small production, the greater will be the proportion of socialised labour, the more powerful will be the concentrated and socialised means of production, the smaller will be the volume of market relations, the greater will be the importance of planned management as compared with unco-ordinated management and the more considerable and universal will be the application of planned management in the sphere of production and distribution.

Provided the proletarian dictatorship carries out a correct class policy, i.e., provided proper account is taken of class-relationships, the technical and economic superiority of large-scale socialised production, the centralisation of all the most important economic key positions (industry, transport, large-scale agiculture enterprises, banks, etc.) in the hands of the proletarian State, planned management of industry, and the power wielded by the State apparatus as a whole (the budget, taxes, administrative legislation and legislation generally), render it possible continuously and systematically to dislodge private capital and the new out-crops of capitalism which, in the period of more or less free commercial and market relations, will emerge in town and country with the development of simple commodity pro-duction (big farmers, kulaks). At the same time by organ-ising peasant farming on co-operative lines, and as a result of the growth of collective forms of economy, the great bulk of the peasant enterprises will be systematically drawn into the main channel of developing socialism. The out-wardly capitalist forms and methods of economic activity that are bound up with market relations (money form of accounting, payment for labour in money, buying and sell-ing, credit and banks, etc.), serve as levers for the socialist transformation, in so far as they to an increasing degree serve the consistently socialist type of enterprises, i.e., the socialist section of economy.

Thus, provided the State carries out a correct policy, market relations under the proletarian dictatorship destroy themselves in the process of their own development by helping to dislodge private capital, by changing the character of peasant economy—what time the means of production become more and more centralised and con-centrated in the hands of the proletarian State—they help to destroy market relations altogether.

In the probable event of capitalist military intervention, and of prolonged counter-revolutionary wars against the dictatorship of the proletariat, the necessity will arise for a war-Communist economic policy (" War Communism "), which is nothing more nor less than the organisation of rational consumption for the purpose of military defence, accompanied by a system of intensified pressure upon the capitalist groups (confiscation, requisitions, etc.), with the more or less complete liquidation of freedom of trade and market relations and a sharp disturbance of the individualist,

economic stimuli of the small producers, which results in
a diminution of the productive forces of the country. This
policy of "War-Communism," while it undermines the
material basis of the strata of the population in the country
that are hostile to the working class, secures a rational distribution of the available supplies and facilitates the military struggle of the proletarian dictatorship—which is the
historical justification of this policy—nevertheless, cannot
be regarded as the "normal" economic policy of the
proletarian dictatorship.

5. Dictatorship of the Proletariat and the Classes

The dictatorship of the proletariat is a continuation of the
class struggle under new conditions. The dictatorship of
the proletariat is a stubborn fight—bloody and bloodless,
violent and peaceful, military and economic, pedagogical
and administrative—against the forces and traditions of the
old society, against external capitalist enemies, against the
remnants of the exploiting classes within the country,
against the upshoots of the new bourgeoisie that spring up
on the basis of still prevailing commodity production.

After the civil war has been brought to an end the stubborn class struggle continues in new forms ; primarily in
the form of a struggle between the survivals of previous
economic systems and fresh upshoots of them on the one
hand, and socialist forms of economy on the other. The
forms of the struggle undergo a change at various stages of
socialist development, and in the first stages the struggle,
under certain conditions, may be extremely severe.

In the initial stage of the proletarian dictatorship, the
policy of the proletariat towards other classes and social
groups within the country is determined by the following
postulates :

(1) The big bourgeoisie and the landowners, a section of
the officer corps, the higher command of the forces, and the
higher bureaucracy—who remain loyal to the bourgeoisie

and the landlords—are consistent enemies of the working class against whom ruthless war must be waged. The organising skill of a certain section of these strata may be utilised, but, as a rule, only after the dictatorship has been consolidated and all conspiracies and rebellions of exploiters have been decisively crushed.

(2) In regard to the technical intelligentsia, which was brought up in the spirit of bourgeois traditions and the higher ranks of which were closely linked up with the commanding apparatus of capital—the proletariat, while ruthlessly suppressing every counter-revolutionary action on the part of hostile sections of the intelligentsia, must at the same time give consideration to the necessity of utilising this skilled social force for the work of socialist construction ; it must give every encouragement to the groups that are neutral, and especially to those that are friendly towards the proletarian revolution. In widening the economic, technical and cultural perspectives of socialist construction to its utmost social limits, the proletariat must systematically win over the technical intelligentsia to its side, subject it to its ideological influence and secure its close co-operation in the work of social reconstruction.

(3) In regard to the peasantry, the task of the Communist Parties, is, while placing its reliance in the agricultural proletariat, to win over all the exploited and toiling strata of the countryside. The victorious proletariat must draw strict distinctions between the various groups among the peasantry, weigh their relative importance, and render every support to the propertyless and semi-proletarian sections of the peasantry by transferring to them a part of the land taken from the big landowners and by helping them in their struggle against usurer's capital, etc. Moreover, the proletariat must neutralise the middle strata of the peasantry and mercilessly suppress the slightest opposition on the part of the village bourgeoisie who ally themselves with the landowners. As its dictatorship becomes consolidated and socialist construction develops, the proletariat must proceed from the

policy of neutralisation to a policy of durable alliance with the masses of middle peasantry, but must not adopt the viewpoint of sharing power in any form. The dictatorship of the proletariat implies that the industrial workers alone are capable of leading the entire mass of the toilers. On the other hand, while representing the rule of a single class, the dictatorship of the proletariat at the same time represents a special form of class alliance between the proletariat, as the vanguard of the toilers, and the numerous non-proletarian sections of the toiling masses, or the majority of them. It represents an alliance for the complete overthrow of capital, for the complete suppression of the opposition of the bourgeoisie and its attempts at restoration, an alliance aiming at the complete building up and consolidation of socialism.

(4) The petty urban bourgeoisie, which continuously wavers between extreme reaction and sympathy for the proletariat, must likewise be neutralised and, as far as possible, won over to the side of the proletariat. This can be achieved by leaving to them their small property and permitting a certain measure of free trade, by releasing them from the bondage of usurious credit and by the proletariat helping them in all sorts of ways in the struggle against all and every form of capitalist oppression.

6. *Mass Organisations in the System of Proletarian Dictatorship*

In the process of fulfilling these tasks of the proletarian dictatorship, a radical change takes place in the tasks and functions of the mass organisations, particularly of the Labour organisations. Under capitalism, the mass labour organisations, in which the broad masses of the proletariat were originally organised and trained, i.e., the trade (industrial) unions, serve as the principal weapons in the struggle against trustified capital and its State. Under the proletarian dictatorship, they become transformed into the principal lever of the State ; they become transformed into a school of Communism by means of which vast masses of the proletariat are drawn into the work of socialist management of production ; they are transformed into organisations directly connected with all parts of the State appartus, influencing all branches of its work, safeguarding the permanent and day-to-day interests of the working class and fighting against bureaucracy in the departments of the State. Thus, in so far as they promote from their ranks leaders in the work of construction, draw into this work of construction broad sections of the proletariat and aim at combating bureaucracy, which inevitably arises as a result of the operation of class influences alien to the proletariat and of the inadequate cultural development of the masses, the trade unions become the backbone of the proletarian economic and State organisation as a whole.

Notwithstanding reformist Utopias, working-class co-operative organisations under capitalism are doomed to play a very minor rôle and in the general environment of the capitalist system not infrequently degenerate into mere appendages of capitalism. Under the dictatorship of the proletariat, however, these organisations can and must become the most important units of the distributing apparatus.

Lastly, peasant agricultural co-operative organisations (selling, purchasing, credit and producing), under proper management, and provided a systematic struggle is carried on against the capitalist elements, and that really broad masses of the toilers who follow the lead of the proletariat take a really active part in their work, can and must become one of the principal organisational means for linking up town and country. To the extent that they were able to maintain their existence at all under capitalism, co-operative peasant enterprises inevitably became transformed into capitalist enterprises, for they were dependent upon capitalist industry, capitalist banks and upon capitalist economic environment. Under the dictatorship of the proletariat, however, such enterprises develop amidst a different system of relationships, depend upon proletarian industry, proletarian banks, etc. Thus, provided the proletariat carries out a proper policy, provided the class struggle is systematically conducted against the capitalist elements outside as well as inside the co-operative organisations, and provided socialist industry exercises its guidance over it, agricultural co-operation will become one of the principal levers for the socialist transformation and collectivisation of the countryside. All this, however, does not exclude the possibility that in certain countries the consumers' societies, and particularly the agricultural co-operative societies led by the bourgeoisie and their social-democratic agents, will at first be hotbeds of counter-revolutionary activity and sabotage against the work of economic construction of the workers' revolution.

In the course of this militant and constructive work, carried on through the medium of these multifarious proletarian organisations—which should serve as effective levers of the Soviet State and the link between it and the masses of all strata of the working class—the proletariat secures unity of will and action, and exercises this unity through the medium of the Communist Party, which plays the leading rôle in the system of the proletarian dictatorship.

The Party of the proletariat relies directly on the trade unions and other organisations that embrace the masses of the workers, and through these relies on the peasantry (Soviets, co-operative societies, Young Communist League, etc.) ; by means of these levers it guides the whole Soviet system. The proletariat can fulfil its rôle as organiser of the new society only if the Soviet Government is loyally supported by all the mass organisations ; only if class unity is maintained, and only under the guidance of the Party.

7. The Dictatorship of the Proletariat and the Cultural Revolution

The rôle of organiser of the new human society presupposes that the proletariat itself will become culturally mature, that it will transform it own nature, that it will continually promote from its ranks increasing numbers of men and women capable of mastering science, technique and administration in order to build up socialism and a new socialist culture.

Bourgeois revolution against feudalism presupposes that a new class has arisen in the midst of feudal society that is culturally more advanced than the ruling class, and is already the dominant factor in economic life. The proletarian revolution, however, develops under other conditions. Being economically exploited, politically oppressed and culturally downtrodden under capitalism, the working class transforms its own nature only in the course of the transition period, only after it has conquered State power, only by destroying the bourgeois monopoly of education and mastering all the sciences, and only after it has gained experience in the great work of construction. The mass awakening of Communist consciousness, the cause of socialism itself, calls for a mass change of human nature, which can be achieved only in the course of the practical movement, in revolution. Hence revolution is not only necessary because there is no other way of overthrowing the ruling class, but also because only in the process of revolution is the overthrowing class able to purge itself of the dross of the old society and become capable of creating a new society.

In destroying the capitalist monopoly of the means of production, the working class must also destroy the capitalist monopoly of education, that is, it must take possession of all the schools, from the elementary schools to the universities. It is particularly important for the proletariat to train members of the working class as experts in the sphere of production (engineers, technicians, organisers, etc.), as well as in the sphere of military affairs, science, art, etc. Parallel with this work stands the task of raising the general cultural level of the proletarian masses, of improving their political education, of raising their general standard of knowledge and technical skill, of training them in the methods of public work and administration, and of combating the survivals of bourgeois and petty-bourgeois prejudices, etc.

Only to the extent that the proletariat promotes from its own ranks a body of men and women capable of occupying the key positions of socialist construction, only to the extent that this body grows and draws increasing numbers of the working class into the process of revolutionary cultural transformation and gradually obliterates the line that divides the proletariat into an " advanced " and a " backward " section will the guarantees be created for successful socialist construction and against bureaucratic decay and class degeneracy.

However, in the process of revolution the proletariat not only changes its own nature, but also the nature of other classes, primarily the numerous petty-bourgeois strata in town and country and especially the toiling sections of the peasantry. By drawing the wide masses into the process of cultural revolution and socialist construction, by uniting and communistically educating them with all the means at its disposal, by strongly combating all anti-proletarian and narrow craft ideologies, and by persistently and systematically overcoming the general and cultural backwardness of the rural districts, the working class, on the basis of the developing collective forms of economy, prepares the way for the complete removal of class divisions in society.

One of the most important tasks of the cultural revolution affecting the wide masses is the task of systematically and unswervingly combating religion—the opium of the people. The proletarian government must withdraw all State support from the Church, which is the agency of the former ruling class ; it must prevent all church interference in State-organised educational affairs, and ruthlessly suppress the counter-revolutionary activity of the ecclesiastical organisations. At the same time, the proletarian State, while granting liberty of worship and abolishing the privileged position of the formerly dominant religion, carries on anti-religious propaganda with all the means at its command and reconstructs the whole of its educational work, on the basis of scientific materialism.

8. The Struggle for the World Dictatorship of the Proletariat and the Principal Types of Revolution

The international proletarian revolution represents a combination of processes which vary in time and character ; purely proletarian revolutions ; revolutions of a bourgeois-democratic type which grow into proletarian revolutions ; wars for national liberation ; colonial revolutions. The world dictatorship of the proletariat comes only as the final result of the revolutionary process.

The uneven development of capitalism, which became more accentuated in the period of imperialism, has given rise to a variety of types of capitalism, to different stages of ripeness of capitalism in different countries, and to a variety of specific conditions of the revolutionary process. These circumstances make it historically inevitable that the proletariat will come to power by a multiplicity of ways and degrees of rapidity ; that a number of countries must pass through certain transition stages leading to the dictatorship of the proletariat and must adopt varied forms of socialist construction.

The variety of conditions and ways by which the proletariat will achieve its dictatorship in the various countries may be divided schematically into three main types.

Countries of highly-developed capitalism (United States of America, Germany, Great Britain, etc.), having powerful productive forces, highly centralised production, with small-scale production reduced to relative insignificance, and a long established bourgeois-democratic political system. In such countries the fundamental political demand of the programme is direct transition to the dictatorship of the proletariat. In the economic sphere, the most characteristic demands are : expropriation of the whole of the large-scale industry ; organisation of a large number of State Soviet farms and, in contrast to this, a relatively small portion of the land to be transferred to the peasantry ; unregulated market relations to be given comparatively small scope ; rapid rate of socialist development generally, and of collectivisation of peasant farming in particular.

Countries with a medium development of capitalism (Spain, Portugal, Poland, Hungary, the Balkan countries, etc.), having numerous survivals of semi-feudal relationships in agriculture, possessing, to a certain extent, the material prerequisites for socialist construction, and in which the bourgeois-democratic reforms have not yet been completed. In some of these countries a process of more or less rapid development from bourgeois-democratic revolution to socialist revolution is possible. In others, there may be types of proletarian revolution which will have a large number of bourgeois-democratic tasks to fulfil. Hence, in these countries, the dictatorship of the proletariat may not come about at once, but in the process of transition from the democratic dictatorship of the proletariat and peasantry to the socialist dictatorship of the proletariat. Where the revolution develops directly as a proletarian revolution it is presumed that the proletariat exercises leadership over a broad agrarian peasant movement. In general, the agrarian revolution plays a most important part in these countries, and in some cases a decisive rôle : in the process of expropriating large landed property a considerable portion of the confiscated land is placed at the disposal of the peasantry ; the volume of market relations prevailing after the victory of the proletariat is considerable ; the task of organising the peasantry along co-operative lines and, later, of combining them in production occupies an important place among the tasks of socialist construction. The rate of this construction is relatively slow.

Colonial and semi-colonial countries (China, India, etc.) dependent countries (Argentine, Brazil, etc.), have the rudiments of and in some cases a considerably developed industry—in the majority of cases inadequate for independent socialist construction—with feudal mediæval relationships, or " Asiatic mode of production " relationships prevailing in their economies and in their political superstructures. In these the principal industrial, commercial and banking enterprises, the principal means of transport, the large landed estates (*latifundia*), plantations, etc., are concentrated in the hands of foreign imperialist groups. The principal task in such countries is, on the one hand, to fight against the feudal and pre-capitalist forms of exploitation, and to develop systematically the peasant agrarian revolution ; on the other hand, to fight against foreign imperialism for national independence. As a rule, transition to the dictatorship of the proletariat in these countries will be possible only through a series of preparatory stages, as the outcome of a whole period of transformation of bourgeois-democratic revolution into socialist revolution, while in the majority of cases, successful socialist construction will be possible only if direct support is obtained from the countries in which the proletarian dictatorship is established.

In still more backward countries (as in some parts of Africa) where there are no wage workers or very few, where the majority of the population still lives in tribal conditions, where survivals of primitive tribal forms still exist, where the national bourgeoisie is almost non-existent, where the primary rôle of foreign imperialism is that of military occupation and usurpation of land, the central task is to fight for national independence. Victorious national uprisings in these countries may open the way for their direct development towards socialism and their avoidance of the stage of capitalism, provided real and powerful assistance is rendered them by the countries in which the proletarian dictatorship is established.

Thus, in the epoch in which the proletariat in the most developed capitalist countries is confronted with the immediate task of capturing power—that in which the dictatorship of the proletariat already established in the U.S.S.R. is a factor of world significance—the movement for liberation in colonial and semi-colonial countries, which was brought into being by the penetration of world capitalism, may lead to social development—notwithstanding the immaturity of social relationships in these countries taken by themselves—provided they receive the assistance and support of the proletarian dictatorship and of the international proletarian movement generally.

9. Struggle for the World Dictatorship of the Proletariat and Colonial Revolution

The special conditions of the revolutionary struggle prevailing in colonial and semi-colonial countries, the inevitably long period of struggle required for the democratic dictatorship of the proletariat and the peasantry and for the transformation of this dictatorship into the dictatorship of the proletariat, and, finally, the decisive importance of the national aspects of the struggle, impose upon the Communist Parties of these countries a number of special tasks, which are preparatory stages to the general tasks of the dictatorship of the proletariat. The Communist International considers the following to be the most important of these special tasks :

(1) To overthrow the rule of foreign imperialism, of the feudal rulers and of the landlord bureaucracy.

(2) To establish the democratic dictatorship of the proletariat and the peasantry on a Soviet basis.

(3) Complete national independence and national unification.

(4) Annulment of State debts.

(5) Nationalisation of large-scale enterprises (industrial, transport, banking and others) owned by the imperialists.

(6) The confiscation of landlord, church and monastery lands. The nationalisation of all the land.

(7) Introduction of the 8-hour day.

(8) The organisation of revolutionary workers' and peasants' armies.

In the colonies and semi-colonies where the proletariat is the leader of and commands hegemony in the struggle, the consistent bourgeois-democratic revolution will grow into proletarian revolution in proportion as the struggle develops and becomes more intense (sabotage by the bourgeoisie, confiscation of the enterprises belonging to the sabotaging section of the bourgeoisie, which inevitably extends to the nationalisation of the whole of large-scale industry). In the colonies where there is no proletariat, the overthrow of the domination of the imperialists implies the establishment of the rule of people's (peasant) Soviets, the confiscation and transfer to the State of foreign enterprises and lands.

Colonial revolutions and movements for national liberation play an extremely important part in the struggle against imperialism, and in the struggle for the conquest of power by the working class. Colonies and semi-colonies are also important in the transition period because they represent the *world rural district* in relation to the industrial countries, which represent the *world city*. Consequently the problem of organising socialist world economy, of properly combining industry with agriculture is, to a large extent, the problem of the relation towards the former colonies of imperialism. Hence the establishment of a fraternal, militant alliance with the masses of the toilers in the colonies represents one of the principal tasks the world industrial proletariat must fulfil as leader in the struggle against imperialism.

Thus, in rousing the workers in the home countries for the struggle for the dictatorship of the proletariat, the progress of the world revolution also rouses hundreds of millions of colonial workers and peasants for the struggle against foreign imperialism. In view of the existence of centres of socialism represented by Soviet Republics of growing economic power, the colonies which break away from imperialism economically gravitate towards and gradually combine with the industrial centres of world socialism, are drawn into the current of socialist construction, and by skipping the further stage of development of capitalism, as a dominating system, obtain opportunities for rapid economic and cultural progress. The Peasants' Soviets in the backward ex-colonies and the Workers' and Peasants' Soviets in the more developed ex-colonies group themselves politically around the centres of proletarian dictatorship, join the growing Federation of Soviet Republics, and thus enter the general system of the world proletarian dictatorship.

Socialism, as the new method of production, thus obtains world-wide scope of development.

V. THE DICTATORSHIP OF THE PROLETARIAT IN THE U.S.S.R., AND THE INTERNATIONAL SOCIAL REVOLUTION

1. The Building Up of Socialism in the U.S.S.R. and the Class Struggle

The principal manifestation of the profound crisis of the capitalist system is the division of world economy into capitalist countries on the one hand, and countries building up socialism on the other. Therefore, the internal consolidation of the proletarian dictatorship in the U.S.S.R., the success achieved in the work of socialist construction, the growth of the influence and authority of the U.S.S.R. among the masses of the proletariat and the oppressed peoples of the colonies, signify the continuation, intensification and expansion of the international social revolution.

Possessing in the country the necessary and sufficient

material prerequisites not only for the overthrow of the landlord and the bourgeoisie, but also for the establishment of complete socialism, the workers of the Soviet Republic, with the aid of the international proletariat, heroically repelled the attacks of the armed forces of the internal and foreign counter-revolution, consolidated their alliance with the bulk of the peasantry and achieved considerable success in the sphere of socialist construction.

The contacts established between proletarian socialist industry and small peasant economy, which stimulates the growth of the productive forces of agriculture, and at the same time assures a leading rôle to socialist industry ; the linking up of industry with agriculture in place of capitalist production for the satisfaction of the unproductive consumption of parasitic classes that was the system formerly ; production, not for capitalist profit, but for the satisfaction of the growing needs of the masses of the consumers ; the growth of the needs of the masses, which in the final analysis greatly stimulates the entire productive process ; and, finally, the close concentration of the economic key positions under the command of the proletarian State, the growth of planned management and the more economic and expedient distribution of the means of production that goes with it—all this enables the proletariat to make rapid progress along the road of socialist construction.

In raising the level of the productive forces of the whole economy of the country, and in steering a straight course for the industrialisation of the U.S.S.R.—the rapidity of which is dictated by the international and internal situation—the proletariat in the U.S.S.R., notwithstanding the systematic attempts on the part of the capitalist Powers to organise an economic and financial boycott against the Soviet Republics, at the same time increases the relative share of the socialised (socialist) section of national economy in the total means of production in the country, in the total output of industry and in the total trade turnover.

Thus, with the land nationalised, by means of the levers

of State trade and rapidly growing co-operation, and with the increasing industrialisation of the country, State socialist industry, transport and banking are more and more guiding the activities of the small and very small peasant enterprises.

In the sphere of agriculture especially the level of the forces of production is being raised amidst conditions that restrict the process of differentiation among the peasantry (nationalisation of the land, and consequently the prohibition of the sale and purchase of land ; sharply graded progressive taxation ; the financing of poor and middle class peasants' co-operative societies and producers' organisations ; laws regulating the hiring of labour ; depriving the kulaks of certain political and public rights ; organising the rural poor in separate organisations, etc.). However, in so far as the productive forces of socialist industry have not yet grown sufficiently to enable a broad, new technical base to be laid for agriculture, and consequently to render possible the immediate and rapid unification of peasant enterprises into large public enterprises (collective farms), the kulak class tends to grow and establish, first economic and then political contacts with the elements of the so-called " new bourgeoisie."

Being in command of the principal economic key positions in the country, and systematically squeezing out the remnants of urban and private capital, which has greatly dwindled in the last few years of the " New Economic Policy "—restricting in every way the exploiting strata in the rural districts that arise out of the development of commodity and money relationships ; supporting existing Soviet farms in the rural districts and establishing new ones ; drawing the bulk of the peasant simple commodity producers, through the medium of rapidly growing co-operative organisations, into the general system of Soviet economic organisation, and consequently into the work of socialist construction, which, in the conditions prevailing under the proletarian dictatorship, and with the economic leadership of socialist industry, is identical with the development of socialism ; passing from the process of restoration to the process of expanded reproduction of the entire productive and technical base of the country—the proletariat of the U.S.S.R. sets itself, and is already beginning, to fulfil the task of large-scale capital construction (production of means of production generally, development of heavy industry, and especially of electrification), and developing still further selling, buying and credit co-operation, sets itself the task of organising the peasantry in producing co-operatives on a mass scale and on a collectivist basis, which calls for the powerful material assistance of the proletarian State.

Thus, being already a decisive economic force determining, in the main, the entire economic development of the U.S.S.R., socialism by that very fact makes still further strides in its development and systematically overcomes the difficulties that arise from the petty-bourgeois character of the country and the periods of temporarily acute class antagonism.

The task of re-equipping industry and the need for large investments in capital construction unavoidably give rise to serious difficulties in the path of socialist development which, in the last analysis, are to be attributed to the technical and economic backwardness of the country and to the ruin caused in the years of the imperialist and civil wars. Notwithstanding this, however, the standard of living of the working class and of the broad masses of the toilers is steadily rising and, simultaneously with the socialist rationalisation and scientific organisation of industry, the seven-hour day is gradually being introduced, which opens up still wider prospects for the improvement of the conditions of life and labour of the working class.

Standing on the basis of the economic growth of the U.S.S.R. and on the steady increase in the relative importance of the socialist section of industry ; never for a moment halting in the struggle against the kulaks ; relying upon the rural poor and maintaining a firm alliance with the bulk of the middle peasantry, the working class, united and led by the Communist Party, which has been hardened in revolutionary battles, draws increasing masses, scores of millions of toilers into the work of socialist construction. The principal means employed towards this aim are : the development of broad mass organisations (the Party, as the guiding force ; the trade unions, as the backbone of the entire system of the proletarian dictatorship ; the Young Communist League ; co-operative societies of all types ; working women's and peasant women's organisations ; the various so-called "voluntary societies" ; worker and peasant correspondents' societies ; sport, scientific, cultural and educational organisations) ; full encouragement of the initiative of the masses and the promotion of fresh strata of workers to high posts in all spheres of industry and administration. The steady attraction of the masses into the process of socialist construction, the constant renovation of the entire State, economic, trade union and Party apparatus with men and women fresh from the ranks of the proletariat, the systematic training in the higher educational establishments and at special courses of workers generally and young workers in particular as new socialist experts in all branches of construction—all these together serve as one of the principal guarantees against the bureaucratic ossification or social degeneration of the stratum of the proletariat directly engaged in administration.

2. The Significance of the U.S.S.R. and its World Revolutionary Duties

Having defeated Russian imperialism and liberated all the former colonies and oppressed nations of the Tsarist Empire, and systematically laid a firm foundation for their cultural and political development by industrialising their territories ; having guaranteed the juridical position of the Autonomous Territories, Autonomous Republics and

Allied Republics in the Constitution of the Union and having granted in full the right of nations to self-determination—the dictatorship of the proletariat in the U.S.S.R., by this guarantees, not only formal, but also real equality for the different nationalities in the Union.

Being the land of the dictatorship of the proletariat and of socialist construction, the land of great working-class achievements, of the union of the workers with the peasants and of a new culture marching under the banner of Marxism, the U.S.S.R. inevitably becomes the base of the world movement of all oppressed classes, the centre of international revolution, the greatest factor in world history. In the U.S.S.R., the world proletariat for the first time acquires a country that is really its own, and for the colonial movements the U.S.S.R. becomes a powerful centre of attraction.

Thus the U.S.S.R. is an extremely important factor in the general crisis of capitalism, not only because it has dropped out of the world capitalist system and has created a basis for a new socialist system of production, but also because it plays an exceptionally great revolutionary rôle generally ; it is the international driving force of proletarian revolution that impels the proletariat of all countries to seize power ; it is the living example proving that the working class is not only capable of destroying capitalism, but of building up socialism as well ; it is the prototype of the fraternity of nationalities in all lands united in the World Union of Socialist Republics and of the economic unity of the toilers of all countries in a single world socialist economic system that the world proletariat must establish when it has captured political power.

The simultaneous existence of two economic systems ; the socialist system in the U.S.S.R. and the capitalist system in other countries, imposes on the Proletarian State the task of warding off the blows showered upon it by the capitalist world (boycott, blockade, etc.), and also compels it to resort to economic manœuvring and the utilisation of economic contacts with capitalist countries (with the aid of the monopoly of foreign trade—which is one of the fundamental conditions for the successful building up of socialism, and also with the aid of credits, loans, concessions, etc.). The principal and fundamental line to be followed in this connection must be the line of establishing the widest possible contact with foreign countries—within limits determined by their usefulness to the U.S.S.R., i.e., primarily for strengthening industry in the U.S.S.R., for laying the base for its own heavy industry and electrification, and finally, for the development of its socialist engineering industry. Only to the extent that the economic independence of the U.S.S.R. in the capitalist environment is secured can solid guarantees be obtained against the danger that socialist construction in the U.S.S.R. may be destroyed and that the U.S.S.R. may be transformed into an appendage of the world capitalist system.

On the other hand, notwithstanding their interest in the markets of the U.S.S.R., the capitalist States continually vacillate between their commercial interests and their fear of the growth of the U.S.S.R., which means the growth of international revolution. However, the principal and fundamental tendency in the policy of imperialist Powers is to encircle the U.S.S.R. and conduct counter-revolutionary war against it in order to strangle it and to establish a world bourgeois terrorist régime.

3. The Duties of the International Proletariat to the U.S.S.R.

The systematic imperialist attempts politically to encircle the U.S.S.R., and the growing danger of an armed attack upon her, do not, however, prevent the Communist Party of the Soviet Union—a section of the Communist International and the leader of the proletarian dictatorship in the U.S.S.R.—from fulfilling its international obligations and from rendering support to all the oppressed, to the

Labour movements in capitalist countries, to colonial movement against imperialism and to the struggle against national oppression in every form.

In view of the fact that the U.S.S.R. is the only fatherland of the international proletariat, the principal bulwark of its achievements and the most important factor for its international emancipation, the international proletariat must on its part facilitate the success of the work of socialist construction in the U.S.S.R., and defend it against the attacks of the capitalist Powers by all the means in its power.

> The world political situation has made the dictatorship of the proletariat an immediate issue, and all the events of world politics are inevitably concentrating around one central point, namely, the struggle of the world bourgeoisie against the Soviet Russian Republic, which must inevitably group around itself the Soviet movements of the advanced workers of all countries on the one hand, and all the national liberation movements of the colonial and oppressed nationalities on the other.—(Lenin.)

In the colonies, and particularly the colonies of any imperialist attacking the U.S.S.R., the international proletariat must retaliate by organising bold and determined mass action and struggle for the overthrow of the imperialist governments with the slogan of : Dictatorship of the proletariat and alliance with the U.S.S.R.

In the colonies, and particularly the colonies of the imperialist country attacking the U.S.S.R., every effort must be made to take advantage of the diversion of the imperialist military forces to develop an anti-imperialist struggle and to organise revolutionary action for the purpose of throwing off the yoke of imperialism and of winning complete independence.

The development of socialism in the U.S.S.R. and the growth of its international influence not only rouse the hatred of the capitalist States and their social-democratic agents against it, but also inspire the toilers all over the world with sympathy towards it, and stimulate the readiness of the oppressed classes of all countries to fight with all the means in their power for the land of the proletarian dictatorship, in the event of an imperialist attack thereupon.

Thus the development of the contradictions within modern world economy, the development of the general capitalist crisis, and the imperialist military attack upon the Soviet Union inevitably lead to a mighty revolutionary outbreak which must overwhelm capitalism in a number of the so-called civilised countries, unleash the victorious revolution in the colonies, broaden the base of the proletarian dictatorship to an enormous degree, and thus, with tremendous strides bring nearer the final world victory of socialism.

VI. THE STRATEGY AND TACTICS OF THE COMMUNIST INTERNATIONAL IN THE STRUGGLE FOR THE DICTATORSHIP OF THE PROLETARIAT

1. Ideologies among the Working Class Inimical to Communism

In its fight against capitalism for the dictatorship of the proletariat, revolutionary Communism encounters numerous tendencies among the working class, which to a greater or less degree express the ideological subordination of the proletariat to the imperialist bourgeoisie, or reflect the ideological influence exercised upon the proletariat by the petty-bourgeoisie, which at times rebels against the shackles of finance capital, but is incapable of adopting sustained and scientifically planned strategy and tactics or of carrying on the struggle in an organised manner on the basis of the stern discipline that is characteristic of the proletariat.

The mighty social power of the imperialist State, with its auxiliary apparatus, schools, press, theatre and church—is primarily reflected in the existence of religious and reformist tendencies among the working class, which represent the main obstacles on the road towards the proletarian social revolution.

The religious-sectarian tendency among the working class finds expression in religious-sectarian trade unions, which are frequently connected directly with corresponding bourgeois political organisations, and are affiliated to one or other of the church organisations of the dominant class (Catholic trade unions, Young Men's Christian Association, Jewish Zionist organisations, etc.) All these tendencies, being the most striking product of the ideological enslavement of certain strata of the proletariat bear, in most cases, a romantic feudal tinge. By sanctifying all the abominations of the capitalist régime with the holy water of religion, and by terrorising their flock with the spectre of punishment in the world to come, the leaders of these organisations serve as the most reactionary units of the class enemy in the camp of the proletariat.

A cynically commercial, and imperialist-secular mode of subjecting the proletariat to the ideological influence of the bourgeoisie is represented by contemporary " socialist " reformism. Taking its main gospel from the tablets of imperialist politics, its model to-day is the deliberately anti-socialist and openly counter-revolutionary " American Federation of Labour." The ideological dictatorship of the servile American trade union bureaucracy, which in its turn expresses the ideological dictatorship of the American dollar, has become, through the medium of British reformism and His Majesty's Socialists of the British Labour Party, a most important ingredient in the theory and practice of international social-democracy and of the leaders of the Amsterdam International, while the leaders of German and Austrian social-democracy embellish these theories with Marxian phraseology in order to cover up their utter betrayal of Marxism. " Socialist " reformism, the principal enemy of revolutionary Communism in the labour movement, which has a broad organisational base in the social-democratic parties and through these in the reformist trade

unions, stands out in its entire policy and theoretical outlook as a force directed against the proletarian revolution.

In the sphere of foreign politics, the social-democratic
parties actively supported the imperialist war on the pretext
of " defending the fatherland." Imperialist expansion and
" colonial policy " received their wholehearted support.
Orientation towards the counter-revolutionary " Holy
Alliance " of imperialist Powers (" The League of
Nations "), advocacy of ultra-imperialism, mobilisation of
the masses under pseudo-pacifist slogans, and at the same
time, active support of imperialism in its attacks upon the
U.S.S.R. and in the impending war against the U.S.S.R.—
are main features of reformist foreign policy.

In the sphere of home politics, social-democracy has set
itself the task of directly co-operating with and supporting
the capitalist régime. Complete support for capitalist
rationalisation and stabilisation, class peace, " peace in
industry " ; the policy of converting the labour organisations into organisations of the employers and of the predatory imperialist State ; the practice of so-called " industrial democracy " which in fact means complete subordination to trustified capital ; adoration of the imperialist State
and particularly of its false democratic labels ; active participation in the building up of the organs of the imperialist
State—police, army, gendarmerie, its class judiciary—the
defence of the state against the encroachments of the revolutionary Communist proletariat ; and the executioner's rôle
played in time of revolutionary crisis—such is the line of
social-democratic reformist home policy. While pretending
to conduct the industrial struggle, reformism considers its
function in this field to be to conduct that struggle in such a
manner as to guard the capitalist class against any kind of
shock, at all events to preserve in complete inviolability
the foundations of capitalist property.

In the sphere of theory, social-democracy has utterly and
completely betrayed Marxism, having traversed the road
from revisionism to complete liberal bourgeois reformism

IIM

and avowed social-imperialism. It has substituted in place of the Marxian theory of the contradictions of capitalism the bourgeois theory of its harmonious development ; it has pigeon-holed the theory of crisis and of the pauperisation of the proletariat ; it has turned the flaming and menacing theory of class struggle into prosaic advocacy of class peace ; it has exchanged the theory of growing class antagonisms for the petty-bourgeois fairy-tale about the " democratisation " of capital ; in place of the theory of the inevitability of war under capitalism it has substituted the bourgeois deceit of pacifism and the lying propaganda of " ultra-imperialism " ; it has exchanged the theory of the revolutionary downfall of capitalism for the counterfeit coinage of " sound " capitalism transforming itself peacefully into socialism ; it has replaced revolution by evolution, the destruction of the bourgeois State by its active upbuilding, the theory of proletarian dictatorship by the theory of coalition with the bourgeoisie, the doctrine of international proletarian solidarity by preaching defence of the imperialist fatherland ; for Marxian dialectical materialism it has substituted the idealist philosophy and is now engaged in picking up the crumbs of religion that fall from the table of the bourgeoisie.

Within social-democratic reformism a number of tendencies stand out that are characteristic of the bourgeois degeneracy of social-democracy.

Constructive socialism (MacDonald and Co.), which by its very name suggests the struggle against the revolutionary proletariat and a favourable attitude towards the capitalist system, continues the liberal philanthropic, anti-revolutionary and bourgeois traditions of Fabianism (Beatrice and Sidney Webb, Bernard Shaw, Lord Olivier, etc.). While repudiating the dictatorship of the proletariat and the use of violence in the struggle against the bourgeoisie as a matter of principle, it favours violence in the struggle against the proletariat and the colonial peoples. While acting as the apologists of the capitalist State and preaching

State capitalism under the guise of socialism, and in conjunction with the most vulgar ideologists of imperialism in both hemispheres—declaring the theory of the class struggle to be a " pre-scientific " theory—" constructive socialism " ostensibly advocates a moderate programme of nationalisation with compensation, taxation of land values, death duties, and taxation of surplus profits as a means of abolishing capitalism. Being resolutely opposed to the dictatorship of the proletariat in the U.S.S.R., " constructive socialism," in complete alliance with the bourgeoisie, is an active enemy of the Communist proletarian movement and of colonial revolutions.

A special variety of " constructive socialism " is " *co-operativism* " or " *co-operative socialism* " (Charles Gide & Co.), which also strongly repudiates the class struggle and advocates the co-operative organisation of consumers as a means of overcoming capitalism, but which, in fact, does all it can to help the stabilisation of capitalism. Having at its command an extensive propagandist apparatus, in the shape of the mass consumers' co-operative organisations, which it employs for the purpose of systematically influencing the masses, " co-operativism " carries on a fierce struggle against the revolutionary Labour movement, hampers it in the achievement of its aims, and represents to-day one of the most potent factors in the camp of the reformist counter-revolution.

So-called " *Guild socialism* " (Penty, Orage, Hobson and others) is an eclectic attempt to unite " revolutionary " syndicalism with bourgeois Liberal Fabianism, anarchist decentralisation (" national industrial guilds ") with State capitalist centralisation and mediæval guild and craft narrowness with modern capitalism. Starting out with the obstensible demand for the abolition of the " wage system " as an " immoral " institution which must be abolished by means of workers' control of industry, guild socialism completely ignores the most important question, viz., the question of power. While striving to unite workers, intellectuals,

and technicians into a federation of national industrial
" guilds," and to convert these guilds by peaceful means
(" control from within ") into organs for the administration
of industry within the framework of the bourgeois State,
guild socialism actually defends the bourgeois State,
obscures its class, imperialist and anti-proletarian character, and allots to it the function of the non-class representative of the interests of the " consumers " as against the
guild-organised " producers." By its advocacy of " functional democracy," i.e., representation of classes in capitalist
society—each class being presumed to have a definite social
and productive function—guild socialism paves the way for
the Fascist " corporate State." By repudiating both parliamentarism and " direct action," the majority of the guild
socialists doom the working class to inaction and passive
subordination to the bourgeoisie. Thus guild socialism represents a peculiar form of trade unionist Utopian opportunism, and as such cannot but play an anti-revolutionary rôle.

Lastly, *Austro-Marxism* represents a special variety of
social-democratic reformism. Being a part of the " left-
wing " of social-democracy, Austro-Marxism represents
a most subtle deception of the masses of the toilers. Pros-
tituting the terminology of Maxism, while divorcing themselves entirely from the principles of revolutionary Marxism
(the Kantism, Machism, etc., of the Austro-Marxists in the
domain of philosophy), toying with religion, borrowing the
theory of " functional democracy " from the British reformists, agreeing with the principle of " building up the
republic," i.e., building up the bourgeois State, Austro-
Marxism recommends " class co-operation " in periods of
so-called " equilibrium of class forces," i.e., precisely at the
time when the revolutionary crisis is maturing. This theory
is a justification of coalition with the bourgeoisie for the
overthrow of the proletarian revolution under the guise of
defending " democracy " against the attacks of reaction.
Objectively, and in practice, the violence which Austro-
Marxism admits in cases of reactionary attacks is converted

into reactionary violence against the proletarian revolution. Hence the "functional rôle" of Austro-Marxism is to deceive the workers already marching towards Communism, and therefore it is the most dangerous enemy of the proletariat, more dangerous than the avowed aderents of predatory social imperialism.

All the above-mentioned tendencies, being constitutent parts of "socialist" reformism, are agencies of the imperialist bourgeoisie within the working class itself. But Communism has to contend also against a number of petty-bourgeois tendencies, which reflect and express the vacillation of the unstable strata of society (the urban petty-bourgeoisie, the degenerate city middle class, the *lumpenproletariat*, the declassed Bohemian intellectuals, the pauperised artisans, certain strata of the peasantry, etc.). These tendencies, which are distinguishable by their extreme political instability, often cover up a right-wing policy with left-wing phraseology, or drop into adventurism, substitute noisy political gesticulation for objective estimation of forces. They often tumble from astounding heights of revolutionary bombast to profound depths of pessimism and downright capitulation before the enemy. Under certain conditions, particularly in periods of sharp changes in the political situation and of forced temporary retreat become disrupters of the proletarian ranks and, consequently, a drag upon the revolutionary movement.

Anarchism, the most prominent representatives of which (Kropotkin, Jean Graves and others) treacherously went over to the side of the imperialist bourgeoisie in the war of 1914–18, denies the necessity for wide, centralised and disciplined proletarian organisations and thus leaves the proletariat powerless before the powerful organisations of capital. By its advocacy of individual terror, it distracts the proletariat from the methods of mass organisation and mass struggle. By repudiating the dictatorship of the proletariat in the name of "abstract" liberty, anarchism deprives the proletariat of its most important and sharpest weapon against the bourgeoisie, its armies, and all its organs of repression. Being remote from mass movements of any kind in the most important centres of proletarian struggle, anarchism is steadily being reduced to a sect which, by its tactics and actions, including its opposition to the dictatorship of the working class in the U.S.S.R., has objectively joined the united front of the anti-revolutionary forces.

" *Revolutionary* " *syndicalism*, many ideologists of which, in the extremely critical war period, went over to the camp of the Fascist type of " anti-parliamentary " counter-revolutionaries, or became peaceful reformists of the social-democratic type, by its repudiation of political struggle (particularly of revolutionary parliamentarism) and of the revolutionary dictatorship of the proletariat, by its advocacy of craft decentralisation of the labour movement generally and of the trade union movement in particular, by its repudiation of the need for a proletarian party, and of the necessity for rebellion, and by its exaggeration of the importance of the general strike (the " fold arms tactics "), like anarchism, hinders the revolutionisation of the masses of the workers, wherever it has any influence. Its attacks upon the U.S.S.R., which logically follow from its repudiation of dictatorship of the proletariat in general, place it in this respect on a level with social-democracy.

All these tendencies take a common stand with social-democracy, the principal enemy of the proletarian revolution, on the fundamental political issue, i.e., the question of the dictatorship of the proletariat. Hence, all of them come out more or less definitely in a united front with social-democracy against the U.S.S.R. On the other hand, social-democracy, which has utterly and completely betrayed Marxism, tends to rely more and more upon the ideology of the Fabians, of the Constructive Socialists and of the Guild Socialists. These tendencies are becoming transformed into the official liberal-reformist ideology of the bourgeois " socialism " of the Second International.

In the colonial countries and among the oppressed

peoples and races generally, Communism encounters the influence of peculiar tendencies in the labour movements which played a useful rôle in a definite phase of development, but which, in the new stage of development, are becoming transformed into a reactionary force.

Sun Yat-Senism in China expressed the ideology oι petty-bourgeois democratic " socialism." In the " Three Principles " (nationalism, democracy, socialism), the concept " people " obscured the concept " classes " ; socialism was presented, not as a specific mode of production to be carried on by a specific class, i.e., by the proletariat, but as a vague state of social well-being, while no connection was made between the struggle against imperialism and the perspectives of the development of the class struggle. Therefore, while it played a very useful rôle in the first stage of the Chinese revolution, as a consequence of the further process of class differentiation that has taken place in the country and of the further progress of the revolution, Sun Yat-Senism has now changed from being the ideological expression of the development of that revolution into fetters of its further development. The epigones of Sun Yat-Senism, by emphasising and exaggerating the very features of this ideology that have become objectively reactionary, have made it the official ideology of the Kuomintang, which is now an openly counter-revolutionary force. The ideological growth of the masses of the Chinese proletariat and of the toiling peasantry must therefore be accompanied by determined decisive struggle against the Kuomintang deception and by opposition to the remnants of the Sun Yat-Senist ideology.

Tendencies like Ghandism in India, thoroughly imbued with religious conceptions, idealise the most backward and economically most reactionary forms of social life, see the solution of the social problem not in proletarian socialism, but in a reversion to these backward forms, preach passivity and repudiate the class struggle, and in the process of the development of the revolution become transformed into an openly reactionary force. Ghandism is more and more becoming an ideology directed against mass revolution. It must be strongly combated by Communism.

Garveyism which formerly was the ideology of the masses, like Ghandism, has become a hindrance to the revolutionisation of the Negro masses. Originally advocating social equality for Negroes, Garveyism subsequently developed into a peculiar form of Negro " Zionism " which, instead of fighting American imperialism, advanced the slogan : " Back to Africa " ! This dangerous ideology, which bears not a single genuine democratic trait, and which toys with the aristocratic attributes of a non-existent " Negro kingdom," must be strongly resisted, for it is not a help but a hindrance to the mass Negro struggle for liberation against American imperialism.

Standing out against all these tendencies is proletarian Communism. The sublime ideology of the international revolutionary working class, it differs from all these tendencies, and primarily from social-democracy, in that, in complete harmony with the teachings of Marx and Engels, it conducts a theoretical and practical revolutionary struggle for the dictatorship of the proletariat, and in the struggle, applies all forms of proletarian mass action.

2. The Fundamental Tasks of Communist Strategy and Tactics

The successful struggle of the Communist International for the dictatorship of the proletariat pre-supposes the existence in every country of a compact Communist Party, hardened in the struggle, disciplined, centralised, and closely linked up with the masses.

The Party is the vanguard of the working class, and consists of the best, most class-conscious, most active and most courageous members of that class. It incorporates the whole body of experience of the proletarian struggle. Basing itself upon the revolutionary theory of Marxism and representing the general and lasting interests of the whole of the working class, the Party personifies the unity of proletarian principles, of proletarian will and of proletarian revolutionary action. It is a revolutionary organisation, bound by an iron discipline and strict revolutionary rules of democratic centralism—which can be carried out owing to the class-consciousness of the proletarian vanguard—to its loyalty to the revolution, its ability to maintain inseparable ties with the proletarian masses and to its correct political leadership, which is constantly verified and clarified by the experiences of the masses themselves.

In order that it may fulfil its historic mission of achieving the dictatorship of the proletariat, the Communist Party must first of all set itself to accomplish the following fundamental strategic aims :

Extend its influence over the majority of the members of its own class, including working women and the working youth. To achieve this the Communist Party must secure predominant influence in the broad mass proletarian organisations (Soviets, trade unions, factory councils, co-operative societies, sport organisations, cultural organisations, etc.). It is particularly important for this purpose of winning over the majority of the proletariat, to capture the trade unions, which are genuine mass working-class organisations closely bound up with the every day struggles of the working class. To work in reactionary trade unions and skilfully to capture them, to win the confidence of the broad masses of the industrially organised workers, and to remove from their posts and replace the reformist leaders, are all important tasks in the preparatory period.

The achievement of the dictatorship of the proletariat pre-supposes also that the proletariat acquires leadership of wide sections of the toiling masses. To accomplish this the Communist Party must extend its influence over the masses of the urban and rural poor, over the lower strata of the intelligentsia, and over the so-called " small man," i.e., the petty-bourgeois strata generally. It is particularly important that work be carried on for the purpose of extending the Party's influence over the peasantry. The Communist Party must secure for itself the whole-hearted support of that stratum of the rural population that stands closest to the proletariat, i.e., the agricultural labourers and the rural poor. To this end the agricultural labourers must be organised in separate organisations ; all possible support must be given them in their struggles against the rural bourgeoisie, and strenuous work must be carried on among the small allotment farmers and small peasants. In regard to the middle strata of the peasantry in developed capitalist countries, the Communist Parties must conduct a policy to secure their neutrality. The fulfilment of all these tasks by the proletariat—the champion of the interests of the whole people and the leader of the broad masses in their struggle against the oppression of finance capital—is an essential condition precedent for the victorious Communist revolution.

The tasks of the Communist International connected with the revolutionary struggle in colonies, semi-colonies and dependencies are extremely important strategical tasks in the world proletarian struggle. The colonial struggle pre-supposes that the broad masses of the working class and of the peasantry in the colonies must be won over to the banner of the revolution ; but this cannot be achieved unless the closest co-operation is maintained between the proletariat in the oppressing countries and the toiling masses in the oppressed countries.

While organising under the banner of the proletarian dictatorship the revolution against imperialism in the so-called civilised States, the Communist International supports every movement against imperialist violence in the colonies, semi-colonies and dependencies themselves (for example, Latin-America) ; it carries on propaganda against all forms of chauvinism and against the imperialist mal-treatment of enslaved peoples and races, big and small (treatment of negroes, " yellow labour," anti-semitism, etc.), and supports their struggles against the bourgeoisie of the oppressing nations. The Communist International especially combats the chauvinism that is preached in the Empire-owning countries by the imperialist bourgeoisie, as well as by its social-democratic agency, the Second International, and constantly holds up in contrast to the practices of the imperialist bourgeoisie the practice of the Soviet Union, which has established relations of fraternity and equality among the nationalities inhabiting it.

The Communist Parties in the imperialist countries must render systematic aid to the colonial revolutionary liberation movement, and to the movement of oppressed nationities generally. The duty of rendering active support to these movements rests primarily upon the workers in the countries upon which the oppressed nations are economically, financially or politically dependent. The Communist Parties must openly recognise the right of the colonies to separation and their right to carry on propaganda for this separation, i.e., propaganda in favour of the independence of the colonies from the imperialist State. They must recognise their right of armed defence against imperialism (i.e., the right of rebellion and revolutionary war) and advocate and give active support to this defence by all the means in their power. The Communist Parties must adopt this line of policy in regard to all oppressed nations.

The Communist Parties in the colonial and semi-colonial countries must carry on a bold and consistent struggle against foreign imperialism and unfailingly conduct propaganda in favour of friendship and unity with the proletariat in the imperialist countries. They must openly advance, conduct propaganda for, and carry out the slogan of agrarian revolution, rouse the broad masses of the peasantry for the overthrow of the landlords and combat the reactionary and mediæval influence of the priesthood, of the missionaries and other similar elements.

In these countries, the principal task is to organise the workers and the peasantry independently (to establish class Communist Parties of the proletariat, trade unions, peasant leagues and committees and—in a revolutionary situation, Soviets, etc.), and to free them from the influence of the national bourgeoisie, with whom temporary agreements may be made only on the condition that they, the bourgeoisie, do not hamper the revolutionary organisation of the workers and peasants, and that they carry on a genuine struggle against imperialism.

In determining its line of tactics, each Communist Party must take into account the concrete internal and external situation, the correlation of class forces, the degree of stability and strength of the bourgeoisie, the degree of preparedness of the proletariat, the position taken up by the various intermediary strata, etc., in its country. The Party determines slogans and methods of struggle in accordance with these circumstances, with the view to organising and mobilising the masses on the broadest possible scale and on the highest possible level of this struggle.

When a revolutionary situation is developing, the Party advances certain transitional slogans and partial demands corresponding to the concrete situation ; but these demands and slogans must be bent to the revolutionary aim of capturing power and of overthrowing bourgeois capitalist society. The Party must neither stand aloof from the daily needs and struggles of the working class nor confine its activities exclusively to them. The task of the Party is to utilise these minor everyday needs as a starting point from which to lead the working class to the revolutionary struggle for power.

When the revolutionary tide is rising, when the ruling classes are disorganised, the masses are in a state of revolutionary ferment, the intermediary strata are inclining towards the proletariat and the masses are ready for action and for sacrifice, the Party of the proletariat is confronted with the task of leading the masses to a direct attack upon the bourgeois State. This it does by carrying on propaganda in favour of increasingly radical transitional slogans (for Soviets, workers' control of industry, for peasant committees, for the seizure of the big landed properties, for disarming the bourgeoisie and arming the proletariat, etc.), and by organising mass action, upon which, all branches of Party agitation and propaganda, including parliamentary activity, must be concentrated. This mass action includes : strikes ; a combination of strikes and demonstrations ; a combination of strikes and armed demonstrations and finally, the general strike conjointly with armed insurrection against the State power of the bourgeoisie. The latter form of struggle, which is the supreme form, must be conducted according to the rules of war ; it pre-supposes a plan of campaign, offensive fighting operations and unbounded devotion and heroism on the part of the proletariat. An absolutely essential condition precedent for this form of action is the organisation of the broad masses into militant units, which, by their very form, embrace and set into action the largest possible numbers of toilers (Councils of Workers' Deputies, Soldiers' Councils, etc.), and intensified revolutionary work in the army and the navy.

In passing over to new and more radical slogans, the Parties must be guided by the fundamental rôle of the political tactics of Leninism, which call for ability to lead the masses to revolutionary positions in such a manner that the masses may, by their own experience, convince themselves of the correctness of the Party line. Failure to observe this rule must inevitably lead to isolation from the masses, to putschism, to the ideological degeneration of Communism into " leftist " dogmatism, and to petty-bourgeois " revolutionary " adventurism. Failure to take advantage of the culminating point in the development of the revolutionary situation, when the Party of the proletariat is called upon to conduct a bold and determined attack upon the enemy, is not less dangerous. To allow that opportunity to slip by and to fail to start rebellion at that point, means to allow the initiative to pass to the enemy and to doom the revolution to defeat.

When the revolutionary tide is not rising, the Communist Parties must advance partial slogans and demands that correspond to the everyday needs of the toilers, and combine them with the fundamental tasks of the Communist International. The Communist Parties must not, however, at such a time, advance transitional slogans that are applicable only to revolutionary situations (for example workers' control of industry, etc.). To advance such slogans when there is no revolutionary situation means to transform them into slogans that favour merging with the capitalist system of organisation. Partial demands and slogans form generally an essential part of correct tactics ; but certain transitional slogans go inseparably with a revolutionary situation. Repudiation of partial demands and transitional slogans " on principle," however, is incompatible with the tactical principles of Communism, for in effect, such repudiation condemns the Party to inaction and isolates it from the masses. United front tactics also occupy an important place in the tactics of the Communist Parties throughout the whole pre-revolutionary period as a means towards achieving success in the struggle against capital, towards the class mobilisation of the masses and the exposure and isolation of the reformist leaders.

The correct application of united front tactics and the fulfilment of the general task of winning over the masses pre-supposes in their turn systematic and persistent work in the trade unions and other mass proletarian organisations. It is the bounden duty of every Communist to belong to a trade union, even a most reactionary one, provided it is a mass organisation. Only by constant and persistent work in the trade unions and in the factories for the steadfast and energetic defence of the interests of the workers, together with ruthless struggle against the reformist bureaucracy, will it be possible to win the leadership in the workers' struggle and to win the industrially organised workers over to the side of the Party.

Unlike the reformists, whose policy is to split the trade

unions, the Communists defend trade union unity nationally and internationally on the basis of the class struggle,
and render every support to, and strengthen, the work of
the Red Trade Union International.

In championing universally the current everyday needs
of the masses of the workers and of the toilers generally, in
utilising the bourgeois parliament as a platform for revolutionary agitation and propaganda, and subordinating all
partial tasks to the struggle for the dictatorship of the
proletariat, the Parties of the Communist International
advance partial demands and slogans in the following
main spheres :

In the sphere of Labour, in the narrow meaning of the
term, i.e., questions concerned with the industrial struggle :
the fight against the trustified capital offensive, wages
questions, the working day, compulsory arbitration, unemployment ; which grow into questions of the general
political struggle, big industrial conflicts, fight for the right
to organise, right to strike, etc. ; in the sphere of politics
proper : taxation, high cost of living, Fascism, persecution
of revolutionary parties, white terror and current politics
generally ; and finally in the sphere of world politics, viz.,
attitude towards the U.S.S.R. and colonial revolutions,
struggle for the unity of the international trade union
movement, struggle against imperialism and the war
danger, and systematic preparation for the fight against
imperialist war.

In the sphere of the peasant problem, the partial demands
are those appertaining to taxation, peasant mortgage
indebtedness, struggle against usurer's capital, the land
hunger of the peasant small-holders, rent, the metayer
(crop-sharing) system. Starting out from these partial
needs, the Communist Party must sharpen the respective
slogans and broaden them out into the slogans : confiscation of large estates, and workers' and peasants' government
(the synonym for the proletarian dictatorship in developed
capitalist countries and for a democratic dictatorship of

the proletariat and peasantry in backward countries and in certain colonies).

Systematic work must also be carried on among the proletarian and peasant youth (mainly through the Young Communist International and its Sections) and also among working women and peasant women. This work must concern itself with the special conditions of life and struggle of the working and peasant women, and their demands must be linked up with the general demands and fighting slogans of the proletariat.

In the struggle against colonial oppression, the Communist Parties in the colonies must advance partial demands that correspond to the special circumstances prevailing in each country such as : complete equality for all nations and races ; abolition of all privileges for foreigners ; the right of association for workers and peasants ; reduction of the working day ; prohibition of child labour ; prohibition of usury and of all transactions entailing bondage ; reduction and abolition of rent ; reduction of taxation ; refusal to pay taxes, etc. All these partial slogans must be subordinate to the fundamental demands of the Communist Parties such as : complete political national independence and the expulsion of the imperialists ; workers' and peasants' government, the land to the whole people, eight-hour day, etc. The Communist Parties in imperialist countries, while supporting the struggle proceeding in the colonies, must carry on a campaign in their own respective countries for the withdrawal of imperialist troops, conduct propaganda in the army and navy in defence of the oppressed countries fighting for their liberation, mobilise the masses to refuse to transport troops and munitions, and in connection with this, to organise strikes and other forms of mass protest, etc.

The Communist International must devote itself especially to systematic preparation for the struggle against the danger of imperialist wars. Ruthless exposure of social chauvinism, of social imperialism and of pacifist phrase-mongering intended to camouflage the imperialist plans of the bourgeoisie ; propaganda in favour of the principal slogans of the Communist International ; everyday organisational work in connection with this in the course of which constitutional methods must unfailingly be combined with unconstitutional methods ; organised work in the army and navy—such must be *the activity of the Communist Parties in this connection. The fundamental slogans of the Communist International in this connection must be the following : " Convert imperialist war into civil war " ; defeat the " home " imperialist government ; defend the U.S.S.R. and the colonies by every possible means in the event of imperialist war against them. It is the bounden duty of all Sections of the Communist International, and of every one of its members, to carry on propaganda for these slogans, to expose the " socialistic " sophisms and the " socialistic " camouflage of the League of Nations, and constantly to keep to the front the experiences of the war of 1914–18.

In order that revolutionary work and revolutionary action may be co-ordinated and in order that these activities may be guided most successfully, the international proletariat must be bound by international class discipline, for which first of all, it is most important to have the strictest international discipline in the Communist ranks.

This international Communist discipline must find expression in the subordination of the partial and local interests of the movement to its general and lasting interests and in the strict fulfilment, by all members, of the decisions passed by the leading bodies of the Communist International.

Unlike the social-democratic Second International, each Section of which submits to the discipline of " its own," national bourgeoisie and of its own " fatherland," the Sections of the Communist International submit to only one discipline, viz., international proletarian discipline, which guarantees victory in the struggle of the world's workers for world proletarian dictatorship. Unlike the Second International, which splits the trade unions, fights against colonial peoples, and practises unity with the bourgeoisie, the Communist International is an organisation that guards proletarian unity in all countries and the unity of the toilers of all races and all peoples in their struggle against the yoke of imperialism.

Despite the bloody terror of the bourgeoisie, the Communists fight with courage and devotion on all sectors of the international class front, in the firm conviction that the victory of the proletariat is inevitable and cannot be averted.

" The Communists disdain to conceal their views and aims. They openly declare that their aims can be attained only by the forcible overthrow of all the existing social conditions. Let the ruling class tremble at a Communistic revolution. The proletarians have nothing to lose but their chains. They have a world to win.

" Working men of all countries, Unite ! "

APPENDICES

GLOSSARY OF NAMES

Aristotle (384–322 B.C.). Celebrated Greek philosopher, called by Marx " the Hegel of the ancient world."

Axelrod, P. B. (1850–1928). Russian Menshevik leader after the Social Democratic Labour Party split in 1903.

Babeuf, F. N. (1764–97). A radical republican (Jacobin) in the great French Revolution, guillotined for plotting for a Communist state.

Bakunin, M. A. (1814–76). Famous Russian revolutionary and leader of the Anarchist wing of the First International.

Bauer, Bruno (1809–82). " Young Hegelian " philosopher.

Bauer, Otto (1882–   ). Leader of Austrian Social Democracy, and prominent theoretician of the Second International.

Bebel, Auguste (1840–1913). One of the founders of the German Social Democratic Party. Leader of the Second International before the war.

Berkeley, G. (1684–1753). Famous idealist philosopher.

Bernstein, Eduard (1850–   ). Prominent German Social Democrat, member of the Reichstag, leader of the Second International.

Bismarck, Otto von (1815–98). Chancellor of the German Empire. Author of the *Anti-Socialist Laws*.

Blanc, Louis. French Utopian Socialist and historian, who entered the French Provisional Government in 1848 as a " workers' representative."

Blanqui, A. (1805–81). French revolutionary Socialist who advocated " putchist " tactics as a substitute for mass action.

Bonaparte, Louis (1808–73). Nephew of Napoleon I. He was elected French President in 1840, and proclaimed himself Emperor in 1851 by *coup d'état*. Overthrown in 1870, after defeat in Franco-Prussian war.

Buchanan, G. W. (1854–1924). British Ambassador to Russia, 1910–18.

Büchner, L. (1824–99). German doctor, materialist writer.

Caussidière (1808–61). French revolutionary.

Chernov, Victor (1876–   ). Leader of the Russian Socialist Revolutionary Party. Opponent of the Bolsheviks.

Chkheidze, N. S. (1864–1926). Menshevik leader from the Caucasus.

Dan, F. J. (1871–   ). Menshevik leader.

Danton, G. (1759–94). A Jacobin leader in the great French Revolution.

Darwin, Charles (1809–1882). English naturalist, famous for his development of the theory of Evolution.

David, E. (1863–   ). German Social Democrat opportunist.

Denikin. Tsarist general ; in 1918–19 commanded the counter-revolutionary forces in South Russia.

Descartes (1596–1650). French philosopher, whose work contains elements of both materialism and idealism.

Desmoulins, Camille (1760–94). A Jacobin leader in the great French Revolution.

Diderot (1713–84). French materialist philosopher.

Dietzgen, Joseph (1828–88). German socialist and self-educated philosopher. A tanner by trade.

Favre, Jules. French Foreign Minister, in the Thiers Government, February 1871.

Feuerbach, Ludwig (1804–72). " Young Hegelian " philosopher who turned to materialism, influencing Marx and Engels.

Fichte, J. G. (1762–1814). German idealist philosopher.

Fourier C. (1772–1837). French Utopian Socialist.

Gapon, G. (died 1906). A priest who organised the mass demonstration on " Bloody Sunday " which precipitated the 1905 Revolution.

Goethe, W. (1749–1832). German classical writer.

Golay, Paul. French Socialist. During the war edited a socialist paper in Lausanne.

Gompers, S. (1850–1924). Reactionary president of the American Federation of Labour.

Gorter, H. (1864–1927). Dutch left-wing Socialist, later Communist.

Guchkov, A. I. (1862–   ). Rich Moscow capitalist. Minister of War in the First Provisional Government, 1917.

Guizot (1787–1874). French Conservative. Representative of the Finance aristocracy.

Habakkuk. Hebrew prophet.

Haeckel, Ernst (1834–1919). German biologist.

Hegel, G. W. F. (1770–1831). German philosopher who developed the dialectical theory as an idealist.

Hilferding, Rudolph (1877–   ). Leading theoretician of German Social-Democracy. Attempted to reconcile Marxism with opportunism.

Hobbes, T. (1588–1697). English materialist philosopher.

Hobson, J. A. (1858–   ). English economist.

Höglund, Z. (1884–   ). Leader of Swedish Left Socialist Party before the war. For a short time Communist.

Holyoake, G. J. (1817–1906). English co-operator.

Hume, David (1711–76). English "sceptical" philosopher.

Huxley, T. H. (1825–95). English biologist, "Agnostic" philosopher.

Jouhaux, L. (1876–   ). Secretary of the French General Confederation of Labour and leader of the Amsterdam (trade union) International.

Kant, Emmanuel (1724–1804). Classical German philosopher.

Kautsky, Karl (1854–   ). Former leading Marxist theoretician, sank into Opportunism during the Great War, and opposed the Bolshevik Revolution.

Kerensky, A. F. (1881–   ). Socialist-Revolutionary, Premier in the Provisional Government that was overthrown by the Bolshevik Revolution.

Kornilov, L. G. (1876–1918). Tsarist General. Marched on Petrograd in September 1917, in an unsuccessful attempt to set up a military dictatorship.

Kropotkin, P. A. (1842–1921). Founder of Anarcho-Communism.

Lamarck, J. (1744–1829). French naturalist.

Lamartine, A. (1790–1869). French poet.

Laplace, P. (1749–1827). French astronomer and mathematician.

Lassalle, Ferdinand (1825–64). One of the outstanding leaders of the early German labour movement. Orator, publicist ; non-Marxist.

Ledru-Rollin, A. (1807–74). Bourgeois Republican leader.

Legien, K. (1861–1920). German reformist Trade Union leader.

Liebknecht, Karl (1871–1919). Left German Social-Democrat ; militant Internationalist and opponent of the Imperialist War ; murdered by German officers.

Liebknecht, Wilhelm (1826–1900). One of the founders of German Social-Democracy. Father of Karl Liebknecht.

Lincoln, Abraham (1809–65). United States President and leader of the Capitalist North in the Civil War.

Linnaeus, C. (1741–83). Swedish naturalist.

Locke, J. (1632–1704). English materialist philosopher.

Lunarcharsky, A. V. (1875–1934). Bolshevik. People's Commissar for Education after the Boshevik Revolution.

Lvov, Prince (1861–1925). Large landowner and member of the Provisional Government, 1917.

Macaire. Type of swindler from French play.

Mach, Ernst. German eclectic philosopher who vacillated between idealism and materialism.

Maine, H. S. (1822–88). English jurist and historian.

Malpighi, M. (1628–94). Italian anatomist.

Martov, L. (1873–1923). Leader of the Mensheviks at the Russian Social Democratic Labour Party split in 1903.

Martynov, A. S. (1865–1934). Theorist of " Economism," later Menshevik. Became a Bolshevik after the Bolshevik Revolution.

Metternich (1773–1859). Chancellor of the Austrian empire, and leader of the European reaction.

Mignet, F. (1796–1884). French historian.

Miliukov, P. (1859–   ). Leader of Constitutional Democratic Party (" Cadets ") and of Russian Liberalism. Bitter opponent of the Soviet Government.

Millerand, A. (1859–   ). French politician. First Socialist to join a bourgeois cabinet (1899–1902). Later expelled from the Socialist Party.

Moleschott (1822–93). Dutch naturalist with materialist views.

Moll, Joseph. German watchmaker, member of the Communist League. In London associated with Chartist movement. Fell in the German revolutionary struggles of 1849.

Montesquieu, C. (1689–1755). French historian.

Newton, Isaac (1642–1727). Mathematician, astronomer, physicist. Famous for his work on Gravitation.

Noske. German Social-Democrat who suppressed the revolutionary risings of the German workers after the war.

Ostwald. German chemist, writer on philosophical questions.

Owen, Robert (1771–1858). English Utopian Socialist. Pioneer of the Co-operative Movement.

Philippe, Louis (1773–1850). Duke of Orleans. Became " King of the French " as a result of July 1830 revolution. Deposed by February 1848 Revolution.

Plekhanov, George (1856–1918). Founder of Russian Marxism. Supported Lenin in his controversies with the idealists, but became a social-patriot during the war, and opposed the Bolshevik revolution.

Potresov, A. N. (1869–   ). Old Russian Social-Democrat. Leader of extreme right wing of the Mensheviks. Social-patriot during the war.

Proudhon, P. J. (1809–65). Petty-bourgeois Utopian Socialist.

Rakovsky, C. (1873–   ). Rumanian Socialist, then Communist and Soviet official ; later in Trotskyist opposition.

Rasputin, Gregory (1872–1916). Siberian priest who attained great influence at the Russian Court.

Renan, E. (1823–92). French historian.

Renner, Karl (1871–   ). Leading theorist of Opportunism in the Austrian Social-Democratic Party.

Ricardo, David (1772–1823). English Banker and Economist.

Robespierre, Maximilien (1758–1794). French Jacobin ; leader in the Great French Revolution.

Rodbertus-Jagetzow (1805–75). A rich Prussian landowner, theorist of " Prussian Junker " socialism.

Roland-Holst, Henrietta (1869–   ). Dutch writer and Marxist.

Romanov. Family name of the Russian Tsar Nicholas II.

Rousseau, J. J. (1712–78). French writer, author of the *Social Contract* ; expressed bourgeois revolt against the rule of the feudal aristocracy.

Royer-Collard, P. (1763–1845). French liberal.

Saint-Just, A. L. (1767–94). Jacobin. Outstanding figure in the French revolution.

Saint-Simon (1760–1825). French Utopian Socialist.

Say, Jean Baptiste (1767–1832). Leading French economist, and apologist of free-trade capitalism.

Scheidemann, P. (1865–   ). Right Wing German Social-Democrat. Together with Noske he organised the crushing of the Spartacist rising in 1919.

Sismondi (1773–1842). French historian and economist.

Skobelev, M. I. (1885–   ), Menshevik, member of the Fourth Duma.

Smith, Adam (1723–90). Classical English economist.

Stirner, Max (1808–56). Associated with " Young Hegelians."

Strauss, D. F. (1800–74). German " Young Hegelian " philosopher.

Struve, Peter (1870–   ). Russian economist. Originally opportunist Social-Democrat, later Liberal.

Sun-Yat-Sen. Leader of Chinese bourgeois revolution. Founded Kuomintang Party in 1912. In control of Canton from 1916 until his death in 1925.

Thiers, A. (1797–1877). Leader of government that suppressed the Paris Commune in 1871.

Thierry, A. (1795–1856). French historian.

Trochu, L. J. (1815–96). Military Governor of Paris, after September 4th, 1870, President of the " Government of National Defence."

Trotsky, L. (1879–   ). Leading Russian Social-Democrat, who vacillated between the Bolsheviks and Mensheviks after the Party split in 1903, being continually in opposition to Lenin. He joined the Bolshevik Party just before the Bolshevik Revolution and filled leading posts during the Civil War. Later he became a leader of anti-party fractional struggles and was expelled from the Party.

Tseretelli, I. G. (1882–   ). Menshevik. Became a Minister of the First Coalition Government in May 1917.

Turati, F. (1857–   ). Leader of right wing in Italian Socialist Party.

Turgenev, I. S. (1818–83). Famous Russian novelist.

Vogt, Karl (1817–98). German naturalist, vulgar materialist and petty-bourgeois democrat.

Vollner, G. von (1850–1922). German Social-Democrat and outstanding defender of Imperialism.

Zubatov (1864–1917). Head of the Tsarist Secret Police in Moscow.

SUPPLEMENTARY LIST OF
THE MORE IMPORTANT OTHER WORKS
BY MARX, ENGELS, LENIN AND STALIN

(Where no publisher is mentioned, no English edition is available)

KARL MARX

A Critique of the Hegelian Philosophy of Right (1844).
On the Jewish Question (1844). Martin Lawrence, 1935.
The Holy Family (written jointly with Engels in 1845).
Wage Labour and Capital (1849). Martin Lawrence, 1935.
Revelations about the Cologne Communist Trial (1852).
Herr Vogt (1860).
Critique of the Gotha Programme (1890). Martin Lawrence, 1933.
Value, Price and Profit (1865). Allen & Unwin, 1925.
Theories of Surplus Value.
Civil War in America. Martin Lawrence, 1935.
Letters to Kugelmann. Martin Lawrence, 1934.
Karl Marx and Friedrich Engels : Correspondence. Martin Lawrence, 1935.

Among reprints of articles, collections under the titles of *Palmerston* and *The Eastern Question* exist in English editions.

FRIEDRICH ENGELS

The Condition of the Working Class in England (1845). Allen & Unwin.
Critical Essay of Political Economy (1845).
The Economic Development of Russia (1892).
The Peasant War in Germany. Allen & Unwin.
Dialectics of Nature.
The Franco-German War of 1870–71. (Articles written in English for the *Pall Mall Gazette.* Collected edition in German only.)

V. I. LENIN

Several volumes of Lenin's Collected Works have already been published in English by Martin Lawrence. These are :

The Iskra Period. (Two volumes.)
The Imperialist War, 1914–15.
Towards the Seizure of Power, 1917. (Two volumes.)
The Revolution of 1917. (Two volumes.)

Some of the articles contained in the above have also been reprinted in the " Little Lenin Library " (Martin Lawrence). Most of these smaller volumes have been mentioned in the extracts from Lenin given on earlier pages. Others include :

The War and the Second International.
The Paris Commune.
Religion.
The Threatening Catastrophe.
Will the Bolsheviks Maintain Power ?

Other volumes of articles and speeches also published by Martin Lawrence :

Marx, Engels—Marxism.
Lenin on Britain.
Voices of Revolt.

A number of pamphlets containing separate articles or speeches have also been published in English, including :

The Deception of the People.
The Foundation of the Third International. (Containing Lenin's Theses on Bourgeois Democracy and Proletarian Dictatorship.)
The Historic Significance of the Third International.
Democracy and Trade Unions.

The *Labour Monthly, Communist International,* and *Communist Review* have also published a number of other articles or speeches of Lenin's.

J. STALIN

The most important collection in English of Stalin's articles and speeches is :

Leninism. (Two volumes.) Allen & Unwin, 1928 and 1932.

Other collections and separate articles and speeches published by Martin Lawrence include :

Lenin.
Stalin Reports on the Soviet Union (1933).
From the First to the Second Five Year Plan (1934).
Socialism Victorious (1935).

GLOSSARY OF UNFAMILIAR TERMS

Anti-Socialist Laws (Germany). Introduced by Bismarck in 1878 to suppress the Social-Democratic organisation. The organisation, however, developed, and when elections were held after the repeal of these laws in 1890, the Social Democratic Party secured 1½ million votes.

Artel. A group of workers or peasants engaged in co-operative production.

Black Hundreds. The most reactionary landlord group in Russia under the Tsars.

Boxer Rebellion. Chinese national revolt against foreign oppression (1900).

Bund. The Jewish Labour League in Poland and Russia, established in 1897.

Cadets. Constitutional-Democratic Party in Russia.

Decembriseur. Member of " Society of December 10th," described by Marx in his *Eighteenth Brumaire.*

Duma. Russian " parliament " granted by Tsar after 1905 revolution.

Gotha Programme. Programme adopted by the German Social-Democratic Party on the occasion of its formation by the amalgamation of the two previously existing workers' parties (1875).

Guildmaster. A full member of a craft guild.

Holy Alliance. Alliance of counter-revolutionary monarchies of Russia, Austria and Prussia. Founded in 1815.

Jacobins. Radical Republicans, the most radical party representing the petty-bourgeoisie in the French Revolution, 1789.

Junkers. Large landowners of Prussia.

Kienthal (Switzerland). The second international conference of Socialist groups opposing the war was held there in 1916.

Kulak. Rich peasant, also village usurer and exploiter.

Kustar industry. Small scale home industry, mainly handicraft.

Legitimists. Supporters of the older or " legitimate " branch of the Bourbon Royal family of France, who represented particularly the landlords.

Liquidators. Reformist Socialist—Mensheviks—who proposed the liquidation of the underground party organisation and instead favoured only legal activities.

Lumpenproletariat. " Ragged proletariat "—The lowest stratum of the town working-class.

Muzhik, mujik. Russian peasant.

Narodniks. A Russian petty-bourgeois revolutionary group.

Octobrists. A Russian (constitutional) political party formed in 1905, when the Tsar promised a Duma.

Orleanists. Supporters of the junior branch of the Bourbons (descendants of Louis Philippe). The Party of the merchants, bankers and landlords.

Phalanstères. Socialist colonies planned by Charles Fourier.

Praetorian. In ancient Rome, the personal bodyguard of a general or emperor.

Sachsenwald. The extensive estate presented to the German Chancellor Bismarck.

Spartacus League. The anti-war organisation of Karl Liebknecht during the war. (He signed his illegal leaflets " Spartacus"—Spartacus was the leader of a slave revolt in ancient Rome).

Tuileries. Traditional residence of the French Kings

Vedas. Hindu Sacred Books.

White Guards. The general term used by the Bosheviks (the " Reds ") to describe the counter-revolutionary forces (the " Whites ") after November 1917.

Zemstvo. Elected provincial representative assembly in Russia. The zemstvos were used by the Liberal bourgeoisie for agitation against the autocracy.

Zimmerwald (Switzerland). The first international conference of Socialist groups opposing the war was held there in 1915.

INDEX

INDEX

ACCUMULATION, historical tendency of capitalist, 401
— on an enlarged scale, 480
— secret of primitive, 375
Adultery, 303, 306
Agahd, 712
Agrarian programme, Lenin's, 786
Agricultural armies, establishment of, 46
— artel, 935-7
— policy in U.S.S.R., 1017
— population expropriated from the land, 379
— revolution of fifteenth century, 386
— — reaction on industry, 386
Agriculture and proletarian dictatorship, 995
— in Asia, 183
— separated from handicraft, 320, 322
Aguinaldo, 712
Aikin, John, 400
Albert, 101, 104, 112
All-Russian newspaper for propaganda, 607
Allies, Lenin on the, 801
Alsace-Lorraine, annexation of, 83, 720
America, and U.S.S.R., 926
— antagonism between Japan and, 982
— as economic centre, 982
— conflict with the United States of, 982
— gold and silver discovered in, 391
— Imperialism in, 711
— industrial activity in, 204
— Irish emigrants in, 196
— official corruption in, 331
— railways of, 699
— slavery in, 356
— war of, with Spain, 711

American Federation of Labour, 1024
— Redskins, 314
— trade union bureaucracy, 1024
Amsterdam Federation of Trade Unions, 978
— International, 1024
Anarchism, 1029
— distinction from Marxism, 788
— Lenin on, 846
Anarchists, distinction from communists, 774
— Engels's conclusions against, 736
— Lenin on, 684
Ancient Society (Morgan), 301
Anderson, A., 387, 400
Anderson, James, 387
Angora, 899
Anti-Corn Law League, 203
Anti-Dühring (Engels), 232 *et seq.*, 636
Anti-Leninism, 931
Anti-revolt Bill, 94
Anti-Socialist law, 83
" Appeals to Action," Lenin on, 598
Apprenticeship system, 399
Archives of World Economy, 710
Aristocracy, " finance," 96 *et seq.*
— landed, 206
— morality of, 248
" Aristocrat " bureaucrats, 951
Aristotle, 1045
— on moneylending, 448
Armaments, growth of, 919
Armed masses, organisation of in communism, 747
— men and the State, 726-9
Armenia, national council of, 817
Armies, growth of, 88
Army, abolition of, 145
— in Russia, 622
— of early tribes, 321

Kᴋᴍ

Artel in relation to the commune, 936
— the agricultural, 935–7
Aryan tribes, 315
Asia, capitalism in Eastern, 697
— horticulture introduced into, 316
— public works in, 182 et seq.
— social revolution in, 186
Asiento Treaty, 400
Asquith, Herbert, 872
Astronomy, an exact science, 242
Augier, 401
Aurelles de Paladine, L. J. B., 138, 140
Austria annexes Cracow, 101
— industrial growth in, 80
— revolution in, 975
— universal suffrage in, 632
Austrian social-democrats, 819
Austro-Marxism, 1028
" Austrophilism," 569
Autocracy, political exposure of, 589
Avenarius, Richard, Bemerkungen, 648, 655
— Bogdanov on, 656
— Der Menschliche Weltbegriff, 644, 654, 655
— philosophy of, 644–5, 647 et seq., 654 et seq.
— Prolegomena, 644
— relativity of, 666
Aviation, Chemical and Defence League, 948
Axelrod, P. B., 847, 854, 1045
Azerbaijan, national council of, 817

Babeuf, François Noel, 55, 1045
Babushkin, 863
Bachofen, 311
Bad, antithesis between good and, 247
Bailiffs, 385
Bakunin, M. A., 222, 1045
Balfour, A. J., 201
Bancroft, H. H., 315
Bank of England founded, 396
Bankers, opposition to social reform, 98
— rule of, in France, 96

Banks, collapse of, 914
— origin of, 395
— proletarian nationalisation of private, 996
Barbarism, Engels on, 313
— highest stage of, 319
Barbon, Nicholas, 407
Barricades of 1848, 101
— effect of, 86
Barrot, C. H. Odilon, 92, 101
Basle Congress, 976
— Manifesto, 683, 764
Bastiat, Frédéric, 97
Bauer, Bruno, 222, 1045
Bauer, Otto, 1045
— national cultural autonomy of, 687, 819
Bazarov, Outlines of, 653
Bebel, Ferdinand August, 84, 740, 1045
— correspondence with Engels, 745
Being in contrast to reasoning, 233
— relation to thinking, 214–15
Belgium and the franchise, 90
Bengal, agrarian revolution in, 193
Bérard, Victor, England and Imperialism, 712
Berkeleianism, 637, 640
Berkeley, Bishop, 1045
— philosophy of, 638–40, 643, 647, 660
Bernstein, Eduard, 800, 1045
Bernsteinism in Russia, 597
Bismarck, Prince Otto von, 77, 81, 84, 93, 137, 161, 204, 332, 1045
Bismarck régime in Germany, 731
Black Hundred workers' meetings, 863
Black Sea fleet, 623
Blackett, Mr., 180
Blanc, Louis, 58, 101, 104, 110, 112, 1045
Blanqui, L. A., 165, 1045
Blanquism, 799, 800
Blanquist party, 167–8
Bleichröder, 332
Blood circulation, 243
" Bloody Sunday," 609, 610, 614, 616
Bogdanov, A., 634
— Empirio-Monism, 644, 647, 660
— on Avenarius,
— on Engels, 660

Bogdanov, A.—*continued*
— on Marxism, 667
— on relative truth, 663
— philosophy of, 673
Boguslawski, Herr von, 91, 93
Bolingbroke, Viscount, 174, 396
Bolshevik work and socialism, 941
Bolsheviks, 784
— and Kautsky, 838
— and parliamentary struggles, 891
— and the State, 725
— " Left," 870
— sixth congress of, 792
— strategy of, 856, 857
Bolshevism and Socialist Revolutionary Party, 867
Bombay, agrarian revolution in, 193
Bonaparte, Louis, 81, 82, 1045
Boncour, Paul, 977
Bordeaux protests, 97
Bourgeois civilisation, hypocrisy and barbarism of, 193
— demand for equality, 253
— democracy and workers, 828
— domination, 732
— government and fascism, 980
— inequalities of, 993
— institutions, 365
— monarchy of Louis Philippe, 123
— morality, 248
— Parliaments, Lenin on, 864–7
— power, overthrow of, by proletariat, 991
— production, economists' views of, 350
— republic, 122, 124
— revolutions, 120
— rights, Lenin on, 750, 751, 753, 755
— Socialism, 53
— wealth, 378
Bourgeois-Democratic revolution in Germany, 569
Bourgeoisie, achievements of, 25
— and opportunism, 681
— and proletariat, Marx on, 567
— antagonistic character of, 367–8
— birth of, 251
— conditions for existence of, 36
— control of commercial crises, 29
— definition of, 22
— divisions of, 127
— English, exploit Irish poverty, 195

Bourgeoisie—*continued*
— evolution of, 24
— family relations of, 42
— freedom of, 40
— hatred of *Ateliers*, 110
— in imperialist countries, 970
— in the Colonies, 971
— industrial development of, 105
— — rule of, 106
— marriage among, 43
— peasantry under, 151
— petty, 49, 101
— — a transition class, 129
— — allied with workers, 127
— proletariat struggle with, 31
— proletariat within, 367
— Prussian, 52
— struggle with aristocracy, 33
— working-class, creation of, 30
Boxer rebellion in China, 718
Boyle, Robert, law of, 246, 664
Bracke, 740
Brahman mythological chronology, 181
Brentanoism, 682
Brest-Litovsk, peace of, 928, 977
British capital invested abroad, 701
— communists, Lenin on, 880
— double mission in India, 188
— East India Company, 181
— Empire, railways of, 699
— imperialism, Schulze-Gaevernitz on, 705
— — Lenin on, 706
— Labour movement, Engels on, 197
— — Party, 977, 1024
— policy of *laissez-faire*, 183
— rule in India, Marx on, 180
— — results of, 187
— Socialist Party, 868, 874
— supremacy in India, cause of, 187
— trade-unionism, Lenin on, 593
— workers, political struggle of, 600
Buchanan, G. W., 766, 1045
Büchner, L., 1045
Bukharin, 897, 899
Bulgaria and the franchise, 90
— uprising in, 975
Bulygin Duma, 626, 627

Bureaucracy, Lenin and, 847
— Stalin on, 948, 950
Buzançais hunger riots, 100

CABET, ETIENNE, 57
Cadets in Russia, 795, 796, 797, 801
Cadres, Stalin on, 962
Calculus, differential, 261, 264
Calver, Richard, *An Introduction to World Economy*, 696
Canton, 899
— Kuomintang, 904
— National government of, 901, 904
— period of Chinese revolution, 897
Capital and payment of wages, 200
— and use-value, 437
— cheapening of existing, in development of industry, 504
— circulating, 477
— conditions essential for, 36
— constant, 471, 473, 477
— — cheapening of elements of, 504
— contradictions in general formula of, 440 *et seq.*
— conversion of money into, 450
— epoch of industrial, 964
— fixed, 477
— general formula for, 431
— in railroads, 698
— invested in colonies, 507
— — in foreign trade, 506
— — in production, 478
— merchants', 440 *et seq.*
— monopoly of, 404
— nature of, 39, 438
— of moneylenders, 448
— origin of, 450
— over-production of, 517
— primitive accumulation of, 258
— starting point of, 431
— surplus of, 516
— the barrier of capitalist production, 515
— variable, 471, 473, 477
Capital (Marx), 373 *et seq.*, 558-60, 562
Capitalism and imperialism, 688 *et seq.*
—and imperialist wars, 969
— and machinery, 966, 968

Capitalism—*continued*
— and nationalities, 563
— and U.S.S.R., 945
— British, features of, 708
— changes effected by modern, 562
— decay of, 700 *et seq.*
— dynamic laws of, 964
— general crisis of, 918, 974 *et seq.*
— history of, 964 *et seq.*
— imperialism and the downfall of, 972, 973
— in agriculture, 558
— in Eastern Asia, 697
— in factories, 31
— in Russia, 697
— in the Colonies, 696
— revolutionary collapse of, 980 *et seq.*
— the crisis of, 978-80
— transition of, to communism, 741 *et seq.*, 836
— — to proletariat dictatorship, 988 *et seq.*
— world system of, 964 *et seq.*
Capitalist accumulation, historical tendency of, 401
— combines, industrial production in, 915, 916
— countries, economic crisis in, 912-18
— — political situation in, 918 *et seq.*
— democracy, 741
— economy, 690
— farmer, genesis of, 385
— functions of, 207
— industrial genesis of, 390
— monopolies and competition, 689, 709
— production, breakdown of, 291
— — capital the barrier of, 515
— — mode of, 280 *et seq*
— — of use-value, 460
— — traits of, 531
— society, changes in, 966
— stabilisation, contradictions, 980 *et seq.*
— states and the U.S.S.R., 925-31
— world, antagonism to U.S.S.R., 982
Capitation, development in the colonies, 983
Carnegie, A., Lenin on, 706

Categories, logical sequence of, 350, 359
Catholic morality, 247
— trade unions, 1024
Cattle as commodity, 316, 322
Caussidière, 116, 1045
Cell, discovery of the, 226, 243
Censorship in autocratic Russia, 607
Central Committee of Bolsheviks, 799
" Central Europe," creation of, 696
Central Executive Committee in Russia, 897
— Lenin's letter to, 808 et seq.
— tasks of the, 949, 950
Charles II, King, 174
Chartist movement, 198
Chartists, Marx on the, 567
Chatterboxes, Stalin on, 951, 952
Chauvinism, 161
Chemistry, Engels on, 236
— hypothesis in, 242
Chernov, V., 666, 754, 801-2, 1045
Chiangkai Shek's *coup d'état*, 902, 903
Child labour, 399
— abolition of, 46
Children, exploitation of, 42
— free education of, 46
— public care and education of, 304
China, expansion of soviet regions in, 920
— Hobson's economic valuation of, 704
— Lenin on, 896
— rebellion in, 983
— revolutions in, 632, 677, 895, 907, 975
— soviet revolution in, 907
— Stalin on, 894 et seq.
— war with Japan, 911
— war-plans against, 922
Chinese Communists, 901
Chkheidze, N. S., 785, 787, 1045
Christian colonial system, 391
— distinction from philosopher, 352
— morality, 247
— Socialism, 49
Christianity and equality, 250
Christians, persecution of, 94
Church and the proletarian dictatorship, 1009
— land, confiscation of, 381

Churches, disendowment of, 145
Churchill, Randolph, 875
Civil Wars, Lenin on, 633, 683
Civilisation, characteristics of, 335
— definition of, 333
— Engels on, 313
— Fourier on, 337
— marriage for, 303
— Morgan on, 337
— slavery in, 335
Class antagonisms and the State, 722, 724, 726-8
— consciousness, Marx on, 566
— " dangerous," 34
— decay, 34
— domination and the State, 725
— middle. *See* Middle class
— Society and the State, 722 et seq.
— struggles, 22, 1015
— — in France, Engels on, 71-2 ; Marx on, 95
— transition, 129
Classes, abolition of social, 297
— capitalist middle, 206
— cleavage of society into, 320
— demand for abolition of, 254
— development of the, 272 et seq.
— disappearance of, 985
— exploitation of each other, 336
— producing, 206
— proletarian dictatorship and the, 1003-5
Classic School of economists, 369
Clive, Lord, 193
Clynes, J. R., 869, 871
Coal industry in Germany, 699
Cobbett, William, 395, 397
Coin, introduction of minted, 323, 335
Collective farm movement, 936, 937, 940
Colonial monopoly, 709
— question and proletarian dictatorship, 998
— revolution and proletarian dictatorship, 1013-15
— system, 391
Colonies, bourgeoisie in the, 971
— capital invested in, 507
— capitalism in, 696
— monopoly of ownership of, 701
Combination Laws of 1824, 198

Commerce, Annals of (Anderson), 400

Commodities as products of labour, 407
— average profit of, 486
— cause of rise in price of, 426
— circulation of, 290, 422
— — and capital, 431 *et seq.*
— commercial knowledge of, 406
— drop in prices of, 914
— exchange value of, 406
— exchangeability of, 415
— fetishism of, 411
— market prices and values of, 483
— Marx on, 405
— mystical character of, 411
— production of, 281
— requirements for sale at value of, 487
— supply and demand of, 486 *et seq.*
— two factors of, 405
— value of, expressed in gold, 422
Common land, enclosure of, 383, 386
Communal life among tribes, 315
— property, institution of, 383
Communard-Blanquists, 881
Commune, abolition of class-property under, 149
— antagonism to State power, 147
— composition of, 144
— financial measures of, 154
— in relation to the artel, 936
— nature of, 141
— origin of term, 25
— significance of, 166
— the government of workers, 153
— *versus* Empire, 151
Communication services and proletariat dictatorship, 994
— centralisation of means of, 46
— control of means of, 207
Communism a power in itself, 22
— and control of labour, 753
— and Ghandism, 1031
— and the distribution of products, 751
— and the means of production, 748
— and the State, 746, 751
— Critical Utopian, 55
— elimination of capitalists from, 745
— higher stage of, 987
— " impossible," 149

Communism—*continued*
— in England, 891–2
— " Leftist " views in, 940
— Lenin on development of, 741
— — on future of, 883 *et seq.*
— Marx's description of, 755
— organisation of armed masses in, 747
— " possible," 149
— scientific difference from socialism, 754
— strategy : fundamental tasks of, 1032 *et seq.*
— transition from capitalism to, 836
— working class ideologists inimical to, 1023–32
— world, 984 *et seq.*
Communist discipline, 1041
— International, 893–4
— — aims of, 1042
— — and imperialist wars, 1040
— — second congress of, 895, 898
— — seventh plenum of the, 900
— — sixth plenum of the, 903
— — strategy of, 1023 *et seq.*
— — tasks of, 1034
— — ultimate aims of, 984 *et seq.*
— League, Congress of 1847, 21
— — dissolution of, 21
— — Marx's address to, 60
— literature, 47
— Manifesto of 1848, 21, 60, 566–7, 963
— parties and revolutionary movements, 1035
— — growth of, 984
— — in colonial countries, 1035
— — in imperialist countries, 1035
— Party and colonial oppression, 1040
— — and the peasant problem, 1039
— — in England, 868, 871
— — Lenin on, 787, 789
— — of Soviet Union, seventeenth congress, 910 *et seq.*
— Society, first phase of, 748–51
— — general phases of, 747
— — higher phase of, 751 *et seq.*
— tactics, 1032 *et seq.*
Communists, abolition of property by, 38
— aims of, 37

Communists—*continued*
— allied with Social-Democrats, 58
— and abolition of the family, 42
— and trade unions, 1038
— Chinese, 901
— distinction from anarchists, 774
— — from other parties, 37
— in Germany, 59
— in relation to opposing parties, 58
— relation to proletarian, 37
— the theoreticians of the proletariat, 369
Companies, jointstock, 292 *et seq.*
Company flotation, 208
Competition, advent of free, 28
— and capitalist monopolies, 689
Compromise, Stalin on, 794
Concepts, production of, 212
Condillac, 443–4
Congress of Austrian Social-Democratic Party, 633
— of Soviets, 798, 806
Consciousness, brain the source of, 219
— determined by life, 213
— Dühring on, 240
— in contrast to being, 233
— nature of, 233
— production of, 212
— relation to nature, 233
Constanza, 623
Constituent assembly in Russia, 611, 613, 860
Constructive socialism, 1026, 1027, 1030
Consumption, means of, 477
Contract, freedom of, 309, 311
Contradictions, Proudhon's system of, 349, 354, 358
Co-operative farming and proletarian dictatorship, 1002
— organisations and the proletarian dictatorship, 1006, 1007
— stores, 208
Co-operativism, 1027
Copernican solar system, 217
Corbon, M., 135
Corn Laws, introduction of, 202
— repeal of, 100, 203
Corps Legislatif, 139
Cosmogony, Engels on, 236

Cotton industry, child labour in, 399
— in England, 202
— in India, 184
Council of soldiers' deputies, 1037
— of workers' deputies, 1037
Countries, abolition of, 43
Country, antagonism between town and, 987
Cracow annexed by Austria, 100
Crapulinsky, 125
Credit and proletarian dictatorship, 997
— system, international, 396
Cremieux, 101
Crimean War, Marx on, 172
— policy leading to, 176
Crises, commercial, 29
Critique of Political Economy (Marx), 209, 370 *et seq.*
Cultural revolution and the proletarian dictatorship, 1008–10
Culture, disappearance of, 41
Cunow on imperialism, 694

Dan, F. J., 854, 1046
Danton, Georges Jacques, 116, 117, 133, 1046
Darwin, Charles, 1046
— theory of evolution, 227
David, E., 763, 1046
Defencism, Lenin on, 784, 803
De Hauranne, 175
Demand, regulation of supply and, 486 *et seq.*
Democracy and bourgeois society, 757
— and equality, 756
— capitalist, 741
— Lenin on, 756
— workers as champions, 601 *et seq.*
Democratic conference, 802
— labels, false, 1025
— republic, 331
Denikin, General, 1046
Denmark and the franchise, 90
Descartes, René, 218, 220, 1046
— philosophy of, 237
Desmoulins, Camille, 117, 1046
De Witt, *Maxims*, 397
Dialectical materialism, 1026

Dialectics, Engels on, 256, 258
— eternal truths in, 245
— Hegel's view of, 223
— nature of, 266
Diderot, Denis, 642, 643, 1046
Dietzgen, Joseph, 225, 864, 1046
— *Excursions*, 664
— philosophy of, 665, 669
Dilke, Sir Charles, 201
Diocletian, Emperor, 94
Discipline and Leninism, 852
Distribution, conditions of, 528
— control of means of, 76
Ditmarsh families, 328
Djugashvili, Joseph. *See* Stalin
Dogmatics (Strauss), 222
Douai, General, 154
Doubleda7, 397
Dream apparitions, 215
Dresden barricade, 86
Dualism, 657
Dühring, Eugen, 649, 737
— and pure mathematics, 235
— and the negation of the negation, 261
— as metaphysician, 239
— metaphysical materialism of, 662
— on cause of economic order, 271
— on dialectics, 245–6
— on force, 278
— on morality, 247
— on result of slavery, 276
— on thought and knowledge, 240
— philosophy of, 232, 636
Duma, the, 766
Dumping, Stalin on, 915
Dupont de l'Eure, 101
Dutch East India Company, 181
— " Lefts," 864
— tribunists, 864

ECONOMIC AGITATION, Lenin on, 594
— concessions, Lenin on, 595
— crisis, factors contributory to, 912–16
— — in capitalist countries, 912–18
— —, Stalin on the, 911, 918
— exposures, Lenin on, 608

Economic—*continued*
— function of capitalist middle class, 207
— life, internationalisation of, 969
— order, political conditions the cause of, 269
— policy of proletarian dictatorship, 999 *et seq.*
— politics, Lenin on, 600
— regions of the world, 696
— reforms and social-democracy, 595
— reforms, Lenin on, 595
— strikes in Russia, 619
— struggle, Lenin on the, 596
— struggles and trade unions, 603
— theories, logical sequence of, 350, 359
Economic Table (Quesnay), 349
Economism, Lenin on, 589
Economists and political agitation, 592
— fatalist, 368
— fundamental error of, 602
— Lenin on the, 603
— schools of, 368
— the scientific representatives of bourgeoisie, 369
— view of bourgeois production, 350
Economy, political. *See* Political economy
Eden, Sir F. M., 383, 398
Education, capitalist monopoly of, 1008
— Communists and, 42
— free, in France, 145
— of children a public matter, 304
Egoism, Lenin on, 670
Elizabeth, Queen, 381
Ellenbogen, 633
Embryology, nature of, 226
Emigrants, property of, confiscated, 46
Emigration from Germany, 707
— from Great Britain, 707
Empire *versus* Commune, 151
Energy, transformation of, 227
Engels, Friedrich, *Anti-Dühring*, 232 *et seq.*, 564, 654, 661, 663–4
— Bogdanov on, 660 *et seq.*
— *Communist Manifesto*, 11
— *Condition of the Working Class in England*, 708

Engels, Friedrich—*continued*
— contrasted with Kautsky, 833
— correspondence with Bebel, 745
— eclecticism of, 660
— *Germany : Revolution and Counter Revolution,* 132
— Introduction to *Civil War in France,* 160
— letters of Marx to, 557, 565–70
— life of, 11
— *Ludwig Feuerbach,* 637, 654
— materialism of, 643, 649
— *Mr. Dühring Revolutionises Science,* 939
— on a democratic republic, 731
— on absolute truth, 663
— on barbarism, 313
— on British trade unions, 708
— on civilisation, 313
— on class struggles in France, 71
— on collaboration with Marx, 223
— on dialectical materialism, 222
— on dialectics, 256, 258
— on Feuerbach, 214
— on free trade, 201
— on German ideology, 209
— on insurrection, 132
— on marriage, 303
— on mental images, 636
— on need for social classes, 205
— on negation of the negation, 258
— on political economy, 267
— on private property, 301
— on public force, 727, 728
— on pure mathematics, 235
— on the British Labour movement, 197
— on the housing question, 338 *et seq.*
— on the modern state, 732
— on the origin of the family, 301, 563–4
— on the State, 301, 563–4, 726
— on thought, 240
— on universal suffrage, 731
— on violent revolution, 737–8
— on " withering away " of the state, 733 *et seq.*
— programme of 1848, 21
— *The Origin of the Family, Private Property and the State,* 563, 564, 724

England and U.S.S.R., 929
— Communism in, 891–2
— Communist Party in, 868, 871
— cotton industry in, 202
— general strike in, 975
— industrial supremacy of, 202
— — wane of, 204
— Irish hatred of, 196
— landlordism in, 195, 206
— " Left-Wing " communism in, 868 *et seq.*, 876
— opportunism in, 709
— social-chauvinism in, 709
English East India Company, 392
— monopoly of tea trade, 392
" Enrich yourselves," Stalin on the slogan, 940
Equalitarianism and socialism, 935, 939
Equality, Marxian conception of, 938
— modern demand for, 249, 253
— of rights, 250
Equilibrium, relativity of, 237
— unconditional, 239
Equivalents, exchange of, 268
Error, antithesis between truth and, 246
Eschwege, 410, 712
Essence of Christianity (Feuerbach), 229
Estates, " clearing " of, 384
Esthonia, uprising in, 975
Eudes, General, 165
Evolution, Darwin's theory of, 227
Ewald on introjection, 659
Exception law against socialists in Germany, 570
Exchange, control of, 76
— Indian lack of means of, 189
— of equivalents, 268
— of products, 323
— origin of, 28
— production for, 286, 333
— value, 406
— confusion with use-value, 443
Exploiters and exploited, Lenin on, 831
— suppression of, 990
Exposures, all-national, 608
— and social-democracy, 609

Expropriation of property, forms of, 258 *et seq.*
— of the expropriators, 994 *et seq.*

FABIAN IMPERIALISTS, 710
— Society, opportunism of, 710
Fabianism, liberal, 1027
— traditions of, 1026
Factions and Leninism, 851–3
Factory discipline in the State, 758
— organisation, 30, 282
— reforms, Lenin on, 595
— system, Marx on the, 562
Family, abolition of, 42
— division of labour in, 314, 318
— Engels on the origin of, 301
Farm contracts, 386
— wages, 386
Farmer, genesis of the capitalist, 385
Fascism, aims of, 979
— and bourgeois government, 980
— in Germany, 920
— Stalin on, 920
Fashoda affair, 719
Fatalist economists, 368
Faucher, Leon, 97
Favre, jules, 135, 136, 1046
February revolution in France, 823
Federation of soviet republics, 815, 825, 1015
Feodosia, 623
Feudal inequalities, 252
— institutions, 365
— morality, 247
— privileges, 253
— production, 366, 380
— state, 330, 331
— tenure of land abolished, 382
Feudalism destroyed by bourgeoisie, 25, 28
Feuerbach, Ludwig, 1046
— and materialism, 217, 219, 643, 667
— as philosopher, 222
— Engels on, 214
— *Essence of Christianity*, 229
— Marx's theses on, 227 *et seq.*

Feuerbach, Ludwig—*continued*
— " metaphysics " of, 218
— philosophy of, 672
Fichte, J. G., 1046
— philosophy of, 671
Fielden, on apprentice system, 399
Fifteenth Party Congress, C.P.S.U., 931
Finance and political alliances, 719
— aristocracy in France, 96 *et seq.*
— capitalism era of, 967–9
Finland, independence of, 818
— liberation of, 825
— recognition of independence of, 814
— republic in, 782
— revolution in, 975
— uprising of workers in, 816
First International, 676
— —foundation of, 133
Five-Year Plan, 937, 953
Flocon, 101
Force, Dühring on, 278
— establishment of a public, 329
Foreigners in France, 707
— in Germany, 707
Fourier, François Charles Marie, 287, 290, 291, 1046
— Communist system of, 55
— on civilisation, 337
Fox, Charles, 174
France and U.S.S.R., 927
— *Civil War in*, 133 *et seq.*
— — Engels's introduction to, 158
— class struggles in, Engels on, 72
— commercial treaty with, 201
— Communists allied to Social-Democrats, 58
— Constituent National Assembly in, 111 *et seq.*
— demand for equality in, 103, 253
— February Revolution of 1848, 101 *et seq.*, 119, 823
— First Empire in, 142, 161
— foreigners in, 707
— industrial growth in, 80
— Marx on class struggles in, 95
— — on history of, 75
— Ministry of Labour in, 104
— Mobile Guards in 108 *et seq.*
— National *Ateliers* in, 109
— — Guard in, 108
— peasantry in, 152–3

France—*continued*
— Provisional Government of 1848, 101
— railways of, 699
— religious problems in, 174–5
— Second Empire in, 138, 143, 153, 161
— socialist and communist literature in, 49 *et seq.*
— state expenditure in, 98
— steam power introduced into, 202
— struggle between bourgeois and proletariat in, 76
— universal suffrage in, 84
Franklin, 448
Fraternisation, Lenin on, 784
— of soldiers, 684
Frederic II, Emperor, 387
Free competition and industrial capitalism, 968
Free Trade, 55, 201
— established by bourgeoisie, 25
Freedom, abolition of, 39
— and the State, 752
— definition of, 40
— nature of, 255
— of the Press, in Russia, 628
— — Lenin on, 829
— relation between necessity and, 255
French Chauvinism, 161
— proletariat, Marx's warning to, 569
— Republic, 103 *et seq.*, 111, 134
— — a " social " republic, 159
— — proclaimed, 81, 103
— Republican Convention of 1793, 175
— Revolution of 1848, 75 *et seq.*, 95 *et seq.*, 675
— — abolition of property, 38
— — contrasted with Russian Revolution, 617
— — lack of religious belief after, 174
— — prologue to, 121
— — reasons for failure of, 822
Friedrich Wilhelm IV, Emperor, 278
" Functional " system, 950

GALEN, CLAUDIUS, 243
Gallacher, W., 869, 870

Galle, Johann Gottfried, 218
Gambetta, Leon, 136
Ganesco, 153
Gapon, George, 612, 614, 1046
Garveyism, 1032
General Congress of Soviets, 829
Gens organisation of society, 313 *et seq.*
Geology, nature of, 226
Georgia, national council of, 817
German Empire, establishment of, 81
— fascism, Stalin on, 928
— ideology, Marx and Engels on, 209
— imperialism in 710
— iron industry, loss to, 298
— " Lefts," 864
— liberalism of 1848, 62
— philosophy, idealism of, 210
— revolution in, 975
— Social Democratic Party, 232, 681
— Socialism, 50
Germany and the Versailles Treaty, 982
— and the War, Stalin on, 921
— and U.S.S.R., 928
— bourgeois-democratic revolution in, 569
— coal industry in, 699
— Communists in, 58
— democratic party in, 63
— fascism in, 911, 920
— foreigners in, 707
— free trade in, 204
— industrial growth in, 80
— iron industry in, 699
— petty bourgeois class in, 53
— railways of, 699
— *Revolution and Counter-Revolution in* (Engels), 132
— social-democracy in, 743
— — growth of, 83
— socialist and communist literature in, 51
— steam power introduced into, 202
— universal suffrage in, 83
— withdrawal from League of Nations, 919
Ghandism and communism, 1031
Gibbon, Edward, 174
Gide, Charles, 1027

Giffen, Sir Robert, 298
Girondins, 147
Gladstone, W. E., 201
Godunof, Boris, 382
Golay, Paul, 681, 1046
Gold as money-commodity, 422
— discovery of, in America, 391
— effects of change in value of, 425
Gompers, S., 860, 863, 1046
Good, antithesis between bad and, 247
Gorki, Maxim, *Materialism and Empirio-criticism*, 635
Gorter, H., 683, 1046
Gotha Programme, Marx on the, 741, 748
Government, alliance with Stock Exchange, 331
Grandin, 96
Graves, Jean, 1029
Great Britain, coal industry in, 699
— conflict with the United States, 982
— foreign policy of, 719
— iron industry in, 699
— sport of, 706
— treaty of, with Japan, 719
— unemployment in, 706
— wealth of, 298
Greece, slavery in, 325
Ground-rent, genesis of capitalist, 558
— Marx's analysis of, 558
Guchkov, A. I., 762, 765-6, 768, 771, 776, 781, 1046
Guild masters, 23, 24
— socialism, 1027, 1030
Guiod, Alphonse Simon, 136
Guizot, François Pierre Guillaume, 1046
— opponents of, 96
— opposition to Communism, 22, 101
Gvozdev, 763, 770

Haeckel, Ernst, 1046
— materialism of, 642
Haidah tribes, 315

Handicraft separated from agriculture, 320, 322
Hastings, Warren, trial of, 393
Haussmann, 341
Haxthausen, August von, 23
Hegel, Georg W. F., 349, 1046
— and civil society, 371
— and metaphysical thought, 226
— and world creation, 216
— dissolution of school of, 222
— on dialectics, 223, 667
— on freedom in relation to necessity, 255
— on metaphysics, 349
— on nature, 221
— on repetition of facts, 116
Henderson, Arthur, 860, 863, 869, 871, 877
— Lenin on, 887
Hervé, Edouard, 156
Hilderbrand, Gerhard, opportunism of, 705
Hilferding, Rudolph, 700, 977, 1046
— on imperialism, 712, 713, 720
Hill, David Jayne, *History of Diplomacy in the International Development of Europe*, 719
Hindostan religion, 180
History of Commerce (Anderson), 387
History of Diplomacy in the International Development of Europe (Hill), 719
History of Political Economy, 365
Hobbes, Thomas, 218, 1046
Hobson, J. A., 1027, 1046
— economic valuation of China, 704
— *Imperialism*, 693
— on emigration, 707
— on Fabian imperialism, 710
— on imperialism, 700-1, 703-5, 712, 716
Hogg, Sir J., 180
Höglund, Z., 867, 1047
Holland, capital wealth of, 396
— colonial administration of, 392
Holyoake, George Jacob, 1047
— Marx on, 567
Hong Kong strike, 898, 904
Horticulture introduced into Asia, 316
Housing question and the proletarian dictatorship, 998

Housing question—*continued*
— Engels on, 338 *et seq.*
— origin of, 345
— Proudhon and the, 339
— Sax on, 344
Howitt, W., 391
Human morality, 249
— thought, nature of, 240
Humanitarian school of economists, 368
Humanity, Proudhon and, 361
Hume, David, 174, 666, 1047
— and cognition of the world, 217
— philosophy of, 671
Hungary, industrial growth in, 80
— revolution in, 975
Huxley, T. H., 1047
— materialism of, 659

ICARIA, 57
Idea, absolute, 218
Idealism, contrasted with materialism, 214 *et seq.*
— negated by materialism, 265
Idealist conception contrasted with materialist, 210
Ideas, production of, 212
Ideological influence and proletarian dictatorship, 999
— political leadership, 932 *et seq.*
Ideology, German, 209
Illingworth, Mr., 201
Immortality, theory of, 215
Imperialism, aggressive, 701
— and capitalism, 688 *et seq.*
— and Marxism, 693
— and monopoly, 700
— and national oppression, 720
— and socialism, 687
— and the downfall of capitalism, 972, 973
— and the labour movement, 690
— and the October revolution, 819
— and wars, 973
— as a State power, 144
— Cunow on, 69
— forces of, 969-72
— Hilferding on, 712, 713

Imperialism—*continued*
— Hobson on, 700, 701, 703, 704, 705, 712, 716
— in Germany, 710
— in the United States, 711
— Kautsky on, 691, 693–5, 711-15, 719-20
— Lenin's critique of, 687, 709 *et seq.*
— — definition of, 690
— priviliged workers under, 707
— Russian revolution and, 821
— twentieth century, 708
Imperialist countries, bourgeoisie in, 970
— and U.S.S.R., 984
— Lenin on the, 729
— war and communist international, 1040
Imthurn, B., 215
Income tax, 46
Independent Labour Party, 869, 872, 878, 977
India, British double mission in, 188
— British rule in, Marx on, 180
— — supremacy in, cause of, 187
— cotton industry in, 184
— ferment in, 975, 983
— importance of railways in, 190
— industrial energy of workers in, 192
— irrigation in, 273
— lack of means of exchange in, 189
— political unity of, 188
— public works in, 183 *et seq.*
— revolution in, 898
— social revolution in, 186
— village system in, 184
Individual, definition of, 40
— mode of life of the, 211
Industrial capitalist, genesis of, 390
— production in capitalist countries, 915, 916
— — in Russia, 915, 916
— — statistics of, 915, 916
— supremacy in nineteenth century 202
Industrialisation of U.S.S.R., 1016
Industry and materialism, 218
— capitalism in, 31
— development of, 24 *et seq.*
— — and proletariat, 32
— in India, 191

Industry—*continued*
— petty, nature of, 402
— reaction of agricultural revolution on, 386
— services and proletariat dictatorship, 994
— Stalin on creation of, 958
Inheritance, abolition of right of, 46
Inkpin, 874
Insull Company, 914
Insurrection, nature of, 132
Inter-Allied debts, 914
Interest on money introduced, 324
Inter-imperialist alliances, 718
International contradictions, 196
— credit system, 396
— peace statistics, 712, 713
— rebuilding the, 787
— situation in 1927, 893 *et seq.*
— social revolution, 1015-19
— Working Men's Association, 133, 157, 569
— — and the Irish question, 194, 196
Introjection, doctrine of, 657
Ireland, clearing of estates in, 384
— landlordism in, 195
— peasants exploited by English bourgeoisie, 195
— the cause of British standing army, 196
Irish hatred of English, 196
— working-class ; relations with English, 194
Iron age, 319
— industry in Great Britain, 699
Irrigation in Asia, 182, 189
— in India, 273
Iskra, 589, 594-5, 598-9, 608-9
Italy and the franchise, 90
— and U.S.S.R., 926
— uprising in, 975

Jacob, 410
Japan and annexation of Korea, 721
— and U.S.S.R., 930
— and war, inflation boom, 917
— antagonism between America and, 982

Japan—*continued*
— rice riots in, 795
— treaty with Great Britain, 719
— war with China, 911, 919
— withdrawal from League of Nations, 919
Jaubet, Count, 157
Jewish Labour League, Fourth Congress, 591
— Zionist organisations, 1024
Jews in Russia, 630
Joint stock companies, bankruptcy of, 914
Jouhaux, L., 860, 863, 1047

Kaledin, 817
Kamenev, Leo, 799, 899, 903
Kant, Emmanuel, 666, 1047
— and cognition of the world, 217
— philosophy of, 671,
— theory of origin of solar system, 221
Kapp, Wolfgang, 885
Kautsky, Karl, 374, 630, 681-2, 787-8, 1047
— and State organisation, 828
— and the Bolsheviks, 838
— as leader of the Second International, 819
— contrasted with Engels, 833
— — with Marx, 833
— Lenin on, 692, 714-15, 718
— Marxism of, 713, 714, 717
— on imperialism, 691, 697, 711-15, 719-21
— social-chauvinism of, 684
— *The Dictatorship of the Proletariat*, 837
— the renegade, 826 *et seq.*
Kautskyism, Lenin on, 681, 723, 725
Kemalists, 898
Kerensky, A. F., 796, 801, 807, 1047
— and the Ukraine, 812
— Government, 730
Khuli Khan, 181
Khvostism, 844
Khvostists, 605
Knowledge, criterion of practice on theory of, 667 *et seq.*

Knowledge—*continued*
— Dühring on, 240
— main departments of, 242
Köller, Herr von, anti-revolt bill of, 94
Kolpino, rise of workers in, 611
Korea, annexation of, by Japan, 721
— uprising in, 975
Kornilov, L. G., 817, 885, 1047
— affair, 801, 802, 809
Kreuger concern in Sweden, 914
Kropotkin, P. A., 1029, 1047
Kugelmann, 665
— Marx's letter to, 569
Kuibyshev, 953
Kuomintang people, 901, 1031
— at Huhan, 908
— in China, 902, 904, 905
Kwantung province, 904

LABOUR, capacity for, meaning of, 451
— commodities as products of, 407
— conditions of, under proletarian dictatorship, 997
— effect of machinery on, 32, 199
— emancipation of, 148 *et seq.*
— expenditure of, in relation to value, 407 *et seq.*
— exploitation of, 499
— in the family, division of, 314, 318
— Ministry of, in France, 104
— movement, Engels on British, 197
— Party, 872, 874
— — Lenin on British, 881
— planned division of, 282
— power, buying and selling of, 450
— — meaning of, 451
— — value of, 454 *et seq.*
— process, general character of, 458
— productive power of, 511
— proletarian hours of, 997
Laffitte, Jacques, 90
Laissez-faire, British policy of, in India, 183
Lamarck, J., 1047

Lamartine, Alphonse Marie de, 101 *et seq.*, 107, 1047
Land, confiscation of Church, 381
— feudal tenure of, abolished, 382
— individual ownership of, 324, 335
— mortgaging of, 325, 335
— nationalisation of, 557
— ownership, a fetter on production, 265
— private ownership of, 557
— rents, confiscation of, 46
— thefts of State, 382
Landlordism in Ireland, 195, 206
Landlords *versus* tenants, 342
Lansburgh, A., 712
— *Die Bank*, 702
Laroche-Jaquelin, Marquis de, 103
Lassalle, Ferdinand, 84, 1047
— Marx on, 568, 569, 749
— on the worker and his labour, 748, 749
— *System of Inherited Rights*, 336
Lassalleanism, Marx's criticism of, 739
League of Nations, 977, 1025
— Japan's withdrawal from, 919
— Lenin on, 590, 591
— object of, 981
— Stalin on, 911
— withdrawal of Germany, 919
Ledru-Rollin, Alexandre Auguste, 58, 101, 1047
Left communists in England, 876
" Left-Wing " communism in England, 868 *et seq.*
Left-Wing Communism (Lenin), 849–51, 855 *et seq.*
" Leftist " views in communism, 940
Legien, K., 860, 863, 1047
Legitimists in France, 103, 111, 125
Leibniz, G. W., 261
Lenin, Vladimir Ilyich, agrarian programme of, 786
— and bureaucracy, 847
— *Communist Manifesto*, 743
— *Critique of the Gotha Programme*, 787
— definition of imperialism, 690
— lecture on the 1905 Revolution, 614 *et seq.*
— letter to central committee, 808
— *Letters from Afar*, 759 *et seq.*

Lenin—*continued*
— life of, 13
— on anarchism, 846
— on appeals to action, 598
— on bourgeois parliaments, 864-7
— — rights, 750-1, 753
— on British Communists, 880
— — imperialism, 706
— — Labour Party, 881
— — Liberal Party, 872, 874
— — trade unionism, 593
— on Carnegie, 706
— on China, 896
— on Civil Wars, 633
— on Communist Party, 787
— on criterion of practice, 667 *et seq.*
— on defencism, 784, 803
— on democracy, 756
— on development of communism, 741
— on distortion of Marxism, 723, 724
— on economic agitation, 594
— — concessions, 595
— — exposures, 608
— — politics, 600
— — reforms, 595
— on economism, 589
— on Economists, 603
— on egoism, 670
— on exploited and exploiters, 831
— on fraternisation, 784
— on future of communism, 883 *et seq.*
— on Henderson, 887
— on imperialism, 678, 687
— on imperialist war, 729
— on Kautsky, 691, 714-15, 718
— on Kautskyism, 681, 685, 723, 725
— on League of Nations, 590, 591
— on Liberal Party in England, 872, 874
— on Lloyd George, 876-80, 887
— on Machism, 669
— on Martynov, 595
— on Martynov's economic theory, 602
— on Marxism and revolution, 799 *et seq.*
— on materialism, 641
— on Menshevism, 882
— on monopoly, 689

Lenin—*continued*
— on national liberation, 687
— on nationalisation of land, 786
— on nationality, 687
— on nihilism, 846
— on opportunism, 676, 681
— on pacifism, 686
— on parasitism,.700 *et seq.*
— on peasant war, 823
— on Peter Struve, 616
— on political agitation, 599
— on political education, 589
— on political exposure, 596-7
— on political exposures, 608
— on proletarian democracy, 827 *et seq.*
— on proletarian revolution in the West, 824
— on propagandism, 604, 605
— on qualifications of a Social-Democrat, 597
— on rentiers, 701, 702, 703
— on revolution of 1905, 609 *et seq.*
— on self-determination, 817, 820
— — of nations, 686
— on slogans, 939
— on Social-Democracy, 588, 741
— on social-pacifists, 615
— on task of Social-Democrats, 599, 601, 605, 607
— on teaching of Marx, 675 *et seq.*
— on the Allies, 801
— on the October revolution in Russia, 810 *et seq.*
— on the Mensheviks, 725
— on the term social-democracy, 787, 788, 789, 791
— on trade unionism, 603
— on trusts, 698
— on Tsarist monarchy, 765
— on ultra-imperialism, 695
— on " United States of Europe," 705
— on violent revolution, 739
— party, tasks for the, 945, 946
— quotes Engels on insurrection, 132
— *Socialism and War*, 687 *et seq.*
— *The State and Revolution*, 721 *et seq.*, 837
— *Two Congresses*, 591
— works of, 1051

Leninism and dictatorship of proletariat, 849–51
— and discipline, 852
— and existence of factions, 851–3
— and opportunism, 853–5
— and technical resources, 958, 959
— and the workers, 841 *et seq.*
— as class organisation of the proletariat, 847–9
— as organised detachment of
 working class, 844–7
— foundations of, 839 *et seq.*
— party of, 840 *et seq.*
— problems of, 933, 934
— victory of, 931
Leon, Daniel, de, 861
Letters from Afar, Lenin's, 759 *et seq.*
Leverrier, Urbain J. J., 217
Liberal fabianism, 1027
— Party in England, 872
Liberalism in Germany, 62
Liebknecht, Karl, 867, 1047
Liebknecht, Wilhelm, 72, 1047
— Marx on, 569
Life a contradiction, 257
Life of Jesus (Strauss), 222
Lincoln, Abraham, 1047
Linnaeus, C., 1047
Liquidators, 768
Liverpool and the slave trade, 400
Lloyd George, David, 872–3, 875,
 877
— Lenin on, 876–80, 887
Lloyd Morgan, materialism of, 642
Locke, John, 118, 1047
Logic, eternal truths in, 245
Longuet, 787
Louis XV, King of France, 349
Louis XVIII, King of France, 118
Louis Bonaparte. *See* Napoleon III
Louis Philippe, King of France, 96,
 98 *et seq.*, 121, 147
— bourgeois monarchy of, 123
Lumpenproletariat, 108, 123
Lunarcharsky, A. V., 634, 1047
— philosophy of, 653
Luther, Martin, 117
Luxembourg Commission, 106 *et seq.*
Lvov, Prince, 812, 1048

MACAIRE, ROBERT, 99, 1048
MacDonald Government, 977

MacDonald, J. Ramsay, 787, 869,
 871, 1026
Mach, Ernst, 1048
— *Analysis of Sensations*, 638, 639,
 670
— *Die Mechanik in ihrer Entwickelung*, 636
— " Elements " of, 656, 660
— *Erkenntnis und Irrtum*, 669
— on cognition, 669
— on criterion of practice, 668
— on the problem of science, 635
— philosophy of, 650
— positivism of, 671
— relativity of, 666
Machinery and capitalism, 966, 968
— effect on labour, 32, 199
— in production, 288
— labour-saving, 204
Machism contrasted with Marxism,
 669
— in Russia, 656, 658
— Lenin on, 669
— principles of, 636 *et seq.*
MacIver, Mr., 201
M'Culloch, 367
Madras, agrarian revolution in, 193
Maine, Sir H. S., 308, 1048
Malpighi, M., 243, 1048
Man, distinction from animals, 211
— equal rights of, 250 *et seq.*
— evolution of, 227
— practical process of development
 of, 213
— productive relationships of, 371
Manchester School, 201–2, 204
Manchuria, occupation of, 911
Manilovism, 844
Manufacture, origin of, 251
— system of, introduced, 24
Marche, decree of, 104
Marie (French Minister), 109, 110
Marxist theory on imperialism and
 colonial revolt, 179
Market prices and values, Marx on,
 383
Markowski, 153
Marrast, 118
Marriage by purchase, 308
— forms of, 303
— freedom of, 311
— in middle ages, 307
— indissolubility of, 312

Marrov, L., 1048
Martov, L., 845, 847, 854,
Martynov, A. S., 590, 1048
— doctrine, 904
— economic theory of, 595, 602
— Lenin on, 595
— on Social-Democracy, 592
— theory of stages, 594
Marx, Karl, address to Communist
League (1850), 60 et seq.
— address to First International,
134
— analysis of ground-rent, 558
— Capital, 373 et seq., 558–60, 562
— Civil War in France, 133
— Class Struggles in France, 559
— Communist Manifesto, 11, 563,
566–7, 674
— contrasted with Engels, 833
— criticism of Lassalleanism, 739
— Critique of the Gotha Programme,
739
— Critique of Political Economy,
209, 370
— Engels on collaboration with, 223
— expelled from France, 371
— historical fate of teaching of,
674 et seq.
— Lenin on teaching of, 537 et seq.,
657 et seq.
— letters to Engels, 557, 565–6,
568–70
— letter to Kugelmann, 569, 665
— life of, 11
— materialism of, 643
— on British rule in India, 180
— on capitalism in agriculture, 558
— on class struggles in France, 95
— on commodities, 405
— on decay of religious authority,
172
— on expropriation of property, 258
— on German ideology, 209
— on history of France, 75
— on Holyoake, 567
— on land nationalisation, 557
— on Lassalle, 568–9, 749
— on Liebknecht, 569
— on metaphysics of political economy, 349
— on money, 422
— on Most, 570
— on negation of the negation, 258

Marx, Karl—continued
— on primitive accumulation, 375
— on proletarian tactics, 565
— on relations between Irish and
English working classes, 194
— on the Gotha Programme, 741,
748
— on the Chartists, 567
— on the Crimean War, 172
— on the modern State, 732
— on the peasantry, 822
— on use-value and value, 405
— Poverty of Philosophy, 348 et seq.,
566–7
— programme of 1848, 21
— teachings of, on the State, 723
— The Peasant Problem in France
and Germany, 564
— theses on Feuerbach, 228
— warns French proletariat, 569
— works of, 1051
Marxian socialism in relation to
nationality, 562
Marxism and absolute truth, 665
— and imperialism, 693
— and opportunism, 738
— and revolution, Lenin on, 799 et
seq.
— and the State, 724
— betrayal of, by social democracy,
1025
— Bogdanov on, 667
— conception of equality in, 938
— distinction from anarchism, 788
— dogmatism of, 673
— international, 680
— Kautsky's, 713, 714, 717
— Lenin on distortion of, 723, 724
— philosophic, 636
— spread of, 676
Marxists, the Narodniks on Russian, 694
Mass organisation and proletarian
dictatorship, 1005–7
Materialism advanced by science
and industry, 218
— contrasted with idealism, 213 et
seq.
— defects of earlier, 564
— dialectical, 222, 635
— eighteenth-century, 220
— Feuerbach and, 219
— Lenin on, 641

Materialism—*continued*
— negation of the old, 265
— principle underlying, 279
— standpoints of old and new, 231
Materialism and Empirio-criticism
(Maxim Gorki), 634 *et seq.*
Materialist conception contrasted
with idealist, 210
Mathematics an exact science, 242
— Dühring on pure, 235
— origin of, 236
Matter, relation to motion, 237
Maurer, Georg Ludwig von, 23
Maxims (De Witt), 397
Mechanics an exact science, 242
Mensheviks, 609, 731, 784, 794, 797,
802, 807, 836, 855, 859–61, 878
— and the State, 725
— Lenin on the, 725
— Stalin on the, 845
Menshevism, Lenin on, 882
Merchant class, creation of, 323, 335
Merchants, capital of, 440 *et seq.*
Merrheim, 860
Metal-workers' strikes in Russia, 620
Metaphysical thought, 226
Metaphysics of political economy,
349
Metternich, Prince, opposition to
Communism, 22, 1048
Middle-class and the Commune, 147
— and the October revolution, 821
et seq.
— and the proletariat, 31
— capitalist, 206 *et seq.*
— conservatism of, 34
— property owners, abolition of, 40
Mignet, F., 1048
Mikhailovsky, 727
Militarism in revolutions, 625
Miliukov, P., 760, 762, 765–6, 768,
771, 776, 781, 795
Miliukov-Kerensky government,
812 *et seq.*
Minorities, revolution the means of
overthrowing, 77
— submission of, to majority, 846
Minority movements, 35
Mohammedan League in Russia,
629
Moleschott, 219, 1048
Moll, Joseph, 61, 1048
Molotov, V. M., 953
Monck, Mr., 201

Money as standard of price, 425
— circulation of, 290
— — and capital, 431 *et seq.*
— converted into capital, 450
— functions of, 422, 425
— introduction of metallic, 323, 335
— loaning of, 324
— the basis of capital, 431
Moneylenders, capital of, 448
Monogamy, 303–4, 320
— Morgan on, 313
Monopolies, national and interna-
tional, 980
Monopoly and imperialism, 700
— Lenin on, 689
Montesquieu, Baron Charles de,
147, 1048
Morality a class morality, 249
— Engels on, 247
Morgan, Lewis Henry, 23, 301, 313
— on civilisation, 337
Morocco, uprising in, 975
Mortgages on land, 325, 335
Moscow, strike in, 611
— uprising in, 631
Most, Marx on, 570
Motion, in relation to matter, 237
— — to rest, 239
Movement, abstraction of, 352
Mutinies in Russia, 623, 624

NANKING, 908
Napoleon Bonaparte, 118, 119
Napoleon III, 139, 140, 147, 160
— and Eighteenth Brumaire, 116 *et
seq.*
Narodniks on Russian Marxists, 694
Nation as product of social development, 563
National *Ateliers*, 109 *et seq.*
— assembly of early tribes, 321
— bourgeois governments, 816
— council of Armenia, 817
— — of Azerbaijan, 817
— — of Georgia, 817
— councils, 811
— debt, 395 *et seq.*
— Defence, Government of, 161
— governments, formation of, 815

National—*continued*
— Guards, 108, 129, 139
— liberation, Lenin on, 687
— oppression and imperialism, 720
— question, Stalin on, 943
Nationalisation of estates and proletarian dictatorship, 995
— of land, Lenin on, 786
— of production, 1000
Nationalism, effect of bourgeoisie on, 27
Nationality, abolition of, 43
— Lenin on, 687
Nature, interconnection of phenomena of, 234
— relation of consciousness to, 233
— transformation of forces of, 227
Necessity, relation between freedom and, 255
Negation of the negation, 258
Negro " zionism," 1032
Negroes, 1032
Nepenin, Admiral, 776
" New Economic Policy," 1017
Newton, Isaac, 1048
Neymarck, A., international peace statistics of, 712
Nicholas II, Tsar, 765, 775, 795
Niebuhr, K., 328
Night-work, 400
Nihilism, Lenin on, 846
Nootka tribes, 315
Noske, 977, 1048

OCTOBER REVOLUTION in Russia, 810 *et seq.*
— and the middle strata, 821 *et seq.*
— in relation to imperialism, 819
— international importance of, 818 *et seq.*
— Lenin on the, 810 *et seq.*
Octobrist cadet government, 767, 768
Odessa, revolution in, 623
— strike in, 611
Officials as organs of State power, 730
Olivier, Lord, 1026

Opportunism and Leninism, 853–5
— and Marxism, 738
— and the bourgeoisie, 681
— and Trotsky, 682
— in England, 709
— Lenin on, 676, 681
— of Fabian Society, 710
Orage, A. R., 1027
Organisation committee and Russia, 785
Organisational leadership, problem of, 946 *et seq.*
Organisms, investigation of living, 243
Orleanists, 111, 125
Ostwald, Wilhelm, 646, 647, 1048
Outlines of Marxian Philosophy, 635
Over - centralisation, the struggle against, 147
Overpopulation, relative, 505
Over-production, epidemic of, 29
Owen, Robert, 229, 1048
— Communist system of, 55
Ownership of property, private v. common, 267

PACIFIC, struggle for the, 919
Pacificism, Lenin on, 686
— Stalin on, 912, 919
Palchinsky, 731
Palermo rising, 100
Palmerston, Lord, 177
Pankhurst, Sylvia, 868, 869, 872, 874, 875
Pannekoek, 683
Paris, army abolished from, 108
— barricades, 86
— betrayal of, 154
— capitulation of, 135–6
— Commune, 82, 144 *et seq.*, 625, 675, 683, 730, 735, 773, 788, 822, 828, 833, 835
— June insurrection in, 123
— massacre of, 113
— police abolished in, 145
— proletarian revolutions in, 159
— Revolution of 1870, 161
— siege of, 140
Parisitism, Lenin on, 700 *et seq.*

Party-of-Order Republic, 142–3, 152
Pastoral tribes, 315
Pearson, Karl, 659, 660
Peasant enterprises and proletarian dictatorship, 1000
— farmers, 379
— movement in Russia, 622
— problem and the communist party, 1039
— riots in Russia, 628, 629
— war, Lenin on, 823
Peasantry and the proletarian dictatorship, 1004
— and the Russian revolution, 822
— attitude of Marxian socialism towards, 564
Peasants and the Commune, 151
— exploitation of, 559
— soviets of, 1015
Pecqueur, 402
Penty, 1027
People, nature of, 129
— rights of, 129
Père la Chaise cemetery, 155, 166
Persia, revolutions in, 632, 677
Petrograd, population of, 778
Petrov, 623, 624
Petzoldt, 638, 648
— Einführung in die Philosophie der reinen Erfahrung, 651
— on Avenarius, 651, 652
— relativity of, 666
Phalansteres, definition of, 57
Philanthropic school of economists, 369
Philippines, annexation of, 712, 721
Philosopher, distinction from Christian, 352
Philosophers and world creation, 216
Philosophy, basic question of, 214
— Marxist theory on, 233
— natural, Engels on, 236
— need for, 234
— of reality, 247
— poverty of, 348
— predilection for, in eighteenth century, 174
Philosophy of Poverty (Proudhon), 348 et seq.
Physics, an exact science, 242
— Engels on, 236
Physiology, nature of, 226

Picard, 157
Pisarevsky, Rear-Admiral, 623
Plekanov, George, 634, 763, 770, 788, 890, 1048
— materialism of, 653
— philosophy of, 671
— social-chauvinism of, 684
Poland and U.S.S.R., 927
— Commune's attitude to, 153
— Communists in, 58
— industrial growth in, 80
— uprising of school children, 629
Police abolished in Paris, 145
Political action and the proletariat, 970
— agitation and the Economists, 592
— — Lenin on, 599
— consciousness, Lenin on, 596
— economy, Engels on, 267
— — Marx's Critique of, 370
— — metaphysics of, 349
— — primitive accumulation in, 376
— — social fairness decided by, 198
— education, Lenin on, 589
— exposures in social-Democracy, 607
— — Lenin on, 596–8, 608
— power, definition of, 46
— recognition of poverty, 331
— situation in 1917, Stalin on, 792 et seq.
— strikes in Russia, 619
Polygamy, 303
Pomyalovsky, 753
Poor-rate, introduction of, 381
Popular representation in Russia, 626
Population, effect of bourgeoisie on, 28
— increase of, 211
— surplus of, 516
Postal reform, 98
Potresov, A. N., 763, 770, 847, 854, 1049
Poverty of Philosophy (Marx), 349, 566, 567
Price, definition of, 429
— money as standard of, 425
Price-form, 426, 429
Prices, cause of fluctuations in, 426
— market, 483 et seq.

Prison reform, 55
Prisons and the State, 726–9
Processes, natural, interconnection of, 225 *et seq.*
Production, anarchy of social, 285–6
— as a creation of value, 461
— capital invested in, 478
— capitalist, breakdown, of, 291
— — capital the barrier of, 515
— — mode of, 280 *et seq.*
— — traits of, 531
— collective, 333
— conditions of distribution and, 529
— conflict between expansion of, and creation of values, 511
— control of, 76
— cosmopolitan nature of, 26
— development of world, 987
— economists' views of, 350
— feudal, 366, 380
— for exchange, 286, 333
— in mediæval society, 285
— land ownership a fetter on, 265
— machinery in, 288
— means of, 477
— mental, 212
— nationalisation of, 1000
— of natural subsistence, 211
— prices of, regulated by law of value, 487
— social means of, 281 *et seq.*
— social seizure of means of, 298
— State control of means of, 292
Productive capacity, growth of, 982
— relationships, 371
Profit determining price of production, 486
— falling tendency of rate of, 494
Proletarian demand for equality, 253
— democracy, Lenin on, 827 *et seq.*
— dictatorship, 744, 991
— — and communication services, 994
— — and conditions of labour, 997
— — and co-operative farming, 1002
— — and co-operative organisations, 1006, 1007
— — and credit, 997
— — and cultural revolution, 1008–10
— — and housing, 998

Proletarian—*continued*
dictatorship and ideological influence, 999
— — and industry services, 994
— — and mass organisation, 1005–7
— — and nationalisation of estates, 995
— — and peasant enterprises, 1000
— — and technical intelligentia, 1004
— — and the church, 1009
— — and the classes, 1003–5
— — and the housing question, 998
— — and the peasantry, 1004
— — and the sexes, 998
— — and trade, 996
— — and transport services,
— — conditions of life under, 997
— — economic policy for, 999 *et. seq.*
— — transition period from capitalism, 988 *et seq.*
— militia, 770 *et seq.*
— morality, 248
— nationalisation of private banks, 996
— revolution, 824, 826 *et seq.*
— struggle and social-Democracy, 604
— tactics, Marx on, 565
Proletariat, a revolutionary class, 34, 48
— and bourgeoisie, Marx on, 567
— and political action, 970
— and the conquest of power, 989
— concentration of, 32
— control in Paris, 141
— definition of, 22
— development of, 30 *et seq.*
— — of industrial, 105
— duties of the international—to the U.S.S.R., 1021–3
— *foncier*, 152
— Leninism and dictatorship of the, 849–51
— Leninism as class organisation of, 847–9
— militant, 82
— organisation of, 772, 773
— organised into a political party, 33
— overthrow of bourgeois power by, 991

Proletariat—*continued*
— position of, in Russian revolution, 769, 770
— relation to Communists, 37
— revolution of, in France, 76, 82
— self-emancipation of, 332
— struggle with bourgeoisie, 31
— — with colonial revolution, 1013 *et seq.*
— — with other types of revolution, 1010–13
— tactics of class struggle of, 564 *et seq.*
— tasks of, in the Russian revolution, 783 *et seq.*
— within bourgeoisie, 367
Proletary, 609
Propaganda, Lenin on, 604, 605
Property, abolition of, 38, 40, 46, 149
— expropriation of, 258 *et seq.*
— founded on force, 267 *et seq.*
— inequality in ownership of, 267
— institution of communal, 383
— landed, in Scotland, 364
— political recognition of, 331
— private, abolition of, 985
— — character of, 401
— — Engels on, 301
Prostitution, 303 *et seq.*
— abolition of, 43
Protection and capitalism, 968
— system of, 397
— *versus* free trade, 201
Protestant morality, 247
Proudhon, Pierre Joseph, 222, 1049
— and human reason, 361–2
— and principle of association, 167
— and providence, 364
— and slavery, 357
— and the housing question, 339
— contradictions of, 349, 354, 358
— *Philosophy of Poverty*, 54, 348
Proudhonist party, 167
Providence, Proudhon and, 364
Provisional government, Stalin on the, 798
Prussia and working class movement, 568,
Prusso-Austrian War of 1866, 161
Public debts, 395 *et seq.*
— force, Engels on, 727, 728

Public—*continued*
— force, establishment of, 329
— works in Asia, 182 *et seq.*
Puttkamer, von, 626

QUESNAY, DR., 349

Rabocheye Dyelo, 589, 599
Rabochaye Mysl, 588, 599
Radek, 894
Raffles, Sir Stafford, 181
Railroad, capital in, 698
Railway statistics, 698
Railways, importance of, in India, 190
— ownership of, 207
— state control of, 292
Rakovsky, C., 1049
Ranizin, 927
Raspail, François Vincent, 102
Rasputin, Gregory, 761, 1049
Reactionism in trade unions, 859
Reality, philosophy of, 247
Reason, absolute, 362
Reasoning in contrast to being, 233
Red Army Academy, Stalin's address to graduates of, 956 *et seq.*
Red Trade Union International, 1039
Redskin tribe, 314
Regnault, Henri Victor, 246
Religion of Hindostan, 180
— theologians and, 365
Religious authority, Marx on decay of, 172
— dogmas, eighteenth century disbelief in, 174
— sectarian trade unions, 1024
Renan, Joseph Ernest, 222, 1049
Renner, Karl, 687, 819, 1049
Rent, differential, Ricardo on, 557
Rentiers, Lenin on, 701, 702, 703
Reproduction on an enlarged scale, 480
— simple, 475 *et seq.*, 481
Republic, bourgeois, 122, 124
— democratic, 331
— Engels on a democratic, 731

Republic—*continued*
in France, 103 *et seq.*, 111, 134
— social, 142
Repudiation of state debts to capitalists, 997
Rest the result of motion, 239
Reval, strike in, 611
Revolution, forces of, 969–72
— in Russia, 610 *et seq.*
— Lenin on, 739
— of 1905, Lenin on, 609 *et seq.*, 614 *et seq.*
— results of, 77
— right to, 91
— social, in Asia, 186
— violent, 733 *et seq.*
Revolutionaries and reactionary Trade Unions, 857, 864
Revolutionary activity, 229
— crisis and counter revolutionary social democracy, 976
— defencism, Lenin on, 784
— party in Russia, growth of, 616
Rhine, possession of left bank of, 161
Ricardo, David, 349, 1049
— and foreign trade, 506
— mission of, 368
— on differential rent, 557
— on value of commodities, 485
Riesser on finance and political alliances, 719
Riga, strike in, 619
Rights, equality of, 250
Robespierre, Maximilien, 116, 117, 1049
Rodbertus-Jagetzow, 1049
Rodichev, Cadet, 782
Roland-Holst, Henrietta, 682, 1049
Roman Empire, revolution in, 93
Romanovs, 761, 1049
Romantic School of economists, 368
Rössler, Herr, 93
Rothschild, firm of, 98
Rousseau, Jean Jacques, 1049
Royer-Collard, P., 1049
Rumania and the franchise, 90
Rurals, Assembly of, 138, 144, 151, 153, 154
Russell family, 175
Russia, army in, 622
— cadets in, 795, 796, 797, 801
— capitalism in, 697

Russia—*continued*
— central executive committee in, 797
— Church authority in, 178
— constituent assembly in, 860
— counter-revolutionary period in, 761, 795
— freedom of the Press in, 628
— growth of revolutionary party in, 616
— industrial growth in, 80
— — production in, 915, 916
— Jews in, 630
— Mohammedan League in, 629
— mutinies in, 623, 624
— naval mutiny in, 623
— October revolution in, 810 *et seq.*
— peasant movement in, 622
— peasant riots in, 628, 629
— political inertia of workers in, 597
— railways of, 699
— strikes in, 619–21, 627, 631
Russian February revolution and the national question, 811–13
— October revolution and the national question, 813–18
— — and the peasants, 822
— revolution, 610 *et seq.*
— — and the world war, 762
— — and world imperialism, 821
— — contrasted with Chinese, 895–7
— — contrasted with French revolution, 617
— — forces in the, 793 *et seq.*
— — international significance of, 856
— — of 1905, reasons for failure of, 822
— — of 1905, significance of, 632
— — of 1917, 760 *et seq.*
— — position of proletariat in, 769, 770
— — tasks of the proletariat, 783 *et seq.*
— Social-Democracy, tasks of, 601
— Social-Democrats, 634
— trade union membership, 948
Russo-Japanese war, 622
Ryotwar, 189

SAINT HILAIRE, GEOFFROY, 387
Saint-Just, Louis Antoine, 117, 1049
St. Petersburg, strike in, 611, 619
— uprising in, 612
St. Simon, Claude Henri, Count, communist system of, 55, 1049
Sax, Dr., 344, 345
Say, Jean Baptiste, 1049
Scheidemann, P., 763, 1049
Schilder, 702
School-children in Poland, demands of, 629
Schubert-Soldern, 649
Schulze, philosophy of, 67
Schulze-Gaevernitz, 702
— on British imperialism, 705
Science and materialism, 218
— natural, nature of, 226
— positive, 234
Sciences, exact, 242
— historical group of, 243
Scotland, clearing of estates in, 384
— landed property in, 364
Scottish Workers' Council, 869
Second Congress of Third International, 856
Second Five-Year Plan, 933, 953
Second International, 679, 691, 788, 790, 819, 823, 831, 840, 864, 882-3, 896, 976, 1041
Sejm, dispersion of, 812
Self-determination, Lenin on, 817, 820
— of nations, Lenin on, 686
Self-emancipation group in Russia, 592
Semite tribes, 315
Sensations and complexes of sensations, 635 et seq.
Serfdom, 36
— disappearance of, 379
Seventeenth Party Congress, C.P.S.U., 933
Sex-love, individual, 305
Sexes, conditions of, under proletarian dictatorship, 998
— social inequality of the, 304 et seq., 985
Shanghai, 899
— strike in, 904
Shaw, G. Bernard, 1026
Siberian " government," downfall of, 817

Sismondi, Jean Charles Léonard de, 50, 1049
Sixteenth Party Congress, C.P.S.U., 932
Skobelev, M. I., 770, 1049
Skrypnik, fall of, 943
Slagg, Mr., 201
Slave trade, 400
— an economic category, 356
— in civilisation, 335
— in the social system, 320 et seq.
— sequel to, 274
Slogans, Lenin on, 939
Smith, Adam, 1049
— mission of, 368
— previous accumulation of, 375
Smith, Norman, 659
Snowden, Philip, 869, 871, 875, 877
Social changes, ultimate causes of, 279
— classes, abolition of, 297
— — need for, 205
— fairness, 198
— forces, subjugation of, 294
— imperialism, 976
— life a practical one, 231
— means of production, 281 et seq.
— pacifists, Lenin on, 615
— patriotism, 976
— production, sections of, 477
— reform in India, 192
— reforms and wage reductions, 347
— republic, 142
— revolution in Asia, 186
Social-Chauvinism, 679, 680, 709
Social-Democracy and contact with classes, 604
— and economic reforms, 595
— and the proletarian struggle, 604
— and the workers, 588
— and trade unions, 603
— betrayal of Marxism by, 1025
— character of, 128
— democratic tasks of, 601
— functions of international, 596
— in Germany, 743
— in Russia, advance of, 606
— Lenin on, 744, 787-91
— — on tasks of, 601, 605, 607
— Martynov on, 592
— propaganda of, 606, 607
— revolutionary, 594

Social-Democratic movement in Russia, 592
— Party, formation of, 127
— — in Germany, 232, 570, 705, 710
Social-Democrats in Austria, 819
— in France, 58
— Lenin on qualifications of, 597
— — on task of, 599
Socialism and Bolshevik work, 941
— and equalitarianism, 935, 939
— and the State, 563
— bourgeois, 53
— building up of, in U.S.S.R., 1015-19
— Christian, 49
— clerical, 49
— conservatism, 53
— critical Utopian, 55
— feudal, 47 et seq.
— German, 50
— Marxian, attitude of, towards the peasantry, 564
— — in relation to nationality, 562
— Marx's description of, 755
— petty bourgeois, 49
— position of modern, 279
— principles of, and the War, 679 et seq.
— scientific difference from communism, 754
— true, 50
— working class, distinct from other forms, 75
Socialism and War (Lenin), 678 et seq.
Socialist construction for different countries, 1012
— Engels's definition of, 21
— industry : contact with peasant economy, 1016
— Labour Party, 868
— literature, 47 et seq.
— movement in Switzerland, 634
— representation in Parliaments, 90
— revolutionaries, 797
— revolutionary party and Bolshevism, 867
— State, economic prerequisites of, 757
Socialists and imperialist war, 685
— and the bourgeoisie, 763
— Democratic, in France, 58

Socialists—continued
— in Germany, Exception Law against, 570
— the theoreticians of the proletariat, 369
Society, first cleavage into classes, 320
— Hegel's " civil," 371
— history of, 22
Solar system, Copernican, 217
— Kantian theory of, 221
Soltykow, Prince, 192
Soul, immortality of the, 265
— theory of the, 215
South America, struggle for, 696
South Wales Socialist Society, 868
Soviet democracy, 993
— form of State, 991
— of agricultural labourers' deputies, 786
— of agricultural workers, 770
— of peasants' deputies, 770, 786
— of workers' and soldiers' deputies, 763, 767-8, 770, 778, 794, 819
— of workers' deputies, 628-9, 773-4, 782, 785-6, 788-9
— Union, foreign relations of, 911
— — influence on world workers, 981
Soviets and the bureaucracy, 831
— formation of, in China, India, and Persia, 818
— of deputies, 815
Spain, fascism in, 911
— revolution in, 920
— War with the United States, 711
Spencer, Herbert, 727
Stages, Martynov's theory of, 594
Stalin, Joseph, address to graduates of Red Army Academy, 956 et seq.
— life of, 14
— on bureaucracy, 948
— on cadres, 962
— on chatterboxes, 951, 952
— on China, 894 et seq.
— on compromise, 794
— on dumping, 915
— on fascism, 920
— on foundations of Leninism, 839 et seq.
— on German fascism, 928

Stalin, Joseph—*continued*
— on Germany and the War, 921
— on imperialistic war plans, 922–4
— on pacifism, 912, 919
— on problems of organisational leadership, 946 *et seq.*
— on technique, 960
— on the economic crisis, 911
— on the League of Nations, 911
— on the Mensheviks, 845
— on the national question, 943
— on the political situation in 1917, 792 *et seq.*
— on the provisional government, 798
— on the slogan "enrich yourselves," 940
— on the Trotskyists, 944
— on Tsarism, 792, 793
— works of, 1052
Starcke, on Feuerbach, 214, 218
State, abolition of the, 734
— ancient, 330
— and armed bodies, 726–9
— and class antagonisms, 722, 724, 726–8
— and class domination, 725
— and communism, 746, 751
— and prisons, 726–9
— as instrument of exploitation, 729 *et seq.*
— control of means of production or communication, 292
— debts, 329
— disappearance of the, 986
— economic base of "withering away" of, 739 *et seq.*
— Engels on, 301, 726, 732–3
— feudal, 330, 331
— free people's, 296
— freedom and the, 752
— lands, thefts of, 382
— loans, 729
— Marx on the, 723, 732
— Marxism and the, 724
— origin of the, 327 *et seq.*
— ownership, Communist furtherance of, 46
— power and forces of society, 729
— — officials as organs of, 730
— right to exact taxes, 329
— Socialism and the, 563
— "syndicate," 757

State—*continued*
— the combining link in civilised society, 335
— views of Marx and Engels on, contrasted, 740
— "withering away" of the, 733 *et seq.*, 739 *et seq.*
State and Revolution (Lenin), 721 *et seq.*
States the product of contract, 93
Steam power, effect on industry, 202
Stein, Lt. Col., 623
Steklov, 785
Steuart, Sir James, 380
Stirner, Max, 222, 1049
Stock exchange, alliance with government, 331
— speculation, 208, 293
Stolypin, 776
Strauss, David Friedrich, 222, 1049,
Strikers in Russia, 622
Strikes in Russia, 611, 627, 631
— statistics of, 617, 618
— use of, as a weapon, 1037
Struve, Peter, 1049
— Lenin on, 616
Struveism, 682
Stuttgart International Socialist Congress, 680, 976
Subsistence, production of means of, 211
Suffrage under the Commune, 146
— universal, the measure of maturity of workers, 332
— workers' use of, 83, 84
Sun Yat-Sen, 1031, 1050
Superabundance, crises of, 290
Supply and demand, regulation of, 488 *et seq.*
Surplus capital, 516
— population, 516
— — relative, 505
— value, distribution of, 340
— — nature of, 435
— — origin of, 449
— — process of producing, 458
— — reason for creation of, 445
— — rise and fall in mass of, 503
Suzanne, General, 136
Sweden, resumption of Crown lands in, 382–3
Swiss separatist war, 100

Switzerland and the franchise, 90
— Communists in, 58
— Socialist movement in, 634
— universal suffrage in, 84
Syndicalism, revolutionary, 1030
Syria, uprising in, 975
System of Inherited Rights (Lassalle), 336

Tableau Économique (Quesnay), 349
Tariffs, prohibitive, 918
Taxation, modern system of, 397
Taxes, introduction of, 329
Tea trade, English monopoly of, 392
Technical intelligentia and the proletarian dictatorship, 1004
— progress, artificial restriction of, 700
— resources and Leninism, 958, 959
Technique, development of, 980
— Stalin on, 960
Tenants *versus* landlords, 342
Textile-workers' strikes in Russia, 620
Theologians and religion, 365
Thierry, A., 1050
Thiers, Louis Adolphe, 82, 134, 135, 137 *et seq.*, 153 *et seq.*, 165, 175, 376
Thing-in-itself, theory of, 217
Thinking, relation to being, 214-5
Third Estate, 25
Third International, 864, 869, 883, 891
— formation of, 855
— programme of, 936 *et seq.*
Thirty Years War, 279
Thomas, Albert, 977
Thought, nature of human, 233, 240
Torrens, Col., 446
Town, antagonism between country and, 987
Trade and proletarian dictatorship, 997
— crises, 290

Trade—*continued*
— foreign, and capital, 506
Trade Union bureaucracy, American, 1024
— work in Russia, 588
Trade Unions and communists, 1038
— and economic struggles, 603
— and Left Communists, 862
— and Social-Democracy, 603
— Engels on British, 708
— formation of, 32
— membership of Russian, 948
— reactionism in, 859
— religious sectarian, 1024
— statistics, English, 862
Trading enterprises, proletarian nationalisation of, 997
Transport, centralisation of means of, 46
— services and proletariat dictatorship, 994
Trélat (French Minister), 112
Tribes, cattle as commodity exchange, 316
— communal life among, 315
— development of, 314
— industry among barbaric, 317
— pastoral, 315
— wars among, 321
Trochu, Louis Jules, 134, 135, 140, 1050
Trotsky, Léon, 894, 904, 906, 1050
— and opportunism, 682
Trotskyist opposition, 893
Trotskyists, Stalin on the, 944
Trusts, formation of giant, 980
— Lenin on, 698
Truth, absolute and relative, 660 *et seq.*
— antithesis between error and, 246
Truths, eternal, 241 *et seq.*
Tsar and the proletariat, 610
— introduces popular representation, 626
Tsarism and the Jews, 630
— Stalin on, 792, 793
— uprising against, 613, 620
Tsarist monarchy, Lenin on, 765
Tsereteli, I. G., 754, 783, 785, 801, 1050
Turanian tribes, 315
Turati, F., 787, 1050
Turgenev, I. S., 1050

Turkey and U.S.S.R., 926
— revolution in, 632, 677, 898, 975
Two Congresses (Lenin), 591

UKRAINE and Kerensky, 812
— nationalism in the, 944
— Skrypnik group in, 943
— uprising of workers in the, 816
Ukrainian question, Stalin on the, 795
Ultra-imperialism, Lenin on, 695, 697, 716
Unemployed, official returns of, 919
Unemployment in Great Britain, 706
" United States of Europe," Lenin on, 705
Universal suffrage, Engels on, 731
Urban bourgeoisie and the proletarian dictatorship, 1004
— life, development of, 27
Use-value and capital, 437
— capitalist production of, 460
— confusion with exchange value, 443
— Marx on, 405
U.S.S.R., agricultural policy in, 1017
— and capitalism, 945
— and England, 929
— and France, 927
— and Germany, 928
— and imperialistic war, 984
— and Japan, 930
— and Poland, 927
— and the capitalist states, 925–31
— and the United States, 926
— and Turkey, 926
— antagonism to capitalist world, 982
— attitude towards Versailles treaty, 928
— building up of socialism in, 1015–19
— duties of international proletariat to, 1021–3
— foreign policy of, 931

U.S.S.R.,—*continued*
— impending war against, 1025
— industrialisation of, 1016
— peace policy of, 926
— significance of the, 1019–21
— workers and world proletariat, 955
— world revolutionary duties of the, 1019–21
Usury, origin of, 324
Utopian Socialism and Communism, 55 *et seq.*
Utrecht, Peace of, 400

VALENTIN, 138
Value, exchange, 406
— identification of identity of, 438
— market, 483
— measure of, 422
— of commodities, factors determining, 408 *et seq.*
Vandervelde, Emile, 977
Vendôme column, 154
Verkhovsky, 808
Versailles, Treaty of, 977
— and Germany, 982
— attitude of U.S.S.R. towards, 928
Vienna barricade, 86
— uprising in, 975, 977
Village system in India, 184
Villeneuve-Bargemont, M. de, 365
Vinoy, 138, 140
Vladimir, Grand Duke, 610
Vogt, Karl, 1050
Vollner, G. von, 1050
Voltaire, François-Marie, 174
V period, 609

WAGE, a fair day's, 197–8
— reduction after social reforms, 347

Wage-labour, 268
— a form of slavery, 335
— antagonism to capital, 38
— competition in, 36
— life-long, 284
— price of, 39
Wages, depression below their value, 503
— source of, 200
— system, equalitarianism in, 949
Walpole, Horace, 174
Waltershausen, Sartorius von, *National Economic System of Foreign Capital Investments*, 702
War among early tribes, 321
— inflation boom, effects of, 917
— of 1870–71, 82, 83
— of 1914–15, and socialism, 679
— plans, Stalin on imperialist, 922, 923, 924
— socialists and imperialist, 685
" War-Communism," 1003
Warren, Col., on importance of railways, 190
Wars and imperialism, 973
Warsaw, strike in, 619
Wealth, bourgeois, 367
— growth of, in iron age, 319
— indirect power of, 731
Webb, Beatrice, 593, 1026
Webb, Sidney, 593, 1026
Weber, Max, 631
Westphalia, Treaty of, 172
Wilhelm II of Germany, 765
William of Orange, 382
Willy, Rudolf, 644, 648
— philosophy of, 652
Women, community of, 42–3
— emancipation of, 318
Wood, Sir Charles, 180–1
Work, a fair day's, 197–8
— a right to, 75
— equal obligation of all to, 46
Workers and peasants, soviets of, 1015
— and political consciousness, 602
— and the Paris Commune, 150
— as champions of democracy, 601 *et seq.*
— *Ateliers* of, 109 *et seq.*

Workers—*continued*
— coalition with petty bourgeoisie, 127
— Commune the Government of, 153
— dwellings of, in towns, 341
— economic struggle of, 600
— exploitation of, 31
— Marxian theory adopted by French, 168
— Marx's instructions to (1850), 66
— motto of British, 197
— ownership of raw materials, machinery, etc., 200
— political consciousness of, 601
— private property of, 402
— relations between Irish and British, 194
— revolution of March 18, 141
— Socialist Federation, 868
— trade union movement among, 32
— universal suffrage the measure of maturity of, 332
— use of franchise by, 84
— win bourgeois republic, 104
Working-class consciousness, 596
— evolution of, 30
— ideologies inimical to communism, 1023–32
— Leninism as organised detachment of the, 844–7
— machinery and, 30
World communism, 984 *et seq.*
— dictatorship, struggle for, 1010–13
— economy after the world war, 981
— literature, origin of, 27
— market, development of, 24, 25
— proletariat and U.S.S.R. workers 955
— revolution, first phase of, 974 *et seq.*
— revolutionary duties of the U.S.S.R., 1019–21
— union of socialist republics, 1020
— war, the revolutionary crisis, 974 *et seq.*
Wuhan, kuomintang at, 908
Wundt, W. M., 649
— idealism of, 658, 659

YEOMANRY, 381
Young Communist League, 947–9, 1007, 1019
Young Men's Christian Association, 1024

Zarya, 589
Zemindaree, 189
Zemstvo chiefs, Lenin on, 590
Zinoviev, G. E., 799, 899, 903–4, 906
Zubatov, 863, 1050

BOOKS PUBLISHED BY MARTIN LAWRENCE

MARX-ENGELS

Communist Manifesto (both)
Wage Labour and Capital (M)
The Eighteenth Brumaire of Louis Bonaparte (M)
Anti-Dühring (E)
Letters to Dr. Kugelmann (M)
The Housing Question (E)
Class Struggles in France (M)
Germany: Revolution and Counter-Revolution (M)
Correspondence of Marx and Engels
Critique of the Gotha Programme (M)
The Civil War in France (M)
Ludwig Feuerbach (E)
The British Labour Movement (E)
Marx on the Jewish Question
Poverty of Philosophy (M)

LENIN

Iskra Period
Materialism and Empirio-Criticism
Imperialist War
Revolution of 1917
Towards the Seizure of Power
Teachings of Karl Marx, War and Second International, Socialism and War, What Is to be Done ?, Paris Commune, Revolution of 1905, Religion, Letters from Afar, Tasks of the Proletariat, April Conference, Threatening Catastrophe and How to Avoid It, Will the Bolsheviks Maintain Powers ?, On the Eve of October, State and Revolution, Imperialism, " Left - Wing " Communism, Two Tactics, Proletarian Revolution and the Renegade Kautsky, Marx-Engels-Marxism, Lenin on Britain.

STALIN

Stalin Reports on the S.U., The October Revolution.